W9-BKR-556

# THE 50% SOLUTION

## I. WILLIAM ZARTMAN

*HOW TO BARGAIN SUCCESSFULLY WITH HIJACKERS, STRIKERS, BOSSES, OIL MAGNATES, ARABS, RUSSIANS, AND OTHER WORTHY OPPONENTS IN THIS MODERN WORLD*

$3.95

# THE 50% SOLUTION

# THE 50% SOLUTION

How to Bargain Successfully with Hijackers, Strikers, Bosses, Oil Magnates, Arabs, Russians, and Other Worthy Opponents in This Modern World

*I. William Zartman*

ANCHOR BOOKS
ANCHOR PRESS/DOUBLEDAY
GARDEN CITY, NEW YORK
1976

Library of Congress Cataloging in Publication Data

Main entry under title:

The 50% solution.

   Bibliography
   Includes index.
   CONTENTS: Zartman, I. W. The analysis of negotiation.—Permanent negotiations: Félice, F. B. de. Negotiations, or the art of negotiating. Morse, E. L. The bargaining structure of NATO: multi-issue negotiations in
an inter-dependent world. Strauss, A., et al. The hospital
and its negotiated order.—Structural analysis and its alternatives: Schuler, G. Henry M. The International oil
negotiations. Wriggins, W. H. Up for auction: Malta bargains with Great Britain, 1971. Rothchild, D. Racial
stratification and bargaining: the Kenya experience. [etc.]
   1. Diplomatic negotiations in international disputes—
Addresses, essays, lectures. 2. Negotiation—Addresses, essays, lectures. I. Zartman, I. William.
JX4473.F53    341.5′2

ISBN: 0-385-09656-9
Library of Congress Catalog Card Number: 75-14851
Copyright © 1976 I. William Zartman

TO ALEXANDER,
FROM THE BEGINNING,
WITH LOVE, AND HOPE, AND FAITH.

# ACKNOWLEDGMENTS

My first thanks go to my graduate classes in Negotiation and Diplomacy in 1968, 1970, 1971, and 1974, and my undergraduate class the last year as well. Out of this helpful collectivity, I would particularly like to cite Bert Spector and Bob Janosik. I am also grateful for useful exchanges and encouragement from Joe Johnson, Ed Barrett, Alan Coddington, and Paul Kattenburg, and to the pleasantly catalytic effects of Elizabeth Knappman of Anchor Press.

Among the publishers, I am particularly grateful to the Canadian Association of International Studies, and also to Sage Publications for their encouragement of the study of negotiations.

Finally, my great gratitude goes to Daniele, my wife, who joined me in the search for articles, kept me on the project, and kept life flowing smoothly about me, and all the while this was being put together was busy on her own creation, to whom this book is dedicated.

This study is part of the Negotiations Project of the Center for Research in International Studies of New York University. This book was completed under a senior fellowship from the National Endowment for the Humanities.

# CONTENTS

# PART I
# The Analysis of Negotiation

# INTRODUCTION

## I. William Zartman

Ours is an age of negotiation. The fixed positions and solid values of the past seem to be giving way, and new rules, roles, and relations have to be worked out. The hard lines and easy cognitive recognition systems of the Cold War have first multiplied and then melted, revealing the necessity and the possibility of talking things over and out. Even lesser conflicts whose issues used to be nonnegotiable and where friend and enemy once were easily identifiable—such as those of the divided nations, the Indians and the Pakistanis, even the Arabs and Israelis—are showing themselves susceptible to discussion. It has been asserted that ideology is waning, which means that dogmatic formulas, strong feelings of righteousness, black-and-white perceptions, beliefs in historical inevitability, and disinclinations to compromise are all being softened. Instead, people become aware that they share both goals and problems, and that a useful way of achieving separate as well as joint ends is through discussion and bargaining. People and nations who knew their place before are questioning that concept, and individuals and countries who were inclined to put others in their place in the past are no longer sure of their power or of the proper order of things. New orders must therefore be defined.

Two types of situations characterize this age. One involves a ansition from one order of things to another. When existing ystems prove inadequate for current needs, replacements ıust be devised or defined, invented or discovered. Either relaons need restructuring to meet some future image of desirale affairs, or their new form must be ratified to reflect real hanges that have already taken place. Conceptually, these fforts are shaped by justice, as the basis of the future ideal, nd by power, as the past determinant of reality, and so justice nd power become basic elements in the process of negotiation ıat characterizes the transition. Few would doubt that the urrent age is one of transition, although a transition to what is ot always clear. From bipolarity to polycentrism, from olonialism to independence, from nuclear stalemate to disarıament, from a single gold standard to floating currencies— ıese are all changes, none of them yet completed, that are in rocess as the fourth quarter of the century begins. The transion, in each case, requires negotiation.

The other type of situation involves a change from fixed ıles and roles to flexible ones. If the existing order proves indequate, the replacement may be not a new order but an abınce of set systems, a "transition" so prolonged as to appear ermanent. The shift to a dynamic from a static system charcterizes many current developments. Those who see permaınt revolution in the American or Russian system, or in the ıltural revolution of China, identify this type of change. The rocess of economic development, with its takeoff and self ıstaining growth, incorporates such a dynamic equilibrium, ınd to the extent that political or social development can be ınceived on a parallel image, it too involves a shift from deıed to continually redefined relations. Even within esıblished institutions, the dominant *modus operandi* is often ıe of bargaining and accommodation, as studies of the ′orld Court, the World Bank, and the American foreign ılicy process have shown (Gross 1962, Coplin 1969, Bald in 1965, Allison 1969, 1971). In such cases, negotiation ıcomes not a transition but a way of life, with a continuing ıle for power and justice.

These characteristics, and the associated process of negotia ın, are often identified with diplomacy and international rela ıns, as many of the examples illustrate, but the age of negoti

ation extends deeper down into domestic life. The mos
obvious occurrence is in labor relations, where collective bar
gaining has overtaken the unilateral use of power—throug
edict or strike—to determine wages and working conditions
But negotiation has replaced other decision-making processe
in other areas of domestic governance than simply labor rela
tions. Adversary pleading and adjudication have been joine
and partially replaced by plea bargaining in the courts and ne
gotiated settlements out of court. Even the bureaucratic do
main has been invaded by demonstrations and sit-ins tha
require explanation and group decision-making. Election an
legislation still remain important parts of governance, bu
behind each lies a process of bargaining and horse tradin
that is clearly negotiatory. Indeed, in the wake of Watergate
President Gerald Ford proclaimed a motto of "communica
tion, conciliation, compromise, and co-operation," negotiatio
politics more appropriate to this era than the politics of victor
and defeat.

More surprising is the new predominance of negotiation as
form of decision-making in nonpolitical areas where othe
orders have traditionally reigned. "Rapping" has crept int
American life at all levels. Wherever action was designated b
command—in the schoolroom, the family, the hospital, eve
the Army—new styles have added more collective and partici
patory ways of arriving at decisions. Followers, obeyers, con
formers, and workers have become demanders, discussants
contestants, and participants in a shift of roles and processe
that clearly reflects a shift in rules and accepted ways an
orders.

Indeed, some have seen such changes as particularly char
acteristic of all America. Herbert Gans, writing in the New
York *Times Magazine* (February 6, 1972), noted that i
America the gap between aspirations and expectations wa
closing, but the gap between expectations and achievemen
has increased.

As a result, matters previously decided by fiat, consensus o
the application of traditional values now have to be nego
tiated, and in many ways America has become a negotiatin;
society. . . . Politicization and the demand for negotiatio

not only complicate the life of the political decision-maker but also contribute to the malaise. They bring political conflict out in the open, raising popular awareness of the conflict, and increasing the dissatisfaction of those on the losing end.

In this view, the current concern with conflict-solving processes only increases conflict.

Yet the age of negotiations continues. On a "typical" day such as March 27, 1973, when the lead story in the newspaper was about the final agreement for the release of the Vietnam prisoners negotiated by the Four-party Joint Military Commission in Saigon, other front-page news included the failure of the Saigon and Vietcong delegations to agree on an agenda for negotiations leading to a national election, the opening of the twenty-state ministerial commission in Geneva to negotiate world monetary reform, and the agreement of striking students to begin negotiations of grievances with university authorities in Athens. Other stories in the same issue of the newspaper noted that public protest over the Forest Hills housing project has abated in a year of negotiation and compromise, lawyers for Joan Baez and David Harris were negotiating a divorce settlement, Connecticut bus service was restored after a new agreement was negotiated, and "the atmosphere of the National Invitation Tournament is becoming more and more like a high-pressure market place where college basketball scholarships are up for grabs, coaches are job-hunting, and agents and pro scouts are in almost constant negotiation."

At the end of the year, on the day the world prepared to commemorate the Armistice negotiated to end the First World War, the French newspaper *Le Monde,* in another "typical" day's reporting, carried articles on the acceptance of the Kissinger plan by Egypt and Israel, the consideration of periodical European Community summit meetings, a negotiating session between Chancellor Brandt and President Sadat, a schedule for Nixon Round tariff negotiations, the breakdown of collective bargaining in the Netherlands, and, in France, attempts by professional unions to negotiate with government representatives, by trade unions and left-wing parties to reach an agreement on priority goals, and by strikers at the Renault factory to win a raise. Other such typical days could be chosen at random to show that the age of negotiations is worldwide.

If negotiation is such a pervasive aspect of modern life, it is important to understand what goes on in the process, what the accompanying characteristics are, and how outcomes are determined. Since the process is not a new invention, one would expect to find a good deal of study and wisdom accumulated on the subject, and indeed there is. At the same time, however, more recent modes of scholarship have only begun to develop to their fullest in the analysis of negotiation, since its pervasive characteristic is only a recent phenomenon. It is therefore appropriate to turn attention to this important political process first to understand its nature and then to examine the various ways in which it has been analyzed. In the end, we are interested in understanding how the political process works and how negotiators make their decisions—as distinguished from other political processes or ways of making decisions—or at least in learning what we have left to learn to find out these answers.

We are also interested in providing analytical tools and examples to facilitate further work by others for the analysis of the variety of negotiating experiences in more helpful terms. The most striking fact about the subject is the small number of studies available, and the large communications gap between those who practice negotiations and those who study it. The two aspects are related. Most works today fall into two categories: The descriptive account of the encounter and the abstract conceptual study or experiment on the theoretical phenomenon. The first is often uninteresting to the scholar and the second is incomprehensible to the negotiator. Perhaps even more striking, there has been little attempt to bring the two together, as people or as studies. Possibly because the theoretical, conceptual, and methodological work has only been establishing itself with some confidence in the 1950s and 1960s, there have been very few studies of real-life encounters that use or test notions derived from theoretical or experimental studies.

This collection is compiled in the hope of inspiring or challenging further work in this direction. It would be comforting to be able to note that the two traditional areas of interest in negotiation—diplomacy and labor relations—provide enough solid studies for students to be able to proceed to newer subjects. Yet this is not so: few diplomatic encounters have received adequate study, and there are almost no detailed accounts of labor-management negotiation cases. Access to information, as much as conceptual sophistication, remains a problem in both areas. In the area of newer subjects, the family as a negotiating situation, hostage and holdup bargaining, the drafting of a resolution in committee, patterns of market haggling, comparative typologies of colonial independence negotiations, commodity agreements, and auction behavior can all be studied with rigor and imagination within a negotiation framework of analysis.

I

Negotiation has been defined in many ways, but most of the definitions contain common components. To begin with, negotiation is considered one of the basic processes of decision-making, along with legislation and adjudication, among others (see Dahl 1955, Coddington 1973). That is to say, it is a dynamic or moving event, not simply a static situation, and an event concerning the selection of a single value out of many for implementation and action. This decision-making event is a sociopolitical process involving several parties, and not simply one individual's making up his mind.

But now three additional components of this process-event have been brought to the light. One is the *parties* or sides that engage in the process as actors. Whether groups or individuals, they may be conceived of as having their own internal dynamics, but it is the interaction among parties that interests the analyst of negotiations in the first place. Second is the element of *values* or interests or demands presented by the parties for the purpose of collective choice. Such values are "things" that matter to the parties and may be positive or negative, as benefits and costs. Third is the *outcome,* which presents a slightly more complicated matter to conceptualize. Negotiations may be successful or unsuccessful, depending on whether or not a single agreed value has been chosen as the result of the process; an agreement is acceptable as *prima facie* evidence of "success," since it can be assumed that no party would agree to a value that he viewed as being worse than the value of nonagreement. But successful or unsuccessful, any negotiation has an outcome, in the sense of an agreed, jointly-determined value, even if that outcome is only the breakoff of negotiation and the agreement to disagree. (Unilateral breakoff, however, may prove a special case.) This view of outcomes raises further problems, which will be dealt with later, but it is a helpful and logical component of the present definition.

A final logical element is *mutual movement,* the beginning point in the process and one that is conceptually necessary only to separate the event from a mere situation. It will be assumed that negotiation begins when some movement has taken place from the parties' initial positions, since it is common sense that merely stating positions does not constitute negotiation, much as it may lead to it. However, once admitted, this assumption creates other definitional limitations that will prove useful to analysis. It means that if one side does not give in at all but forces the other side to make all the concessions, *Diktat* and not negotiation has taken place, even though other elements of the definition appear to apply (see Lall 1966, p. 288). Actually, this assumption is not as restrictive as might appear, since there are few such encounters in the real world in which one side does not give in a little, even if the other does give in a lot.

These four elements—parties, values, outcomes, and movement—are crucial to an understanding of negotiation, but they do not distinguish it from other basic political processes. All four are common to the two other modes of decision-making—legislation and adjudication—but other elements mark the difference. Legislation or voting involves a twofold choice (pass-fail) and so represents a 0-sum situation; values are constant, and decision is made by aggregating a larger number of the parties on one side than on the other; the immediate source of power is therefore found in numbers of parties (and size, in weighted-vote situations) and their order of appearance. Adjudication or choosing involves a single choice out of a plural or infinite field; there is only one party involved in the choosing, and so there is a conflict only in values, not in parties. It should be clear that these terms are being used as conceptual labels for separate theoretical modes of decision-making and not as descriptive summaries for all that goes on in a parliament or a court, for, as already suggested, these bodies in the real world engage in mixed processes. In order for the distinction to be pursued, it is necessary to identify the additional elements that are peculiar to negotiation, assumptions that both definitionally and operationally provide the necessary and sufficient conditions for its occurrence (for a similar exercise, see Rapoport 1966, pp. 18–21).

The first assumption is the *mixed-motive* nature of the process. Most studies of negotiations, from the implicit wisdom of De Callières and De Felice to the explicit analysis of Nash and Rapoport, note that negotiations take place when common and conflicting goals are present among the parties. If the situation were only one of conflicting goals, it would be impossible for the process to begin and hence impossible to analyze it. The moment there is a decision to negotiate, there is *prima facie* evidence of at least one common goal (the agreement itself). On the other hand, if the situation were one of common goals only, it would be uninteresting. At most, agreement would be a matter of discovery, and although discovery is a common aspect of the negotiation's interchange of views, it is scarcely the only component of the process. There is also a third category of values (beyond the residual category of those things that neither side cares about), which may be termed complementary, values that matter only to one side or to the other but not to both, and that can be used as tradeoffs against each other during the negotiating process. Some such values are sometimes called side payments by game theorists, but too little attention has been paid to them within the process of negotiations.

Although it is in both parties' interest to reach agreement on an acceptable reallocation of values, it is also in the interest of each to end up with as much of the pile as it can or to give up as little and gain as much as possible, depending on whether the reference is to a single contested value or to several exchangeable or complementary values. Nevertheless, as the previous assumption on satisfactory outcomes indicated, the expected value of the outcome to each side, and hence the total value of the outcome, must be positive, or there would be no incentive to engage in negotiations or to accept the outcome. In negotiations, both parties win (are better off than at no agreement) or they would not come to agreement; they are not competing for an unsharable victory, as in a vote. Each party wants the other to be satisfied too, not because they care about each other per se, but so that the other will make and keep the agreement that gives the first party its share. Thus, the second assumption is the *nonzero-sum* nature of the encounter.

To yield a nonzero sum, either things must be valued differently by the different parties or there must be side payments that are newly available because of the agreement. In the first case, each party presumably gives up its less valued items in exchange for items it values more, or gives up a part of the single value it prizes in order to get (as it otherwise would not) the remainder, again depending on whether it is complementary or contested values that are at stake. As Homans' (1961, p. 62) theorem has it:

> *The more the items at stake can be divided into goods valued more by one party than they cost to the other and goods valued more by the other party than they cost to the first, the greater the chances of successful outcome.*

In the second case, the agreement itself must be counted as a good, since it is the successful outcome that creates the situation for the realization of the other positive values. "The goal of the participants in a mixed-motive or bargaining situation," according to Gruder (in Swingle 1970, p. 111), "is to reach some agreement as to how to divide between themselves the total outcome available from their relationship." In many cases, the "opportunity benefit" of the agreement (as opposed to opportunity costs) is the most important value, since the absence of a peace treaty or cease-fire would mean more war.

It may be easier to portray this assumption by a few examples. The simplest situation for negotiation is the one where a quantity of goods is made available to two parties provided they can agree on an acceptable allocation of the goods between themselves. It may be a matter of a handful of candy offered to John and Mary or of Algeria's iron deposits at Tindouf, which are only economically available if they can be evacuated through neighboring Morocco. If we stick with John and Mary as a schematic example, we might imagine initially that every piece of candy won by Mary would be a piece of candy lost to John, a typically zero-sum situation (line A–B in Fig. 1). But that is not the whole story. It is more likely that both John and Mary would consider that any deviation to the advantage of the other party from an equitable standard such as a fifty-fifty division of the candy pile would require some additional compensation for the party with the smaller pile; this compensation could be made either through side payments, such as marbles, or through nonmaterial additions

FIGURE 1.
*The propensity to compromise*
*(All Disarmament Negotiations 1946-60)*

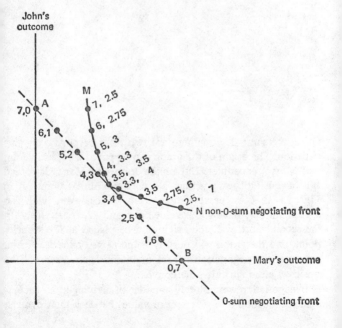

to the values involved, such as appeals to rights and to reason. *The farther the deviation from the solution of justice, the more side payments required,* resulting in a nonzero-sum situation. Thus a contested-value encounter is likely to give a concave negotiations front (line M–N).

A more complex situation—if only because there are more values involved—concerns the complementary values encounter. If Bill and Jack decide to barter their prized possessions, they will do so only if and in ways that each will be better off at the end. Unlike the encounter as described between John and Mary, Bill and Jack can be better off because they value the goods involved differently; Jack can buy some things he values highly with goods that he values less than those he receives, and vice versa. An evaluation or utility scale might look as follows:

|  | | value to Bill | value to Jack |
|---|---|---|---|
| book | | 2 | 4 |
| whip | | 2 | 2 |
| ball | Bill's goods | 2 | 1 |
| bat | | 2 | 2 |
| box | | 4 | 1 |
| | | 12 | |
| pen | | 10 | 1 |
| toy | | 4 | 1 |
| knife | Jack's goods | 6 | 2 |
| hat | | 2 | 2 |
| | | | 6 |

Using the same device, there are two ways of portraying this situation. The origin of the graph can be put at zero, as in John and Mary's encounter. But unlike John and Mary, Jack and Bill have a fallback position—a security or threat point (A in Fig. 2)—that is greater than zero, since even with no agreement they have goods valued at 6 and 12, respectively. In the second portrayal, the origin can be placed at the security point, and the graph will portray value gains or losses. Again, however, the negotiation's front or indifference curve will be positive, although this time convex.

If negotiation were merely a matter of arriving at an acceptable reallocation of a given set of values between their owners,

**FIGURE 2.**
*(Points represent some possible outcomes. Points not on the
negotiating front are not Pareto-optimal, since one party can
improve his position—by advancing to the front—
without depriving the other.)*

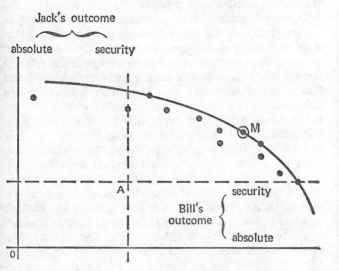

two simple utility scales listing how much each value is worth
to each party would show a clear result in most cases. This
result (point M in Bill's and Jack's horse trading) is known
as the Nash solution and is located at the place where the
product of the parties' values is the greatest. Under such assumptions, the study of negotiation could be reduced to a
study of outcome and ignore process. But reality is not that
simple, and it is three additional complexities that separate the
study of negotiations from the current body of efforts to
analyze a more stylized type of bargaining. Since it is each
party's interest to get a little more while giving a little less, and,
in Homans' terms, to value the things that it is giving a little
less than those it is getting, it is also in each party's interest to
control each other's knowledge of its own utility lists. Thus, a
third assumption is *imperfect information*, with the amount of

information and its veracity under control of the parties involved. Indeed, since negotiation is by nature a communications encounter, not a physical encounter (like war) or a mechanical encounter (like voting) or some other sort, the controlled exchange of partial information is the very essence of its decision-making process.

The verbal encounter of the process is not designed to reveal a given reality, in this case a fixed hierarchy of utilities. Instead, it is designed to shape a new reality, for the values in question are at least partially alterable as well as partially unknown. While many parties enter negotiations with a rather firm notion of what they want under what terms, they are quite unlikely to come out of the encounter with all of these values intact. More precisely, it is definitionally impossible that both sides emerge with both their shopping lists and budgets filled. If they do, it is not negotiations that will have taken place, but, again, simple discovery. If controlled communication is the essence of negotiation, the essence of that communication is *variable values,* the fourth assumption of negotiation. As a result, it unfortunately becomes very difficult to portray the process analytically as a simple matter of scales and curves (see Valavanis 1958, Ikle and Leites 1962). The single-function negotiation curve or frontier or set so commonly used is at best an illustration, not a depiction, and a misleading one at that, for—like the other commonly used device, the matrix—it shows value choices as unalterable givens. Such illustrations are graphic and convenient, and have heuristic value, but must be used advisedly lest they be taken literally to the point of distorting the analysis. Thus, John might well be able to convince Mary that she doesn't like chocolates in red wrappers or, in the old days, that as a male he deserved or needed more chocolates than she, and Bill would try to persuade Jack that one can play ball without a bat or read a book without a whip. Kissinger has said that the main obstacle to agreement in the Nixon-Brezhnev summit conference of 1974 on permanent limitations for offensive nuclear arms was the difficulty of agreeing upon how to balance missile vs. warhead totals (New York *Times,* July 5, 1974). Such problems must be portrayed through new value diagrams, assuming it is possible in the first place to give accurate portrayals to evaluations, for they represent efforts to alter rather than work within the given negotiation set.

But even within the given evaluations, Mary might decide that she doesn't want John to have more than a particular number of chocolates because they are bad for his health (without her valuing them more highly for herself), and Bill might discover that he would be better off if he didn't give up his ball in exchange for the pen, toy, and knife, just as Jack would be better off if he didn't give up his knife in order to get the book, whip, ball, and bat. These new problems in the negotiation process introduce the most important and most misunderstood element, the matter of *power*.

In the verbal and nonverbal exchanges that comprise negotiation, information is manipulated for the purpose of changing the other party's evaluation of the values involved, in order to bring about convergence or agreement at a point more favorable to one side than to the other. Power is defined as the volitionally controlled ability of one party to produce such movement or re-evaluation on the part of the other party, often more generally as the ability of one party to cause another to change behavior in an intended direction. Such a definition indicates neither a thing nor a variable, nor even a thing symbolizing a relationship, but an "ability." It is merely a label for a causal relation, an area for inquiry rather than a concept of inquiry. Hence, on the first round, the identification of power as an assumption of negotiation has led back simply to a search for a causal explanation for the movement that produces outcomes.

The matter should be pursued further, however. There are at least two ways of handling the assumption that outcomes do not just happen but are caused. One is to rephrase the question as, What is the best variable to explain outcomes? and to look for a causal theory. There is no overabundance of such theories, but a few of them have been devised, notably those in terms of concession rates and utilities (Cross 1969, Edgeworth 1881, Zeuthen 1930). These will be reviewed at appropriate places below. Their general characteristic, within this discussion, however, is that, paradoxically, they have no place for the connotations of will and skill that hover about the term "power." Quite to the opposite, all the causal theories and explanatory variables devised to date are "cataclysmic," in Coddington's word (1968, p. 79); once the process has been set into motion, it runs its course and determines its outcomes, impervious to any human tinkering. (Another generic criticism that can be made, as Hamermesh has done in this volume, is that the variables in terms of which the theory explains outcomes are inoperationalizable, a separate point that will also be taken up later.) There is one set of theories that is not impervious to human hands in the same sense, however, since they depend entirely on choice strategies. But these, the game theory explanations of outcomes, cannot answer the original question about the cause of outcomes, either, since they have nothing to do with process; they explain only why a particular choice is made (in terms of their assumptions about rationality) among given values, not the process of changing behavior by altering those values. They too are cataclysmic, since the choice is determined by an array of potential outcomes that is given.

The other way of meeting the causal question in terms closer to the common-sense connotations of "power" is to identify the types of human behavior, the settings in which they are effective, and the resources they use, in causing other human behavior to change. The operational assumption of this approach is that bargaining behavior causes and is caused by other bargaining behavior, and so the main variable is identified. The qualifications—type, setting, and source—are important, since they break down the concept of power into analytical components, permitting refinement and testing of the general proposition that certain types of action, employing certain resources in certain situations, have certain effects on the other party (who in turn initiates and responds with actions that can be analyzed in the same way).

This restatement of the problem also gets over the major conceptual dispute over power as a possession and power as a relation. It has already been seen that power is neither a thing nor a variable. Contrary to common usage, power is not something one "has." In this sense, the original definition is misleading, since grammatically one can "have" a capability. Indeed, too many of the standard discussions of power, such as Dahl's or March's or Harsanyi's, say that it is something "A *has* over B" (in Bell, Edwards, and Wagner 1969, pp. 80, 181, 239). However, there is something that a negotiator can have in regard to power, and that is resources, which he uses in a particular way to create a causal relationship. Thus it is more nearly correct to say that power is a relation. Yet within even that understanding, what the analyst really wants to know is what causes the relation or the effect of one party on the other. To be complete, an explanation must not merely correlate effects or assert a causative relation, but also must, in its chosen terms, tell what it is in one element that causes another. Hence the identification of "power" as a causative relation leads one back to the search for components and variables, such as resources (base), their use (means), and the setting. In this circular confusion, it is as much the common-sense vs. the analytical semantics of the term that causes the trouble as anything else. What is idiomatic ("to have power over someone") is not scientific, and what is scientific ("to be in power —i.e., a causal relationship—toward someone") is hardly idiomatic.

The last aspect of the power confusion relates to the setting of process vs. outcomes. "Power is present" in a negotiation situation when one party shifts another from its initial positions and toward the positions of the first party, because the first party has caused the second to move. Such a notion allows the analyst to compare the amount of movement effected by each party, as an index of the ability of each to cause the other to change, or, in other words, of their power. But effect is not cause, only an indicator of it (just as, in regard to power as a possession, resources are not use, but only a basis for it). From movement, one can infer a motivating force, but one cannot tell what it is in the "ability" that causes the movement. To do so, the analyst must look into the process, not simply the outcomes.

Furthermore, it has already been seen that there are some theories that explain "natural" outcomes through a cataclysmic process, without taking power into account. Thus, there are already partial explanations accounting for some of the movement, rendering an examination of outcomes alone a poor measure of power. It may therefore be more useful to the understanding of the role of agent causality to explain deviation from cataclysmic processes and outcomes rather than simply change from initial positions.

In summary, the recognition that there is a volitional causal relationship between parties negotiating over values that accounts for movement from beginning to outcome leads to a search for explanatory elements in the type, basis, and setting of related behaviors. It is only by looking into negotiators' behavior that negotiated outcomes can be explained. The operational problem that remains is how to translate different types of behavior, using different resources very differently, into comparable elements for analysis.

II

The problem of explaining the outcomes of negotiation has intrigued students for centuries, but little progress toward a solution has been achieved until recently. Probably the reason is that for a long time analysts asked their questions and sought their answers in terms of single cases and so were thrown back to situational and historical descriptions of essentially unique events. Only with the attention that economists brought to more abstract analysis of general situations in symbolic or mathematical language has the interest turned to theoretical answers and to the analysis of negotiation rather than the study of particular negotiations. As has already been suggested in the discussion on variable values, these attempts are still not adequate for the negotiation process. They have been a step in the right direction, but they pose two further questions: What is the best variable for analyzing the process? How can theoretical variables be translated into practical terms? In their search for the proper variable in terms of which to explain the process, modern analysts have produced a number of different approaches to analysis and theory. That search continues, for, despite all claims, there is not yet a satisfying theory of negotiation and, perhaps even more important for the present discussion, there is still no explanation in terms of fully operationalizable variables that can be applied to real cases.

The interesting questions are simple enough. What caused a particular outcome? is the basic challenge underlying any account of negotiations. Generalized into a more abstract analytical inquiry, the question becomes, What causes particular outcomes? When a complete answer to this question has been devised, it can be said that the outcomes are determinate within a theory or causal explanation. If the answer can be calculated in probabilities, the outcomes can be called partially determinate within a stochastic theory.

Some people, including the most imaginative analysts, such as Bartos (in this volume), have sometimes suggested that no theory is possible, since human imponderables play too large a role in negotiation. Others of a different school, such as Pen (1952), have stated that negotiations theory is possible but presently deficient, a statement of hope that has not yet been justified. It may seem as if any sort of determinacy would be totally unrealistic if it means, as it appears to, that observers, and hence participants, could know the outcome from the start.

Yet determinacy need not have precisely that meaning. It can also refer to a situation where a model or ideal-type solution is defined, but where reality is likely to differ precisely because men are not machines. Indeed, in such a situation, it is probably quite rational for men not to give over negotiations to machines, because it is always a reasonably good bet that the opponent will make some human errors of his own. Chess is a fully determinate process, but it still takes people to play it. Since each individual has a certain confidence in his skills, he may well think that he can outsmart his opponent or make fewer errors—and he is certainly entitled to the chance. In that case, it may be objected, it is useless to go to the efforts of devising or learning from models, since mutual attempts at outsmarting are what negotiation has been all about from time immemorial. Yet it is not unreasonable to suggest that outsmarting can, and often does already today, go on at a higher level. The highly sophisticated calculations that went into the background preparation for the disarmament talks of the 1960s and 1970s are a case in point.

The problem of determinate models, like the problem of any theory, is that explanations must be given in terms of relevant variables—variables that are independent, meaningful, applicable, and evaluable (even if not necessarily measurable).

There are perfectly sound explanations of winning at negotiations "because the winner is stronger" or "because the winner is more skillful." But even if they were not circular, these would not tell us much, since it has been impossible thus far to operationalize "strength" or "skill" satisfactorily. Thus, De Callières (1963 [1716], p. 42), one of the best early analysts of negotiating skills, advises every student of negotiation to read the Letters of Cardinal Arnaud d'Ossat (1698),

> one of the most profitable readings I know for this purpose. . . . He will see how Monseigneur d'Ossat profited by everything, how he is firm as a rock when necessity demands, supple as a willow at another moment, and how he possessed the supreme art of making every man offer him as a gift that which it was his chief design to secure.

Unfortunately, there is still no way of knowing when necessity demands rockiness and when it demands willowiness, or of what is composed that admittedly crucial art. But by the same token, more modern writers with greater pretentions at scientificness are no more help. Pen's (1952) ophelimity, Cross's (1969) concession rates, and even Rapoport's (1966) utilities are no easier to operationalize. Yet De Felice (in this volume), De Callières, and their modern successors who write of skills are important to the study of negotiations in ways that will be detailed later in this volume.

From among all the imperfect ways of studying negotiations, it is possible to distinguish at least seven different schools. Each explains outcomes in terms of a different variable and each has something to tell to both the observer and the practitioner, although it must be said that the line between any two schools is not always very sharp. The first approach is through *historical* description, explaining a given outcome through a particular set of ingredients or through one unique element. Whether one tries to work up from a specific case study or to work down from a set of theorems, it is impossible to apply the causal question to reality without a solid understanding of what actually took place and, more specifically, who said what to whom and with what effect. There are a number of burning questions of timely interest that could have formed the basis of revealing studies in this collection, such as the Strategic Arms Limitation Treaty (SALT) talks or the Kissinger Round of Middle East negotiations, if only the intimate facts were known. Often the problems of fact-finding have been so great that students have attempted to devise other ways of analyzing the process, on the basis of external indicators rather than of internal details. Such attempts, as by Spector and by Holsti, Brody, and North (in this volume), are often quite imaginative, and in their success with the assigned problem often also indicate deeper elements of the negotiation process; in focusing on indicators, or indirect measures of the encounter, both of these chapters also unearthed some findings about the nature of the communication process itself, the very core of the event. But indicators cannot replace the need for blow-by-blow accounts.

Such accounts seek the same sorts of answers as more analytical studies. They focus on crucial moments in the negotiatory interchange when telling points were made, and then they attempt to relate the momentary point to more generalized sources of the power exercised. Even though the concern of the historian may not go beyond the particular event, he is obliged by his use of language to incorporate more general terms. Thus when Schuler (in this volume) writes that Dr. Amouzegar "raised the threat of letting the OPEC Conference proceed and the bugaboo of ending up with the most radical demands as the common denominator," or Kennedy (1969, p. 109) tells Ambassador Dobrynin that "I was not giving them an ultimatum but a statement of fact . . . if they did not remove those bases, we would remove them," the words "threat" and "bugaboo," "ultimatum" and "statement of fact" are as much conceptual terms as Schelling's (1960) "threat" and "warning," and have the same meaning. The difference, however, lies in the preciseness and consciousness of their use; Schuler and Kennedy use the concepts in a common-sense way, without the concern that Schelling and his successors show for drawing clear distinctions between the two phenomena.

There is a way in which clearer distinction can be forced on common-sense concepts, and that is through comparison or the use of parallel cases. By conducting several case studies, chosen for their similarity in a number of important aspects, the analyst can relate the differences in outcome to the remaining differences in "input" into the cases. Such attempts at control are simply efforts to move a bit closer toward the scientific experiment, sacrificing some science for realism without any of the reverse. Such studies as O. Young's (1968) on a series of international crises, Randle's (1973) on ending hostilities, George, Hall, and Simons (1971) on coercive diplomacy, or Zartman's (1971) of five rounds of Eur-African negotiations allow concentration on a few variables, while others are held constant or controlled. They try to avoid being dominated by the event rather than by the analysis, as they do something more than simply letting the whole encounter speak for itself in terms of its intuitively most striking features. They follow a selective focus on variables identified beforehand, and hence are attempts to answer the causal question in chosen terms, while operating within the explanatory chronology of the historical event.

The second approach might also be termed historical, since it finds its explanation in the chronology of the event, but here it will be called *contextual*, to distinguish it from the preceding type of study. Contextual studies of negotiations see outcomes determined by a particular phaseological interpretation of history, referring either to the history of the negotiation itself or to the larger phase of history into which it fits. A number of writers have detected phases within the negotiation process itself that call for different types of tactics or that determine different types of outcomes. For example, in her comprehensive treatment of labor bargaining, Douglas (1957) identifies three successive phases in which the range of demands is first established, then reconnoitered for possible agreements, and then a decision-making crisis is precipitated by one party's final offer posed as an acceptable ultimatum to the other party. Such phases are quite applicable to other than labor negotiations, and other analysts have identified similar elements of phasing such as "crests" or points of change from unstable to stable concession rates in relation to diplomatic bargaining (see Zartman 1974, p. 393). Such phasing has also been tested experimentally (see Sawyer and Guetzkow 1965, pp. 500–1; Bartos 1974). Admittedly, it does not tell which outcome out of a spectrum of alternatives will be chosen, but it does explain how the choosing goes on. And it may explain, in Jensen's and Spector's examples (in this volume), why out-of-phase negotiations are less successful (much as Zartman, in this volume, shows how such phasing is the key to understanding the type and details of the outcome).

Another explanation of outcomes in terms of phasing examines the context and evolution of the subject under negotiation to determine the evolutionary history of its course. Kapoor (in this volume and 1974) finds agreement in negotiations between host developing countries and multinational corporations to be a function of the times. The life cycle of the project then establishes its own content, leaving only details to be talked out. An attempt to prolong a life cycle, or to introduce a new project out of phase, would make agreement a more difficult outcome than usual. Finally, most broadly, the outcome might be determined by more generalized historical contextual variables. These are the wave-of-history explanations, and like any others, they can range from the insightful to the banal. The analysis that explains the outcome of the U.S.-Panama negotiations of the 1960s and 1970s over the fate of the Canal by saying that such territorial concessions are outmoded, or that accounts for the success of nationalist negotiations with colonial states by citing the age of the end of empire, has identified important elements in history, and may provide insight into the dynamics of their operations. Even if the nationalists are going to win sooner or later, for example, this trend may be manipulated by both sides to alter its speed or attach conditions to suit its own purposes, thus providing the major context of the negotiations, as Rothchild's study of Kenya (in this volume and 1973) aptly discerns. But often these explanations merely generalize the particular case into a self-affirming tautology, and one that does not explain either the particular moment of agreement or the outcome of similar negotiations that have failed.

The third approach is *structural,* finding its explanation of outcomes in patterns of relationships between parties or their goals. Probably the most common structural explanation states that negotiations reflect the relative strengths of the parties, again a judgment that can be either perspicacious or circular.

Such statements often merely cite outcomes as an indicator of relative power positions and apply that conclusion elsewhere, although at worst, the power position is somehow intuited beforehand—often on the basis of resources conceived as power—and then used as a sort of obvious description of negotiating conduct. "In international negotiation," Lall (1966, p. 344) writes, "a powerful state tends to be inflexible whatever its form of government; it may, nevertheless, show considerable maneuverability." Taken most simply, such structuralist "explanations" could obviate negotiation. However, others use structural explanations in the sense of a determinate model, testing actual behavior against an array of possibilities opened up to optimal utilization by a particular power relationship, or indicating the tactics appropriate to particular configurations.

Structural explanations have responded to a fascination with the paradox of the weak negotiating with the strong: Despite the definitional inequality, negotiations frequently (one might say always) involve a weaker and a stronger party, with the former often winning something. Analysis generally identifies compensatory arrangements—grouping, *faits accomplis*, coercive deficiency, heartstrings appeals, clever skills—that can overcome the structural weakness during negotiations. Alternatively, structural analysis also shows the level of power necessary for either party to move the other, since, in the absence of compensation, the weaker party or the party in a weaker position would be expected to require less power to be won over by its opponent than vice versa. The problem remains one of defining power before—and hence, independently of—outcome.

Structural explanations are also related to the composition of the sides, in terms of numbers, organizations, or factions. Underdal (1973) has written that the probability of success in multilateral negotiations is a direct function of intracoalition power rankings and reward structures. Since, as already noted, sides can always be analyzed as coalitions, structural explanations of this type can be both useful and elusive. Structural analyses of diplomatic encounters in terms of bureaucratic roles and pressures (Allison 1969, 1971; Davis 1972; Janis 1972; Halperin 1974) open a new dimension to foreign-policy analysis; although concerned with parties rather than their interaction, it can provide the background for new propositions on the relation between parties and tactics or communications.

Another type of structural explanations focuses on the structure of issues. Ikle's (1964) identification of normalizing, extensive, innovative, and redistributive situations, as developed further by Walton and McKersie (1965) in regard to labor and international negotiations and as discussed by Druckman (1973), are prominent examples of different types of goals whose structures are seen to impose particular tactics, alternatives, dynamics, and outcomes on the participants. Unfortunately, pure types are infrequent occurrences, and predominantly mixed cases have less clearly determinate characteristics.

Structural explanations, whether drawn from the strength, numbers, or goals of the parties, remain highly attractive because they permit theoretical prediction of outcomes and hence a comparison of reality with theory in order to test the latter and to identify deviant or nontheoretical ingredients in the former. One of the most significant theoretical constructs of a structural nature was devised by Nash in his analysis of bilateral monopoly based on the structure of utility scales, as portrayed in Jack's and Bill's barter lists, used above. Nash demonstrated that the outcome for a two-person positive-sum game that fulfills the conditions of Pareto optimality, independence of linear transformations, independence of irrelevant alternatives, and symmetry of utility scales is a point along the compact convex negotiation set where the product of the parties' utilities is greatest. Here "strength" of the parties is unrecognized; they are without power or personality, armed only with a shopping list and a single-minded rationality to do their collective best in the exchange. There is only justice. Nash's solution brings out a crucial point, but by itself it is not a formula for the analysis of negotiation. It is its pure utility structuralism that makes it both useful and unreal, two characteristics that are highly appropriate for a piece of theory. It is an ideal type, helpful for identifying deviations for further analysis. To some observers, however, such structural explanations appear mechanistic, since they ignore process and skill, much like a theory that explains elections without taking into account campaigns and voting.

A fourth approach, closely related to the structural approach applied to values, is called *strategic*. It focuses on the element of choice, as determined by the structure of the values at stake and also by the other party's patterns of selection. In this approach, the independent variables are the value structure and the selection patterns and the dependent variable, the outcome, but selection patterns also depend in part on preliminary outcomes. Skill and power are purposely abstracted from the analysis, and indeed the parties are considered to be interchangeable, each making the same choice in the same situation under the assumption of rationality. It is also assumed that values can be clearly, unchangingly, and quantitatively established and preferentially ordered. This approach is best expressed through game theory.

Unlike the historical or structural approaches, game theory has no long tradition behind it in the study of negotiation, and yet it is a simple logical analysis whose appearance has depended only on the notion of quantifiable utilities. From a simple choice of "3 over 2" it has moved to an analysis so complex that it can throw light on such notions as threats, dilemmas, and even power. Its greatest use, however, is not in the analysis of negotiations but in the suggestion of insights, particularly as exploited by Schelling (1960, 1966) and Rapoport (1966). For strategic solutions are essentially normative solutions. They tell us how to do the best we can in a situation where the other side has access to the same kind of advice. Like Nash points, they provide solutions of justice within given assumptions, and so can be best used as baseline constructs, as Bartos and Hamermesh have done (in this volume). Surprisingly there are few attempts at a game-theory portrayal of real situations as the basis for analysis of outcomes, like that used very simply in the analysis of the Vietnam negotiations (in this volume).

Yet game theory in the end depends on three assumptions that separate it from many real situations: minimax rationality (making the best of things under symmetrical circumstances), occasion to replay (in its more complex instances), and precise invariable values established before the analysis begins. The variability of values might be handled by successive matrical depictions (thereby placing the analysis outside of the matrices, however), and the laboratory replays could be applied to the negotiating chambers to compare reality and theory. But the minimax rationality (although it could also be used for comparative purposes) is the element that seems most foreign to real-world bargainers, for whom "good enough" is not usually good enough and who are often as interested in interdicting as in obtaining.

Another treatment that used the strategic-choice approach but as an interpretive device rather than as a means of selecting among precise values is Ikle's (1964) discussion of the threefold choice. The essence of negotiation lies in the fact that it does not involve a dichotomous choice either of the coercive type ("take it or else") or of the voting type ("take it or leave it"), but a threefold choice: Take it, leave it, or come up with something else. The approach loses the quantitative precision of the negotiating front, but it shows that available values constitute an almost infinite spectrum or field and that the job of negotiation is to reduce that spectrum or field to a unique choice of values agreeable to both sides. However, studies of real encounters using the decision tree by which the threefold choice and its precise implications could be portrayed are also very rare (see Forward 1971).

The fifth approach uses *personality types* to explain outcomes, combining some of the insights of the structuralists with those of the behavioralists in the search for a single key to negotiation. Like a number of others, this approach too reveals some important characteristics of negotiation, but it can also end up in a helpless caricature. A prominent example of the approach is found in Nicolson's (1964) warriors and shopkeepers, or zero-sum and positive-sum negotiators. "The greatest danger of all is the inability of the military school to understand the sincerity of the civilian school and the failure of the shopkeepers to realize that the warriors are inspired by a totally different idea of the means and purposes of negotiation. . . . This difference in conception creates, on one side, resentment; on the other, contemptuous suspicion" (ibid., p. 26). The dichotomy has been extended into all areas of political activity through the personality types of the agitators and administrators identified by Lasswell (1930, pp. 124 f, 151 f). As a diplomat from the Nation of Shopkeepers, Nicolson was above all offering analytical advice on how to run a smooth diplomacy, with an explanation on the side as to why one can't do business with the Germans and the Russians. The explanation foreshadowed, in human terms, the message that Nash's solution expressed in terms of utilities: There is an optimal outcome for men of goodwill and limited aims, and people who do not play in those terms are neither rational nor gentlemanly. "In a successful negotiation everybody wins," writes Nierenberg (1973, p. 195), a shopkeeper *par excellence*. "Negotiation, then, is not a game—and it is not war."

The problems with such explanations are many. Just as there are few pure structure situations, there are few pure personality types, and there is doubtless a little warrior in every shopkeeper. Negotiations among shopkeepers may be more gentlemanly, but a warrior among shopkeepers may be less likely to lose and may win more if he can bully the others into continuing to play, as Bartos shows (in this volume). Hence, the next interesting question after Nash's solution is: What happens when warriors negotiate with shopkeepers? Nogee's answer (in this volume) shows that everybody becomes a warrior, blustering for propaganda advantage, since the real stakes are placed beyond bargaining by the zero-sum mentality. Another answer at the tail end of the Cold War period was to turn that zero-sum mentality into a positive-sum outlook by adding new values ("seek common interests with the Russians").

But personality types are not only attitudes toward negotiation; they also imply tactics during negotiation, and can also be used to explain responses to appropriate and inappropriate use of various means of persuasion and coercion (Deutsch 1974). When tested experimentally, studies of personalities generally reinforce intuitive notions about their effects: Flexible personalities bargain more easily but give in more, whereas authoritarian personalities play the game less easily but win more if they can avoid frightening the opponent away (see Terhune in Swingle 1970). But other, less intuitive relations can also be explored by reference to work on attitude change, short-term learning, cognition, and perception (see Kelman

1965; Marlowe, Gergen, and Doob 1966; Zimbardo and Ebbeson 1969).

The sixth approach focuses on *behavioral skills,* and is nearly as old as the school of historical description. The great diplomatic treatises of the Renaissance and the Enlightenment were manuals of good conduct for successful diplomats, encouraging them to firmness and suppleness and other appropriate qualities. Negotiators were admonished not to kill their opponents, molest the ladies, or in other ways stray from the path of perfect gentlemanliness, but they were also told to reciprocate concessions but retain flexibility, wheedle information but always negotiate in good faith, put oneself in the other's shoes but always follow up a threat with its enactment. A kind of realistic morality was the message of Bacon, a number of French diplomatic chroniclers such as De Callières (1716), his rival Pecquet (1737), and De Felice (in this volume), Schopenhauer (1896), and then the contemporary commentators and participant observers such as Nicolson (1964), Ikle (1964), Karrass (1970), Lall (1966), Nierenberg (1973), as well as others. Such admonitions undoubtedly have their place in the training of negotiators, especially when, as in the Renaissance, the Fascist period, and the Cold War, there is room for doubt whether both sides really enter negotiations in good faith and the spirit of things. Nevertheless, such admonitions are by nature prescriptive, and by themselves they are of only limited help in the analysis of outcomes. It would be hard to maintain that particular outcomes resulted from proper adherence to diplomatic codes of conduct, even if gentlemanliness were held to be helpful to one's cause in general and boorishness were considered counterproductive.

It has only been in very recent times that skills, attitudes, and personality have been thought of rigorously and used to analyze process and outcomes. The entrance of social psychologists into the study of negotiations has meant that for the first time in history, the impact of specific behavioral traits on negotiations has been subject to analysis. Traits such as toughness, trust, and threats have been examined for conduciveness to agreement and tested for appropriateness against the opponent's use of similar skills. Yet such studies often seem to end up back in the world of De Callières without advancing knowledge about the negotiating process. Firmness and flexibility have their moments, but these moments are partly defined by the behavioral ingredients from the other side and partly dependent on a multitude of psychological considerations that multivariate analysis has not yet put into order. Identification of variables and dominance in reality thus becomes practically impossible, as yet, as does advice to practitioners based on this approach, and analyses tend to be either very general or so detailed as to be almost anecdotal.

As Bartos himself has pointed out, the problem of behavioral skills is a problem of symmetry. (For a good discussion of symmetry in another context, see Clive Granger and Oskar Morgenstern, *Predictability of Stock Market Prices* [Lexington, Mass.: Heath, 1970], pp. 15, 25–26). If firmness is effective against softness, then there is no point in any party's not being firm. But firmness against firmness reduces chances of agreement: Symmetry produces stalemate, a point the students of disarmament and deterrence have used to good advantage, but one that runs counter to the different assumptions of negotiation, such as movement and nonzero-sum outcomes. The dilemma is still that left by Cardinal d'Ossat, and calls for a more complex analysis of situational, tactical, and resource variables in the search for power explanations.

The seventh approach deals with *process variables*. Unlike previous approaches, which depended for their explanations on the outcome derived from various types of initial input factors, process explanations look at negotiation as a challenge-and-response encounter in which the moves are the inputs, and negotiating is a learning process. Parties use their bids both to respond to the previous counteroffer and to influence the next one; the offers themselves become an exercise in power. In part, this approach has been devised out of dissatisfaction with the needs of those who work with utilities. If there is an infinite field of values from which to choose and if these values are variable under negotiation as well, it may be easier to ascertain the changes during the process than to ascribe fixed valuation to the stakes. In an attempt to get away from "utils" as an unrealistically cardinal measure of values, rates of change become the process variable. Such is the approach that Cross

1969) has used with skill and imagination to confirm some
intuitive notions and discover some counterintuitive ones
about negotiation. "Whenever a party increases his demand,
he increases the payoff which he expects to receive at the time
of settlement, but he also delays the date of that settlement by
an amount of time determined by his opponent's rate of
concession. . . . Sudden large concessions from one player
tend to encourage increased demands on the part of the
other. . . . Whenever both actual concession rates are less
than the expected rates, both parties will converge toward an
agreement. . . ." But "The better a learner he is [in perceiving
changes in the other party's concession rate and adjusting to
them], the more the outcome will go against a player. . . .
The faster a player expects his opponent to concede, the
greater will be his own demand. . . . The best bluff is no bluff
at all!" (ibid., pp. 47, 50, 51, 60, 73, 171).

Cross's work immediately gave rise to a number of other important investigations of the negotiating process, adding on
new patterns of interaction. Coddington (1966, 1968) posed
the possibility of characteristically mixed (unstable followed
by stable) concession rates, producing a long holdout and then
a rush to agreement under conditions resembling the stages
identified earlier by Douglas (1957). Bartos (1974) called
a similar pattern "endgame," and he also supported Cross's
work experimentally and tested models of reciprocal and
exploitive concession behavior (behavior positively and nega-
tively related), finding support for the latter. Study of actual
cases, however, suggests that there are other processual patterns to be explored: mutual toughness until an agree macro-
nage is defined, and then mutual co-operation (Zartman
1975; similar to the outcome analysis in Raiffa 1953, and
Braithwaite 1955); concessions as primarily communication
behavior to establish trust or co-operation, with detailed positions, then constituting a discovery rather than a negotiating
process; concessions to lure the other party toward agreement,
followed by mounting toughness to freeze the process at a
desirable outcome (see George, Hall, and Simons 1971). All
of these variations depend essentially on broken or mixed rates
of concession and on specific negotiation phases, and all invite

further analytical attention (along with the discovery of stil other process patterns).

In addition to these seven substantive approaches to an ex planation of negotiated outcomes, there is an eighth, which cuts across many of them and which may be termed proce dural. While studies of negotiations for centuries have been limited to observation and cogitation, *experimentation and simulation* have been added in the postwar decades as a new method of checking experience and theory. Both experiment and simulations are similar uses of artificial or "laboratory" situations to approximate spontaneous reality, but they diffe from each other in that experiments involve subjects whe "play" themselves, whereas simulations involve participants playing (and therefore learning) some other role. Experiment are their own reality; simulations try in controlled ways to ap proximate external reality. Both can be used to test the ability of particular variables to explain for difference in outcomes and are particularly useful for developing and testing proposi tions about structural, behavioral, and processual variables Some of the most insightful works on negotiation have evolved around experimental reconstructions of the process, notably those reported by Siegel and Fouraker (1960), by Barto (1974), by Morton Deutsch (1974), and by Spector (1975)

## III

The problem of negotiated outcomes is the subject of analy sis from many different approaches, but none of them alone seems to bear the promise of a comprehensive explanation o the process. Instead, most analysts are working on short-range correlations and explorations of particular ingredients in the process. Yet this effort is important, for negotiation is a complex process, with many of its complexities still unexplored. A bit like a problem of solving two simultaneous equations with four unknowns, it now seems to resist complete analysis, or rather seems susceptible to solutions only in terms of indecipherable variables. The effect of toughness on conces sion rates, for example—to focus on two different tools of ex planation recently used by Bartos and Cross—can only be explored after some knowledge has already been acquired about the operation of toughness as a skill and the functioning of concession rates within the process.

Yet in the end, outcome can never be understood without an investigation of the means by which negotiating positions are inflected. The point missed by both strategic and processual models is that the participating parties to negotiations are people making decisions on how to change the others' stands and undergoing the effects of the others' decisions for the same purpose. The process is neither a matter of independent choices nor one of inexorable mechanisms but one of choice and mechanism related. For this, more work is needed in the aspect of power that is most relevant to negotiations, that of political persuasion.

Persuasion involves *contingent gratification and deprivation*. While immediate gratification and deprivation are occasionally used in negotiation, primarily to change reality or confirm credibility as an adjunct to bargaining (see George, Hall, and Simons 1971, Schelling 1966), delayed obligation imposed by a present agreement for future benefits is more common. Even where past events (*faits accomplis*) are used for persuasion, it is the implicit idea of gratification or deprivation involved in undoing them that provides the element of contingency. ("You know I can't do that" means "I want you to believe that the cost would be too high for me to do that.") It is this contingency that makes persuasion a matter of *commitment* (of one's self) or *obligation* (of the other), and hence a matter of some uncertainty. (On the importance of uncertainty, see Schelling 1966.)

Contingent sanctions used for persuasion fall further into two types, those referring to volitional acts and those referring to nonvolitional events. The difference between volitional *threats* ("I'll cut off your cabbage supply if you don't come to terms") and nonvolitional *warnings* ("Your people will starve if you don't come to terms") has been more frequently analyzed than the corresponding difference between *promises* ("I'll open up a cabbage credit for you if you come to terms") and *predictions* ("Your economy will prosper if you come to terms"). The threats and promises cited here have been stated as commitments, tying our hands; they can also be used as obligations, tying the other party's hands ("You announced that rejection of your association would mean exclusion from the cabbage trade," and "You have always extended massive cabbage credits to friendly countries," respectively). Interestingly, the common form of warnings and predictions is obligatory, constraining the other party, but these too can be stated as commitments, the one sometimes termed coercive deficiency ("My economy will collapse if you don't come to terms") and the other as yet unnamed ("My people will finally be able to defend themselves [against the common foe, for example] if you come to terms").

There are many advantages to a typological exercise of this kind. By isolating the exercise of persuasion within the power question, one is able to distinguish the use of specific tactical devices from the general search for causal explanations. Then again, the identification of such types of persuasion enables further inquiry into their properties such as that pursued by Schelling (1960, 1966), Fisher (1969), Lockhart (1974), Deutsch (1974), and Baldwin (1971c). The notion, for example, that "promises tend to cost more when they succeed while threats tend to cost more when they fail" (Baldwin 1971c, p. 28) is an important implication of the original distinction that reveals in turn further, often paradoxical implications: Bigger threats are cheaper than bigger promises; overthreat devalues credibility but overpromise devalues currency; bluff is an element of threat, not promise; gratification tends to lead to sympathy, continuity, exploitation, and blackmail, whereas deprivation tends to imply hostility, avoidance and conditioning. Other propositions on the appropriateness of the various types of persuasion and their implications can be developed. Since theory involves the discovery of regular relationships among concepts, work of this type is a further step toward theory.

Furthermore, such concepts have an important place in the total grasp of the negotiation process. If negotiation can be conceived as a process of mutually adjusting cost/benefit conditions or of inflecting utility curves, then the different means of persuasion can be portrayed as positive or negative values to be added onto the evaluations of the stakes under discussion. A threat to cut off the cabbage supply represents a presumably large negative increment to the threatee and probably a small negative increment to the threator as well, whereas a promise to open a cabbage credit contains a presumably large positive increment for the promisee and a variable increment for the promisor. The side payments of persuasion attached to the original stakes become part of them. This formulation is not a theory, nor is it a recipe for assigning quantitative values to apples and oranges. But it is a conceptual means of handling both power and interest on the same plane, an important step toward the analysis of the negotiation process.

The notion of contingency also allows further conceptual thinking about response and countermoves, as well as initial offers. On one hand, any offer can be met with a response that is either a defense or an attack. The defense would be to heighten the element of contingency or doubt about implementation. This could take the form of moral impediments at the sources ("You wouldn't do a thing like that because of your concern for your reputation") or physical impediments at the target ("You couldn't do a thing like that because we no longer eat cabbages" or ". . . because we grow our own"). The attack would take the form of a different means of persuasion launched to annul the initial move ("We will decrease —or increase—our supply to you of inkwells"). Particular means of persuasion are susceptible to particular forms of response, under certain conditions, providing hypothetical relations for research to verify.

A further possibility for analysis can also be introduced by identifying more clearly the value forms or "pressure points" to which the means of persuasion are applied. Any negotiator has three "points" in mind, his offering point and his acceptance point—the point of his current public bid for agreement and the minimum point that he would accept—plus his threat point or security point—the quantity available at no agreement.

But he is also aware that these three points are on the mind of the other party as well. Each party is therefore juggling his own offer, accept, and security points and his estimate of the other party's three points. Furthermore, these points are potentially movable, and hence defensible. A serious error of many portrayals of negotiation (and of some practitioners as well) has been to consider one or more of these points as fixed, thus missing an understanding both of the nature and of the opportunities of the process. It is the job of the means of persuasion to bring about—that is, to cause—this movement, against any defense or countermove. By being attached, or added, to the latest bid (offering point) to make it more expensive or more rewarding to the bidder, to the other party's acceptance point to reduce his expectations, or to the security point to make his no-agreement position less satisfying than it originally appeared, the means of persuasion raise or lower the value of various alternatives and related reference points, and render other alternatives relatively more or less attractive. Negotiation then is a matter of bringing several "images into focus" by adding values to the original offers until desires and offers on both sides coincide, a much more complex reality than that analyzed by models based on concession rates or other changes in offering points alone.

Three levels of model-building seem most appropriate for the pursuit of such analysis. One is a simple convergence analysis focusing on the means required to bring the parties' offering points into convergence at a point of agreement. The amount of movement effected through the use of various means of contingent gratification and deprivation, related to various resources and to particular situations, is an important measure of causation that even the experiments and simulations on convergence have so far ignored. The analysis can be expanded further by a study of means of persuasion used as countermeasures, again related to resources and setting. It also depends on the formulation of propositions on relationships among offer, acceptance, and security points. Such analysis requires detailed information on the unfolding process of negotiations in the cases studied; it cannot rest on mere accounts of outcomes. For even pretheoretical propositions to be tested in such cases, relations within and among the general categories of variables need to be identified. To do so requires either induction from case studies or reasoning from logical constructs. Yet the approach is probably the simplest and immediately most promising.

The second-level models are deviance analyses and are more complex. It is possible to take normative outcomes like Nash's or other game solutions or cataclysmic processes like Cross's concession rates as ideal types and use an analysis of the means of persuasion to explain deviance from these ideal solutions. Although it is most tempting—because it is simplest—to apply this approach to Nash's solution, this does not provide the most useful ideal type, since it only concerns outcomes, not the process of arriving at them. Nevertheless, the Nash point could be considered a fixed standard during the process, and the Cross process a series of successive standards. (For that matter, persuasion and movement could also be considered a matter of deviance, in which the use of power explains change from the initial positions considered as two normative points at which either party got all, as compared with Nash's normative point, at which both parties got most.) In the second-level model as in the first, theoretical relations among variables remain to be elaborated. But despite its complexity, the model has the particular advantage of permitting a comparison between the effects of process and of persuasion in determining outcomes.

The third-level models are also more complex, based on a cybernetic analysis of a self-stabilizing (i.e., outcome-reaching) process of output and feedback. In its most famous application, cybernetics has been used as the basis for a servomechanism correcting gunfire on a moving object by cranking in feedback information on target movement and gun error. The cybernetic analysis of negotiation involves "a pair of linked servomechanisms" (Coddington 1968, p. 55), each seeking to hit the same target as the other and at the same time to use its fire to cause the other to hit one target rather than several others. Output and feedback then become complex, interdetermined events, above all because they have a dual purpose: both to bid and to persuade. This dual quality makes the reality of negotiations a matter both of learning and of persuasion, combining such elements as Bartos' notions of toughness with Cross's notions of concession rates, but also including for analysis the types of power—the means of persuasion—used. For this purpose, the notion of added value seems most appropriate. A number of students of negotiation have pointed out the potentiality that cybernetics has for the analysis of the subject, but none has developed the suggestion or succeeded in working in the element of agent-induced value change.

IV

The discussion so far has been in Morgenthalian terms of power and interest, looking at actors and interactions and looking for the explanation of outcomes in party and process, structure and communication. But it has not provided any overarching criterion by which to judge negotiations, negotiators, or negotiated outcomes. Is there no justice? Earlier parts of the discussion have suggested that there is, and that it serves along with power as a limit to negotiation. In fact, there are several types of justice, each with a special type of limiting relationship to the process, although it will be seen that this very plurality reflects and expresses the basic impossibility of any overarching criterion, equivalent on its level to the absence of any underlying determinacy.

One kind of justice, the kind most frequently referred to, may be called substantive or partial justice. In any negotiating situation, each side believes that it represents the just solution, that the best outcome in a perfect world would be the adoption of its position, and that negotiation and compromise are necessary in the first place only because the forces of error, if not of evil, have enough power to prevent true justice from being enacted. Such a description is no caricature, and it is necessary to remind too fervent partisans of negotiation—from De Callières' gentlemen to Nicolson's shopkeepers to Morton Deutsch's co-operative personalities—that negotiation is required precisely because both sides think that they are right and the other wrong. Such feelings often interfere with analysis as well, when students of the process develop overly strong sympathies with one side and so have difficulty admitting that the "bad" side has used skills, strategies, or strengths that have enabled it to outdo the "good guys." Analytically, the argument enters the old and unnecessary domain of value-free research. There is a time for objective analysis of the negotiating process, like any other political process, in order to understand how it works. There is also a time for taking sides on

ubstantive issues and using the analytical knowledge gained to
ood purpose. If "good purpose" may appear obvious in some
ituations, however, there are far many more over which there
s never agreement or on which agreement changes with the
ontext and the age. It is in the nature of the bumpy world that
ruths about the best way to achieve outcomes through negoti-
tion will be available to good guys and bad alike, and that the
bad" may occasionally be "better" in procedural skills. That
vould seem to be all the more reason to find out how and why.

Substantive justice legitimizes inputs, but it does not explain
utcomes. If presented as an explanation, it would exclude
ower, obviate process, and invalidate negotiation. As an
ngredient among others in the process, however, it mobilizes
ower, and screens the use of the means of persuasion. It thus
ecomes very important to analysts and practitioners alike, as
 source of power (as Underdal [1973] and others discuss).
ls a single explanatory or evaluative referent external to
ecision-making, justice has its own process, called adjudica-
on, that is not negotiation but an alternative to it, with its
wn assumptions and analysis. (It should be noted that there
 both a real and an analytical difference as well between two
losely associated variants on these processes: arbitration, a
orm of adjudication, and mediation, a special catalytic form
f negotiation—negotiation *à trois,* in which the third party has
nly procedural interests. A special literature has grown up
n the subject of mediation but is not treated here; see Ed-
read 1971.)

There is, however, another kind of justice, which may be
alled procedural or impartial. Procedural justice is quite
ifferent from substantive, and if anything is more important
 the negotiating process, it is the justice of the conciliator,
ne structural justice drawn from the basic equality of the par-
es found in the ideas of democracy and the Enlightenment,
nd it is antithetical to any notion of inherent or substantive
istice in the stand of one party or the other. If substantive jus-
ce says one side, or each, is right and therefore deserves the
ntire outcome, procedural justice—recognizing the claims of
oth sides—says that the just solution lies in the middle. A
umber of studies have shown split-the-difference or its
ariants to be a "natural" solution and one that responds best

to demands for a meeting of the minds or a reference poir
when all arguments have been exhausted and an equitable ou
come is sought (Schelling 1960, Nash 1950). Yet the impa:
tial justice of the midpoint is also an alternative to negotiatio
a pure co-operation point in contrast to the pure conflict solv
tions of partial justice, the solution of Good Guys and Shop
keepers in a world free of Bad Guys and Warriors (Youn
1968, pp. 25–26; Cross 1969, p. 42). Like the pure solution c
partial justice, therefore, it can also serve analysis as a baselin
or ideal solution, and is even more useful in this light since :
represents a point of high legitimacy, deviation from whic
can be accounted for by the exercise of power.

The final aspect of justice is that it represents its own undc
ing: Evoked in a search for an overarching criterion for judg
ing negotiations, it gradually leads the analyst into the sam
paradoxes, dilemmas, and components as did the study c
power and interest. It has been seen that the study of justic
must begin with a recognition of the claims to partial justice o
each side, and must then proceed by reaction to the substantiv
incompatibility of these claims to a recognition of imparti:
justice in the middle. But just as impartial justice is an answe
to the internal incompatibility of partial justice, so the searc
continues for an answer to the incompatibility of partial *an*
impartial justice; one can no more enforce the two at the sam
time (and there is something to say—some justice—fc
each) than one can enforce both elements of partial justice :
the same time. The search for an agreed Olympian solutio
has only complicated the problem. The answer then comes in
third and fourth type of solution, beginning first with an ou
come of distributive justice. Combining elements of procedur
and substance, this says that the outcome should be split, nc
equally, but according to need (Homans 1961). Distribu
tive justice is antithetical to both partial and imparti:
justice, and its outcome is not as immediately obvious as th
other two. Since need is vulnerability and weakness, it is th
strategy of the weak and seeks to use weakness as the basis fc
power—as a referent for the means of persuasion. The fin:
type of solution should now be evident: It is the mirror imag
of distributive justice, and it says that the outcome should b
split, neither equally nor by need, but according to the partie

.bility to do without or according to their fallback position, or
n other words according to their power (Shapley 1953). By
now it can be seen that the argument has come full circle. The
search for an irrefutable criterion for the right solution has led
ight back to the analysis of negotiation as an arena of power,
n which legitimacy and process, need and power, are essential
lements.

Thus to say that there is no just solution is in itself justifica-
ion for negotiation, but it is also quite similar to saying that
here is no determinate outcome. Indeed, it is quite impossible
-or it is not yet possible-to indicate that, given X, a particu-
ar outcome will or should be attained, unless there is
greement beforehand on the assumptions of power and/or jus-
ice. Yet to obtain such agreement would mean merely trans-
erring the negotiating problem to its analytical components
nd would neither determine nor justify anything at all. At the
resent point, barring new analytical breakthroughs, the
rocess of negotiation remains operative within two limits that
ave been previously identified as running through the con-
epts of power, justice, and process itself. On one hand, negoti-
tors seek to increase common interests and expand co-opera-
ion in order to broaden the area of agreement to cover the
em under dispute. On the other, each seeks to maximize his
wn interest and prevail in conflict, in order to make the
greement more valuable to himself. No matter what angle
nalysis takes, it cannot eliminate the basic tension between
o-operation and conflict that provides the dynamic of negotia-
ion.

# PART II
## Permanent Negotiations

# INTRODUCTION

This is not the first work to identify its point in history as [an] era of negotiations. Lall (1966) so identified the previou[s] decade, Klaiber et al. (1973) the present, and Nicols[on] (1954, 1964) saw a number of contemporary and historic[al] periods characterized by diplomacy, "old" or "new." Som[e]what earlier, Thucydides recorded a classic case of negoti[a]tions with the Lacedaemonians, while Roman chronicl[es] report a losing encounter between Tarquin, justly surnam[ed] The Proud, and the Sybiline Oracle. Perhaps the earli[est] recorded instance, against a formidable adversary, was wh[en] Abraham bargained the Lord down to ten righteous souls[,] the minimum requirement for saving the town of Sodom fr[om] destruction (Genesis 18:20-32), even though Abraham cou[ld] not deliver the goods in the end. Yet against these impressi[ve] claims of previous eras, ours seems to stand out for its barga[in]ing spirit. Negotiation is the sign of our particular times f[or] uniquely historical reasons, which may probably be su[m]marized as a disillusionment with the predominant notions [of] force and justice in the immediately preceding era. But mo[re] generally, negotiation is a sign of times that value parti[ci]pation, provide a role in shaping one's own destiny, proclaim[s] faith in process rather than a belief in outcome, a respect f[or] complexity rather than a reduction to simplicity.

It is therefore most appropriate to begin a study of the analsis of negotiation with a writer from the Enlightenment who, ar ahead of the analytical tools of his times, saw many of the spects of negotiation that more modern analysts have developed, as well as noting other characteristics that were common o his contemporaries' discussion of the subject. De Felice born in 1723 in Rome) was a professor of physics who exanded the work of the Encyclopedists and made their work vailable beyond France to a larger audience. His largest vork, the *Dictionnaire universel raisonné des connaissances umaines* (1770–80), ran to fifty-eight volumes, including ables and supplements, and his article "Negotiations, or the \rt of Negotiating," translated here for the first time, apeared in a similar work of thirteen volumes at the same time. )e Felice identifies negotiation with all activities of human fe, and with all periods of human history to a greater or lesser xtent. Although using a premodern notion of theory, he notes nat the theory of negotiation is broader than merely diplomatic affairs, and he speaks of the means of persuasion and the oncept of interest in terms ahead of his times. Unlike many of is famous predecessors and contemporaries, such as De Callières, he maintains that good negotiators can be trained as vell as being born into their art, and he sees their activity as ne involving the interaction of wills according to sparse ormulas and a limited number of variables. He also is aware f the possibilities of psychological analysis of attitude change. 'hus De Felice lays the ground for the study of negotiation as permanent phenomenon, susceptible to scientific analysis— ven if his language is drawn above all from the humanist radition.

It is therefore less of a leap in concept than in time to roceed to an analysis, two centuries later, of the Western allince as a situation of permanent negotiations. De Felice had alled for the negotiation of a permanent zone of peace and seurity in the European system; Morse examines the permanent haracteristics of bargaining that accompany the pervasive inerdependence of the ensuing Atlantic community, and he does o with persuasive description and tight propositional analysis. he characteristic interdependence tempers the equally char-

acteristic assymetries of power and relations, leading to contin
ual stalemates on the procedural (core vs. coalition) and sub
stantive (defense, economics, and innovation) levels. *Th
greater the interdependence, the greater the pressures t
reduce one's own vulnerability and to increase that of th
other parties.* Thus the dynamic tension is set into motion t
create a situation of permanent bargaining, quite the opposit
effect of the same proposition stated by Rothchild (in the fo
lowing section) in his analysis of transitional negotiations. I
the world is getting smaller and moving toward broader inter
dependence, however, the proposition suggests that permaner
negotiations will be even more broadly the sign of the times c
the last decades in this century.

It is perhaps more of a leap from these concerns into th
negotiated order of the hospital, although again De Felice ha
at least prepared the way for an understanding of nondiplo
matic relations in terms of negotiations. The analysis b
Strauss and his associates is a striking application of the ap
proach nonetheless, for it would have seemed that a hospita
above all, should stand as a case of authority relationships, n
of bargaining. It is the strength of the article that it shows th
reverse to be true, as a sign of the times to be sure, but also a
a deeper penetration into basic human relationships. Negotia
tions operate on two indistinguishable levels: as part of th
means authority figures use to implement their roles beyon
the formal rules of their authority, and also as the means avai
able to the subjects of authority to change the rules of their in
stitution. If such analysis is applicable to a hospital, how muc
more applicable it is to other institutions—legislatures, bureauc
racies, management—where negotiation is a more visible pa
of the *modi operandi*. It is merely an extension of the inter
dependence proposition into broader areas to note that *th
greater the division of labor, the greater the reliance on negoti
ation* both to define and to implement roles. Once again, neg
tiation is demonstrated to be a sign of the times, for these time
are continually analyzed as being characterized by increasin
division of labor. Not only is interdependence broadening, bu
specialization is also increasing, and with it the need to negot
ate.

# 1. NEGOTIATIONS, OR THE ART OF NEGOTIATING*

*Fortune Barthélémy de Felice, Universities of Naples and of Berne*

n common usage, the term "negotiation" means the art of
andling the affairs of state as they concern the respective in-
erests of the great and supposedly independent societies in-
eracting in a free state of nature. It is not surprising that the
llure of matters of this kind is such that the art of handling
hem receives a name that should really be applied to the art of
andling affairs in general, whether they be public or private.
t is the greater interest of the nation that determines the value
f an idea, and it is this value that is expressed in terms con-
eyed exclusively through a language.

However, negotiation is not limited to international affairs.
t takes place everywhere where there are differences to concil-
ate, interests to placate, men to persuade, and purposes to ac-
omplish. Thus, all life could be regarded as a continual nego-
iation. We always need to win friends, overcome enemies,
orrect unfortunate impressions, convince others of our views,

* Translated from *Dictionnaire de justice naturelle et civile: Code
e l'Humanité, ou la Législation universelle, naturelle, civile et
olitique comprise par une société de gens de lettres et mise en ordre
lphabétique par de Félice* (Yverdun, 1778).

and use all appropriate means to further our projects. There are some private matters which, by the confrontation of passions, the friction of characters, and the difference in the parties' way of thinking, become so embroiled that their successful resolution requires just as much art and skill as a treaty of peace between the greatest of powers. I have observed the handling of an insignificant matter that posed as much difficulty in bringing together a large number of persons from different states, nations, religions, and sentiment, required as much diplomacy and finesse, and caused as much trouble, as the most important affair of state.

Although the art of negotiating public affairs has drawn in the past and continues to draw our attention by preference, the extent and the usefulness of negotiations in general are such that we should not neglect them. Their examination is all the more necessary because the theory of negotiation, taken in its most universal sense, is common to matters of all kinds, and public and private negotiations differ only in their object and in a few details of execution, as befitting the diversity of the circumstances. It is, therefore, useful to conduct research into the rules of negotiation in general and to apply them afterward to public negotiations, with the required modifications. . . .

In private matters, the person who is charged with the successful execution of a plan is also the one who has had to formulate it. Thus, he must know how to draw up the project and to combine the different elements so well that they provide support for each other. But this art is different from negotiation which, strictly speaking, is only the science of the proper means of implementing a plan already formulated. In public affairs things are different. The negotiator follows his instructions based on a plan drawn up by his sovereign, and his only glory is in the successful accomplishment of his master's orders. Nevertheless, although he is not able to choose his own project as the basis for his efforts, he will still have to formulate a plan to facilitate the success of his instructions. He will examine all the possible means in order to choose those that he will employ and to order them so well that even those that are absent contribute to the success of his endeavor. It is in this choice that his prudence and skill come to the fore. It is difficult to give rules on the matter: Resources are supplied by circumstance and cannot be made to order, and the only thing anyone can do is to teach the best way to use them.

Once a plan is drawn up corresponding to the nature of the affair and to the need for means appropriate to its execution, it is then that one can properly say that negotiation begins. Whatever may be these means, they can all be reduced to the effects of human will. The instruments of negotiation are therefore individual human beings, and its means are the actions in which we engage those individuals in order to arrive at our goal.

Men are moved by feelings alone. Even actions that at first glance may appear to be farthest from what are commonly called emotional acts have some hidden sentimental motive behind them. One man may appear to give in only to the strength of reason: His firm belief depends on a clearly perceived interest, on the interest of being convinced, and the interest itself is a sentiment that derives from the instinct for preservation. Another may faithfully follow the rules of justice: This love of justice is a sentiment mixed with the love of society and glory, and tempered by other parts of instinct. Indeed, even the purest virtue is an emotion composed of all the most refined elements of man's instinct. Thus, to make men act, to convince them, to persuade them is always a question of putting into motion an emotion that determines the will in the particular case.

Not all men are subject to the same passions, and not all are moved to the same extent. Depending on our temperament, frame of mind, mood, and habits, we feel moved in one direction rather than another, and this predominant direction forms the basis of our character. However, the reign of one emotion is never despotic enough to exclude others nor to prevent them from dominating us in their turn, even though with less power. This infinitely variable and sometimes contradictory mixture of emotions and the instability of their reign within the same individual form the astonishing variety of characters and are the cause of the inconsistency of which we accuse human beings. Thus, to know on which emotions to play in order to make a particular individual act, we must study his character and know the nature of his mind, his habits, and his passions.

This study leads to a knowledge of human nature, an equally necessary and difficult art. Some people have a particular instinct for judging human nature, and one speaks of that instinct as a natural gift. But that marvelous quality, appreciated for its true value, is nothing but a branch of the spirit of observation applied to moral man. The observant mind, always busy deciphering the characteristics that distinguish individuals and phenomena, gives the same attention to the characters and actions of individuals, and infers both the cause from the effect, and the effect from the cause. The ability to judge human nature is thus founded on fine rules, often imperceptible but always invariable, and the realization of these rules is insured by long experience or by conscious usage in a world that provides an infinite number of objects of comparison.

The simplest and apparently the surest way to know human nature would be to judge men by their speech, writings, and acts. But in our times, verbal trade has become so faithless that it is risky to base one's judgments on the word of man: Indeed, to do so is practically an assurance of counterfeit currency. Conclusions drawn from acts are doubtless more exact; it is impossible for a man to carry hypocrisy to the point of always mastering his emotions and holding them for long without their escaping. However, there are men who are false enough to get by during part of their life through simulated actions and to keep their true character from revealing itself in their behavior. Thus, dissimulation is a great obstacle to the understanding of human nature, all the more so because experienced individuals imperceptibly acquire the habit of veiling their words, masking their ideas, hiding their inclinations, and covering up their acts by means impenetrable to the most piercing eyes. Although they are sometimes betrayed by activity and imprudence and reveal the keys to their own undoing, these occasions are rare. Thus, to understand human nature, one must discover other, surer indications against which even the most skilled individual cannot defend himself, or against which he is least on guard. . . .

[Here follows a section on the usefulness of physical characteristics for the understanding of human nature.]

If the examination of external appearances is not sufficient to reveal a character, there are other indications that one can pick up from ostensibly the most ordinary moments. People are on guard only on important occasions; they tire of formality and relax in ordinary circumstances, when they do not suspect any danger of revealing themselves. However, nothing is ordinary in the simplest occasions: The analogy of ideas, which leads us to value only those notions that resemble ours, brings out the hidden tastes of even the most reserved individual. His character is clearly indicated by his friends, his acquaintances, his distractions, and his readings. No less reliable indications are given by his judgments on things going on about him, on the writers that he reads, and on the opinions that he adopts or rejects. The similarity or dissimilarity of ideas penetrates everywhere, if the importance of the subject does not impose its reserves, and these disappear as soon as the weight of the matter has been raised, even if continual dissimulation keeps a man perpetually on his guard. Ingenious questions, offhand insinuations, and careful contradictions scatter the fog in which he hides and reveal him plainly.

Once the character and dominant emotions are known, the next question concerns the way to use them to bring about action on the part of those with whom one is negotiating. Some rules apply to all emotions in general; others are appropriate to particular sentiments. Among the latter are those governing the sentiment of interest in its broadest sense, relating to a concern for all that is useful, remunerative, or pleasurable.

In business, where there are always some interests to discuss or obtain, this sentiment should clearly play the leading role. Indeed, one deals no differently with people of an advanced age who are only concerned with the care of their fortune and are insensitive to most other passions. However, it is wrong to think that all men always act according to their true interests; the limits of their minds, ignorances, prejudices, and the heat of passions darken or dazzle their view, and cause unexpected misperceptions. False interest is often so complicated that it is difficult to unravel. Small minds are particularly likely to seize on these little interests and to use the petty means that they require. Herein, I believe, lies the difference between negotiation and intrigue, which so many authors speak of without explaining. The negotiator seeks above all to bring men to great interests and to convince them through the strength of his mind; the intriguer, on the other hand, takes advantage of small interests that he suspects and finds and that the great man neither imagines nor deigns to use. A very limited individual can become an able intriguer if the love of money inspires him, but it is only a superior mentality that can hope to arrive at the glory of great negotiation.

It is these errors about true interest that are partly responsible for the common saying that men's minds can only be made up by small reasons. In other words, one could say that mediocre men are unable to encompass great interests and get carried away by small passions. They construct false ideas about their own interest and therefore can only be persuaded by means of petty ones. This case is more frequent than imagined, and even great men are no more exempt from these weaknesses than are ordinary individuals. Marshal de Bassompierre languished in the Bastille after the death of Cardinal Richelieu, his persecutor, and the love of justice and glory alone was not able to convince Louis XIII to release him from prison and overcome the shame of having mistreated a man whom he had favored. A member of the court let it be known to the King that the marshal was maintained at the expense of the King, and it was this victorious reason that won the marshal his liberty.

The petty sentiments that compete with ignorance to produce these misapprehensions are many and varied. Love, friendship, hate, vengeance, jealousy, envy, greed—in a word, the whole range of effects of badly controlled instinct ally with interest to confuse and disguise it. In private matters, the evidence is available daily; even in public affairs, it is not too difficult to distinguish. How many small causes of large events are visible in a careful study of history. How many revolutions were caused by rivalries, secret aversions, and minute distinctions on the part of those who governed the people. How many times have the interests of nations been sacrificed for motives shameful to admit, that the author carefully seeks to hide and that posterity later has difficulty in imagining because its effects seem so out of proportion.

Happily, most important matters are handled by enlightened people who are capable of knowing their true interests and of understanding the reasons used to express them. It is with people of this kind that one can use the basic principles of negotiation, and can employ the force of reason to its fullest. Perspicacity and exactitude of thought, and order and clarity of ideas are necessary to find the arguments that convince, to organize these arguments in natural order, and to display them conveniently. A man who is gifted in the art of reasoning and inventive in his thinking will not only persuade enlightened minds but will also dominate that group of cold, careful thinkers whose dead imagination does not come up with enough ideas to furnish proofs, but who nevertheless can grasp these ideas, confront them, and draw the proper consequences when they are presented. Minds of this kind cannot be made up and convinced on their own, but they can do so with a little help. In fact, properly revealed truth triumphs over all, if contradictory ignorance and passion does not get in its way. . . .

[There then follows a discussion of the problems of laziness, age, stupidity, and greed as obstacles to reasoning and persuasion.]

If we want to dominate the emotions of others, we must master our own. Otherwise we will always be off on false adventures; we will not be able to await the proper moment or seize the right occasion, because we have been carried away. We will not be able to use gentle insinuations and charming words. Our emotions will warn others to be wary of us, and will make us imagine interests that often we do not have. They will blind us to the nature of the resources that we must use and to the ways of using them. Indeed, a man who wishes to succeed in negotiations must be able to hide his emotions to the point of appearing cold when he is overwhelmed with sorrow and calm when he is shaken with passion. Since it is impossible to eliminate all emotion—indeed, it would be dangerous to be free of it entirely—one must at least learn to keep it in check and out of sight. It is often useful to appear to be shaken with emotion but of a different kind than that which is actually at work. An impassioned man gives hope of being won over, whereas a reserved man puts others on guard. In fact, a man who feigns emotions distracts those who are trying to get the upper hand on him. Such acting is permitted and is in no way contrary to proper behavior. . . .

[There then follows a discussion of the virtues of good looks, friendship, and eloquence.]

Once character and the means of persuasion are well known, there are still other considerations that result from a combination of the nature of the affair and the skill of the individuals with which one deals. One often meets men who are as difficult to convince as they are to arouse and who disdain all ideas other than their own. Neither a lack of intelligence nor a lack of sentiment is the cause of this difficulty: It is rather their attachment to their own thoughts, their vanity of never learning anything from anyone else, their suspicion of formal propositions, which renders men deaf to the voice of persuasion. With characters of this kind one must use insinuation, which is a roundabout way of suggesting ideas so that the hearer believes he has invented them himself. Since the little passions that block these minds' entrance to truth are very common and are found somewhere in every character, the art of insinuation is of more general usage than that of direct persuasion.

The very nature of business often requires insinuation. Some matters dare not be proposed formally, either because they are too contrary to sentiments or because they are too distant from the way of thinking of the individuals with whom one deals. Others cannot succeed at once and are brought to maturity only by long preparations. Still others cannot be proposed during discussion, and yet it is advantageous at the end to have appeared to have proposed them. In all these cases it would be imprudent to try to convince openly: One arrives at the goal only by casting indirect references and seeds of an idea, which will develop bit by bit, gradually producing the thoughts and movements as planned. In such moments generalizations are useful: By producing maxims without affectation and by relating facts simply, the matter for application is provided, and ideas germinate. Insinuations also give rise to what might be called overtures and illuminations, which are usually vague and indeterminate propositions that lead to more direct ones and that serve as conversation. Prudence often requires this approach, but only when used soberly and carefully, lest it degenerate into trickery. If people discover that one is out to surprise them by superficiality or artificiality, they close their minds even to solid notions and to those whose acceptance is in our interest.

Although one cannot choose the characters with which one negotiates an affair, it is nonetheless necessary to take into account the relation between strengths of character and the importance of the subject. The old compliment of a man, that he was never above or beneath that which he undertook, was wise praise. In fact, business prospers only in the hands of those whose character contains qualities proportionate to the means their subject requires. Yet little attention is paid to this and failure often results, simply because the extent of people's ability was not understood and matters were proposed to a degree that surpassed their faculties.

Nowhere is the effect of this disproportion more noticeable than in negotiating with timid or courageous minds. A risky matter that requires firmness is beyond the fearful man; if the matter is important and difficult, he will simply not dare to undertake it, or, if he does, or is obliged to, he will upset everything by false starts inspired by the fear of failure. On the other hand, a courageous man enters carelessly into daring and even frightening projects, and even if these projects are well thought out and organized, he always goes too far, and his confidence in his abilities carries him astray from the safe path. The first always needs the spur and the second the rein: One can never suggest important matters to the former, nor minor matters or those of limited scope to the latter.

Nevertheless, there is more to be gained from a character inspired by courage than from one deflated by timidity. Fear is doubtless one of the most unmanageable emotions, with such diversified and dissimilar effects that they often appear contradictory. Usually it is only curable by a higher dose of the same emotion, and if one has to deal with timid people, they can only be made to move by leading them continually to the brink and exaggerating its danger in order to force them to jump from the lesser precipice at hand. In speaking of courage in business one also speaks of firmness; this type of courage depends on strength of character and awareness of resources, whereas warlike courage or valor strictly speaking is a mechanical effect derived from the awareness of physical and temperamental strength. Those who expose themselves with

the greatest intrepidity to bodily dangers may well lack the first
type of courage, and often the bravest people demonstrate an
astonishing weakness in the events of civil life. It is mental
courage that gave Augustus, whose valor was rather doubtful,
a marked ascendency over Marc Anthony, a brave soldier but
a weak mind, and it is said that the spirit of the latter trembled
before Augustus.

Irresolution is a natural consequence of timidity. A man
who fears everything including himself has difficulty in making
up his mind, and the impression of fear puts uncertainty in
each step. However, there is still another source of irresolution, the absence of the kind of emotion necessary to decide a
particular case. Even people of the highest capacity are often
as irresolute as the most limited individuals. Their contradictory inspiration serves to suspend the decisiveness of their
will, by letting them see on both sides a host of reasons of
almost equal force that keep their animation suspended. It is at
that moment that the additional weight of a passion is necessary to swing the balance and start the will moving, for nothing sets back and upsets matters more than uncertainty of direction on the part of those who handle them. Nothing should
be spared to set their direction early and keep will on course.
If irresolution and inconsistency are caused by timidity, they
must be counterbalanced either by a greater fear or by
courage; if they come from the absence of passion, reason will
do no good. They will only be overcome by attracting and
maintaining exactly that kind of passion that can surmount in-
decision and stop vacillation. . . .

[Then follows a discussion of effects of changing wind,
mood, firmness, patience, passion, and *sang-froid*.]

Flexibility is related to patience, but it is also joined to a fa-
cility for leaning with the ideas and sentiments of others. It is a
necessary quality when dealing with all kinds of characters:
Rarely is it advisable to meet prejudices and passions head on.
Instead, it is best to appear to conform to them in order to gain
time to combat them. One must know how to sail with a contrary wind and to tack until one meets a wind in the right direction. But flexibility should not turn into artifice or falseness,
for if artifice is revealed, it discredits its author. It is permissible first to appear to be on the side of the person one seeks to

convince, in order to bring him around bit by bit through good reasoning without arousing him by premature contradictions. A pope once said of Abby de Polignac, "This young man always seems to be of my opinion and at the end of the conversation I find that I am of his."

It would also be useful to distinguish flexibility, which is a tactic of such great help in business, from that which is simply in the local character. The latter can become dangerous through the habit of weakness that it imparts. Easy manners are a very equivocal merit and are most often the mark of a small heart. A man who is in favor of everything, without distinction, is ordinarily a man good for nothing except to fill in the gaps in lazy societies. The flexibility of the negotiator is the unbending of a superior man, who puts himself within the reach of others; ordinary flexibility is only a servile custom that gives up the liberty of its ideas and its sentiments to the first claimant.

All business runs on conventions, to which truth alone can give consistency. If honesty is absent in contracts, if the parties are out to catch each other's errors, negotiation becomes a game where nothing is decided, where no advantage becomes stabilized, and where the parties must continually begin all over again. One cannot fool the same people repeatedly, and if a reputation for duplicity becomes attached to a negotiator, he can hope for no success in his undertakings. Honesty is therefore an indispensable basis for business, and every appearance of frankness and sincerity is necessary for handling affairs.

It is often suggested that a particular thing is good politics but not good morality; that assertion is contradictory because politics and morality are a single science and share the same principles. This paradoxical distinction is the subterfuge of vulgar politicians who are not able to arrive at their goals by direct means and who instead seek to cover up their petty schemes. A true politician who knows good morality will always be able to reconcile these apparent contradictions and to control his moves so that they do not clash with virtue. Wisdom needs no artifice to find the cleanest ways for its plans to succeed, and prudence disdains trickery when executing the plan drawn up by wisdom.

Sincerity greatly facilitates the conduct of affairs; dealings can be expedited when they involve people known for their truthfulness, and one can save the time that would be required to unveil the lies of those who do not have truth in their reputation. Honest parties do not have to waste time in soundings, in examinations, and in unmasking each other, and confidence smoothes all difficulties. Truth is also most useful when one finds oneself before deceitful and suspicious characters with whom one has to deal. Such individuals judge others by the standards of their own corruption, hearing truth as falsehood and thus fooling their own selves. For this reason Sir William Temple always maintained that truthfulness was the only ruse that always worked. A Spanish ambassador complained of the falseness of Cardinal Mazarin and warned his successor of the need to meet him on his own terms. "To the contrary," responded the latter, "I will always catch the Cardinal because I will always tell him the truth." . . .

[There then follows a section on the further advantages of the appearances of frankness, the avoidance of trickery, and the need to be ready for the unexpected.]

As a whole, the rules of conduct that derive from the different natures and varied combinations of affairs are a matter of intelligence. Without going into useless—and even impossible—detail, we must remain on the level of rather unsatisfactory generalities on the subject. It is enough to lay out the principles and to show what faculties of the mind and qualities of the soul are necessary to make a man capable of behaving properly under the circumstances, and which of these faculties and qualities he must use to arrive at a successful ending. Flashes of genius are not learned, but one prepares for them by skillful use of sentiment and by profound reflection on the relationship between causes and effects.

It is more natural to apply the general theory of negotiations to public affairs than the ordinary politician might suspect. They say that it is wrong to think that a man is capable of high-level negotiations simply because he has shown a superior ability in the conduct of business in ordinary life. Doubtless, unless he adds some basic knowledge on the affairs of state to his capabilities, this man will not be able to jump right into the handling of public affairs. But if he is able to grasp the necessary modifications required by public affairs, the same abilities will help him deal with them just as well as he had handled private matters. The prejudice of these politicians is a result of their ignorance and of their interests: They are not bright enough to feel the affinity between business and talent, and they are interested in presenting their profession as one of difficult access and long apprenticeship. In this way they resemble those old and narrow-minded doctors who scorn knowledge and intelligence and who talk only of experience, which they themselves were never able to acquire.

Cardinal Janson, as good a courtier as a skilled negotiator, felt otherwise. Louis XIV asked him one day where he learned so much about negotiation. "Sire," replied the cardinal, "it was while I was still bishop of Digne and I had to find a mayor for Aix-en-Provence without showing my hand." Indeed, the whole difference in the way of handling matters that at first glance appear to be of such different natures, only comes from the depth, the importance, and the complexity of public matters and from the position, the sensitivity, and the skill of the people involved in them. All that has been said about negotiation in its broadest sense applies to public affairs without exception, and any other specifics that could be added involve only a few reflections.

There have doubtless been negotiations as long as there have been societies with interests to discuss. The savages of America sent ambassadors to each other to conclude treaties and to settle the claims of their compatriots. But the form of negotiations is determined by the customs, development, and constitution of a people, and by the international system to which they belong. The states of old, separated by their customs and having few communications through travel and trade, ordinarily had only momentary interests to untangle: a war to terminate, a boundary to establish, a temporary alliance to set up. To this end, ancient peoples used ambassadors on short missions, and since their task was mostly one of persuading a large number of people, individuals known for their eloquence were chosen so that the name "orator" became synonymous with that of public minister. During the Middle Ages, when everything including justice was decided by force alone and where Gothic government brought together all the small states through their position and separated them at the same time through their interests, negotiation had little power on wild and isolated people who neither knew nor valued any means for ending their quarrels except that of arms. Negotiation was practically reduced to the art of arranging cease-fires and setting ransoms.

It is only in modern Europe, where the inhabitants are closely united by similar customs, common religious basis, frequent commerce, and continual intellectual communication, that negotiation has been raised to an art and become stable. This change has been brought about by the rise of common interests and the creation of a political system unknown to the ancients, which has made Europe a kind of republic of allies and has brought its rulers to maintain resident ministers in all the courts of our continent. Some people have wished to honor Cardinal Mazarin by crediting him with the introduction of the art of negotiation in France and the perfection of that art in general. However, even before his time, France and other states of Europe produced the most able of negotiators, and since his time great men have seemed to follow methods that were quite different from his. This minister, filled with petty tricks, brought his penchant for artifice into negotiation and, far from having perfected this art, appears to have embroiled it, altering its simplicity and retarding its progress.

However that may be, the custom of negotiating without interruption, or at least the possibility of doing so at any time, has made public negotiation more complex. The delays that that custom imposes on affairs demand greater firmness and patience and a surer hold on passions than would have been required by a more expeditious negotiation. The habit of negotiating without interruption teaches all the ruses that the politicians use to fool each other, and its slowness gives all the time necessary to use them both to tire and to surprise each other. There are continual occasions to sound out, examine, and abuse the sentiments of others.

The necessary complexity of public affairs already causes enough difficulties, even beyond those encountered in private matters. So many hidden and obscure sources work together to produce political events; so many disguised sentiments are involved in the behavior of great men; so many separate interests

form the national interest, so that it is impossible to set into
motion or direct such mechanisms without knowing all their
components well. One must be able to discover these sources,
manipulate their effects, and use them appropriately. It is this
multiplicity of considerations necessary to ascertain a single
fact, this quantity of subordinate causes to arrive at a single
effect, that make politics the most difficult science and that
render the application of its theory to practice so unsure. A little wheel is ignored or neglected, and the whole machine
grinds to a halt. In the affairs of civil life, these resources are
fewer, simpler, and dependent upon a smaller framework of
understanding.

The complexity of public affairs requires greater wisdom in
planning, but their importance also requires greater prudence
in execution. In civil life a false step is easily corrected, and
there are a thousand ways to repair the effect of an unfortunate event. But everything that concerns the interest of states
confers the greatest importance on each move, and in case of a
misstep the remedies are not so easy to find. Rulers have no superior judge to make up for the imprudence of their behavior
or for bad faith in their commitments, and they cannot go to
court—as a minister of the past century tried to do—against a
neighbor who tries to take advantage of them. They have to
rely on their own resources, on those of their allies, and on
their own good conduct. The minister whom they trust with
the conduct of their affairs needs all the skill and circumspec-
tion possible, along with an unusual prudence in innovation
and in the choice of expedients. . . .

[Hereafter follows a discussion of the difficulties of dealing
with great men because their high position, their idiosyncrasies
and their susceptibility to flattery, as well as their high expectations of quality in their company.]

By these considerations it is easy to see that the public negotiator should have the necessary qualities for the conduct of
affairs to a much higher degree than one who deals with
private matters. Along with the intelligence necessary to his
calling, he needs a deep knowledge of men and their affairs, a
rare talent for exploiting the sentiments of others and controlling his own, an art of speaking and writing agreeably, forcefully, and easily, and indomitable courage tempered by a gen-

tleness without condescension, an open appearance accompanied by noble and endearing manners, a superior wisdom, a sharply discerning mind, an enlightened honesty, consummate prudence untrammeled by trickery, an inventive spirit through difficulty, and finally an elevation of heart and mind to keep him out of trivia. Such spiritual superiority is required by public affairs where the taste for trivia that characterizes small minds has most dangerous consequences.

Of these qualities, those that are not a happy gift of nature can be gained only through study, meditation, practice, and experience. The life of a man is too short for him to gain experience and capability in all kinds of affairs. Thus, one prepares one's own experience through a study of the experiences of others, in the light of the great intellectual discoveries of history. Some say that an author can only produce a work of the highest quality if he has had an active role in the matters that he writes about; but one could say, more correctly, that a man cannot play his role well—particularly in negotiation—if he has not accumulated knowledge and cultivated talent by a familiarity with the best authors. Study is incontestably useful: Meditation digests and assimilates reading. The negotiator will focus his attention most profitably on those aspects of knowledge closest to his vocation: on politics, which supplies him with the principles for his activities; on history, whose collection of the experiences of moral man teaches him to discover the cause of events; on philosophy, which leads him to reason correctly; and on literature, which adds pleasure to his knowledge. Armed with these benefits he can penetrate into the labyrinth of business with assurance and acquire experience and capability rapidly.

Even if these different sorts of knowledge are not absolutely indispensable, they are always advantageous for an indirect reason. The public minister has to join in all kinds of conversations, and in society one speaks only of things or of people. It is obviously of great consequence to speak too much of the latter in situations where the hostility of the single man can cause a negotiation to collapse, not to mention the disagreeableness of such a conversation. If one speaks of things, a man locked up in the ideas of his profession limits his conversation to business matters or is forced into boring silence. It is obvious that prudence forbids conversations so filled with the risk of an easy betrayal of feelings, a discovery of plans, or a revelation of secrets. If the negotiator is widely read, on the other hand, he can supply subjects for an agreeable conversation, making himself more pleasant, drawing the esteem and the friendship of others, and running no danger of exposure. In any case, such conversation will provide welcome distraction from his important occupations and will save him from uselessly dissipating his talents.

For these reasons great political figures have required a great breadth of knowledge from their public ministers. Sully testified that the eloquence and the reputation of Cardinal Duperron were of more use to him in his negotiations than all the tricks of others; he added that it was impossible to resist his subtle and ingratiating conversation, sparkling with diversified enlightenment. Temple looked down on any uncultured minister as a man who lacked an essential part of his political credentials. There is no need to cite the large number of statesmen who shared his point of view. Bacon shows through history that the most skillful politicians were all highly cultured men. . . . [The discussion continues, citing the necessity of a high level of culture for the proper conduct of negotiation and also the difficulties that such superior talent evokes.]

But if a man is blessed with this happy and rare gift of balance among his spirit, his intellect, and his character, he is capable of handling the greatest affairs. However, such men are practically never used, and the fault is partly theirs. When they are well educated, and once they have actively tasted the pleasures of the knowledge of truth, they usually give themselves up enthusiastically to the study of science and letters. Their occupation there is no doubt so high above the level of other employment that it is difficult for them to descend to less satisfying ventures. In so doing, they make a secret sacrifice to the circumstances or to considerations that are far from their true happiness. Indeed, intellectual attainment renders a man rather indifferent to money, and a certain elevation of the soul prevents him from engaging in the necessary activities to eliminate his rivals and to succeed. Unlike times past, one can no longer tear an enlightened man away from his meditation and force him to serve his country in active life.

It is therefore superfluous to give too much attention to the portrait of the perfect negotiator. Indeed, this portrait, like that of other characters, should simply express the perfection of a model that is difficult to find in reality and often even difficult to define in concept. Good men are often available for the post of public ministry, but often one is also obliged to take what is available, either by chance or by reputation or by acquaintance. In the meanwhile, the world will go its own way for—according to the view of the famous Oxenstiern—it needs so little wisdom to be governed.

In reality, opinions seem divided on the usefulness and the importance of negotiation. Sovereigns neglect it through disdain, through a spirit of economy, or through a presumptuous confidence in their own strength. There are whole periods of history that are sterile in negotiation, where a destructive spirit wins over nations and where matters are decided only by recourse to arms. There are others where the pacifying influence of fear appears to dominate and where serious matters are never discussed. Weak and unwarlike states negotiate ceaselessly, for they can meet their enemies only with the defense of prudence and skill. There are some enthusiastic negotiators that maintain that a good ambassador is worth as much to his master as an army of a hundred thousand men.

The greatest crowned rulers and even the conquerors who looked down on negotiation have never scorned it with impunity. By using only power and arrogance they alarm their neighbors and force them to band together against a troubling and formidable power, always ready to throw itself on those who give it the slightest pretext for war. Early negotiations undercut suspicion and can win over some of the princes who might be tempted to ally against us; by showing a tendency for the ways of gentleness and accommodation, one diminishes the fear that a military government inspires. History is filled with examples of monarchs who became overconfident in the success of their arms and neglected to cultivate the friendship and alliance of other powers through negotiation; through their arrogance and imprudence they attracted the greatest misfortunes on themselves. Even conquerers have made their progress easier through the skill of winning over men: Pyrrhu admitted that his sword did not win him as many cities as the eloquence of Cyneas.

Some powers, with very mediocre forces, win support and rid themselves of the most troublesome difficulties. They owe their success to their prudence, to their care in accommodating themselves to conditions around them, to their sharp grasp of occasions favorable to their interests, and to a wise observation of the maxim that it is always best to submit to negotiation those things that one cannot contest by arms. Such conduct depends on continual negotiations and on friends and allies; it is the unique but sure resource of the weak, and it is most useful for tempering the excessive force of the powerful.

However, negotiations are always imperfect and accompanied by a thousand difficulties if they are not supported by real or imagined power. The minister of a victorious prince who is feared and respected finds doors open and all his affairs ready for solid success. What is most advantageous in general is to be able skillfully to combine power and negotiation. Without force negotiation is usually a tool without an edge, and has little effect; without negotiation force is too sharp and too brittle an instrument, which breaks in the hands of its user.

Up till now public negotiation has shown a very equivocal utility for the happiness of men. The uninterrupted number of treaties, instead of assuring international peace, seems only to be a signal for new wars, and the guarantees invented to give solidity to these pacts are more apt to make belligerence spread than to contain it. Yet what praise would sovereigns attract if they would seek to use negotiation to bring about the greatest design of all politics—that of giving greater consistency to the European system. Alongside of their own peace and security, they would win immortal glory and the sweet satisfaction of having arranged the happiness of a large part of the human race.

# 2. THE BARGAINING STRUCTURE OF NATO: MULTI-ISSUE NEGOTIATIONS IN AN INTERDEPENDENT WORLD*

*Edward L. Morse*
*Council on Foreign Relations*

The recent introduction of international monetary and commercial issues into bargaining among the members of NATO has compounded an already complex strategic setting. Negotiations over burden-sharing, force levels, and military strategy have been intricate enough, especially since the onset of détente. The movement toward a relaxation of tensions in Europe has made explicit the contradictory objectives that the United States and its European allies have pursued toward the Soviet Union and the other Eastern-bloc states. It has also raised suspicions between them, just as it has to a lesser degree brought to light the antithetical goals of the Soviet Union and its Warsaw Pact allies with regard to their own security. Now

* Research support for this study was made available through a NATO research fellowship, which the author gratefully acknowledges. The viewpoint represented in the study is the author's and ought not to be attributed to NATO. An earlier version of this chapter was presented to the Annual Meeting of the American Political Science Association in New Orleans in 1972.

the strikingly different attitudes of the governments on either side of the Atlantic toward strategy and tactics involved in either the energy crisis or restructuring the international economic system have reinforced the contradictions imposed by détente on their security objectives; they have also exacerbated the foreign-policy dilemmas that the different governments face. In economic and security matters the governments of the United States and of Western Europe have discovered that they can neither develop autonomous positions nor reconcile their fundamental disagreements.

What is most significant about these contradictions, especially as they relate to the interjection of economic issues into security affairs, is what they imply for the theoretical conceptualization of alliances in general and of NATO in particular. Can existing theory of alliance or coalition behavior account for the mixed-motive strategies that the members of NATO now pursue vis-à-vis one another? Is a general perspective on the political economy of international relations more likely to prove fruitful to this conceptualization than the body of coalition theory that now exists? If so, how useful would be either cost-benefit analysis or the analysis of public goods to an understanding of the contemporary bargaining context in NATO? Most importantly, how has the growth in interdependence among industrialized non-Communist societies been affected by NATO? What have been the effects of interdependence on the bargaining structure of the alliance?

None of these general questions can be approached directly in the brief analysis embodied in this chapter. They raise, however, a set of secondary questions that can be handled more readily, the answers to which can shed some light on more general theoretical issues. For example, is the introduction of economic issues into alliance matters really new? If not, were they latent or recognized throughout the history of NATO? How, if at all, has their context changed and affected the strategic among the members since 1949?

In this chapter I will argue, first, that coalition theory cannot improve our understanding of NATO and that the alliance is one in name only, bearing little resemblance to traditional coalitions in international relations; second, that a more restrictive definition of the bargaining context in NATO is

needed; third, that an analysis of public goods is important to
the understanding of present problems; and fourth, that a
theory of core-periphery relations helps to explain NATO's
bargaining structure.

### NATO AND TRADITIONAL COALITION THEORY

The existence of interdependent economic relations in the
NATO area would alone set this alliance apart from others.
Unlike previous alliances, NATO can be characterized not
only as a "zone of peace" whose members have renounced the
use of force in their mutual relations,[1] but also as part of a system whose economies have been highly integrated and whose
members have developed great economic benefits while also
losing autonomy for independent decision-making. They can
take independent action only at high cost.[2] Even had this
growth in interdependence not occurred, any general theory of
alliances applicable to the world before 1945 would need to be
altered significantly to describe a world of nuclear weapons. In
such a world, fundamental problems of traditional alliances
like the accretion of power or the restraining of an enemy or
an ally, seem antiquated. As Henry Kissinger wrote a decade
ago,

> Nuclear war requires tight command of all weapons, which
> is to some degree inconsistent with a coalition of sovereign
> states. Moreover, the enormous risks of nuclear warfare
> affect the credibility of traditional pledges of mutual assist-
> ance. In the past, alliances held together because it was
> believed that the *immediate* risk of conflict was less than the
> *ultimate* danger of facing a preponderant enemy alone. But
> when nuclear war hazards the lives of tens of millions, some
> allies may consider the outbreak of a war the worst contin-
> gency and, in times of crisis, act accordingly.[3]

While the dilemmas posed for alliances by nuclear weapons
have become significant features of coalition behavior, few
theorists of alliance take note of them. They continue to
proceed, either through the generation of data on alliances in
past eras, or through the exposition of logical models, in the
hope that by gaining an understanding of the way alliances

have been formed or have disintegrated in the past they will shed a significant amount of light on alliance problems in today's world.[4] The study of alliances, like so many other subjects in the study of politics, is composed of writings that embody contradictory hypotheses, fallacies of misplaced measurement, and a fundamentally weak theoretical basis.[5]

Even if one defines NATO as a collective defense arrangement, two impediments to theorizing about the alliance remain. On the one hand, the centralized American control over the deployment and use of nuclear weapons belies any attempt to affirm that NATO is a coalition of autonomous units. This remains the case in spite of the independent nuclear striking forces operated by the British and French governments. Those forces represent more of a potential for future development than either credible, independent and autonomous forces, or triggers on the American force. On the other hand, an alternative conceptualization of NATO in terms of patron-client relations cannot proceed very far. The European allies not only have retained effective autonomy to negotiate with the presumptive "enemy" to the East, but they can also dissociate themselves from American leadership on a variety of strategic and nonstrategic issues. This remains a striking contrast with the Warsaw Pact, whose East European members are far more constrained by the Soviet Union than are the European members of NATO by the United States.[6] Moreover, the autonomy of the West European members of NATO cannot be attributed simply to the free-rider problem outlined by theorists who have concerned themselves with the effects of public goods.[7] The security provided by the American deterrent has not allayed fears of a "Finlandization" of Western Europe. If anything, it has served to exacerbate them by raising the specter of a set of understandings between the governments of the United States and the Soviet Union that would undermine security in Western Europe. In that scenario, the governments of Western Europe would find themselves with limited American support and intra-European cohesion too difficult to attain. Each would then be open to political manipulation by the Soviet Government through adroit use of bilaterally based promises and implicit threats. Fear of "Finlandization," in short, serves to limit autonomy in security affairs and as an incentive to Europeans to maintain alliance cohesion.

Nor can efforts to maintain autonomy be attributed to the theoretical implications of the free-rider problem when NATO is conceptualized as a public good. In particular, those theorists who have argued that as the size of a group increases there are greater incentives for members to receive a free ride either argued inconsistently with the tenets of rational behavior or have left out exogenous variables. At best, as Frohlich and Oppenheimer have pointed out, the assumptions that the marginal valuation of a good decreases with group size or that there is a higher probability that others will donate to the supply of the good "only suffice to bring about ever smaller donations by an individual, with increasing group-size. Thus, even further restrictions would be needed to produce a relation between group-size and a free-rider problem."[8] In fact, as Beer has shown, the institutionalization of NATO "appears to produce new disproportionalities, which, to some extent, may work to offset the old. Large powers overpay for some aspects, while small ones overcontribute to others."[9]

Such difficulties with the applicability of traditional conceptualizations of alliances are not new. Whether one starts from the nuclear dilemma or with attempts to develop an economic theory of alliance, new metaphors are necessary to come to grips with the complex set of motivations that characterize NATO. A fresh look at the "political economy" of NATO should have greater explanatory power than does traditional alliance theory or predominantly economic theories that have focused only on military relations.[10] In order to specify what is meant by this, it is necessary first to define generally the context of relations among the NATO members.

### THE BARGAINING CONTEXT IN NATO

Relationships among the NATO members are too complex to restrict their analysis to a military-security focus alone. The most important members of the alliance are the same ones that have been involved in the negotiation of predominantly economic issues. All of these latter issues have become central to the bargaining framework of NATO in both open and subtle

ays. Former Secretary of the Treasury John Connally, for
example, voiced what had hitherto been a tacit understanding
when he announced in 1971 that the European members of
NATO would be expected to take actions to revalue their currencies if they expected the United States to continue to deploy
troops in Europe. And votes in the U. S. Senate in support of
the Mansfield Resolution in the early 1970s came consistently
from representatives of farming interests who have been irri-
tated by the restrictive levies on American agricultural exports
to Europe.[11]

Bargaining within NATO, in short, takes place in a complex
environment and includes such disparate factors as politics between the executive branch and Congress in the United States,
electoral politics in Europe, East-West relations, monetary and
commercial issues, and disagreements over strategic objectives
and tactics. The inclusion of economic issues in NATO politics
indicates that the alliance is best interpreted in a general context of political economy. In this sense, the security relationships of the major members of NATO compose but one
aspect of a wider set of relationships, which include security,
interdependent economic relationships, and the continuing
efforts of nine governments (almost all in NATO) to forge a
distinct and autonomous political force in Europe. These arrangements have been counterbalanced by the ever-present
urge to national autonomy in decision-making by all of the
major participants. They therefore have also been contradicted
by the frequently and strikingly divergent goals pursued by
these governments toward each other and toward third parties
(especially the Soviet Union and the governments of Eastern
Europe). This is the case whether one speaks of the suspicion
on the part of European governments of direct and bilateral
negotiations between the two superpowers, or of the implications of the next stage in the pursuit of the *Ostpolitik* by the
West German Government, or of the implications of Gaullist
foreign policy as modified by recent French governments.

This overlapping set of structures shows that nonsecurity
issues have always been implicit in the United States-Western
Europe relationship, in the NATO context in particular. Some
revisionist historians, for example, have seen in NATO an instrument for achieving a policy that was "military in emphasis

but aiming at the ERP's economic goals,"[12] i.e., restitution o
the economies of Western Europe to assure markets for Amer
ican products and thereby to stave off depression in the Unite
States and a crisis for American capitalism. Other schola
have argued that even if the thrust of most revisionist theses i
misleading, there is something to the analysis that security an
economic affairs were tied together in NATO from its begir
nings. Robert Gilpin finds, for example, that the United State
like the Soviet Union, sought to fill a power vacuum created b
the collapse of German and Japanese power at the end c
World War II and, as a primarily naval power, "had to orgar
ize a global system of bases and alliances involving an in
mense drain on its balance of payments."[13] In the interest c
maximizing its strategic position against the Soviet Union, th
United States needed to construct these bases and alliances.
did so, in Gilpin's argument, by striking a bargain with th
governments of Western Europe:

> In the interest of security the United States tolerated, and i
> fact promoted, the creation of a preference area in Wester
> Europe which discriminated against American goods.[14]

In this analysis, NATO represents only one part of a mult
ple bargain between the United States and its Europea
members. In return for acceding to the needs of American s
curity, the Europeans received, at least implicitly, advantag
in commercial relations by discriminating against America
products.[15] By looking at this set of bargains Gilpin can rela
the introduction of nonsecurity issues in the alliance fram
work to the realization on the part of both the Americans an
the European members that they are no longer receiving r
turns for their trade-off and thus both are groping
reformulate it. In this sense, Gilpin's analysis has far great
applicability to contemporary problems in NATO and rel
vance to issues of current negotiation than does the bulk
theoretical writings on alliances in the literature on intern
tional politics. Moreover, it has the virtue of embodying a s
of "ultra-Keynesian" notions about growth and change in tl
international system that seem to provide some useful insigh
into the bargaining structure of the alliance. Implicit in Gi

in's analysis is the ultra-Keynesian notion of core-periphery relationships. In order to apply this notion to contemporary politics in the North Atlantic area, we must first define some terms and then summarize the evolution of the structure of politics between the core and periphery over the past quarter century.

The United States and its political-economic system will be regarded as the core area, and Europe its periphery. This distinction has by now become commonplace in both neo-Marxist and ultra-Keynesian analysis. It is used frequently in writings concerning relations between developed and less-developed societies, especially as used by Raul Prebisch and in studies that have been derivative of his.[16] The neo-Marxist position is based on the Leninist law of uneven development,[17] while the ultra-Keynesian view is based on the presumed economies of agglomeration and the economic bases of the expansion of markets.[18] Both emphasize two of the definitional traits of core areas. On the one hand, the leadership of a core area is defined as having an entrepreneurial role. In terms of the analysis of public goods to which we shall return below, such leadership fulfills an entrepreneurial role in establishing individualistically a collective mechanism or a collective good for itself and others (peripheral systems). On the other hand, emphasis is placed on economic growth, which derives from a core area and spreads to peripheral areas. Economic and political growth is typically associated with a process of nucleation. As Schmitt has argued,

> Particular peoples and nations have tended to crystallize around particular concentrations of capital and technology, core areas whose superior rates of economic growth raised expectations of economic reward from political association with them.[19]

What is noteworthy about core areas is that they tend to attract all factors of production (technology, capital, and labor) due to the higher expectation and lower risks they provide. As Schmitt (p. 4) maintains, "Concentrations of capital and technology will thus attract to themselves further innovations that make both capital and labor progressively

more productive and more highly rewarded than elsewhere.
This development contrasts strikingly with the expectations o
neoclassical or liberal theory, according to which capital and
labor should move in opposite directions, the former to area
lacking in capital and the latter to those lacking in labor, give
higher theoretical expectations of return. In terms of a dis
tributive theory of justice, neoclassical theory would predict
more equitable distribution of wealth, or value, if factors o
production were permitted to move freely. Ultra-Keynesia
theory, to the contrary, would predict an increasing maldistri
bution, with the core area getting richer and poorer area
either brought into the core by the nucleation process (losing
their autonomy) or left out and relegated to greater relative
deprivation. This would be the case as a result of the logic o
economic growth, even if there were a relative absence o
entrepreneurship in the core area.

What are the political implications of this nuclear process o
growth for core-periphery relationships? Nucleation from the
core results in real losses at the periphery, where governments
abilities to achieve their political and economic goals decline i
a relatively open world. If they wish to preserve autonomy
they will have to accept costs to the welfare of their societies
Yet they must do exactly that in the short run if they attemp
to create a core area of their own. These costs need not b
viewed as insuperable obstacles. Schmitt (pp. 6–7) maintain
that

> There are several reasons why a citizenry may willingly bea
> such costs. Fear of excessive concentrations of power coul
> in many minds justify even permanent losses in materia
> welfare. Residential preferences of a population with cul
> tural and political memories may not in any case be share
> to the same extent by managements of foreign origin. Fi
> nally, the survival of a distinct culture as a source of collec
> tive pride may be thought precarious in the context of a new
> and amalgamated society.

An inevitable tension therefore develops in the relationshi
between core and periphery areas, even if the initial benefit
were deemed satisfactory. While the model of core-periphery
relationships in the form described above is somewhat mislead

ng as a description of the relationships between the United States and Western Europe, it does shed a good deal of light on the subject.

The American Government has served as a core area in security, monetary, and commercial affairs since the late 1940s. American military predominance in NATO, which was reinforced by the development of a nuclear deterrent force that has remained an American monopoly in the alliance, was paralleled by its economic predominance among the industrial and non-Communist societies at the onset of the Cold War. The latter is obvious from operational indices used for defining core areas. Direct investments have flowed from the United States to Western Europe, with portfolio investment in the opposite direction, and the American economy has spread outward from the United States by means of the vehicle of multinational enterprises just as the American currency has become the major officially and privately held asset. Frictions that have developed between the United States and Western Europe often derive from the desire of the latter to preserve political and cultural values that have been eroded by the nucleation process. Current negotiations between the European communities and the United States thus can be understood as part of a conscious effort by the former to create a new nuclear or core area centered in Europe. That, in fact, was the explicit goal postulated at the summit meeting of the Nine in October 1972. This effort in the political-economic realm has been paralleled by the perceived need in Europe to maintain the wherewithal to build a European-based deterrent force that could be decoupled from the United States by perhaps the mid-1980s.

The relationships between the United States and Western Europe have, in broad outline, conformed to an evolving structure of core-periphery dimensions. This structure has also been described in the literature on public goods as conforming to some of the expected dynamics of group behavior. Before specifying and explaining the evolution of the bargaining structure of U.S.-European relations in the context of core and periphery, let us first look at some implications of that literature for this analysis.

## ENTREPRENEURSHIP AT THE CORE

The analysis of NATO has in recent years focused to a considerable extent on the model of public goods that Olson and Zeckhauser applied in the mid-1960s. Since public goods are distinguished by the difficulty or impossibility of excluding any member of the group from their enjoyment, they were seen to be relevant to the analysis of "goods" consumed internationally and particularly to the analysis of security in an alliance.[20] Research in international relations has recently centered around the accumulation of data to test the notion that public goods have become significant phenomena in alliances.[21] Most of the research has tested a central properties of public goods. Once such a good is supplied for any one unit of a group (be it a person or a collectivity), it can also be provided to other units at either no cost or at very little cost. Since the cost of exclusion is high, "it is of the essence of an organization that it provides an inseparable, generalized benefit."[22] As Olson argued, rational action by the leaders of the group would lead it, in the absence of coercion, to provide suboptimal contributions for the supply of a good. This has been true in organizations like the United Nations and NATO with regard to some activities, but the reasons for this are still in dispute. I mentioned earlier, for example, that Frohlich and Oppenheimer challenged this assumption on theoretical grounds and that Beer has challenged it on the basis of empirical data. In fact, there are a number of reasons more compelling than the free-rider explanation for the inequity in the distribution of contributions to the alliance. One is the differential value that each member government may seek in the collective enterprise and the possibility that exchanges made in the alliance framework provide for benefits and contributions in nonmilitary contexts.

What is shown by this analysis, through the emphasis placed on the different "size" of members with regard to their contributions to the collective undertaking, is the existence and significance of asymmetries among members. Olson and Zeckhauser argued, for example, that there is "a tendency for the 'larger' members—those that place a higher absolute value n the public good—to bear a disproportionate share of the urden."[23] By assuming rational behavior on the part of individual members of a group, an individual's interest and the roup's interest are likely to differ, and individuals

> will not act to advance their common or group objective unless there is coercion to force them to do so, or unless some separate incentive, distinct from the achievement of the common or group interest, is offered to the members of the group individually on the condition that they help bear the costs or burdens involved in the achievement of the group objectives.[24]

Frohlich, Oppenheimer, and Young have questioned the alidity of claims concerning differential payments for the suply of public goods based on the size principle and, instead, ave argued that another asymmetry is likely to carry more exlanatory power. This has to do with the value to the individal of consuming the good or the value received in an xchange for supplying the collective good.[25] With the inoduction of the concept of entrepreneurship to the question f the supply of public goods a new range of analytical posibilities opens that makes the development of this sort of odel of interdependent relationships more relevant to the udy of international politics in general, and NATO in particlar. Thus, Frohlich and Oppenheimer have introduced the oncept of "entrepreneurial role," which "can be concepualized as the set of rewards and costs which an individual an expect to incur by supplying consumption units in xchanges."[26] It is the political entrepreneur whose pecialization is to supply goods collectively. In these terms, hat distinguishes NATO (and, indeed, the Warsaw Pact) om more traditional forms of alliance is that it involves the idividualistic supply of a public good whose profits to the potical entrepreneur, the United States Government, consist of e revenues extracted from the recipients of the good (in adition to the value attached to the act of political entreeneurship).

The public-goods concept also embodies concepts of interest aximization, which have always been central in the study of olitics, and permits an analysis of greater verisimilitude when combined with other models of interdependence. It permits an analyst to look at the general structure of politics within the North Atlantic area, both as a security community (or public good individualistically supplied by the United States) and as a network of interdependent economic relationships, and at the ways that the two affect one another. Such an analysis would look at symmetries and asymmetries within the total system and their interaction in what are, on the face of it, separate aspects of a single set of relationships.

It became obvious, for example, before the monetary crisis of 1971 that "burden sharing" in NATO is fused with the international monetary and commercial network in which the United States and the other industrialized societies have become interdependent. These relationships involve asymmetries and symmetries. In security affairs, there is a distinction between the role of the United States and that of Western Europe. The United States Government has, since the onset of the Cold War, been the provider of collective security if one focuses upon the core of security in the American deterrent force.[27] In the international monetary system, the American Government has been responsible for the provision of the mechanism of the system by providing dollar assets for use as reserves, liquidity, private transactions, intervention in the private markets, and so forth. The American Government has grown reluctant to provide this collective mechanism in international monetary affairs, and Europeans, if one believes their rhetoric, would like to replace the system of individualistic supply of this set of goods to the group with a system that would provide for their collective supply.[28] In commercial affairs, however, the two are now on equal footing, if one looks at the European communities as an individual unit. The Europe of the Nine by 1970 had a population slightly larger than the United States, a GNP of approximately two thirds in size, and a larger proportion of world exports (25 per cent vs. 20 per cent) and imports (25 per cent vs. 17 per cent). The relatively equal weight of the two enterprises in bargaining over the development of rules and procedures for international trade is thus counterbalanced by a fundamental and long-term asymmetry in other situations. This disparity cannot help be

ave an influence on the bargaining strategies that political
uthorities on each side of the Atlantic have followed.

## NATO IN THE "CRISIS ZONE"

The argument presented above represents an effort to define
he general structure of relations among the NATO members.
he American Government undoubtedly struck a trade-off
vith the other governments at the beginning of the integration
rocess in Europe. The U. S. Government encouraged the de-
'elopment of a nucleation process in Europe from the onset of
he Cold War and, until recently, European political and eco-
omic integration was a principal aim of American policy. In
eturn, the U. S. Government ran the security policies of the
on-Communist industrialized societies and received the
enefits of seignorage from the use of the dollar in interna-
ional monetary relationships.[29]

More recently, the American Government has realized that
 has perhaps received a bad bargain. The dominance it gained
 the international monetary system in return for granting
ommercial freedom to the Japanese and to the European
ommunities was questioned at the same time that restrictions
gainst American exports were viewed as causing the deterio-
ating balance-of-payments position of the United States. The
ominance in security affairs was also attacked as some issues
f the Cold War passed away and both the changed strategic
ituation vis-à-vis the Soviet Union and the increased pressures
t home against military expenditures presented opportunities
or military retrenchment.

The three issue areas under discussion—commercial, mone-
ary, and security affairs—have all entered what might be
alled a "crisis zone."[30] In such a zone the potential for bar-
aining between the core and periphery units becomes height-
ned as the issues separating the two are clarified. The interests
nd objectives pursued by both parties are quite different with
espect to the new rules of the game that must be created in
rder to take the system out of a zone of crisis. The core area
'ill try to prevent the emergence of a coalition of periphery
tates against it in bargaining over these new rules, while the
eriphery will be in an optimum strategic bargaining situation

precisely when it is able to construct an effective coalition
Moreover, the core area will likely feel that it is in its interest
to continue to strike bargains in a variety of issue areas simul
taneously so as to maximize its leverage over the periphery
while the latter countries will attempt to separate issue areas to
prevent manipulation.

This situation is precisely the one now found in the relation
among the industrialized societies of the non-Communist
world. The American Government has, especially since the
monetary crisis of 1971, emphasized its bilateral ties with the
governments on the periphery to prevent a unified coalition
from developing.[31] The pursuit of special interests with the pe
riphery stresses the uniqueness of bilateral ties designed to
prevent the emergence of a peripheral coalition. The U. S
Government has continued to stress the security it has
provided to the Federal Republic of Germany in order to im
pede it from committing itself to a new set of monetary rules
within the European Community, which would be antithetic to
American objectives. It has also tried to tie together the struc
ture of reform in NATO, the international monetary system
and new trade negotiations, since, from the view of the core
these are inseparable. Moreover, as a result of the phenomena
growth in systemic interdependencies, especially in financial
matters, the U. S. Government has not hesitated to manipulat
the internal economic and political situation in the societies
along the periphery in order to induce those governments to
accept American aims.

The objectives of the periphery countries are quite to the
contrary. The only way they can compensate for the high cost
of a change in the rules of the game that have benefited the
core area and to minimize the costs of nucleation is by forming
a coalition with which the United States would be willing to
negotiate on equal terms. They also want to prevent the core
from using its manipulative power in different fields. The Ger
man Government, even with its security ties to the United
States, has been unwilling to give in to American demands in
such a way as to antagonize its Common Market partners. The
European governments have also impeded the United States
from tying together reforms of the monetary, commercial, and
security relationships by insisting on separate negotiating

forums for each. Finally, their fear of manipulation of their domestic economies by the United States, especially as manifested in their claims of "imported inflation," serves to heighten anti-Americanism in their own populations so as to permit the development of a new core area and to make acceptable the economic costs of disentanglement from the United States.

Periphery areas are always at a disadvantage in this sort of bargaining situation. This is manifested in the contemporary world by the fact that the United States holds more strings over each of the European governments than any of them can over the United States. The U.S. strength in bargaining over the reform of the monetary system, and, in particular, over the initial settlement of the monetary crisis in 1971, stemmed from the American position in the global market (16 per cent of world trade) coupled with the relative insignificance of the external sector in the U.S. economy (4 per cent of GNP) when compared with the external sectors of other states (frequently at the level of 20 per cent of GNP in Europe). This has meant that by threatening to disrupt world trade, the U. S. Government could be expected to be affected least of all the industrialized societies. Fears, however, of the eventual consequences of such manipulative behavior, and, in particular, the fear that it spurs the periphery on to develop its nucleation process and impede American power damped the vigor of American diplomacy and led to a compromise settlement. And fears on both sides that overt manipulation of the system might lead to its destruction has also toned down some issues in contention.

The growth of a potential core area in Western Europe to challenge the entrepreneurial capacity of the United States has been noteworthy and ought not to be underestimated. This growth has resulted from economic integration within Europe since the founding of the Coal and Steel Community and from the decline in the salience of Cold War issues. Growing bilateralism between the United States and the Soviet Union has raised suspicions regarding ultimate American and Soviet aims, just as it has stabilized the security setting in Europe and opened the way for the complex set of bilateral and multilateral initiatives on all levels of East-West relations. The set-

ting would seem appropriate for an attempt at limited costs or
the part of the Europeans to begin to break their security linkage to the United States by decoupling European security from
American security. But a combination of issues in the security
field itself make that prospect unlikely in the immediate future

An independent European nuclear deterrent force, upon
which any autonomous European security framework must be
based, remains rudimentary. Not only do general social cost:
in France and Britain prevent them from increasing the leve
of research and development or expenditures in the defense
sector, but also intra-European suspicions over the ultimate
aims of British or French policy, or over that of Germany'
*Ostpolitik*, make the prospect of a continued reliance on the
United States more promising than any realistic alternative
The only politically realistic alternative to reliance on the
American nuclear guarantee is the "Finlandization" o
Europe, and the paralysis implied by that in foreign-policy
matters cannot possibly be worth the risk of decoupling. A
Andrew Pierre has recently concluded,

> In the last analysis, the security of Western Europe simpl
> cannot be decoupled from America, because of the fact tha
> there is no European replacement available for the U.S
> nuclear guarantee. Progress in the Eurogroup toward Euro
> pean defense co-operation has been encouraging, but thes
> efforts will necessarily remain limited. In time, with th
> transformation of relations with the East, the need for suc
> a guarantee may disappear, or a politically and militarily in
> dependent Western Europe may be constructed. Neither o
> these prospects is now within sight.[32]

Difficulties in the security area are compounded when th
stakes of financial and commercial autonomy are reviewed. I
financial matters the Europeans have made several quixotic a
tempts since 1970 to form a monetary union that could be th
basis of a system that would rival the dollar. These attempt
have become almost universally viewed within Europe as verg
ing on the disastrous. Not only has the attempt been mad
prematurely, but also the movement toward flexibility in th
exchange rates of the major currencies of the world has bee
recognized as a better way of adjusting international financia

difficulties than most Europeans would have predicted even three years ago. Moreover, the difficulties encountered in maintaining fixed parity relations in the face of economic dislocations associated with the energy crisis rule it out for now. The European Community members have only adhered to a declaratory commitment to achieve monetary union lest a failure in publicly announced goals reflect a general failure of political will in Europe to maintain the vigor of the integration process.

Once the difficulties inherent in the financial and security aspects of European attempts to create a core area are brought out, those associated with the attempt to co-ordinate the two as part of a European-based nucleation process seem insurmountable for the foreseeable future. Three additional constraints make the prospects for the European periphery even worse.

The age of nuclear deterrence has denied to the Europeans what might be considered the normal fruits of nucleation at the periphery. The sorts of conflicts that now exist in commercial and monetary matters between the United States and Western Europe might easily have led to the outbreak of warfare, or at least overt antagonism, in another age, when the erosion of autonomy within the different governments of Western Europe, and especially in areas of domestic economic management, is brought under consideration. The costs of implementing an independent deterrent force impede a European impulse toward autonomy. Even more important, the fear of nuclear warfare, combined with the paradoxical disutility of nuclear force, prevent the governments of Western Europe from placing any realistic hopes in developing a new core at this time.

Equally significant is a second unprecedented development in the relations between Western Europe and the United States: the growth in economic interdependence among all of the highly industrialized societies of the non-Communist world. Interdependence, even asymmetrically developed, has apparently become so high that the costs of unscrambling may in fact now be too great for any government to contemplate. This interdependence is reinforced by the ways in which the development of strategic nuclear power has served to impede interstate rivalries in the contemporary international system.

Most discussions of interdependence focus primarily on what are, on the face of it, economic phenomena. Trade flows, the integration of international financial markets, the spread of inflation, and the increased internationalization of the labor force all smack of the essence of economics. But these phenomena cannot be dismissed as having no political significance. Indeed, there is a danger in equating the growth of interdependence with the consequences of a presumptive American hegemonic position and then arguing that the necessary devolution of American hegemony will bring about the decrease in interdependence,[33] for the phenomenon reflects a fundamental change in the substance of international politics in the contemporary world: the degree to which plays for power and position are acted out in economic relations.

There are many reasons for the progressive politicization of economic affairs after World War II. One has to do with the disutility of force in the nuclear age and the consequences for this on middle-range and smaller powers, for whom bargaining with force has become too costly. But more significant has been the degree to which governments have assumed increased responsibility in a progressively more significant share of domestic activities and have attempted to implement goals that they have never before assumed. This increase in governmental intervention in domestic activities has, by necessity, been predominantly economic, since it is focused upon the need to provide for the basis of a good life, a concept that has inevitable economic bases.

The increased scope of governments has been responsible for the higher sensitivity of domestic political and economic systems to events that occur outside their geographic borders. And it is here that the most significant political implications of interdependence can be seen. Increased sensitivity reflects the decreased autonomy that governments have to select the options that they feel are required for the achievement of their fundamental goals. The desire to preserve autonomy, the behavioral correlate of the concept of sovereignty, strikes at the heart of what governments are about. If they cannot achieve what they are elected to achieve or what they indicate to be their fundamental goals, they and the institutions they comprise will tend to lose their legitimacy in the face of domestic contingencies.

Interdependence has itself complicated the dynamics of core-periphery relations for both the United States and Western Europe. This is because the higher the level of interdependence among a set of political systems, the lower will be the level of asymmetry among the member systems. This is another way of saying that interdependence equalizes the relative power that can be mobilized by governments.[34] Many factors are responsible for this, but it remains true whether one looks at the international economic system or the deterrent relationship between the superpowers and its effects on the relations between superpowers and lesser powers. Among these factors is the increased cost of exercising power in an interdependent world.[35] While interdependence increases the linkages between any units, linkages are mutual, resulting in a stalemate. Even great powers must give up political instruments as they become more interdependent with others. This increases the power of blackmail of lesser powers whose stake in the stability of a system may be viewed as lower than that of the great powers, which have far more to lose as the system becomes less stable.

As a result, the more interdependent a set of political systems, the lower will be the ability of any single one to achieve positive goals and the greater its ability to threaten others with harm.[36] This has been vivid both in nuclear diplomacy between the United States and the Soviet Union and in the recent diplomacy of crisis in the international monetary system, both of which exemplify different types of interdependent relationships. The latter example, since it is less familiar than the former, perhaps offers the best illustration. It also demonstrates the way interdependence serves to equalize power.

The United States Government was unable to rectify the deterioration of its balance-of-payments position before the outbreak of the monetary crisis of August 1971. It had sought to induce surplus countries to revalue their currencies, but was unable, even with its strength at the center of the system, to get them to do so. It was also unable to have them take steps toward trade liberalization, in particular by ending the discriminatory arrangements that the European Community had developed in violation of the principle of the most favored nation that had been embodied in the GATT. Unable to achieve its positive goals, the United States resorted, after August 15, to negative tactics designed to threaten others with harm, by imposing import restrictions of its own and by attempting to force the world onto a system of floating exchange rates. Although the U. S. Government had to accept a compromise in achieving this goal in the Smithsonian Agreement of December of that year, it was largely the negative threats of harm to others, including the collapse of the international payments system, that enabled it to achieve its interim objectives.

Charles de Gaulle had learned the benefits of threats of harm and of negative diplomacy years before Richard M. Nixon practiced it. This was true in the policy of the "tactical no" that De Gaulle pursued in the Common Market by threatening to disrupt it in order to achieve a compromise common agricultural policy that the other members, and in particular the German Government, were reluctant to accept.

Moreover, the higher the level of interdependence among political systems, the greater will be the ability of any one to manipulate the internal affairs of others. This follows for the same reasons that interdependence curtails the autonomy of decision-making within any one society. Since interdependence ties societies together, causing them to lose some of their autonomy, it also results in an increase in the say that other governments have in the decision-making processes, or at least the outcomes of decisions, in any single political system. When the effects, for example, of credit-restriction policies in one society are dependent upon the same sort of policies pursued elsewhere, it also means that the government of that society can manipulate the effectiveness of credit-restriction policies elsewhere. High-interest-rate policy that is designed to curtail expenditure can, in the face of low-interest-rate policy elsewhere, serve to attract funds from abroad. The government of the Federal Republic of Germany has confronted this problem for a decade in its own attempt to curtail the rate of inflation in its economy. Loose-credit policies simultaneously pursued in the United States, however, would result in the outflow of dollars to Germany, thus undermining the anti-inflationary policy of the German Government by causing an increase in the German money supply.

The paradox of interdependence in this realm is that a government can in effect intervene in another society simply by shifting the course of its own domestic policy.[37] Domestic affairs really have become foreign affairs for a wide variety of purposes.

The same phenomena that lie behind the increased ability of governments to manipulate the domestic affairs of others also result in some cases in the playing out of domestic policies within the context of foreign political systems. This was seen in the German legislative elections in 1972 as well as in the domestic debates in Germany over ratification of the set of Eastern treaties that came out of the *Ostpolitik* of the Brandt government. The leaders of both of the major German political parties traveled frequently to the United States to make speeches on German-American relations as part of the electoral and legislative battles that they were pursuing at home.

The nuclear paradox and the effects of interdependence have restricted the capacity of the United States Government to serve as an entrepreneurial core in the North Atlantic Area, just as it has impeded the efforts of the European periphery to break from it. One additional effect of interdependence, when compounded by a third unprecedented phenomenon—the nature of governance in highly industrialized society—effectively stalemates political relations between the United States and Europe. This effect is as follows: The higher the level of interdependence among a set of political systems, the greater are the incentives to any one society of reducing its relative vulnerability to the actions of others and of increasing the vulnerability of others to its own actions. Governments wish to prevent others from manipulating their own domestic affairs, as they readily can when high levels of interdependence exist. The result is a subtle and new brand of politics. These vulnerabilities stem more from transnational activities and their unintended consequences than from Machiavellian governmental strategies. As Pierre Hassner has argued,

> The essential characteristic of this state [of affairs] is neither force nor co-operation but the constant influence of societies

on one another within the framework of a competition
whose goals are less and less tangible, whose means are less
and less calculable, precisely because they involved activities
rather than strategies and because these activities are important as much because of their effects on what societies *are* as
on what they *do*. . . .

The real race may be less to increase one's comparative
power than to decrease one's comparative vulnerability, to
manipulate not only an opponent's weaknesses but one's
own, to encourage exported erosion or to control contagious
explosions, to modify or maintain not so much territorial
borders or even diplomatic alignments as what might be
called the balance of will and the balance of expectations.[38]

As a result, governments in NATO now tend to pursue a
conservative foreign policy. This is another paradox of interdependence, or of politics between core and periphery in the
"crisis zone." Interdependence carries with it an ability to manipulate other societies and therefore to manipulate foreign
and domestic policies in the interest of reordering the international system. Yet, precisely because interdependence ties
together activities pursued in different societies, it also brings
about the possibility of uncontrolled change. Rather than
confront directly such a situation, which carries with it so
many unknown factors, governments would prefer to maintain
the status quo, with whose costs and benefits they are more familiar.

Fear of uncertainties caused by interdependence are reinforced by uncertainties in the domestic governance in modernized and nonmodernized societies alike. But change is far
more costly in the former than in the latter. The stability of
highly modernized societies, which rests on political traditions
that emerged over a century-long process of nation-building, is
balanced by a fragility that stems from the incredibly rapid
rate of change since World War II. The result is that governance in modern industrialized societies in particular has
become based more than ever on daily decision-making with
governments more concerned with maintaining the status quo
and with keeping the machinery of public affairs operating
than with steering a course for the future.

Politics in an interdependent system are akin to politics in a crisis zone, for the higher the level of interdependence among a set of political systems, the greater is the propensity of their system of interactions to undergo crisis.[39] The creation of transnational interest groups in nongovernmental contexts, like the loss of political instruments relative to policy goals, represents a breakdown in governmental controls. As these activities grow beyond the direct and constant observations of governments, they force governments to intervene and often to collaborate. Such situations are especially acute in the international financial system, where the enormous development of short-term flows of liquid capital across borders have eluded the closest governmental controls and have threatened the status quo in a range of policies, from domestic inflationary policies to exchange rate and other policies. Less tangible evidence of this is seen in the spread of ideas concerning habits, fashions, or even rebelliousness on the part of student groups. Such situations are inevitable consequences of interdependent relationships.

In addition, the higher the level of interdependence among a set of political systems, the greater is the potential for the manipulation of crisis as a general strategy of foreign policy. As a result of the increased incidence of crisis in areas of interdependence, and as a result of the growing interrelatedness of issues, two general possibilities have opened up. On the one hand, negotiations normally will involve a wide range of issues for the development of possible trade-offs among governments in reaching group decisions. On the other hand, since issues are tied together, possibilities for political blackmail are also enhanced.

Paradoxically, the higher the level of interdependence among political systems and the greater the incidence of crises among them, the greater will be the reliance of governments upon crises for effective decision-making. As governments have become aware of their inability to cope with the increasing demands that are placed upon them, the consequent undermining of their own legitimacy, and the costs of making effective decisions (in terms of the loss of support by domestic constituents), they have also become more willing to see crises erupt as a means of short-cutting their decision-making processes. Most governments in modernized societies are fearful of change from the status quo. Yet decisions are forced upon them, either through the disruptions associated with an interdependent international system or through domestic unrest. Within the context of crises, however, governments are able to make decisions that they would otherwise rule out. In such circumstances, the taking of forceful action is likely to be valued by their citizens as a good end in itself. Thus, contemporary governance has become crisis governance. And most new institutional arrangements that have been created to deal with interdependence have been formulated in an *ad hoc* fashion through crises.

The factors outlined above seem to constitute a powerful obstacle to the chances of the European periphery breaking away from the American core, just as they imply that the United States Government cannot easily separate itself from its European periphery. The situation represented by politics in the crisis zone in contemporary North Atlantic affairs depends upon the growth in interdependence among a set of countries and the persistent asymmetry that exists between the United States and Europe. No trends now indicate that the levels of interdependence are anywhere decreasing or that existing asymmetries (except in commercial matters) are likely to become reduced. Rather, interdependencies are everywhere on the increase, as the conditions underlying them have spread. Whether one looks at the security of the world as a whole, the growth in the world economy, the spread of ecological problems, the requirements of governments for resources and technological capacity, or general social problems, it can be seen that national autonomy is everywhere on the decrease, and the need to rely on actions of others is virtually ubiquitous.[40]

This is not to say that a general unscrambling of the economies and societies of the NATO system, or a reversal in the growth in interdependence, is unthinkable. Certainly the energy crisis has thus far led governments to stress their separateness from one another as they vie for security of supplies. Interdependence, too, has brought with it major costs, especially to the autonomy of governmental decision-making and the legitimacy of governmental structures. But the cost of unscrambling should not be underestimated. In fact, in a world in which nuclear weapons had not been developed, the tensions engendered by interdependence would long ago probably have resulted in international conflict and attempts to reassert autonomy. But nuclear weapons have not been the only deterrent to conflict. To date, especially among the modernized societies of the non-Communist world, and increasingly between them and the more modernized Communist societies, the benefits of increased interdependence have been recognized and highly valued. These relationships, however, carry a built-in instability and are likely to create the need for the institutionalization at the international level of a framework for co-ordinating domestic and foreign policies that is unprecedented.

## CONCLUSIONS

If the growth in international interdependence is to be valued ambivalently, it is clear that it provides only one set of contextual factors that define NATO's bargaining structures. Since the political communities that compose this interdependent network are not all members of the alliance, the problems that arise from interdependence can never be handled satisfactorily in an alliance framework. Similarly, the existence of bilateral ties between NATO's members and other governments, including those whose societies possess needed raw materials, will continue to interject tensions into alliance relationships. But the context of interdependence, like those contexts provided by a core-periphery perspective on alliance relations and by a view of the alliance as a group of sovereign political communities, must be taken into account in any effort to capture the richness of undertones and overtones that inevitably inhere in intra-alliance bargaining.

The bargaining context is fundamentally complex and rich because the various "layers" of the system that the members of the alliance compose are so contradictory. They also seem to be quite stable. In the absence of a radical shift of international power relationships, they are likely to endure as far into the future as it is wise to predict. Whether the members of the alliance will be able to co-ordinate the countervailing aspects of these relationships is open to question. What is clearer is that the contextual aspects of the bargaining relationships outlined in this chapter represent a new form of politics. It is one to which governments have increasingly shown awareness and with which they have so far been willing to live.

NOTES

1. Stanley Hoffmann, "Discord in Community: The North Atlantic Area as a Partial International System," *The Atlantic Community,* ed. Francis O. Wilcox and H. Field Haviland, Jr. (New York: Praeger, 1963), p. 6.

2. The ramifications of this assertion are not important for present purposes. For details, see Edward L. Morse, *Foreign Policy and Interdependence in Gaullist France* (Princeton, N.J.: Princeton University Press, 1973), Chap. 2.

3. Henry A. Kissinger, *The Troubled Partnership: A Re-appraisal of the Atlantic Alliance* (New York: McGraw-Hill, 1965), pp. 11–12. Italics in original.

4. See, for example, J. David Singer and Melvin Small, "Alliance Aggregation and the Onset of War: 1815–1945," in *Quantitative International Politics: Insights and Evidence,* ed. J. David Singer (New York: The Free Press, 1968), pp. 247–86. This is but one representative piece of a general analysis of alliances and warfare that has focused upon the "correlates of war," or, more precisely, the correlates of international stability.

5. This is quite obvious in the recent attempt to draw up a "propositional inventory" concerning alliances by Ole R. Holsti, P. Terrence Hopmann, and John D. Sullivan. See their *Unity and Disintegration in International Alliances* (New York: John Wiley & Sons, 1973), Chap. 1 and Appendix C.

6. In this sense, the analysis of Raymond Aron, stemming from his contrasting of the internal dynamics of NATO and the Warsaw Pact, remains valid. See his *Peace and War: A Theory of International Relations,* trans. Richard Howard and Annette Baker Fox (Garden City, N.Y.: Doubleday, 1966), Chap. XV. As Aron stated it, "The two blocs are not homogenous. Relations among states depend, to a degree, on their internal systems: the collective organization of democratic states cannot help being different from the collective organization of the Soviet states (whatever order of succession we acknowledge in the formation of the two blocs)," p. 442.

7. See, in particular, Mancur Olson, Jr., and Richard Zeckhauser, "An Economic Theory of Alliance," *Review of Economics and Statistics* XLVII (1966), pp. 266–79, and their *An Economic*

*Theory of Alliances* (Washington, D.C.: RAND Corporation, 1966).

8. Norman Frohlich and Joe A. Oppenheimer, "I Get By with a Little Help from My Friends," *World Politics* XXIII (1970), No. 1, p. 118.

9. Francis A. Beer, *The Political Economy of Alliances: Benefits, Costs, and Institutions in NATO* (Beverly Hills, Calif.: Sage Professional Papers in International Studies Series, 2-008, 1972), p. 23.

10. See, in particular, F. Beer, op. cit., Norman Frohlich, and Joe A. Oppenheimer, "Entrepreneurial Politics and Foreign Policy," *World Politics* XXIV, Supplement (Spring 1972), pp. 151–78, and Bruce M. Russett, ed., *Economic Theories of International Politics* (Chicago: Markham, 1968), Part I.

11. See, for example, Richard N. Cooper, "Trade Policy is Foreign Policy," *Foreign Policy* (Winter 1972–73), No. 9, p. 32.

12. Joyce and Gabriel Kolko, *The Limits of Power: The World and United States Foreign Policy, 1945–1954* (New York: Harper & Row, 1972), p. 475.

13. Robert Gilpin, "The Politics of Transnational Relations," *Transnational Relations and World Politics,* ed. Robert O. Keohane and Joseph S. Nye, Jr. (Cambridge, Mass.: Harvard University Press, 1972), p. 60.

14. Ibid., pp. 61–62.

15. While it is not necessary to recapitulate Gilpin's entire argument, it is important to note that Gilpin's argument is more elaborate and accounts for obvious criticisms. Thus, while he does not deny the perceived need of the Europeans for a security network with the United States, he does document the manner in which some Europeans strove to exaggerate the Soviet threat in order to exact American economic aid; and he also includes a discussion of the implicit bargain between the United States and Western Europe by which the former gained the benefits of running an international monetary system in return for which the latter received commercial benefits in the form of discriminations against third parties, including the United States. Also see Gilpin's more extensive analysis in *Growth and Change in World Politics* (New York: Basic Books, forthcoming). For a similar argument, see David P. Calleo and Benjamin M. Rowland, *America and the World Political Economy; Atlantic Dreams and National Realities* (Bloomington, Ind.: Indiana University Press, 1973), esp. Part II.

16. See, especially, R. Prebisch, *The Economic Development of Latin America and its Principal Problems* (New York: United Nations, 1950), in which Prebisch first introduced the concept.

17. See, for example, Stephen Hymer, "The Multinational Corpora-

tion and the Law of Uneven Development," *Economics and World Order: From the 1970s to the 1990s,* ed. Jagdish N. Bhagwati (New York: Macmillan, 1972), pp. 113–40.

18. See Hans O. Schmitt, "Integration and Conflict in World Economy," *Journal of Common Market Studies* VII (Sept. 1969), No. 1, pp. 1–18, and John Knapp, "Economics or Political Economy?", *Lloyds Bank Review* (Jan. 1973), No. 107, pp. 19–43.

19. "Integration and Conflict in the World Economy," p. 2.

20. Frohlich and Oppenheimer formally define a public good as follows: "Whenever each of the consumers in a given group receives a consumption unit derived from the same production unit, that production unit will be defined as a *public good* for that group." "Entrepreneurial Politics and Foreign Policy," p. 157. Emphasis is theirs.

21. See especially Francis A. Beer, *The Political Economy of Alliances,* and Frederick L. Pryor, *Public Expenditure in Communist and Capitalist Nations* (Homewood, Ill.: Richard D. Irwin, 1968).

22. Mancur Olson, Jr., *The Logic of Collective Action: Public Goods and the Theory of Groups* (Cambridge, Mass.: Harvard University Press, 1965), p. 15.

23. M. Olson, Jr., and R. Zeckhauser, *An Economic Theory of Alliances,* p. 4. The same authors argue that there is a differing incentive for any individual to pay without coercion in high-membership groups and in low-membership groups: the smaller the group, the greater the incentive.

24. M. Olson, Jr., *The Logic of Collective Action,* p. 2.

25. For details, see Norman Frohlich, Joe A. Oppenheimer, and Oran Young, *Political Leadership and Collective Goods,* pp. 145–50.

26. "Entrepreneurial Politics," p. 159.

27. Europeans frequently point out that their contribution to NATO has, in fact, been substantial if one looks at their commitment of ground forces to meet the contingency of conventional warfare. But that contribution is fundamentally a bargaining instrument, few Europeans having the pretention that ground forces provide more than marginally to their security. In fact, their reliance on the American nuclear deterrent is obsessive since they do not wish to countenance the contingency of ground warfare in Europe and do not trust one another's motivations enough to look to each other (i.e., Britain and France) for the provision of a European deterrent.

28. Richard N. Cooper has argued that in fact a fundamental asymmetry will continue to characterize the international monetary

system so long as the Europeans fail to create a unified currency, the start-up costs of which are apparently prohibitive. "The basic asymmetry," he argues, "is the dominant economic size of the United States reinforced by the closely related asymmetries in scale and sophistication of financial markets. . . . These asymmetries in turn lead through a complicated process . . . to two separate but related asymmetries in the operation of international payments: the extensive private use of the U.S. dollar as a medium of exchange, a unit of account, and a temporary store of value; and use of the dollar as an official intervention currency in a payments system that relies on private markets for multilateral clearing. . . . The reasons for these asymmetries are deep-seated, residing in the enormous efficiency of money as an intermediary in the process of exchange." "Eurodollars, Reserve Dollars, and Asymmetries in the International Monetary System," *Journal of International Economics* 2 (Nov. 1972), pp. 327–28.

29. See in particular Robert Gilpin, "The Politics of Transnational Economic Relations," pp. 48–69, and David P. Calleo and Benjamin M. Rowland, *America and the World Political Economy*, pp. 251–59. Also see Benjamin J. Cohen, *The Future of Sterling as an International Currency* (New York: Macmillan, 1971), pp. 34–52, for a discussion of the costs and benefits of an international currency.

30. This term is borrowed from discussions on the international monetary system, where the crisis zone is defined as that area where dollar liabilities are greater than the old backing in the American reserves, a situation that was realized by the middle of the 1960s. It was originally felt that when the international monetary system entered this zone, it would be prone to run on the central bank (i.e., the U.S. gold stock), since there was no lender of last resort to inspire confidence in the value of the dollar. See, for example, *International Monetary Arrangements: The Problems of Choice; Report on the Deliberations of an International Study Group of Thirty-two Economists* (Princeton, N.J.: Princeton University, International Finance Section, 1964), p. 35. See also the criticism of this view in Lawrence Officer and Thomas D. Willett, "Reserve-asset Preferences and the Confidence Problem in the Crisis Zone," *Quarterly Journal of Economics* LXXXIII (Nov. 1969), pp. 688–95. The latter authors argue that the effects of mutual interdependence of states in the monetary system, in terms of the benefits they derive from the operation of the system and of their shared desire to preserve it, make the crisis zone far more stable than had hitherto been believed.

31. For an elaboration of this argument see Edward L. Morse, "La politique americaine de manipulation de la crise," *Revue Française de Science Politique* XXII (Apr. 1972), pp. 348–59.

32. Andrew J. Pierre, "Can Europe's Security Be 'Decoupled' from America?", *Foreign Affairs* LI (July 1973), No. 4, pp. 775–76.

33. This is the argument of David Calleo, "The Political Economy of Allied Relations: The Limits of Interdependence," *Retreat from Empire? The First Nixon Administration*, Robert E. Osgood et al. (Baltimore: The Johns Hopkins Press, 1973), pp. 207–40.

34. Oran Young argues this point when he hypothesizes that "the higher the level of interdependence in a world system, the harder it becomes to maintain qualitatively unequal (i.e., superordinate-subordinate) relations among the units of the system." "Interdependencies in World Politics," *International Journal* XXIV (Autumn 1969), p. 748.

35. Ibid., pp. 746–47. "As the level of interdependence among the component units of a world system rises, the opportunities for any given actor to exercise power over others increases but the costs of exercising power rise at the same time."

36. As Stanley Hoffmann has observed in his portrayal of the United States as Gulliver among the Lilliputians, "Today the most fascinating aspect of the utility of military power is that this once fairly persistent link between military strength and positive achievements has been loosened. The power to coerce has never been so great or so unevenly distributed . . . but its nature is now such that its possessor must restrict its uses. The fullest use of nuclear power is in *denial,* but this must consist in threats—in deterrence—and by definition shuns execution." *Gulliver's Troubles, or the Setting of American Foreign Policy* (New York: McGraw-Hill, 1968), p. 29. Schelling (1966, pp. 69–91) makes the same point by distinguishing "deterrence" from "compellence."

37. Oran Young's version of this hypothesis in fact focuses upon its interventionary features: "The higher the level of interdependence among the component units of a world system, the greater the frequency of intervention on the part of individual units in the affairs of others." "Interdependencies in World Politics," p. 749.

38. Pierre Hassner, "The New Europe: From Cold War to Hot Peace," *International Journal* XXVII (Winter 1971–72), No. 1, pp. 12–13.

39. Young argues similarly that "The higher the level of interdependence among the component units of a world system, the greater the probability of system transformation." This is because "changes of all kinds become more difficult to contain or keep

isolated as the level of interdependence in a world system rises."
"Interdependence in World Politics," p. 742.
40. This is the argument of Lester R. Brown, *World Without Borders* (New York: Random House, 1972).

# 3. THE HOSPITAL AND ITS NEGOTIATED ORDER*†

*Anselm Strauss*
*Leonard Schatzman*
*Danuta Ehrlich*
*Rue Bucher*
*Melvin Sabshin*

### INTRODUCTION

In the pages to follow, a model for studying hospitals will be sketched, along with some suggested virtues of the model. It grew out of the authors' research, which was done on the premises of two psychiatric hospitals. The reader must judge for himself whether a model possibly suited to studying psychiatric hospitals might equally well guide the study of other kinds of hospitals. We believe that it can, and shall indicate why at the close of our presentation; indeed, we shall argue its

* The writing of this chapter is part of a larger project studying psychiatric hospitals, which is being carried on at the Institute of Psychosomatic and Psychiatric Research and Training of Michael Reese Hospital under the State of Illinois Mental Health Fund, Program 1737.

usefulness for investigating other organizations besides hospitals.

Our model bears upon that most central of sociological problems, namely, how a measure of order is maintained in the face of inevitable changes (derivable from sources both external and internal to the organization). Students of formal organization tend to underplay the processes of internal change as well as overestimate the more stable features of organizations—including its rules and its hierarchical statuses. We ourselves take our cue from George H. Mead, who some years ago, when arguing for orderly and directed social change, remarked that the task turns about relationships between change and order:

> How can you bring those changes about in an orderly fashion and yet preserve order? To bring about change is seemingly to destroy the given order, and yet society does and must change. That is the problem, to incorporate the method of change into the order of society itself.[1]

Without Mead's melioristic concerns, one can yet assume that order is something at which members of any society, any organization, must work. For the shared agreements, the binding contracts—which constitute the grounds for an expectable, nonsurprising, taken-for-granted, even ruled orderliness—are not binding and shared for all time. Contracts, understandings, agreements, rules—all have appended to them a temporal clause. That clause may or may not be explicitly discussed by the contracting parties, and the terminal date of the agreement may or may not be made specific; but none can be binding forever—even if the parties believe it so, unforeseen consequences of acting on the agreements would force eventual confrontation. Review is called for, whether the outcome of review be rejection or renewal or revision, or what not. In short, the bases of concerted action (social order) must be reconstituted continually; or, as remarked above, "worked at."

Such considerations have led us to emphasize the importance of negotiation—the processes of give-and-take, of diplomacy, of bargaining—which characterizes organizational

life. In the pages to follow, we shall note first the relationship
of rules to negotiation, then discuss the grounds for negotiation. Then, since both the clients and much of the personnel of
hospitals are laymen, we wish also to underscore the participation of those laymen in the hospital's negotiative processes.
Thereafter we shall note certain patterned and temporal features of negotiation; then we shall draw together some implications for viewing social order. A general summary of the argument and its implications will round out the paper.

<h2 style="text-align:center">A PSYCHIATRIC HOSPITAL</h2>

Before discussing negotiation in hospitals, it will help to indicate two things: first, what was engaging our attention when
research was initiated; and, second, the general characteristics
of the hospital that was studied.[2] At the outset of our investigation, three foci were especially pertinent. The first was an explicit concern with the professional careers of the personnel:
Who was there? Where did they come from? Where did they
think they were going in work and career? What were they
doing at this particular hospital? What was happening to them
at this place? A second concern was with psychiatric ideology:
Were different ideologies represented on the floors of this
hospital? What were these ideologies? Did people clearly
recognize their existence as well as did their more articulate
advocates? And anyway, what difference did these philosophies make in the lives and work of various personnel? A
third focus consisted of the realization that a hospital is par ex-
cellence an institution captained and maintained principally by
professionals. This fact implied that the nonprofessionals who
worked there, as well as those nonprofessionals there as patients, must manage to make their respective ways within this
professionalized establishment. How, then, do they do this—
and vice versa, how do the professionals incorporate the
nonprofessionals into their own schemes of work and aspiration? These directions of interest, and the questions raised in
consequence, quickly led us to perceive hospitals in terms to be
depicted below.

### A PROFESSIONALIZED LOCALE

A hospital can be visualized as a professionalized locale—a geographical site where persons drawn from different professions come together to carry out their respective purposes. At our specific hospital, the professionals consisted of numerous practicing psychiatrists and psychiatric residents, nurses and nursing students, psychologists, occupational therapists, and one lone social worker. Each professional echelon has received noticeably different kinds of training and, speaking conventionally, each occupies some differential hierarchical position at the hospital while playing a different part in its total division of labor.

But that last sentence requires elaboration and amendment. The persons within each professional group may be, and probably are, at different stages in their respective careers. Furthermore, the career lines of some may be quite different from those of their colleagues: thus some of our psychiatrists were just entering upon psychoanalytic training, but some had entered the medical specialty by way of neurology, and had dual neurological-psychiatric practices. Implicit in the preceding statement is that those who belong to the same profession also may differ quite measurably in the training they have received, as well as in the theoretical (or ideological) positions they take toward important issues like etiology and treatment. Finally, the hospital itself may possess differential significance for colleagues: for instance, some psychiatrists were engaged in hospital practice only until such time as their office practices had been sufficiently well established; while other, usually older, psychiatrists were committed wholeheartedly to working with hospitalized patients.

Looking next at the division of labor shared by the professionals: never do all persons of each echelon work closely with all others from other echelons. At our hospital it was notable that considerable variability characterized who worked closely with whom—and how—depending upon such matters as ideological and hierarchical position. Thus the services of the social worker were used not at all by some psychiatrists, while each man who utilized her services did so somewhat differently. Similarly some men utilized "psychologicals" more than did others. Similarly, some psychiatrists were successful in housing their patients almost exclusively upon certain wards, which meant that, wittingly or not, they worked only with certain nurses. As in other institutions, the various echelons possessed differential status and power, but again there were marked internal differences concerning status and power, as well as knowledgeability about "getting things done." Nor must it be overlooked that not only did the different professions hold measurably different views—derived both from professional and status positions—about the proper division of labor; but different views also obtained within echelon. (The views were most discrepant among the psychiatrists.) All in all, the division of labor is a complex concept, and at hospitals must be seen in relation to the professionalized milieu.

### RULED AND UNRULED BEHAVIOR

The rules that govern the actions of various professionals, as they perform their tasks, are far from extensive, or clearly stated or clearly binding. This fact leads to necessary and continual negotiation. It will be worth deferring discussion of negotiation per se until we have explored some relationships between rules and negotiation, at least as found in our hospital; for the topic of rules is a complicated one.

In Michael Reese, as unquestionably in most sizable establishments, hardly anyone knows all the extant rules, much less exactly what situations they apply to, for whom, and with what sanctions. If this would not otherwise be so in our hospital, it would be true anyway because of the considerable turnover of nursing staff. Also noticeable—to us as observers—was that some rules once promulgated would fall into disuse, or would periodically receive administrative reiteration after the staff had either ignored those rules or forgotten them. As one head nurse said, "I wish they would write them all down sometimes"—but said so smilingly. The plain fact is that staff kept forgetting not only the rules received from above but also some rules that they themselves had agreed upon "for this ward." Hence we would observe that periodically the same informal ward rules would be agreed upon, enforced for a short time, and then be forgotten until another ward crisis would elicit their innovation all over again.

As in other establishments, personnel called upon certain rules to obtain what they themselves wished. Thus the nurses frequently acted as virtual guardians of the hospital against some demands of certain attending physicians, calling upon the resources of "the rules of the hospital" in countering the physicians' demands. As in other hospital settings, the physicians were only too aware of this game, and accused the nurses from time to time of more interest in their own welfare than in that of the patients'. (The only difference, we suspect, between the accusatory language of psychiatrists and that of internists or surgeons is that the psychiatrists have a trained capacity to utilize specialized terms like "rigid" and "overcompulsive.") In so dredging up the rules at convenient moments, the staff of course is acting identically with personnel in other kinds of institutions.

As elsewhere, too, all categories of personnel are adept at breaking the rules when it suits convenience or when warrantable exigencies arise. Stretching the rules is only a further variant of this tactic, which itself is less attributable to human nature than to an honest desire to get things accomplished as they ought, properly, to get done.[3] Of course, respective parties must strike bargains for these actions to occur.

In addition, at the very top of the administrative structure, a tolerant stance is taken both toward extensiveness of rules and laxity of rules. The point can be illustrated by a conversation with the administrative head, who recounted with amusement how some members of his original house staff wished to have all rules set down in a house rule book, but he had staved off this codification. As will be noted more fully later, the administrative attitude is affected also by a profound belief that care of patients calls for a minimum of hard and fast rules and a maximum of innovation and improvisation. In addition, in this hospital, as certainly in most others, the multiplicity of medical purpose and theory, as well as of personal investment, are openly recognized: too rigid a set of rules would only cause turmoil and affect the hospital's over-all efficiency.

Finally, it is notable that the hospital must confront the realities of the attending staff's negotiations with patients and their families—negotiations carried out beyond the physical confines of the hospital itself. Too many or too rigid rules would restrict the medical entrepreneurs' negotiation. To some degree any hospital with attending men has to give this kind of leeway (indeed, the precise degree is a source of tension in these kinds of hospitals).

Hence, the area of action covered directly by clearly enunciated rules is really very small. As observers, we began to become aware of this when, within a few days, we discovered that only a few very general rules obtained for the placement of new patients within the hospital. Those rules, which are clearly enunciated and generally followed, can, for our purposes, be regarded as long-standing shared understandings among the personnel. Except for a few legal rules, which stem from state and professional prescription, and for some rulings pertaining to all of Michael Reese Hospital, almost all these house rules are much less like commands, and much more like general understandings: not even their punishments are spelled out; and mostly they can be stretched, negotiated, argued, as well as ignored or applied at convenient moments. Hospital rules seem to us frequently less explicit than tacit, probably as much breached and stretched as honored, and administrative effort is made to keep their number small. In addition, rules here as elsewhere fail to be universal prescriptions: they always require judgment concerning their applicability to the specific case. Does it apply here? To whom? In what degree? For how long? With what sanctions? The personnel cannot give universal answers; they can only point to past analogous instances when confronted with situations or give "for instance" answers, when queried about a rule's future application.

### THE GROUNDS FOR NEGOTIATION

Negotiation and the division of labor are rendered all the more complex because personnel in our hospital—we assume that the generalization, with some modification, holds elsewhere—share only a single, vaguely ambiguous goal. The goal is to return patients to the outside world in better shape. This goal is the symbolic cement that, metaphorically speaking, holds the organization together: the symbol to which all personnel can comfortably, and frequently point—with the assurance that at *least* about this matter everyone can agree! Although this symbol, as will be seen later, masks a considerable measure of disagreement and discrepant purpose, it represents a generalized mandate under which the hospital can be run—the public flag under which all may work in concert. Let us term it the institution's constitutional grounds or basic compact. These grounds, this compact, are never openly challenged; nor are any other goals given explicit verbal precedence. (This is so when a hospital, such as ours, also is a training institution.) In addition, these constitutional grounds can be used by any and all personnel as a justificatory rationale for actions that are under attack. In short, although personnel may disagree to the point of apoplexy about how to implement patients' getting better, they do share the common institutional value.

The problem, of course, is that when the personnel confront a specific patient and attempt to make him recover, then the disagreements flare up—the generalized mandate helps not at all to handle the specific issues—and a complicated process of negotiation, of bargaining, of give-and-take necessarily begins. The disagreements that necessitate negotiation do not occur by chance, but are patterned. Here are several illustrations of the grounds that lead to negotiation. Thus, the personnel may disagree over what is the proper placement within the hospital for some patient: believing that, at any given time, he is more likely to improve when placed upon one ward rather than upon another. This issue is the source of considerable tension between physicians and ward personnel. Again, what is meant by "getting better" is itself open to differential judgment when applied to the progress—or retrogression—of a particular patient. This judgment is influenced not only by professional experience and acquaintance with the patient but is also influenced by the very concept of getting better as held by the different echelons. Thus the aides—who are laymen—have quite different notions about these matters than do the physicians, and on the whole those notions are not quite equivalent to those held by nurses. But both the nurses and the aides see patients getting better according to signs visible from the patient's daily behavior, while the psychiatrist tends to relate these signs, if apprehended at all, to deeper layers of personality; with the consequence that frequently the staff thinks one way about the patient's "movement" while the physician thinks quite otherwise, and must argue his case, set them right, or even keep his peace.[4]

To turn now to another set of conditions for negotiation: the very mode of treatment selected by the physician is profoundly related to his own psychiatric ideology. For instance, it makes a difference whether the physician is neurologically trained, thus somatically oriented, or whether he is psychotherapeutically trained and oriented. The former type of physician will prescribe more drugs, engage in far more electric shock therapy, and spend much less time with each patient. On occasion the diagnosis and treatment of a given patient runs against the judgment of the nurses and aides, who may not go along with the physician's directives, who may or may not disagree openly. They may subvert his therapeutic program by one of their own. They may choose to argue the matter. They may go over his head to an administrative officer. Indeed, they have many choices of action—each requiring negotiative behavior. In truth, while physicians are able to command considerable obedience to their directives at this particular hospital, frequently they must work hard at obtaining cooperation in their programming. The task is rendered all the more difficult because they, as professionals, see matters in certain lights, while the aides, as laymen, may judge matters quite differently—on moral rather than on strictly psychiatric grounds, for instance.

If negotiation is called for because a generalized mandate requires implementation, it is also called for because of the multiplicity of purpose found in the hospital. It is incontestable that each professional group has a different set of reasons for working at this hospital (to begin with, most nurses are women, most physicians are men); and of course colleagues inevitably differ among themselves on certain of their purposes for working there. In addition, each professional develops there his own specific and temporally limited ends that he wishes to attain. All this diversity of purpose affects the institution's division of labor, including not only what tasks each person is expected to accomplish but also how he maneuvers to get them accomplished. Since very little of this can possibly be prefigured by the administrative rule-makers, the attainment of one's purposes requires inevitably the cooperation of fellow workers. This point, once made, scarcely needs illustration.

However, yet another ground of negotiation needs emphasizing: namely, that in this hospital, as doubtless elsewhere, the patient as an "individual case" is taken as a virtual article of faith. By this we mean that the element of medical uncertainty is so great, and each patient is taken as—in some sense—so unique, that action round and about him must be tailor-made, must be suited to his precise therapeutic requirements. This kind of assumption abets what would occur anyhow: that only a minimum of rules can be laid down for running a hospital, since a huge area of contingency necessarily lies outside those rules. The rules can provide guidance and command for only a small amount of the total concerted action that must go on around the patient. It follows, as already noted, that where action is not ruled it must be agreed upon.

One important further condition for negotiation should be mentioned. Changes are forced upon the hospital and its staff not only by forces external to the hospital but also by unforeseen consequences of internal policies and negotiations carried on within the hospital. In short, negotiations breed further negotiations. . . .

### THE PATIENTS AND NEGOTIATED ORDER

The patients are also engaged in bargaining, in negotiative processes. (As some public-administration theorists have put it, clients are also part of the organizational structure.) Again, a significant aspect of hospital organization is missing unless the clients' negotiation is included. They negotiate, of course, as laymen, unless they themselves are nurses or physicians.[5] Most visibly they can be seen bargaining, with the nurses and with their psychiatrists, for more extensive privileges (such as more freedom to roam the grounds); but they may also seek to affect the course and kind of treatment—including placement on given wards, amounts of drugs, and even choice of psychiatrist, along with the length of stay in the hospital itself. Intermittently, but fairly continually, they are concerned with their ward's orderliness, and make demands upon the personnel—as well as upon other patients—to keep the volume of noise down, to keep potential violence at a minimum, to rid the ward of a trouble-making patient. Sometimes the patients are as much guardians of ward order as are the nurses, who are notorious for this concern in our hospital. (Conversely, the nursing personnel must also seek to reach understandings and agreements with specific patients; but sometimes these are even collective, as when patients pitch in to help with a needy patient, or as when an adolescent clique has to be dealt with "as a bunch.")

An unexpected dividend awaits anyone who focuses upon the patients' negotiations. An enriched understanding of their individual sick careers—to the hospital, inside it, and out of it —occurs. In the absence of a focus upon negotiation, ordinarily these careers tend to appear overly regularized (as in Parsons)[6] or destructive (as in Goffman).[7] When patients are closely observed "operating around" the hospital, they will be seen negotiating not only for privileges but also for precious information relevant to their own understandings of their illness. We need only add that necessarily their negotiations will differ at various stages of their sick careers.

What William Caudill[8] and Erving Goffman have written of as patient culture is roughly equivalent to the demands and expectations of the patients; but their accounts require much supplementation by a conception of patients entering, like everyone else, into the over-all negotiative process. How demands and claims will be made and met, by whom, and in what manner—as well as who will make given demands and claims upon them, how, and in what manner—are of utmost importance for understanding the hospital's structure. When patients are long-term or chronic, then their impact upon structure is more obvious to everyone concerned; but even in establishments with speedy turnover, patients are relevant to the social order.

## PATTERNED AND TEMPORAL FEATURES OF
## NEGOTIATION

To do justice to the complexity of negotiative processes would require far more space than can be allowed here. For present purposes, it should be sufficient to note only a few aspects. In our hospital, as elsewhere, the various physicians institute programs of treatment and care for their patients. Programming involves a mobilization and organization of action around the patient (and usually involves the patient's co-operation, even in the psychiatric milieu). Some physicians in our hospital had reached long-standing understandings with certain head nurses, so that only a small amount of communication was necessary to effectuate their treatment programs. Thus a somatically oriented psychiatrist typically would attempt to get his patients to those two wards where most electric-shock treatment was carried out; and the nurse administrators there understood quite well what was expected in handling "their type of patients." It was as if the physician were to say "do the usual things" (they sometimes did)—little additional instruction being needed. We ourselves coined the term "house special" (as opposed to "à la carte") treatment, to indicate that a patient could be assigned to these wards and handled by the ward staff without the physician either giving special instructions or asking for special favors. However, an original period of coaching the nurses and of reaching understandings was necessary. Consequently when personnel leave, for vacations or permanently, then arrangements must be instituted anew. Even with house-special treatment, some discussion will be required, since not every step of the patient's treatment can be imagined ahead of time. The nurses are adept (as in nonpsychiatric hospitals) at eliciting information from the physician about his patient; they are also adept both in forcing and fostering agreements about action vis-à-vis his patient. We have watched many a scene where the nurse negotiates for such understandings, as well as many staff meetings that the nurses and aides consciously convert into agencies for bringing recalcitrant physicians to terms. When physicians choose, they can be equally concerned with reaching firm agreements and understandings.

It is important that one realize that these agreements do not occur by chance, nor are they established between random parties. They are, in the literal sense of the word, patterned. Thus, the somatically oriented physicians have long-standing arrangements with a secretary who is attached to the two wards upon which their patients tend to be housed; this secretary does a variety of jobs necessitated by these physicians' rather medical orientation. The more psychotherapeutically minded physicians scarcely utilize her services. Similarly, the head nurses and the administrative residents attached to each ward reach certain kinds of understandings and agreements, which neither tends to establish with any other type of personnel. These latter agreements are less in evidence when the resident is new; then the nurse in some helplessness turns to the next highest administrative officer, making yet other contracts. Again, when an attending physician is especially recalcitrant, both resident and nurse's aide seek to draw higher administrators into the act, negotiating for support and increased power. This kind of negotiation occurs with great predictability: for instance, certain physicians because of their particular philosophies of treatment use the hospital in certain ways; consequently, their programs are frequently troublesome for the house staff, who must then seek to spin a network of negotiation around the troublesome situation. When the ward is in high furor, then negotiative activity of course is at its most visible!

In sum: there is a patterned variability of negotiation in the hospital pertaining to who contracts with whom, about what, as well as when these agreements are made. Influencing this variability are hierarchical position and ideological commitments, as well as periodicities in the structure of ward relationships (for instance, because of a rotational system that moves personnel periodically on and off given wards).

It is especially worth emphasizing that negotiation—whether characterized as "agreement," "understanding," "contract," "compact," "pact," or by some other term—has a temporal aspect, whether that aspect is stated specifically or not by the contracting parties. As one listens to agreements being made in the hospital, or watches understandings being established, he becomes aware that a specific termination period, or date line, is often written into the agreement. Thus a physician after being accosted by the head nurse—who may in turn also be responding to her own personnel—may agree to move his patient to another ward after this specific ward has agreed "to try for two more days." What he is doing is issuing to its personnel a promissory note that if things don't work out satisfactorily, he will move his patient. Sometimes the staff breaks the contract, if the patient is especially obstreperous or if tempers are running especially high, and transfers the patient to another ward behind the back of the physician. However, if the patient does sufficiently better, the ward's demands may subside. Or interestingly, it often happens that later both sides will negotiate further, seeking some compromise: the staff, for instance, wishing to restrict the patient's privileges or to give him stronger drug prescriptions, and the physician giving in on these issues to gain some ends of his own. On less tender and less specific grounds, the physician and the head nurse may reach nodding agreement that a new patient should be handled in certain ways "until we see how he responds." Thus there exists a continuum running from specific to quite nonspecific termination dates. But even those explicit and long-term permissions that physicians give to nurses in all hospitals—such as to administer certain drugs at night without bothering to call upon the physicians—are subject to review and withdrawal along with later qualified assent.

It should be added that the very terms "agreements" and "understandings" and "arrangements"—all used by hospital personnel—point up that some negotiations may be made with full explicitness, while others may be established by parties who have scarcely talked. The more implicit or tacit kinds of contracts tend to be called "understandings." The difference can be highlighted by the following contrasting situations: when a resident suggests to a nurse that an established house rule temporarily be ignored, for the good of a given patient, it may be left implicit in their arrangement that he must bear the punishment if administration discovers their common infraction. But the nurse may make this clause more explicit by demanding that he bear the possible public guilt, otherwise she

will not agree to the matter. It follows that some agreements
can be both explicit and specific as to termination, while others
are explicit but nonspecific as to termination, and so on. What
might be referred to as "tacit understandings" are likely to be
those that are neither very specific nor very explicitly
discussed. When a physician is not trusted, the staff is likely to
push him for explicit directives with specific termination
clauses.

### NEGOTIATION, APPRAISAL, AND ORGANIZATIONAL CHANGE

We come now to the full import of the above discussion, for
it raises knotty problems about the relationships that exist between the current negotiated order and genuine organizational
change. Since agreements are patterned and temporal, today's
sum total of agreements can be visualized as different from
tomorrow's—and surely as quite different from next week's.
The hospital can be visualized as a place where numerous
agreements are continually being terminated or forgotten, but
also as continually being established, renewed, reviewed,
revoked, revised. Hence at any moment those that are in effect
are considerably different from those that were or will be.

Now a skeptic, thinking in terms of relatively permanent or
slowly changing structure, might remark that from week to
week the hospital remains the same—that only the working arrangements change. This contention only raises the further
question of what relationship exists between today's working
agreements and the more stable structure (of rules, statuses,
and so on).

With an eye on practicality, one might maintain that no one
knows what the hospital "is" on any given day unless he has a
comprehensive grasp of what combination of rules and
policies, along with agreements, understandings, pacts, contracts, and other working arrangements, currently obtains. In
any pragmatic sense, this is the hospital at the moment: this is
its social order. Any changes that impinge upon this order—
whether something ordinary like a new staff member, a
disrupting event, a betrayed contract; or whether unusual, like
the introduction of a new technology or a new theory—will

all for renegotiation or reappraisal, with consequent changes in the organizational order. Mark the last phrase—a new order, not the reestablishment of an old, a reinstituting of a previous equilibrium. This is what we remarked upon earlier as the necessity for continually reconstituting the bases of concerted action, or social order.

That reconstituting of social order, we would hazard, can be fruitfully conceived in terms of a complex *relationship between the daily negotiative process and a periodic appraisal process.* The former not only allows the daily work to get done; it also reacts back upon the more formalized—and permanent—rules and policies. Further elaboration of this point will follow, but first the following illustration taken from our field notes should be helpful. For some time the hospital had been admitting an increased number of nonpaying adolescent patients, principally because they made good supervisory subjects for the residents. As a consequence, the hospital began to get the reputation of becoming more interested in adolescents than previously; also, some attending physicians were encouraged to bring adolescents for treatment to the hospital. Their presence on the wards raised many new problems, and led to feverish negotiative activity among the various actors implicated in the daily drama. Finally, after some months of high saturation with an adolescent population, a middle-level administrative committee formally recognized what was happening to the institution. The committee recognized it primarily because the adolescents, in the mass, were much harder to handle than an equal number of adults. Yet the situation had its compensatory aspects, since adolescents remained longer and could be given more interesting types of therapy. After some debate, the committee decided that no more adolescent patients would be admitted after an additional stated number had been reached. The decision constituted a formal proclamation, with the proviso that if the situation continued, the policy should be reviewed at high administrative levels in light of "where the institution was going." The decision was never enforced, for shortly thereafter the adolescent census dropped and never rose again to such dangerous heights. The decision has long since been forgotten, and if the census were again to rise dangerously, doubtless a new discussion would take place rather than an evocation of the old rule.

But this is precisely how more long-standing policy and many rules become established in what conventionally is called "hospital structure." In turn, of course, the policies and rules serve to set the limits and some of the directions of negotiation. (This latter proposition is implicit in much of our foregoing discussion on rules and negotiation as well as the patterning of negotiation.) We suggest that future studies of complex relationships existing between the more stable elements of organizational order and the more fleeting working arrangements may profit by examining the former as if they were sometimes a background against which the latter were being evolved in the foreground—and sometimes as if the reverse obtained. What is needed is both a concentrated focus upon, and the development of a terminology adequate to handle, this kind of metaphor. But whether this metaphor or another, the question of how negotiation and appraisal play into each other, and into the rules or policies, remains central

### SUMMARY AND IMPLICATIONS

As remarked at the outset of this paper, the reader must judge for himself whether a model possibly suited to studying psychiatric hospitals might equally guide study and understanding of other types of hospitals. The model presented has pictured the hospital as a locale where personnel, mostly but not exclusively professionals, are enmeshed in a complex negotiative process in order both to accomplish their individual purposes and to work—in an established division of labor—toward clearly as well as vaguely phrased institutional objectives. We have sought to show how differential professional training, ideology, career, and hierarchical position all affect the negotiation; but we have also attempted to show how nonprofessionals may affect the total process. We have outlined important relationships between daily working arrangements and the more permanent structure.

We would argue that this mode of viewing hospitals can be very useful. One reason is that it directs attention to the interplay of professionals and nonprofessionals—*as* professionals and nonprofessionals rather than just in terms of hierarchical position. It forces attention also upon the transactions of professionals, among echelons and within echelons. Properly carried out, the approach will not permit, as in many studies, a focus upon the hospital without cognizance of how the outside world impinges upon what is going on within the hospital: a single hospital, after all, is only a point through which multiple careers stream—including the patients' careers. As suggested in the opening page, the approach also pins one's gaze upon processes of change, and of stability also, providing one assumes that "no change" must be worked at within the organization. Among other considerations, it allows focus upon important internal occurrences under the impact of external pressures as well as of internal changes within the establishment. Whatever the purely specific characteristics of psychiatric hospitals as compared with nonpsychiatric ones, it is evident that most of the latter share certain features that make them amenable to our approach. Hospitals are evolving as institutions—and rapidly. They are locales where many different kinds of professionals work—and more are joining the ranks. The very heterogeneity of personnel and of professional purpose, along with the impact of a changing medical technology, bespeaks the kind of world sketched above.[9]

But what of other organizations, especially if sizable or complex—is this kind of interactional model also relevant to them? The answer, we suggest, is strongly in the affirmative. Current preoccupation with formal organization tends to underplay—or leave implicit—the interactional features underscored in the foregoing pages.[10] Yet one would expect interactional features to jump into visibility once looked for systematically. We urge that whenever an organization possesses one or more of the following characteristics, such a search be instituted: if the organization (1) utilizes personnel trained in several different occupations, or (2) if each contains an occupational group including individuals trained in different traditions, then (3) they are likely to possess somewhat different occupational philosophies, emphasizing somewhat different values; then also (4) if at least some personnel are professionals, the latter are likely to be pursuing careers that render them mobile—that is, carrying them into and out

of the organization. The reader should readily appreciate why
those particular characteristics have been singled out. They
are, of course, attributes of universities, corporations, and government agencies, as well as of hospitals. If an organization i
marked by one or more of those characteristics, then the con
cept of "negotiated order" should be an appropriate way to
view it.[11]

NOTES

1. "The Problem of Society—How We Become Selves," *Movement
of Thought in the Nineteenth Century* (Chicago: University o
Chicago Press, 1936), pp. 360–61.
2. Two psychiatric hospitals were studied, but only one will b
discussed here, namely, the psychiatric wing of Michael Reese Hos
pital in Chicago. (The other hospital was a state mental hospita
that, like most, was maintained and run, though not administered a
the very top, by nonprofessionals. Indeed, it is just this that cause
many psychiatrists to despair of such establishments.) The psychia
ric wing of Michael Reese is in a separate building, administere
with considerable autonomy. It consists of five wards, altogethe
containing about ninety beds. The psychiatric hospital is organize
for quick turnover of private patients: their average length of sta
is only one month. There is a high ratio of personnel to patient
with many nurses and aides, as well as one resident administrato
assigned to each ward. Over 100 men are on the attending staff, c
whom about thirty use the hospital with some frequency. The hosp
tal is well regarded both by the general and psychiatric community
It has the reputation of being a psychoanalytically-oriented e
tablishment—many of its attending staff are analysts or analysts-in
training—but on any given day actually a considerable number,
not the majority, of patients will be those of psychiatrists no
especially sympathetic to the analytic viewpoint.
3. Melville Dalton's book, *Men Who Manage* (New York: Wile
and Sons, 1959), is crammed with such instances. See especially pp
104–7.
4. In passing, it is worth suggesting that many physicians do no
regard nurses as true professionals either and that this affects the
transactions with nurses. Their denial of professional status affec
what they will ask a nurse to do, how they will utilize her service
Stated another way: if she believes herself to be a professional, an
he either denies or is dubious about her claim, then, in commo
parlance, "there will be problems." It happens to be one of the mo

common problems in American hospitals, as many nurses, at least, know.

5. In all hospital settings, when the latter appear the situation becomes, as the staff says, "complicated"—complicated because they make additional, or at least additionally different, demands upon the personnel.

6. Talcott Parsons and R. Fox, "Illness, Therapy, and the Modern Urban American Family," *Journal of Social Issues* VII (1952), pp. 31–44.

7. Erving Goffman, "The Moral Career of the Mental Patient," *Psychiatry* XXII (1959), pp. 123–42.

8. William Caudill et al., "Social Structure and Interaction Processes on a Psychiatric Ward," *American Journal of Orthopsychiatry* XXII (1952), pp. 314–34; Erving Goffman, "On the Characteristics of Total Institutions," *Proceedings of the Symposium on Preventive and Social Psychiatry* (Washington, D.C.: Walter Reed Army Institute of Research, 1957).

9. Without drawing the same conclusions, W. S. Sayre, a professor of public administration, has suggested similar features of modern hospitals. "In the health and medical professions together in a hospital these stresses between *organization* and *profession* are made the more complex by a multiplicity of professions, a multiplicity of values and perspectives not easily reconciled into a harmonious organization. . . . The hospital would seem to be an organizational setting where many semi-autonomous cooperators meet for the purpose of using common services and facilities and to provide services to each other, but in a loosely integrated organizational system." See his "Principles of Administration," *Hospitals* (Jan. 16 and Feb. , 1956).

10. Dalton, op. cit., has made the same criticism of this literature.

11. Julius Roth's yet unpublished research on tuberculosis hospitals similarly emphasizes negotiation, although he is less concerned with social order.

# PART III
# Structural Analysis and Its Alternatives

# INTRODUCTION

The following chapters deal with structural analyses of negoti
ations, often combined with other types to overcome the
insufficiencies of a purely structural explanation. In mos
cases, the structural analysis shows the sides to be highl
imbalanced, and yet this description is clearly not an explana
tion of the outcomes attained, since the "weak" side in thes
cases turns out to be the "winner." Thus other approaches ar
needed. Yet the structural base is by no means irrelevant. I
creates the situation that permits the operation of other impor
tant elements, such as tactics, beliefs, and organization. It wa
only because the Lilliputians were small and numerous tha
they could unite, organize, and gang up on their single, gigan
tic opponent in Swift's *Gulliver's Travels*. It was only becaus
the Professor was small and had nothing to lose that his threa
to do crazy things had to be taken seriously by the Londo
police, which was weighed down by responsibilities, i
Conrad's *Secret Agent*. All of these commonplace situatior
are found in the following cases, and their common charac
teristic is the Structural Paradox: *The greater the structur
imbalance, the more likely it is that nonstructural elements wi
come into play and provide the determinants of the outcom*
or, in other words, the stronger the structural characteristics o

the situation, the weaker the case for a structural explanation of outcomes!

The proposition is demonstrated in the struggle by both sides to maintain unity against disunity in the Teheran oil negotiations of 1971. To the extent that the Libyans and the Iranians were able to act alone in the face of the scrambling oil companies, they were able to have their way. Schuler's crisp participant account, delivered as secret testimony before a closed session of a Senate subcommittee, is a historical description, which makes all the more impressive the natural appearance of analytical concepts, such as threat or commitment. Structurally, it was a case of one side losing its unity and the other side learning to stand together for the first time. But this structural characteristic then permitted a decisive role for other elements, notably tactics, which used structure as a resource for persuasion. Leapfrogging and the threat of further leapfrogging, moving the security or threat point through rumors of nationalizing legislation (cf. Cross 1969, pp. 121–22), and the isolation of adversaries are all tactics that are structural in setting but that provide the basis for further uses of persuasion. The account of the bargaining also shows the important relationship between the means of persuasion and their underlying referents, such as fact, principle, and logic, indicating another important terrain for analysis that has not been fully explored in concept or in theory. The main lesson of the encounter, however, may be summarized in the following proposition: *A party is more likely to achieve favorable outcomes the more it is able to isolate and deal separately with component members of its opponent,* a point that the Malta negotiations also confirm and that Kissinger exploited in the Middle East.

The structural characteristics of the negotiations between Malta and Great Britain were even more striking. A tiny island entered the international arena of great powers and proceeded to auction off as little of itself as possible to the highest bidder. In the process, concession rate theories were thrown for a loop; in a case of what is technically termed unstable behavior (see Rapoport 1960, pp. 60–84; Cross 1969, pp. 54–57; Zartman 1974, p. 393) and is also known more commonly as brinkmanship or chicken (Swingle 1970, pp. 235–73), prices rose rather than fell during the bargaining, and future projections became the credible bases for present threats, much like the behavior of the Sybiline oracle (who, on each rejection of her offer of books on the future, maintained her price but lowered the quantity by burning a few of the books). It may be only an accident of history that the oracle lived near Malta! Wriggins' analysis provides a clear examination of the thesis that outcomes are best explained by the tactical use of power sources rather than by the structural disposition of the power sources themselves. If, after Vietnam and Algeria and Kenya and other cases of structural imbalance, there is still any confusion over power as a possession and power as a relation, then the case of Malta should make the difference clear. But there are also other lessons of the encounter, within the topic of tactics. Mintoff was an impressive example of the warning—or coercive obligation—in which the opponent has to act responsibly just because the first party is so irresponsible. He also was a master cliffhanger, another characteristic of unstable bargaining behavior, and he could batter his opponent up against the ropes of a deadline with skill and verve. The pattern that results is somewhat different from other negotiations, for *in deadline bargaining, concessions tend to be greatest at the end of the process, whereas in nondeadline bargaining, concessions tend to be greatest at the beginning.*

In cases such as Malta, bargaining reflected structure, but the structural characteristics are not deeply affected by the outcome of the negotiation. The Kenyan series of negotiations, and all the other negotiations of colonial transition like them, illustrate a more complicated structural situation, where the process—but not the outcomes—is determined by the structure but where the outcome, in turn, imposes profound changes on the structure itself, which then in turn becomes the basis for new and different negotiation processes. Such restructuring negotiations are typical of our era. Indeed, they make it possible, for if restructuring is attainable through negotiation, fiat and force—which have different kinds of processes and outcomes—become unnecessary. As in the case of the Teheran negotiations and the type of restructuring that they represent, Kenyan-type negotiations become possible only when the credible threat of fiat and force changes hands, or at least is held by both sides. Thus transitional negotiation not only effects restructuring, it also reflects a certain amount of restructuring that has already taken place, by other means. Rothchild's account of the Kenyan experience is a clear portrayal of the changing situation and the role of negotiation in it. It is unusual, not only for its command of the train of events, but also for its use of the negotiating approach to study a subject—decolonization—that should have been analyzed more frequently from this point of view. The case is interesting, too, because it applies the negotiation approach to the study of a domestic situation, showing the similarities between domestic and foreign encounters of the same type, as well as the differences. Thus, in the Kenyan case, extreme structural imbalance is seen to be characterized by tacit bargaining, and structural balance with reciprocal interests by direct bargaining, leading to the more general proposition that *in the absence of organic constraints to bargaining, functional bargaining depends on mutual dependence,* which provides both the reciprocal interests and the sources of the means of gratification and deprivation that are necessary to negotiation.

# 1. THE INTERNATIONAL OIL NEGOTIATIONS*

*G. Henry M. Schuler, Hunt International Petroleum Ltd.*

Upon seizing power in Libya on September 1, 1969, Col. Moamer Qaddafi and his Revolutionary Command Council (RCC) quickly adopted a policy of unhesitant confrontation with oil companies as well as governments. Confrontation was designed to achieve four overlapping and complementary goals: firstly, to ignore existing agreements and OPEC-wide pricing standards so as to increase dramatically the government income per barrel of oil produced; secondly, to seize control of producing operations from oil companies, thus enabling the RCC to manipulate oil supplies for political or commercial purposes; thirdly, to demonstrate to people governed by more moderate regimes that revolution and "Arab socialism" are the wave of the future; and, fourthly, to utilize oil and the revenues derived therefrom in "the battle to liberate Palestine."

### ROUND 1—LIBYA, SEPTEMBER 1970

After consolidating power at the end of January 1970, Col. Qaddafi summoned local oil company representatives to their

* Printed with the author's permission.

first and last personal meeting. Col. Qaddafi immediately set the tone for the impending posted price discussions by stating that "People who have lived for 5000 years without petroleum are able to live without it even for scores of years in order to reach their legitimate right." The Minister of Petroleum, Ezzidin Mabruk, and the Chairman of the Price Committee, Omar Muntasser, left no doubt that a very large increase had become the RCC's prime political goal so as to discredit the previous regime. The Libyan position was based upon alleged underposting of Libya's first exports of crude in 1961, upon the enhanced freight advantage subsequent to the closing of the Suez Canal in 1967 and upon low-sulfur qualities. This position was endorsed by the Organization of Arab Petroleum Exporting Countries (OAPEC) which then included Saudi Arabia and Kuwait, and by Iraq and Algeria which were not yet members.

In fact, Libya co-ordinated its rumored goal of about $0.44 increase in posting with the demands Algeria was making upon France, and frequent consultations between the two Arab countries continued throughout 1970. Occidental was the first company to meet individually with the Price Committee, and others were summoned during the first two weeks of February, including Hunt on the 9th. No company volunteered to increase its postings so a second round of meetings commenced February 23 at which companies were to defend their postings in detail.

The accompanying political background should be noted as Minister Mabruk flew off for the first visit of a senior Libyan to Moscow and as the import of Algerian natural gas to the U.S. was challenged by Atlantic Richfield and Phillips whose assets had been expropriated in Algeria. This round of negotiations failed to produce any results so the Price Committee abandoned the industry-wide approach to concentrate on Esso and Occidental. In April, Col. Qaddafi called for mobilization to fight the oil companies which he linked with "world Zionism and local forces of reaction" and put Dr. Mahmud Mughrabi, Libya's first post-revolution Prime Minister, in charge of the Price Committee. Although an able lawyer and oil economist, Dr. Mughrabi was best known for his extreme political views.

Born in Palestine, he was sentenced to jail by the former regime for his efforts to continue the 1967 embargo on oil exports to the United States and Western Europe after the Khartoum Conference had decided to abandon the embargo. Dr. Mughrabi issued a politically-charged statement and called in as consultants, several well known Arab advocates of nationalization, Dr. Nicolas Sarkis and Abdullah Tariki. They subsequently suggested price levels of $2.61 and $3.115, the latter based on Venezuela.

Discussions with Esso and Occidental resumed in May with Dr. Mughrabi clarifying that the demanded sharp increase in posting must be retroactive and would merely serve to "correct" alleged under postings; however, a week's meetings achieved only agreement in principle by the two companies to some increase. On May 7, Libya began a series of limitations on Occidental's permissible production which reduced production from a peak of 800,000 barrels daily in April to 485,000 b/d in June; the government simultaneously refused to permit Esso to commence export of liquefied gas from its $350-million Brega gas project. Subsequently, Amoseas production was slashed by 31% to 275,000 b/d on June 15; Oasis was cut by 12% to 895,000 b/d on July 20; Mobil/Gelsenberg were cut 20% to 222,000 b/d on August 15 and Esso was cut about 15% to 630,000 b/d on September 5. The reduction in available Libyan supply, coupled with the Syrian closure of Tapline, soon drove up the spot market prices for oil and tankers.

Meanwhile, Algeria nationalized all the assets of Shell and Phillips. Price negotiations with Esso and Occidental resumed in late June. On July 4, the local marketing companies of Esso, Shell and ENI were nationalized. Also in mid-July, Algeria announced a unilateral increase in the postings of French companies from $2.08 to $2.855 retroactive to January 1, 1969. In mid-August Esso and Occidental were reported to have made new offers direct to Deputy Premier Major Abdulsalam Jallud. They were considered unacceptable and Occidental's production was reduced to 425,000 b/d a few days later.

With the September anniversary of the Revolution coming up, the ever-increasing rumors of impending unilateral government action or even nationalization increased. On August 30,

Dr. Hammer reportedly flew to Tripoli and left with agreement in principle on September 3. On September 4, the RCC accepted a September 2 proposal from Occidental which accomplished the following:

1. Increased posting of 40° oil by $0.30 from $2.23 to $2.53 effective September 1.

2. Posting to escalate $0.02 per year for five years commencing January 1, 1971.

3. Postings below 40° to be reduced by $0.015 per degree rather than $0.02 as universally accepted.

4. Increased tax rate from 50% to 58%. Although neither the genesis nor calculation of this new form of increase in "government take" has been made public, there have been reports that it was in substitution for future payments on Occidental's Kufra agricultural project in addition to some $56-million owed for Kufra underpayments and $0.30 per barrel retroactivity from January 1, 1970 through August 31, 1970.

5. Occidental's production ceiling was provisionally increased from 425,000 b/d to 700,000 b/d on condition that Occidental satisfy the head of the Ministry's Technical Department that this represented "good oil field practice."

On September 10, the producers of high pour-point (waxy) Libyan crude met in New York to outline possible strategies for resisting the increases agreed by Occidental on the grounds that the marketplace put a $0.30 penalty on high-pour crudes so no adjustment was required. On September 11, all Libyan producers including Occidental met in New York to discuss various matters including the reported Occidental settlement. Occidental representative was unwilling to provide details, pleading government restraint, so the results of the two industry meetings were entirely inconclusive. The focus of much concern and speculation at these meetings was whether this break in the front would encourage the Libyans to legislate a similar basis for all companies. Dr. Mughrabi had made clear that Libya had unilaterally cancelled all arbitration provisions in the concession agreements, and Major Jallud had assured Algeria that Libya would never submit to arbitration, so this avenue of resolution was considered to be closed. Because of the U.S. desire to reopen diplomatic relations with Algeria and the U.S. interest in gas imports, the U. S. Government had reportedly been reluctant to make representations on behalf of American companies whose properties were nationalized by Algeria, so this avenue of recourse was also not promising.

On September 12, the Oasis partners received letters demanding agreement to Occidental's $0.30 increase retroactive to the commencement of production plus $0.10 more over five years. Discussions began on September 18. On September 21, Continental, Marathon and Amerada Hess signed letters "proposing" similar posted price increases and agreeing to increase tax rate by 4% in satisfaction of the government's claims for additional payments on account of the difference between the posted price provided under paragraph 1 above, and the posted price in effect during the period January 1, 1965 through August 31, 1970. The government "accepted" these "proposals" the same day, and reportedly replaced an onerous per well allowable with a field allowable of 900,000 b/d. Between Occidental and the three Oasis partners, Libya now had half its total production assured at vastly increased "government take."

Nonetheless, recognizing the precedential problem, Shell refused to accept the Hobson's choice of five years retroactivity or 4% increase in tax rate and was refused permission to lift oil after September 22. On the same day, the Ministry summoned representatives of Texaco, Socal, Hunt, Gelsenberg, Arco and Grace and gave these companies until September 27 to accede to similar terms. On September 28, Esso, Mobil and BP unilaterally increased their postings by $0.30 per barrel and accepted the new gravity factor. In the face of this industry acceptance of the general increase, the only things left to fight were the $0.05 wax/quality discount for Hunt, BP, Gelsenberg, Socal and Texaco; the Hunt/BP freight factor of $0.02: and the retroactivity/tax rate increase claim.

The Libyans insisted that the additional tax rate required to buy out of the retroactive under-posting must be based upon 1969 operating costs, current allowables, scheduled increases in postings and a 7.5 year pay-out. The Libyans even refused to permit the companies to specify that the $0.02 per year increase was in recognition of sulfur and they required explicit written acknowledgement that there had been an under-

posting ever since 1965 even though this was not in accord
with the facts. After little more than the trappings of a negotiation, the companies were forced to capitulate on September
30, and tax rates were agreed as follows: Hunt (55%); Texaco and Socal (55% plus $150,000 cash in lieu of 0.02%);
Gelsenberg (55.5%); Grace (54%); and Arco (55%). Thus,
Hunt's posting increased by $0.385 to $2.485 plus $0.02 in-
crease per year; "government take" increased to $0.327 ef-
fective upon signing. On October 8, Esso, Mobil and BP
agreed to similar terms.

### CONCLUSIONS TO BE DRAWN FROM ROUND 1

A number of themes and conclusions emerged from the first
encounter between the Libyan RCC and the international oil
industry. Some points may be painfully obvious with the
benefit of hind-sight, but it must be remembered that these
young army officers were completely unschooled in economics
and negotiations and no one knew anything about them, so
both sides could merely feel their way along:

1) The revolutionary government decided upon a strategy
of going first for those companies which were unduly dependent upon Libyan production. It is open to speculation as to
how this change in attitude from that of the former regime developed, but, in any event, it became clear that those producers
which were unduly dependent upon Libyan crude oil would
have to find access to alternative sources of oil if they were to
resist inordinate demands in Libya.

2) The revolutionary government sought to increase its revenues not through the volume increases which had accounted
for Libya's prior rapid development but rather through unit
increases in per barrel "government take."

3) Subsequent to the rapid increase in Occidental's exports
after the beginning of 1968, the independent producers controlled more than 50% of Libya's exports at their peak in June
1970.

4) The Libyans recognized that a combination of huge
increases in unit take (2 above) and sizeable volumes of vulnerable independent production (1 and 3 above) would permit the Libyan Government to survive a shut-in of major oil

company production with few if any adverse economic consequences. More importantly, this situation would be readily apparent to the companies operating in Libya.

5) The Libyans found that a rationale concocted out of state sovereignty, the doctrine of changing circumstances and allegations of monarchical corruption could be claimed as justification for total abrogation of existing commitments and agreements.

6) The Libyans recognized that "conservation" was a "motherhood issue" which had OPEC's blessing and which was so subjective that it could be argued interminably.

7) The young officers worked closely with their Algerian counterparts who were demonstrating that U.S. appetite for gas was such that even the U. S. Government would do little or nothing to support American producing interests in Algeria. They knew that this had to be even more true of European governments which required more than just peak load gas.

8) By combining "conservation" (6 above), the state sovereignty rationale (5 above) and increasing energy demand (7 above) with a healthy dose of cynicism, the Libyans found they could bring companies and governments to their knees by imposing production restrictions under the guise of "conservation." Similarly, they could threaten "unilateral action" or "legislation" with virtual impunity.

9) It became apparent that growing co-ordination of oil policy among producing states on a multilateral basis (e.g. OPEC, OAPEC) and on a bilateral basis (e.g. Libya with Algeria and Libya with Iraq) would not flounder on ideological differences or selfish national considerations. Disputes and differences between producing states were more apparent than real, more contrived than deep-seated, and more transient than lasting.

10) The Libyans discovered that they could wield this arsenal of weapons to obtain retroactive increases as well as prospective increases, but that the companies preferred to spread these over the future rather than make a lump sum settlement. This approach had great tactical as well as substantive advantage because they could make a demand to establish an effective date and then wait for optimum weather, freight or supply conditions to apply the pressure.

11) Qaddafi's speeches and RCC interest clearly demonstrated that oil policy was seen primarily as a political tool which could be used for internal or external purposes.

ROUND 2—THE REST OF OPEC, DECEMBER 1970

The effect of the Libyan settlement upon other Mediterranean exporting countries was immediate. The Iraq Petroleum Company unilaterally raised its Tripoli/Banias posting by $0.20, but the Iraqis demanded the additional $0.10 given to Libya. Instead of giving Iraq more money in the form of increased posting, IPC made an additional £20-million payment as an advance and, in settlement of a long outstanding issue, offered to pay $0.06 per barrel on Mediterranean exports and $0.07 on Gulf exports in lieu of royalty expensing. Similarly, Algeria's demands from the French were strengthened, and they claimed parity with Libya justified a $3.24 posting.

The fall-out was not limited to Mediterranean exports. Kuwait promptly claimed its posting was too low in light of the Libyan increase and demanded negotiations with Gulf and BP. The Shah also demanded increases in volume or unit payments to meet Iran's five-year plan. Effective November 14, the Consortium increased postings by $0.09 for Iranian heavy crude although the light crude oil postings were left unsettled.

At the same time the various companies offered the 55% tax rate to Iran, Saudi Arabia, Kuwait, Iraq, Nigeria and the Gulf sheikhdoms. Kuwait also settled for $0.09 posting increase effective November 14, but Saudi Arabia did not reach agreement with Aramco. Nigerian postings were increased $0.25 effective retroactive to September 1. At the beginning of December, the Venezuelan Chamber of Deputies passed a bill which increased its tax rate to a flat 60% from a graduated scale peaking at 52% and provided for the unilateral setting of tax reference prices. The increase in tax rate was retroactive to January 1, 1970.

Against this background of rapid world-wide increases to match Libya, OPEC met at Caracas. Not only did Iran raise the subject of the light crude postings, but also Saudi Arabia was reported to be dissatisfied with the overall level of increases just given in the Gulf. The meetings lasted from December 9 to 12, and the results were published on December 28. The resolutions passed by the Conference were as follows:

### Resolution XXI 120:

(1) "minimum" 55% tax rate for all Member countries.

(2) eliminate posted price disparities by tying to the highest existing posting taking into consideration gravity and location.

(3) establish "a uniform increase" to reflect general market improvement.

(4) adopt a new gravity escalation system.

(5) eliminate all OPEC allowances.

To accomplish these ends, the Resolution set up a Gulf group and called for negotiations in Teheran within 31 days. The group was to report to OPEC no later than seven days after the negotiations and OPEC would hold a meeting to evaluate results within 15 days thereafter.

*Resolution XXI 121*—set up a committee to discuss "joint production program."

*Resolution XXI 122*—demanded that postings should reflect the devaluation of the dollar and inflation and called for a study of the matter.

*Resolution XXI 123*—supported the Libyan efforts to get more exploration activity.

*Resolution XXI 124*—supported Libyan efforts to get a freight and Suez premium and promised to support "any appropriate measure."

*Resolution XXI 125*—called for members to be alert against oil company retaliation through production discrimination.

### CONCLUSIONS TO BE DRAWN FROM ROUND 2

As previously described, Round 1 led to a number of conclusions about Libya and the RCC which indicated that future negotiations would be difficult if not impossible there; however, some of the international oil companies apparently retained hope that the Gulf states would exercise self-restraint and ignore the Libyan increases. This illusion was shattered by the events of Round 2 in November and December 1970, leading to a number of conclusions on the international level:

1) Concessions given to any single Eastern Hemisphere country such as Libya would promptly and inevitably spread to all other OPEC members and even outside OPEC. In other words, no individual settlement could be isolated and this led quickly to the conclusion that neither could the negotiations be conducted in isolation with one individual state.

2) It was apparent from the support at Caracas by moderate OPEC states for extreme Libyan demands, that either those moderate states were deliberately setting up the companies and consumers for a flim-flam or else they were afraid of internal and external political pressures if they were seen to be less demanding than the revolutionary regimes. In either event, the issue was too political for Western oil companies to handle without the full support of their home governments.

3) The Caracas Resolutions demonstrated the danger of being dazzled by temporary market conditions into abandoning principle and logic in favor of an easy settlement. Although the companies never accepted the logic or evidence for a claimed underposting in Libya of between $0.30 and $0.37 per barrel back to 1965, they signed a letter ascribing their 4% or 5% increase in tax rate to such underposting. The Gulf states also knew that the Libyan claim was unjustified so they demanded and obtained a 55% tax rate as the new standard. On the other hand, if it became the new standard, then the companies' formally admitted underposting in Libya since 1965 remained unremedied. Similarly, if the September 1 increase of $0.30 per barrel went back to 1965, then it must be based upon the Libyan alleged original underposting and Libya was receiving nothing to reflect the post-Suez freight advantage. In both claims Libya was sure to come back.

4) The Caracas Resolution to take "concerted and simultaneous action by all Member Countries" represented a clear threat to oil supplies and indicated an urgent oil company requirement for the support and cooperation of European consumer governments.

ROUND 3—LIBYA, JANUARY 3, 1971

The RCC refused to recognize that the Gulf states should take the lead after Caracas so on January 3, local representatives in Libya were suddenly summoned to a meeting with Major Jallud. He made it entirely clear that the RCC was determined to make the oil companies hurt in order to coerce them to bring pressure upon the U. S. Government to change its Middle East policy. To produce the necessary pain, Jallud called for implementation of the Caracas Resolutions in the following manner:

*1) Resolution 123*—The companies must reinvest in Libya $0.25 for each barrel of oil exported. The proffered rationale was largely a need for new exploration, but it was clear that non-oil projects would also satisfy the requirement.

*2) Resolution 124*—Major Jallud demanded that posted prices be increased by $0.69 to eliminate so-called "excessive windfall profits." Some element of this was to be "temporary" and some or all was to be applied retroactively to the closing of the Suez Canal in 1967.

*3) Resolution 120 (1)*—The September increases in tax rate were to be put on top of the new OPEC standard rate of 55%, producing new rates varying between 59% and 63%.

*4) Resolution 120 (2) through (5)*—Major Jallud made it clear that Libya would expect whatever increases were obtained in the impending Teheran negotiations.

In addition to these OPEC-supported demands, Major Jallud demanded monthly payment of taxes and royalties (in place of quarterly payments) and the right to obtain oil and gas at cost. With regard to this last demand, it was unclear whether it was for Libya's planned export refinery or merely for local consumption and whether "local consumption" might not include Egypt under the then-scheduled merger.

These demands which would boost the cost of Libyan oil to almost double the level three months earlier were accompanied by the now familiar threats of shut-in or nationalization.

On January 9, the local representatives of Hunt and Occidental were summoned for individual meetings with Major

Jallud, Minister Mabruk and Undersecretary Ghiblawi. The demands were reiterated and the companies given one week to accept.

## CONCLUSIONS TO BE DRAWN FROM ROUND 3

The Libyan demands of January 3 served to confirm all the previous concerns and conclusions created by Rounds 1 and 2. It also raised several new elements:

1) For the first time oil prices and policy were being openly used as a political weapon to force the United States to adopt a pro-Arab Middle Eastern policy.

2) The momentum of OPEC demands were accelerating at a fantastic pace which would lead to a full confrontation if it could not be slowed.

3) The RCC's rejection of the five year posted price schedule in its own September agreement demonstrated that there was little hope for long-term commitments even when freely entered into by revolutionary governments.

4) To some, the Libyan reversion to Occidental as one of the lead-off batters demonstrated that acquiescence to Libyan demands in one round would not enable an individual company to buy a back row seat for the next round. Quite the contrary, acquiescence might encourage the Libyans to come back again.

## ROUND 4—NEW YORK, JANUARY 10–14, 1971

As a result of the events described in Rounds 1, 2 and 3, the more far-sighted members of the industry saw that a major effort would have to be mounted to stem the tide. With the publication of the Caracas Resolutions on December 28, OPEC-watchers at Shell determined that a joint negotiation between the industry and all of the OPEC countries was the only way to avoid the inevitable leap-frog of one round of price increases on the back of its predecessor. Preparations toward this end were commenced on an informal and individual company basis. The original intention was to enlist only the major oil companies, but it is understood that the Department of Justice was unhappy about this, and Major Jallud's demands of

January 3 and 9 revealed that Libya intended once again to "make the running" with the previously successful tactics of picking off the most exposed Libyan independents. His January 16 deadline also introduced an element of urgency. Therefore, the joint approach had to be broadened to include the independent oil companies.

Heretofore, I have attempted to generalize this discussion rather than indicate individual company positions. At this point for the sake of fairness to others as well as precision, I will switch to an exposition of the situation as perceived by Hunt representatives. I would emphasize that views from other vantage points may be equally valid.

Hunt was invited to send representatives to join industry discussions which were already underway in New York. I arrived January 10 and Mr. Epsey from Tripoli on January 11. Meetings were virtually continuous until our departure for Rome and Tripoli on the evening of January 14. It seemed, upon my arrival, that the entire emphasis of the industry discussions was upon the need to have OPEC-wide discussions rather than individual country discussions. *Producing company solidarity* was seen to be entirely reasonable and the only effective response to firm *producing country solidarity*. There may have been some low key generalized mention of "protection" for Libyan producers, but the focus was upon *solidarity* not "insurance." For example, on January 11, Hunt representatives briefed the other companies plus State and Justice representatives on the January 9 meeting with Major Jallud and made a plea for industry unity in the face of the politically-charged situation existing in Libya. To the best of my recollection, the industry meetings on January 11 were devoted exclusively to drafting a joint message to OPEC. The original draft stated:

> we have concluded that we cannot further negotiate the development of claims by member countries of OPEC on any other basis than one which reaches a settlement simultaneously with all producing governments . . . (and called for) all-embracing negotiations . . . between representatives of ourselves . . . and OPEC as representing all its member countries . . .

This language was carried through unchanged to the finished document and was the very heart of the message to OPEC. The only thing of substance that changed was to avoid the specific proposals for a $0.15 general increase in posting and a $0.25 temporary freight premium for Libya which were included in the early drafts and which some participants considered necessary to sell the joint approach to OPEC. The final draft was "cleared" by the Justice Department on January 13. On January 12, the industry began to focus upon the other aspect of the problem, to wit: how could the independent producers' dependence upon Libya be reduced so that he could accept some risk in the face of the inevitable Libyan threats? Although Hunt was not a party to the conversations, it is understood that Occidental sought some form of "insurance" before it would subscribe to the message to OPEC.

It bears emphasizing at this point that while Hunt welcomed tangible assistance, it was perceived that any form of "insurance" would be much less than the value of Sarir field. Nonetheless, "insurance" would be very useful since it would give the Libyan independents some alternative to capitulation, and, perhaps more importantly, because it reflected a willingness to share the burden equitably, thereby creating a climate in which solidarity of independent and major companies was possible. The original concept of what ultimately became known as the sharing agreement called for pro-rate sharing among Libyan producers of the burden of a Libyan cutback for six months or up to December 31, 1971. This concept contained a number of drawbacks which Hunt representatives raised either in formal meetings or informal corridor soundings. Specifically, I suggested the following changes and in several instances provided draft language:

1. Limiting the agreement to Libya was unduly restrictive. It should reflect the same broad scope as the message to OPEC. Hunt was fully prepared to extend its portion of any protection to the French companies in Algeria because their capitulation would necessarily toughen the Libyan demands. I proposed that the group should "open the agreement to all companies which produce or explore for oil and gas in OPEC countries and Nigeria" in order to:

a) spread the risk more widely.

b) involve large American companies not represented in Libya, e.g., Gulf, Phillips.

c) involve the governments of certain consumer countries which had companies producing in OPEC outside Libya, e.g., Japan, Italy, France.

2. Whether or not the *benefits* were extended to other OPEC countries, the obligation should be OPEC-wide. Since the Libyan independents were risking a great deal for the benefit of producers everywhere, an individual company's "cost must be commensurate with its OPEC/Nigeria-wide exposure." This would be accomplished by making a Libyan producer's obligation relate to his share of total OPEC/Nigeria production and non-Libyan producers providing oil would make it available c.i.f. at "tax paid cost plus some equitable sharing of the transportation differential."

3. Because the lead-off batter, in this instance Hunt, might be nationalized, there should either be "no time limit on the protection or the other companies must refuse a settlement which we can't get back in under."

4. The "subject-to-the-physical-availability-of-oil" hedge should be clarified or removed.

5. A new paragraph 6 should be added to read:

"All parties to the agreement undertake to make the strongest possible representations to their respective governments in order to seek official support and cooperation in their efforts to provide crude oil supplies at reasonable cost to consuming countries."

As further evidence of Hunt's desire to expand and strengthen the international and consumer flavor of the joint approach, it may be noted that I kept Gelsenberg informed of the course of the discussions through phone calls from New York to Essen, Germany, prior to their inclusion in the group. We also urged that French representatives be invited immediately because of the stalemated Algerian discussions and the close ties between Algeria and Libya. We also proposed that all possible leverage be employed including sending decisions on the SUMED pipeline and Algerian gas imports.

Hunt's efforts to create an OPEC/Nigeria-wide sharing agreement were apparently over-ambitious in the available time. In any event, commencing with a breakfast meeting on

January 13 and coincident with the arrival of additional Occidental representatives, the sharing concept focused on Libya with "back-up oil" from Gulf producers. During that day and the next, the independent and major companies met both separately and together. Out of one of the caucuses of the major companies emerged the idea that members of the agreement might be restrained by OPEC governments from delivering oil, in which case Libyan obligations might be liquidated at $0.25 per barrel and Gulf obligations could be satisfied by an option to pay $0.10 per barrel. This was fought bitterly by the independent producers because a barrel of oil was worth much more than $0.10–0.25. The Gulf producers refused to give up the option but assured that they would not exercise it "in normal circumstances" and even wrote into the agreement that it was their "present intention" to provide oil.

Although Hunt was unsuccessful in broadening the sharing concept or in getting an open-ended sharing of the burden, we did get written into the agreement that:

> it is furthermore the intention of the parties that they will endeavour, before making an agreement with the Libyan Government, to include a requirement that the Libyan Government accept an offer on comparable terms . . . from all other concessionaires. . . .

Thus, although the insurance was inadequate protection, there was assurance of sufficient oil to remain in the international oil business.

Moreover, the statement of intention and the joint message to OPEC offered assurance of real solidarity which would render the "insurance" unnecessary. With considerable elation at this new solidarity which would permit Hunt to resist unreasonable demands, we went directly from the meeting to the airport, bound for Tripoli.

### CONCLUSIONS TO BE DRAWN FROM ROUND 4

1) The joint message to OPEC was the first evidence of a truly world-wide approach to oil negotiations.

2) The commitment to share the burden of a Libyan cut-

back and the willingness to provide back-up oil from the Gulf was an initial if imperfect step toward sharing the burden which the independent Libyan producers were carrying. As in any agreement of this sort, much depended upon the good faith of the parties, but there was considerable evidence that most participants were prepared to forget past animosities and work toward the common good. Gulf Oil Company's willingness to share part of the Libyan burden is particularly noteworthy since Gulf had no Libyan concessions.

3) The promise of endeavors to obtain comparable terms for all meant that the lead-off batter need not fear that he would be left holding the bag if he resisted unreasonable demands which others later accepted.

4) The United States Government had endorsed the joint approach strategy and the message to OPEC. In fact, Under-secretary of State Irwin was to take this view and a message of support from the President to the Shah and other heads of state. The substance had also been discussed with the governments of Britain, France and the Netherlands.

5) Among the signatories of the message to OPEC were companies from France (CFP), Britain (BP), Holland (Shell), Belgium (Petrofina), Germany (Gelsenberg and Elwerath), Spain (Hispanoil) and Japan (Arabian Oil Company). Shell even hoped to persuade the Italian state company, ENI, to join. This group represented a powerful bloc of consuming countries whose support and cooperation could be reasonably anticipated.

6) On the negative side, there seemed no awareness of the enormous significance of Colonel Qaddafi's political ambitions or there was, at least, no willingness to focus on this aspect of the impending negotiations.

### ROUND 5—TRIPOLI, JANUARY 16–24, 1971

On January 16, the message to OPEC was published and a copy delivered by the president of Esso Libya to the Minister of Petroleum at 9:50 a.m. At 10:00 a.m. Hunt representatives met with the Minister and Under-secretary in response to Major Jallud's January ultimatum (Jallud was in Algeria on the 16th). We referred to the joint OPEC-wide negotiations and our desire to achieve an overall settlement which would reflect Libya's particular advantages but not price us out of the market.

The Minister offered threats and enticements to break with the industry "front" and the major oil companies, but we detected that his major concern for separate Libyan negotiations focused on the peculiarly Libyan problems of the September retroactivity buy-out and exploration activity/reinvestment. The Minister gave us two days to change our minds or he would take action. Occidental also met the Minister on the 16th.

On January 18, Hunt was summoned by the Minister for a half hour meeting although Major Jallud had still not returned from Algeria. It was generally a replay of the meeting of the 16th and he refused a five-year deal, but he expressly recognized that overall posted prices revision and inflation escalator were proper to an overall OPEC forum, and we again had the impression that he might be persuaded to recognize that the freight adjustment was an appropriate subject for OPEC. There was some indication that the threatened unilateral action which would be taken against Hunt was legislated price increases. There were no further deadlines so I returned to London.

On January 18, Major Jallud and the Algerian Oil Minister issued a joint communique in Algiers which praised the Caracas Resolutions of OPEC and called for increased producing country unity. The communique was very much restrained in stating objections to OPEC-wide negotiations.

On January 19, the Minister summoned local Esso representatives and harangued on the "poisoned letter." As in earlier meetings, he "half agreed" that the freight supplement might be dealt with on an OPEC-wide basis. Later in the day Occidental was summoned to meet Major Jallud as well as the Minister and Under-secretary, but he had nothing new to offer except the comment that "Libya will defeat the consuming countries and also the oil companies." The local Hunt representative was given the same treatment, with Major Jallud rejecting the oil industry letter and demanding individual negotiations.

His only justification for rejecting an OPEC-wide approach

was that Libya did not want to negotiate with companies which did not operate in Libya, but this had little real substance behind it given the fact that all the major Persian Gulf producers except Gulf Oil Company operated in Libya. Major Jallud referred to his understanding that President Nixon had promised to take care of the independents in Libya, but said Libya would do its duty. Both Hunt and Occidental were given until January 24 to disassociate themselves from the joint approach or they would be subject to "appropriate action."

On January 23, the Esso representative delivered to the Ministry a letter signed by *both Co-Chairmen* of the OPEC negotiating team Lord Strathalmond (BP) and George Piercy (Esso). The letter was similar to that delivered in Teheran on January 21 and contained the sentences:

*"We should prefer,* and we should have thought that it would be beneficial in the interests of time, *that the negotiations should be with a group representing all the OPEC members.* Nevertheless we should not exclude that separate (but *necessarily connected*) discussions could be held with groups comprising fewer than all OPEC members. However, if we are to embark on such separate but necessarily connected negotiations it is important that it be realized that any negotiated settlement *must be acceptable overall* and *will not lead to further leapfrogging.* It would be our intention to table *one comprehensive document* embodying the proposals referred to above" (emphasis supplied).

As the Minister had gone to Teheran for the OPEC meeting and Major Jallud was not interested in seeing us, Hunt representatives met with Undersecretary Ghiblawi on January 24 in compliance with the deadline issued by Major Jallud on January 19.

The Undersecretary asked if we had decided to disassociate ourselves from the OPEC-wide negotiations and whether we could accept Major Jallud's five demands. We replied along the lines of the "separate-but-necessarily-connected" letter and tried to sell it as made up of delegated representatives of individual companies. We refused to increase tax over 55%, recognized a freight premium per message to OPEC, described compulsory reinvestment as unnecessary and self-defeating, stated preference for existing tax schedule phase-out and offered to consider oil and gas for internal consumption. Prior to this meeting we had prepared a press release in anticipation of being shut-in, but *we did not even receive a threat*.

### CONCLUSIONS TO BE DRAWN FROM ROUND 5

Although these conclusions were never tested, they were strongly indicated at the time:

1) The ability of Hunt and others to face-down three consecutive ultimatums from Major Jallud himself must have proved the soundness of the joint approach agreed in New York. It should have demonstrated also that much of the Libyan bravado was still bluff at that point in time.

2) Prior to his trip to Teheran, the Minister appeared willing to concede OPEC-wide negotiation of everything except exploration/reinvestment and replacement for the September retroactivity buy-out which were in fact peculiarly Libyan problems.

3) Algeria seemed to be exercising considerable caution in its reaction to the proposed OPEC-wide negotiation, presumably because of its desire to obtain U.S. financing and market for its gas liquefaction and its awareness that the U. S. Government supported the message to OPEC. The Algerian influence on Major Jallud was thought to be particularly strong at this time.

### ROUND 6—TEHERAN, JANUARY 15–31, 1971

Although prospects for the joint approach seemed relatively good in radical Libya, things were going much more badly with our "moderate friends" in Teheran. With the benefit of hindsight, the Shah-watchers may find this opposition unsurprising, but it was certainly contrary to what the Libya-oriented companies had been led by the New York meetings to expect.

Early in the morning of January 16, on instructions from London, the senior representative of Iranian Oil Participants (The Consortium), Mr. Van Reeven, presented the message to OPEC to Dr. Amouzegar. After reading the message to

OPEC, Dr. Amouzegar immediately challenged the concept of OPEC-wide negotiations, although there was some indication that his chief concern was that this approach would delay commencement of substantive negotiations in the Gulf. He appreciated the companies' desire to avoid leapfrogging, but argued that OPEC could not stop Libya from making what he characterized as "crazy demands." He promptly raised the threat of letting the OPEC conference proceed and the bugaboo of ending up with the most radical demands as the common denominator. He was to play these tunes repeatedly in the coming weeks. Of a more helpful nature, Dr. Amouzegar raised "the possibility that any settlement which might be reached between the Persian Gulf countries and the oil companies concerned be made subject to an overall settlement between the oil companies and OPEC."

On January 16, Undersecretary of State John N. Irwin commenced a trip to Iran, Saudi Arabia and Kuwait at the published request of President Nixon. Hunt representatives understood that he intended to express high level official support for the message to OPEC and the joint negotiation strategy behind it. Undersecretary Irwin and Ambassador MacArthur met for two hours with the Shah and Minister of Finance Amouzegar on January 18 and a further hour with the Minister alone. Ambassador MacArthur briefed his British, Dutch and French colleagues as well as Lord Strathalmond, Mr. Piercy and Mr. Van Reeven on January 19. That briefing has been reported in several cables.

All accounts agree that Dr. Amouzegar claimed to have taken the lead at Caracas to split the negotiations into three parts whereas *some OPEC members had sought an overall approach*. We are told that both the Shah and Dr. Amouzegar insisted that a collective approach was a "most monumental error" since the "moderates" could not restrain Venezuela or Libya at an OPEC Conference, thereby ending up with the highest common denominator. Ambassador MacArthur's January 19 briefing left the additional impression that the Shah had told Undersecretary Irwin that the joint approach smacked of being a "dirty trick" against OPEC in which case "the entire Gulf would be shut down and no oil would flow."

This impression was reported to London by the British

Ambassador, Sir Denis Wright, and by the industry negotiators, but Ambassador MacArthur subsequently clarified on January 20 that the subject of "Gulf only" negotiations had not even come up during Undersecretary Irwin's meeting with the Shah. Furthermore, the Shah had not threatened to organize a Gulf embargo. Apparently, these threats and demands had come up only in earlier conversations with Dr. Amouzegar.

Although we have no record of the response made by the American diplomats to Dr. Amouzegar, we know that Ambassador MacArthur strongly recommended to Washington that the companies would be well advised to negotiate with the Persian Gulf group and have separate discussions in Libya. In fact, the Ambassador reported that Secretary Rogers had conveyed this message to Mr. John J. McCloy for relay to the companies. The British Ambassador supported this recommendation, but the Dutch Ambassador, Mr. Jonker, recognized that this represented an immediate retreat from the three-day-old message to OPEC. The industry negotiators feared that Ambassador MacArthur failed to appreciate "the essence of the combined strategy."

While it may not be entirely clear who-said-what-to-whom-at-what-time, the record demonstrates that the Iranians were convinced that the U. S. Government was prepared to abandon OPEC-wide negotiations. We are informed of a conversation between the deputy manager of IOP and the Venezuelan Ambassador, wherein the latter describes Dr. Amouzegar as being "most evasive" in response to a request for "his assessment as to how much pressure the governments of the U.K. and the U.S.A. were exerting on Iran to change to a 'global approach'."

He might have been "evasive" with other governments, but he adopted an air of complete confidence with the industry representatives. For example, in response to Mr. Piercy's efforts to push the joint approach on January 19, Dr. Amouzegar said, "If you think you have a problem with your governments, I am quite confident that they will agree to a regional or Gulf approach." Similarly, on January 20, the Shah told the British Ambassador that he was "under the impression that the Americans accepted the 'Gulf only' procedure."

The negotiators' appraisal was stated as follows:

"It was perfectly clear that Dr. Amouzegar believes he and H.I.M. have convinced American Government in recent discussions of the correctness of their position on a Gulf negotiation coming first with the result that our negotiating stand on procedure to be adopted is by no means an easy one."

Against this background of diplomatic contact, the industry representatives met with Dr. Amouzegar, Saudi Oil Minister Yamani and Iraqi Oil Minister Hamadi on January 19. The two-hour meeting was devoted exclusively to the question of a "global approach." Dr. Amouzegar's opposition continued to stress that a global approach was neither logical nor practical; that the authorizing OPEC resolution was limited to the Gulf; that this was merely a question of approach and procedure, not substance, and that it would produce the highest common denominator.

As a method of meeting the problem, the industry representatives suggested that OPEC set up a Mediterranean Committee which could work within a general framework, but the "answer" was a categoric "no." However, the Gulf producers subsequently "suggested" that they might "try" to get a Mediterranean Committee on which they would "endeavor" to have Saudi Arabia and Iraq represented provided that there was a Gulf settlement by February 1. For the first reported instance, Dr. Amouzegar raised the point that the Gulf would insist that any special freight supplement given to Libya would have to be removed when the Suez Canal opened. This problem was glanced over at the January 19 meeting, but it was to become the major focus of the Gulf companies at a later stage. In summary, the Gulf countries gave the companies a 48-hour deadline to agree to "Gulf only" negotiations. Amouzegar would postpone the OPEC meeting from January 23 to January 25 to give the companies a chance to get a "final answer" by January 21 to commence Gulf only negotiations by January 23 to be completed by February 3. If the companies refused to abandon the global approach by January 21, Amouzegar, et al., would hold the OPEC conference and decide whether to legislate or have a global conference to obtain Venezuelan terms. At the conclusion of the meeting, the appraisal of Strathalmond and Piercy was as follows:

> It is not easy to advise what should be done. If we commence with Gulf negotiations we must have very firm assurances that stupidities in the Mediterranean will not be reflected here. On the other hand, if we stick firm on the global approach, we cannot but think . . . that there will be a complete muddle for many months to come. Somehow we feel the former will in the end be inevitable.

In order to develop the requisite joint position vis-à-vis OPEC, a London Policy Group (LPG) was set up in London on January 20 to include all subscribers to the message to OPEC. It is interesting to note that the agenda for the first meeting included the following statement:

"We originally envisaged a rather broad overall negotiation with OPEC generally, i.e., merely covering the four points outlined in the message to OPEC and, stemming from which their application to each country would be agreed, after which more detailed terms would be developed individually with member governments, within the parameters set by the overall agreement concluded by individual concessionaires.

"There would appear to be no reason to change this approach provided OPEC responds in terms which permit its development, i.e., are prepared to sort themselves out as requested in Paragraph 2 of the message to OPEC. It has never been the intention that the individual negotiations of the several companies with the several governments should be carried out to the last detail by a central, and therefore monstrous, overall negotiation."

Although it is largely a question of emphasis, this assertion that an "overall negotiation" was never intended is not supported by the entire record and might be seen as the first indication of an effort to accommodate Amouzegar in the face of the resistance encountered in Teheran. In response to the reports from the negotiators in Teheran and their expressed view that we must eventually give in, the LPG at its first meeting on January 20, debated what approach to take. Hunt representatives expressed concern that the industry not back off the so-called "global approach," because of the following considerations:

1. Amouzegar's "highest-common-denominator-argument" was no threat to the Libyan producers since we were sure to be the highest common denominator in any event.

2. Assurances were worthless because even the companies with Gulf operations "questioned whether there was anything in the record from dealings in this area that would give us any confidence."

3. Although there was talk of a Mediterranean Committee, it was clear that all the Gulf states including Iran opposed this approach.

4. It was clear that the only difference between "parallel" and "separate" negotiations was one of emphasis.

Nevertheless, at the end of the day the LPG unanimously approved movement off the single negotiation approach in the following terms:

"We would prefer, and we would have thought that it would be mutually beneficial in the interests of time, that the negotiations should be with group representing all the OPEC members. Nevertheless, we would not exclude that separate (but necessarily connected) discussions could be held initially with groups comprising fewer than all OPEC members. However, if we are to embark on such separate but connected negotiations it is important that it be realized that any negotiated settlement must be acceptable overall and will not lead to further leapfrogging. It would be our intention to table one comprehensive proposal."

In addition to the formal and public position taken in the letter, the LPG advised the negotiators that "our present feeling is that if there are separate discussions it will be necessary that we should in fact use substantially the same team for the discussions . . . (and) we shall somehow have to take into account the question of fitting Venezuela and Indonesia into the pattern. Thus, notwithstanding the pleas of the negotiators in Teheran at the close of business in London on January 20, it was clear that the LPG was still insisting on a "global negotiation" although agreeing to a "procedure" which provided for geographically-separated meetings.

It should be noted that the separate but "necessarily connected" approach was expressly cleared with the Departments of State and Justice because Mr. McCloy recognized the dangers inherent in it. He described the situation as follows:

"State Department takes the view that parallel negotiations with Gulf and Libya might be favorable *provided that they were linked* in such a way as to ensure that they were within the principles and framework of our OPEC message. The problem as I see it is to link negotiations in such a form and way as to maintain the basis on which our clearances have been obtained, namely, *the need to remove the negative aspect and the chain reaction inherent in separate negotiations. I would imagine the companies would repose little faith in assurances by Iran and others* that they would stand still even if more favorable terms were granted the Libyans. *Substantially unrelated but parallel negotiations might,* I fear, *impair* the basis not only on which Justice Department based its concurrence respecting statement to OPEC, but also *the rationale of the objectives of the entire operation from the industry's point of view.* In advice of Katz of State Department that propriety, from the legal point of view, of parallel negotiations has been raised by Ambassador MacArthur in cable to State Department Wednesday. This being explored by State Department with Justice Thursday morning." (Emphasis supplied.)

Later that day Mr. McLaren advised Mr. Katz that he could understand the need for this approach but indicated that his clearance did not provide for "procedural deviations."

In implementing the "necessarily connected" approach the LPG intended to employ the following procedure as a "fallback":

"A. The 'specific proposals' promised in our letter of January 21 should be presented simultaneously in Teheran and Libya . . .
"B. The team would be split into two halves, each half of which should contain representatives from the majors and Libyan independents. The Libyan half should include Piercy and . . . the Gulf half including Strathalmond . . .
"C. Each half of the team would make it clear that it was only one half of one team and would use best endeavors to persuade Libya and the Gulf countries to get together . . .
"D. It is absolutely essential that neither half of the team

should be prepared to negotiate on the proposals or counter-proposals. The line to be taken would be that any counter-proposal must be considered by the team in one whole . . . so that the team as a whole may consider what new terms, if any, it is prepared to put forward to both groups. . . .

To ensure that there is no doubt as to what we are intending we should perhaps repeat that the first effort of each half of the team would be directed at bringing the producing countries together. . . ."

Prior to receipt . . . January 20, Lord Strathalmond saw Dr. Amouzegar at his home to explore what would happen if no agreement to abandon the global approach was reached by January 21. Dr. Amouzegar again threatened an OPEC Conference on the 25th and implied Venezuelan terms. Three propositions to justify a delay in the OPEC Conference "emerged jointly."

1. "We could request clarification on the assurances that the Gulf states will give regarding unreasonable terms which they fully recognize will have to be granted to Libya." (Comment: this observation expressly recognizes that the Gulf states will not hold Libya back from unreasonable demands. For the first time the emphasis on assurances shifts to protecting Gulf producers against a leap-frog back from Libya which, of course, offers no joy to the Libyan producer. This was pointed out to the negotiators and they agreed to drop any emphasis on it.)

2. "We can announce that we are trying to bring one of two independents in Libya or Algeria to hear from the Persian Gulf Committee why it feels negotiations should take place on the Persian Gulf first in their interests as they would then have backing of Persian Gulf countries in their battle." (Comment: reliance on such "backing" is surely unjustified.)

3. Ask for "their terms in regard to the Persian Gulf and spend a few days considering them."

Strathalmond and Piercy decided to play for time with propositions (1) and (2) and urged that independents join the Teheran negotiations even if they were not American companies. (Comment: this implied suggestion was apparently designed to avoid any anti-trust difficulties.)

Upon receiving the letter and "necessarily connected"

approach from the LPG, the negotiators cabled back strong objections complaining that "it can only put us back to square one in the Gulf." However, they subsequently relented and tried the letter out privately with Dr. Amouzegar on January 21 prior to the scheduled meeting. It is noted that the conditional voice was changed from the "would prefer" of the London draft to "should prefer" in the Teheran submission. Dr. Amouzegar agreed to circulate the "necessarily connected" letter to OPEC and to postpone the scheduled January 25 OPEC meeting.

However, he claimed to be under great pressure from Algeria, Libya and Iraq because the companies were "stalling and infringing on sovereignty of nations." During the afternoon of January 21, the two company negotiators met for 4½ hours with the three Gulf representatives (Amouzegar, Attiki and Hamadi because Yamani had not yet arrived). The company representatives introduced the "necessarily connected" letter which had already been circulated by Amouzegar. Hamadi immediately began to challenge because *the letter precluded a Gulf settlement prior to a settlement with Libya and Algeria. The company representatives confirmed his understanding of this point on two occasions during the meeting.* Dr. Amouzegar insisted that the companies should start negotiating with the Gulf immediately and contended that Libya had no claim on the "OPEC allowances" or "gravity escalation" so these could serve as the starting point and justification for postponing the January 25 OPEC meeting. The company negotiators pointed out that Dr. Amouzegar's contention was factually inaccurate and argued at length; however, the companies finally gave in to Dr. Amouzegar's insistence that this was a break-point.

Piercy stated, "We most assuredly do not want to break on procedural matters. We will discuss this matter as long as it is appreciated that such discussion does not compromise our position given in the letter just handed you . . . (which) meant we were committed to a global basis." (Comment: it was a valiant effort and legal position was preserved, but the damage was done because negotiations had begun with the Gulf only group even though they had continued to reject the "global approach.")

Having opened the door, Dr. Amouzegar insisted that negotiations on all Caracas points recommence on January 23, renewing the threat of the January 25 OPEC meeting. The company negotiators refused to be stampeded before the comprehensive proposal promised for January 28 whereupon Dr. Amouzegar settled for technical level discussions of "OPEC allowances" and "gravity escalation" on January 24. Dr. Amouzegar threatened to give the companies a written reply on January 22 to the message to OPEC and subsequent letter which would lay down certain conditions:

1. Company experts to discuss gravity and allowances from January 24.

2. A package deal on overall Caracas to be submitted January 28.

3. "They (Gulf countries) will not agree that the settlement in the Persian Gulf should be dependent on another area although they will give *all the assurances we want* on no leapfrogging" (emphasis supplied).

4. Negotiations to be finished by February 1 with OPEC conference to be delayed until February 3.

Lord Strathalmond and Mr. Piercy offered the following confidential appraisal: "we are far from home particularly in regard to a Gulf settlement not being dependent on a settlement elsewhere. We are sure this will not repeat not be agreed to here and if we push for a global settlement this will only lead to a demand for Venezuelan terms everywhere." Their public position was not much different since they avoided answering besieging newsmen's questions as to whether the companies were still on a world-wide basis but admitted that negotiations on "Gulf only matters" had commenced even though the Gulf countries had not submitted all of their demands as required by the message to OPEC.

Upon learning of Amouzegar's threat to give Lord Strathalmond a letter containing unacceptable conditions, the LPG recognized that our global approach would be seriously eroded and sent the following message:

"Please inform Strathalmond that unanimous view of companies meeting here is that he should do everything possible to ensure that Amouzegar does not deliver letter envisaged . . . If Amouzegar insists on handing over letter we shall be forced to send reply reasserting the position set out in our previous letter and in addition taking issue about the deadline."

Several hours later they advised Lord Strathalmond that if he were successful in short-stopping Dr. Amouzegar's letter, then he should submit a company letter on the following lines:

"The companies feel that they must reiterate their firm conviction that a broad settlement is necessary, since they believe, as stated in their message of January 16, that it is in the long-term interest of both producing and consuming countries alike, as well as that of the oil companies that there should be stability in the financial arrangements with producing governments. The companies therefore regret that they cannot agree to settlement in the Gulf which would be independent of other areas."

Lord Strathalmond received [these messages] on the evening of January 22, Mr. Piercy having departed to New York. On the advice of Ambassadors Wright and MacArthur, Lord Strathalmond rejected the unanimous instructions of the LPG and refused to attempt to stop delivery of Dr. Amouzegar's letter. The situation is clearly described in Lord Strathalmond's cable:

"Firstly: Your [message] arrived when Wright and MacArthur were with me telling me of a lengthy discussion with Alam and Amouzegar today.

"Secondly: They both say very forcefully that in the light of that discussion to attempt to do as you all ask can only finish everything here and now.

"Thirdly: Reasons are:

"a) Letter was ruse he used to gain postponement Monday meeting.

"b) Grave suspicion we are all stalling discussions until Libya settled.

"Fourthly: Moreover I saw Attiki who helped draft letter and apparently all it awaits is Yamani's signature and he is on way from Saudi Arabia to do this. Letter I believe is at least polite.

"Fifthly: In any event we must face position set out your letter which Amouzegar described as a poor lawyers' effort. I too am a bit lost on it.

"Sixthly: The rigidity of the timetable I think can be eased but only if talks of substance get going.

"Seventhly: I have therefore decided not to try and stop delivery of letter which anyway I think would be fruitless."

The next day, January 23, Lord Strathalmond was given a letter signed by Ministers Amouzegar, Yamani, Hamadi and Attiki. The letter recites the history of the post-Caracas discussions from the Gulf countries' point of view. For example relative to the January 19 meeting with Strathalmond and Piercy, the letter says, "Although the logic of the procedure envisaged by OPEC XXI-120 (Gulf-only negotiations) was finally recognized by you during the meeting, however, you expressed the view that since you were committed to a global approach, you would require 48 hours recess to convey our position to the companies concerned . . . it was made absolutely clear that in case you insist upon global approach without accepting in advance the condition referred in (B) above (prior acceptance of the highest common denominator), the negotiations shall be considered as broken . . ." The Gulf letter goes on to criticize the companies' January 21 letter as ambiguous and vague and to reject the "acceptable overall" condition. The letter agrees to a one week recess subject to the conditions previously indicated by Amouzegar, including:

"That negotiations, as we have repeatedly informed you, shall be conducted on behalf of the producing countries bordering the Gulf, and will in no way involve any other country or region. In case our negotiations were concluded satisfactorily, the settlement with regard to countries in this area should not be delayed if the negotiations elsewhere are not yet concluded, neither shall it be dependent upon settlement with any other country." (Comment: note that the reference is to "countries bordering the Gulf," with no distinction based upon whether oil is exported from Gulf terminals or Mediterranean terminals.)

Upon receipt of this letter, Lord Strathalmond returned to London and the war of words moved into the press. The LPG released to the press at 1600 January 22 a statement including:

"The oil companies' objective remains the achievement of an overall settlement covering the producing countries concerned

The companies reaffirm that any settlement with the oil producing governments concerned must be reached simultaneously."

The Gulf countries also recognized the importance of enlisting the press and consumer governments so the Shah himself gave a 2½ hour long press conference on January 24. H.I.M. attacked the "global approach," saying:

"The oil companies grouped together and there was even news that the government of industrial countries had decided to support the oil companies or to use their influence to bring pressure in favor of the oil companies. If this proves to be correct, obviously it will be a precise example of what is called economic imperialism and neocolonialism, which during the course of history has on several occasions influenced the thoughts and ideas of responsible leaders in the world." (Comment: At this point it was easy for the Shah to adopt a tough stance since he was already convinced that the U. S. Government had backed off the "global approach.")

He threatened Venezuela terms, and an embargo of Gulf production if the companies persisted, but he made clear that no matter what the companies did during this round of negotiations "the oil companies . . . or those holding concessions should in my opinion be removed." Western press reports highlighted the press conference as a battle between the "have-not" producing nations and the "have" consuming nations.

If the Libyan Minister of Petroleum Mabruk had left Tripoli with any thoughts of agreeing to OPEC-wide negotiations on at least some of the Libyan demands (see "Conclusions to be drawn from Round 5"), he was disabused of these in Teheran by the hard-line refusal of Dr. Amouzegar and the other Gulf states. On January 25, the Teheran press reported that Mabruk "flatly rejected a demand by major Western oil companies for a global arrangement on oil prices . . [because] we do not want to bind ourselves and restrict our sovereignty." Similarly, the earlier caution of the Venezuelans was dispelled, and Oil Minister La Salvia even expressed his country's disapproval of "indirect" contacts like the Irwin mission. *If the British or the U.S. Governments had anything to discuss they should have adopted a more direct line rather than resort to other ways."* (Emphasis supplied.)

The "Chiefs" met on January 22 and 23 and the LPG met January 23 and 24. (Because the writer left London for Tripoli on the 23rd and therefore missed all meetings until his return the morning of the 25th, the account is less complete at this point.) The substance of the offer which was to be made as promised on the 28th could not have been terribly difficult to determine because the original drafts of the message to OPEC had included $0.15 general increase and $0.25 temporary freight and the January 28 offer was to be $0.15 general increase and only $0.18 temporary freight. On the key question of overall approach, the "Chiefs" apparently agreed to rely upon Eastern Mediterranean postings and the Gulf assurances to keep Libya connected to the Gulf; therefore, they agreed to submit a more accommodating reply to the Gulf states' letter of January 22 than had been drafted by the LPG and rejected by Lord Strathalmond. This January 28 reply forwarding the companies' offer made several points.

1. The Gulf letter erred in saying the companies agreed to tie future posting increases to product prices but was correct in saying that Gulf take must go up unless Libyan take goes down when freight conditions become normal.

2. The companies had merely stated that they "understand your position" regarding the logic of Gulf only negotiations. (Comment: this was to be the first of many "mutual misunderstandings.")

3. "We are fully authorized to proceed with these negotiations and to seek agreement." (Comment: this is the first clear statement of readiness to negotiate all Caracas matters with the Gulf alone.)

4. If the simultaneous negotiations in Libya take longer, then the Gulf shall agree to "some reasonable time" so that companies can try for a Libyan settlement. In the event that a "reasonable time" elapses without a Libyan settlement, the companies would sign a Gulf agreement "provided reasonable assurances are secured." (Comment: note the new emphasis on "assurances.")

5. The Gulf countries will, as they have promised, try to set up a Mediterranean committee. (Comment: this is the first

written request for a separate committee which the Gulf states
had earlier rejected categorically.)

6. Even if it is not possible to set up a Mediterranean
committee, "by then we will have reached a solution with you
regarding Saudi Arabian and Iraqi short-haul crudes and it
would be our hope that it would be generally recognized that
the terms you had negotiated were reasonable and acceptable
to the Mediterranean countries." (Comment: this reflects the
underlying assured assumption that the Gulf committee could
fix *all* postings of the countries which were represented
thereon. This is the so-called "hinge" rationale whereby the
Gulf and Libya would be "necessarily connected.")

The meetings also came up with the assurances which negotiators would obtain. These "Further Amended Final
Draft—Further Assurances" are . . . built on the assumption
that East Mediterranean postings will be fixed and include a
paragraph against *any* form of leapfrogging back to the Gulf.
They also provide that there will be no "reduction, restriction
or limitation" on production *or* export in support of another
government. (Comment: this was of vital importance to the
Libyan producers since the assurance against production limitations in the Gulf guaranteed the availability of back-up
crude under the Sharing Agreement should they be shut-in in
Libya.)

Lord Strathalmond took the letter and assurances to
Teheran on January 26 where he was joined by Messrs.
Tavoulareas, Kircher and De Crane.

On January 25, the LPG selected the two negotiating groups
headed by Lord Strathalmond and Mr. Piercy. Although the
"two-halves-of-one-team-approach" was being implemented, it
is noted that neither team contained representatives of companies which did not operate in Teheran and Tripoli respectively.
Because it demonstrates Hunt's commitment to both the global
approach and to consumer government involvement, it is
noted that Hunt nominated the German company Gelsenberg
to the Libyan team and suggested that the Japanese company
(AOC) be included on the Teheran Team. No one else
nominated non-Anglo-American companies, but Gelsenberg
was agreed while AOC was not.

On January 27, Lord Strathalmond tried out the letter on

Dr. Amouzegar in private. The latter thought one month a "reasonable time" but insisted that the Gulf agreement be retroactive to the date of initialling. Dr. Amouzegar "very much doubts if we can fix Mediterranean terms for Saudi and Iraqi crude in his committee. He fully understands the 'hinge' and will do everything he can to help." (Comment: prior to the resumption of negotiations we learn that the very basis for agreeing to the resumption of negotiations with the Gulf states alone is invalid, i.e., the East Mediterranean postings will not be fixed so as to serve as a "hinge.")

Meanwhile the Tripoli half of the Team was preparing to submit a similar $0.15 to $0.18 proposal in Tripoli, but this was largely a delaying action since all concerned wished to await the outcome of the Teheran meetings. On January 26, Undersecretary Ghiblawi was advised that Mr. Piercy and Team would arrive the 27th and wished to meet Major Jallud on the 28th.

Ghiblawi set an appointment with Major Jallud for Mr. Piercy alone; however, on the 27th, Minister Mabruk returned from Teheran and pointedly announced in an airport statement that Mr. Piercy would be received solely as a representative of Esso. In the event, Mr. Piercy was only able to see Minister Mabruk and the Undersecretary. Emboldened by his colleagues in Teheran, the Minister used the meeting for a denunciation of the oil company "cartel" and refused to receive an industry proposal. The proposal was subsequently sent to the Minister with a covering letter from Mr. Piercy. Later the letter was sent back to Esso, and the team determined that Libya was merely biding time until Teheran was settled so that it could do one better. Therefore, Mr. Piercy sent a letter to the Minister on January 30 advising that the Team was returning to London.

While the Tripoli Team were out of effective communication in Tripoli events moved very quickly on the Teheran "front." The Teheran Team met for six hours on January 28 with Amouzegar, Hamadi and Yamani which meeting led the Team to conclude that it was "difficult to see much hope of reaching settlement anywhere close to what London saw as reasonable." Lord Strathalmond commented that Dr. Amouzegar now appeared very much more confident and re laxed than the previous week. (Comment: one could speculate that he had been afraid that industry and government would persevere in the "global approach.") In addition to a rejection out of hand of the $0.15 general increase, the Teheran Team gleaned the following information:

1. The Gulf states claimed that the $0.32 given to Libya in September 1970 could not be justified on the basis of freight so there existed a disparity between Libya and the Gulf which had to be corrected under Caracas Resolution 120 (2). (Comment: this is a blatant claim for a ratchet back from the excessive settlement in Libya; it goes to the very heart of the need for a global approach.)

2. The Gulf states agreed to divide the total increase they would receive under Resolution 120 (1) (general increase) and (2) (elimination of disparities) in any way the industry wished. (Comment: another trap for the Libyan producer: if the Gulf companies labeled most of it as "general increase," then Libya was clearly entitled to it under 120 (3); on the other hand, if it were labelled "disparity elimination," then Libya would say they had received nothing in September 1970 for what the record called an original under-posting.)

3. "They refuse to talk about the present freight element . . . and it is now clear that if a deal is reached here it does not repeat does not include either Kirkuk or Sidon crude either in regard to increase in price or freight element." (Comment: a clear rejection of the East Mediterranean "hinge" rationale which had been used to justify a separate negotiation with the Gulf group.)

4. If the companies are unable to eliminate or reduce the Libyan "temporary" freight premium when freight conditions reach normal, "then the Persian Gulf will want a corresponding increase in their prices during the five-year period." (Comment: in the next few days this was to become the biggest horror for the Gulf producers because they envisaged the possibility of giving Libya a $0.25 temporary freight premium on the major oil companies' 1-million b/d of Libyan production. Then if they were unable to eliminate it from Libyan postings at more normal later times, the Gulf states would demand $0.25 barrel on *20-million b/d* of Gulf production because a new unjustified disparity would exist.)

The Teheran Team sought an additional $0.05 which they would attribute to a disparity created by the Libyan increase of September 1970. The LPG resisted this request for additional authority but agreed to meet again on the 29th to hear the Teheran Team's arguments.

Meanwhile so-called "technical discussions" plowed steadily ahead on the questions of an "inflation escalator" and the appropriate level of freight/location disparity between Libya and the Gulf. (Comment: both discussions would have a critical effect on the impending Libyan negotiations as follows:

(1.) The Gulf states argued for a low basic normal freight rate just as the companies had done in Libya prior to September 1970; if the Gulf states made their case stick, then the companies had given too much to Libya and the disparity would have to be corrected by an increase in the Gulf. However, establishment of a low basic normal rate also established a low base against which the then high freight market would be compared to establish the "temporary freight premium" for Libya. In other words, all of OPEC won by establishing a low normal rate because the Gulf was entitled to more for Libyan disparities and Libya was entitled to more for "temporary freight premium." It was a classic whip-saw.

(2.) The Gulf states initially sought a flat cents per barrel annual increase for inflation instead of the percentage escalation preferred by the company representatives. If the "inflation escalator" was established as a percentage rather than a flat cents per barrel, it would cost the Libyan producer more than the Gulf producer because it applied to a higher posted price. In addition, an annual percentage increase would increase the disadvantage of the Libyan producer every year during the life of the agreement.)

Subsequent to the formal meeting of the Team with the Gulf states on the 28th, "informal private discussions" took place, following which the Team cabled its assessment of a possible deal including:

3. "No possibility agreement on freight element nor of including Sidon or Kirkuk crude. . . ."

4. "Some fairly reasonable assurances against future leapfrogging except . . . for reduction, restriction or limitation as

provided in paragraph 3 of our further amended final draft further assurances." (Comment: the Gulf states' lawyers argued that the Gulf committee's terms of reference were limited to Resolution 120 and did not extend to 125. This argument is clearly specious, and, as previously noted, this protection was vital to implementation of the Libyan Sharing Agreement). . . .

7. If negotiations break on the 31st, OPEC will hold meeting on February 3 followed by "a world-wide shut down for a week to prove solidarity although doubts about Venezuela and thereafter legislation or minimum posted prices." . . .

10. Senior members of industry should come to Teheran. "Possibly at last moment this could have moderating effect and avoid a shutdown . . ."

11. "The real basic question however is whether there will be legislation." (Comment: this was to become the major focus of industry discussion in coming days.)

12. "The areas which are clearly non-negotiable are those arising out of Libyan September deals. They are so upset over this action . . ." (Comment: this cries out for a global approach in the future.)

The Teheran Team recommended that the assurance re no Gulf support for embargo be watered-down by the elimination of reference to Resolution 125. (Comment: the start of the slide on assurances.)

The LPG met . . . and suggested that visits by high-level company contacts should be on an individual country basis and raised the possibility of "intervention by home governments." The Teheran Team replied that the U.S. and British ambassadors had already alerted their governments of the possible necessity for intervention.

The Teheran Team met with the Gulf group at 14:30 on January 29 which essentially confirmed the Team's assessment of the 28th. Regarding East Mediterranean postings, it was reiterated that they would not be fixed but Yamani promised "that he will not leap-frog back from Sidon to Ras Tanura." Comment: that this "assurance" even needs expression demonstrates the extent to which the Gulf countries were contemplating bad faith and the extent to which the companies were prepared to capitulate.)

With no fixing of Mediterranean postings, assurances became vital and the Team assessment was that "The assurances are not as watertight as we had hoped but are being worked on here tomorrow . . . the two basic points on no leapfrogging nor support of Libyans' unreasonable demands outside OPEC Resolution 120 stand *and were reinforced*." (Comment: emphasis added because the Gulf states later emasculated them completely.)

The Teheran Team then recommended acceptance of the terms outlined . . . because of the feared alternative . . . and dispatched Messrs. DeCrane, Kircher and Parkhurst to London to sell the deal to the LPG.

The Teheran Team members arrived in London early on January 30, and meetings commenced at 0900. They left London that afternoon *before the arrival of the Tripoli Team* who were responsible for looking after the interests of the Libyan producers. (Comment: we might here recall the terms of reference for the "necessarily connected" negotiations: "It is absolutely essential that . . . any counter proposals must be considered by the Team in one whole . . . so that the Team as a whole may consider what new terms, if any, it is prepared to put forward to both groups. . . ." The Tripoli Team members had a limited idea of what was going on in Teheran but did not appreciate the full extent of the deteriorating position until they reached Finsbury Square about 2000 on January 30.

Prior to their arrival, the LPG had been meeting in London, and a rump session of the "Chiefs" had been convened in New York at the Mobil offices. There was no Hunt representation at the LPG because Hunt's two London representatives, Schuler and Rooney, were in Tripoli as Team member and back-up member. These meetings concurred in the recommendations of the Teheran Team and agreed a "final" offer in an effort to avoid a breakdown in negotiation although the cable expressly recognized that the offer might well be unsuccessful in avoiding such a breakdown.

*Most importantly,* for the first time, accepting the assessment of the Teheran Team that the Gulf group would not fix Eastern Mediterranean postings . . . they agreed *to abandon the message to OPEC and to recognize the total separation of the Gulf and Libyan negotiations*. There was to be no global negotiation, no "two-halves-of-one team" approach, no "necessarily connected" requirement, no Mediterranean Committee, and no fixing of Sidon and Kirkuk postings; all that was sought were assurances. The instructions regarding assurances were very complete and included clauses which had already been rejected by the Gulf states including no embargo in the Eastern Mediterranean and no limitation on the production increases which would be necessary to provide back-up oil for the Sharing Agreement . . . In addition, the cable established a Mediterranean settlement as a condition precedent to a Gulf settlement in the following terms:

"If the OPEC Committee insists that negotiations cannot be carried on at this moment as regards Mediterranean exports from Iraq and Saudi Arabia then the assurances listed below would all be necessary . . . If for any reason the Gulf countries cannot give us formal and full assurances, the initialling of an agreement and the effective date in the Gulf should be delayed until the companies have reached heads of agreement in the Mediterranean."

Also for the first time, the companies expressly provided that "if it is agreed that Libya should receive a special transportation differential tied to a freight index and this transportation differential is not in fact reduced by industry generally in accordance with the agreement, as this index falls then Gulf export tax reference prices will rise by an appropriate amount having regard to the amount the Libyan tax reference price should have fallen." (Comment: this is another horror for the Libyan producer because it virtually condones future Libyan Government failure to live up to its agreement and it also encourages the Gulf states to increase their own postings by persuading Libya not to make appropriate future reductions.)

Upon learning of this complete abandonment of the "solidarity" painstakingly put together in New York only two weeks earlier, I expressed my total disagreement with the decision to abandon the entirely logical and equitable requirement that Eastern Mediterranean postings be fixed. My position was reported to the "Chiefs" in New York, and Mr. Jamieson invited me to express my views over the speaker phone to the assembled group. My notes of the position taken on the phone to New York are as follows:

"We are making an offer in the Gulf which we assume will not be accepted. In the process we are giving . . . total destruction of our credibility by abandoning Eastern Mediterranean port link. Destroys credibility:

a. with consuming countries because we present the posture of hagglers in the market place instead of statesmen who made a firm and fair offer.

and

b. with the U. S. Government because we said we would stand together and we are not.

and

c. with Libya because they have succeeded in separating themselves from the Gulf negotiations—this will encourage them to take individual punitive actions.

and

d. with each other."

Upon completion of this plea, Mr. Jamieson thanked me for my forceful presentation and suggested that the "Chiefs" in New York would take it into consideration.

Meanwhile the session of the LPG resumed in the conference room after dinner and Hunt representatives attempted to reopen the consideration of the new position on the ground that the "Chiefs" had not themselves foreclosed further discussion. There was much resistance to this proposal and word was brought that the "Chiefs" wished to know what would be Hunt's position if there were no other company objecting.

I expressed the reluctant recognition that any question of assurances in substitution for Eastern Mediterranean postings was largely a "judgement area." I could not pit my second-hand judgement against the Teheran Team's firsthand confidence that they could get very detailed assurances; nor could I pit my scepticism at the likelihood of Yamani or Hamadi living up to the assurances against the long association of Gulf company representatives with these two men. Therefore, Hunt would have to acquiesce if we were the only company which objected to abandoning East Mediterranean postings.

Hunt representatives then attempted to win other company

support for reopening on the grounds that Hunt was not really alone in objecting. Although private caucuses were held with the other independent Libyan producers, the only company to support Hunt's request to reconsider the earlier LPG/"Chiefs'" decision was Gelsenberg. In the end the Marathon representative terminated the discussion by saying the issue had been decided earlier in the afternoon. It is only fair to note that I did not feel on this occasion that we had been subjected to a "steam-roller" by the Gulf companies, as the "Chiefs" had provided the opportunity to reopen discussions or even to cast a veto. In fact, with an eye to likely future disputes, I expressly advised Mr. Clarke of Esso and Mr. Shapiro or Mr. Jackson of Millbank Tweed that this final abandonment of the global approach resulted from the failure of the other independent Libyan producers to protect their own interests.

With this abandonment of the last link between the Gulf and Libyan discussions, the entire negotiation took on a different complexion so it is an appropriate place to terminate Round 6 and see what conclusions can be drawn therefrom.

## CONCLUSIONS TO BE DRAWN FROM ROUND 6

The following comments will serve essentially as a summary of the preceding descriptive material.

1. The two weeks of discussions and negotiations repeatedly demonstrated why a "global approach" was imperative:

a. The Gulf countries expressed rage at the level of the September 1970 settlement in Libya because it was not justified by the low basic freight rates which they considered appropriate. They therefore demanded elimination of the "disparity" under OPEC Resolution 120 (2) whereas granting this correction would leave Libya's September 1970 demands unresolved.

b. The Gulf countries stressed the highest-common-denominator threat which might worry the Gulf producers but was of no concern to the Libyan producers who expected to be that highest common denominator in any event. It was merely a question of timing, i.e., whether to take the highest common denominator immediately at a global negotiation or later as an individual leap-frog back.

c. As events developed, it became clear that while massive negotiation with all of OPEC at one table might be procedurally difficult, parallel or "necessarily connected" negotiations in two isolated places were procedurally impossible.

d. The Gulf states maintained that Libya would inevitably get too much but held out faint hope to the Gulf companies that they could rely on assurances that these disparities would not be used to justify new demands in the Gulf. If carried out to the letter, this promised that the Libyan producer would be uncompetitive with the Gulf producer.

e. The Gulf states were demanding certain increases not raised at Caracas or in Libya, e.g., the "Shah's point" for future product price increases, but these would have to be granted to Libya on top of their own special demands.

f. The Gulf states demanded and obtained recognition that any subsequently unjustified freight premium retained by Libya would have to come back to the Gulf. This meant that certain Libyan producers would condone Libyan violation of their own agreement and that the Gulf states would benefit if they could persuade Libya to violate their agreement.

g. If the "inflation escalator" was established as a percentage increase, it would hurt the Libyan producers more because of higher postings to which the percentage would apply.

2. The companies demonstrated their readiness to back-off the all-embracing and all-inclusive negotiation envisaged in the message to OPEC provided they could grasp at successive straws which then slipped away. Among the various rationales for retreat were:

a. "separate (but necessarily connected)" negotiations conducted by two-halves-of-one-team.

b. Gulf states promises to urge the establishment of a Mediterranean Committee which would include Yamani and Hamadi.

c. Gulf settlement reached individually but implementation to be conditional upon settlement everywhere. First variant: Gulf settlement effective only after a "reasonable time" (30 days) has elapsed following initialling during which Libya can be settled. Second variant: effective date is retroactive to date of initialling.

d. Fix Eastern Mediterranean postings. First variant: fix only the freight element in Eastern Mediterranean postings.

e. "All the assurances we want." First variant: "fairly reasonable assurances." Second variant: implied general assurances from the Shah to government representatives.

f. Specific commitment to permit increased Gulf liftings if Libya shut-in. First variant: specific commitment to disclaim embargo on Gulf *and* Eastern Mediterranean liftings if Libya shut-in. Second variant: specific commitment to disclaim embargo solely on Gulf liftings. Third variant: moral commitment by Yamani to avoid Eastern Mediterranean embargo. Fourth variant: generalized but carefully hedged statement that Gulf countries satisfied relative to certain OPEC matters.

g. Gulf states to establish a basis for the freight compensation factor and expressly to define it as "reasonable" for Libya. First variant: include the basis for Gulf purposes but avoid characterization as reasonable.

3. As a result of abandoning the Eastern Mediterranean "hinge" and the insistence on a Libyan settlement, the French, Belgian and Japanese oil companies had no immediate interest in a reasonable Libyan settlement, and we lost the support of their governments.

4. The producing state governments knew exactly what their negotiators were up to and employed every tactic from press conferences with the Shah on down. On the other hand, there is less evidence that the U. S. Government understood the full importance of the joint negotiations sought by the companies. This appraisal could be wrong since the press interpreted the eventual settlement as vastly strengthening the Shah's hand in the Gulf and it is, therefore, entirely probable that the U. S. Government fully understood but decided to embark upon a Shah-oriented policy in the Gulf. If the British and American ambassadors had not supported Lord Strathalmond's decision to ignore unanimous instructions, the outcome would have been very different.

5. By demonstrating our inability to stand up to threats of "legislation," "unilateral action" and embargo, we guaranteed that we would hear many more of these threats in the future.

6. By expressly recognizing the right of the Gulf states to

embargo Eastern Mediterranean crudes to coerce a settlement we granted color of legality to a very potent weapon which had never previously been recognized in commercial disputes. Prior thereto, OPEC could not be sure that we would not call upon arbitration or even government action in the face of an embargo. It can be argued that this was the thin edge of the wedge of political embargos which we have felt so painfully in recent months.

7. The consumer paid an extra price for a five year deal when it was readily apparent from the product price rationale expounded by everyone from the Shah to Major Jallud that this purported stability of price was ephemeral.

8. Perhaps the greatest consequences of the abandonment of joint negotiations are the least tangible. At the commencement of the two week period, there was a certain air of caution on the part of the Algerians and Libyans as well as the Venezuelans and Iranians; on the other hand, there was a certain air of confidence on the part of the companies that, for the first time, all companies were ready and willing to work together towards a reasonable settlement. By January 31 these roles were reversed: the OPEC countries were confident of their ability to face-down the oil companies, home governments of those companies and consumer governments; and the companies had reverted to an attitude of narrow self-interest. This was the start of a rapidly accelerating momentum which has brought us to the point where we find ourselves today.

ROUND 7—TEHERAN, JANUARY 31—FEBRUARY 15, 1971

After the abandonment of the joint negotiation approach, the consideration of a Teheran settlement focuses principally on two issues: firstly: how to avoid *in the Gulf* the consequences of the now-inevitable excessive settlement in Libya; and, secondly, how much to give the Gulf so as to avoid legislation. As a result of the abandonment of solidarity and the new Gulf focus, the Libyan producer also refocuses on two issues: firstly, to investigate all avenues for improving his "insurance" under the Sharing Agreement which has become vastly more important; and, secondly, to encourage the Gulf producers to tailor their settlement in such a way that it will not have adverse consequences in Libya, e.g., avoid a lot of "Shah's points" which will be exported to Libya.

On January 31, Lord Strathalmond met privately with Dr. Amouzegar during the morning to discuss the company offer which would be tabled later in the day. Dr. Amouzegar saw "no difficulty" in the assurances drafted in London and agreed effectively that the deadline for an agreement was the morning of February 3 prior to the OPEC meeting. Later in the day, the Teheran Team met with the four Gulf ministers for 1½ hours. It did not take long to lose the assurances which had provided the justification for backing-off East Mediterranean postings:

1. The freight exception to the assurances against leap-frogging from the Mediterranean would be triggered only if the majors operating in Libya failed to insist on right to re-duce freight." (Comment: the split of the negotiations was not 24 hours old when all the old animosities were resurrected by formally recognizing a distinction between the independents and the majors. This distinction appealed to companies with Gulf production because it meant that the inability of the independents to resist in Libya would not produce an automatic increase in Gulf postings, but its very recognition made the independents more vulnerable and threatened to price them out of the market at some future date.)

2. "No Gulf producing country would go beyond their obligation under Resolution 120 to participate in concerted action in support of the claims of governments having Mediterranean outlet oil. However the Saudi and Iraqi indicated they felt that they could shut off their Med oil in support of this demand, while at the same time their Gulf production for Gulf delivery would not be affected. Countries would be free to press for their demands without benefit of concerted action." (Comment: this is full of new holes: (a) the phrase "beyond their obligation under Resolution 120" is subjective and therefore virtually open-ended; and, (b) there is an implication that *individual* embargos would be permitted even in the Gulf provided there was no "concerted action.")

3. The disclaimer of limitations on production was to take

account of "conservation" but was acceptable to the extent "that in case of a shutdown in the Med by Saudi Arabia and/or Iraq, then the Gulf producing companies can take all the oil you want from all repeat all of the Gulf producing OPEC governments." (Comment: we had all seen the application of "conservation regulations" in Libya and the idea of Iraq or Saudi Arabia allowing increases in their Gulf exports while embargoing their Mediterranean exports strains credibility.)

"Amouzegar stated that we apparently had agreed on the assurances and that each side should instruct their lawyers to put them in proper language." Apparently his appraisal was accurate for the company lawyers' draft was substantially the same. (Comment: my contemporaneous comments on these so-called assurances were:

> We're trying to kid ourselves—the best assurances aren't worth a damn and these aren't worth anything, even in their terms!! Doesn't it demonstrate that we're facing an effort to get the best of all worlds and that good faith is completely lacking. Doesn't the position of Hamadi and Yamani indicate that we are going to be unsuccessful in isolating Libya on straight commercial grounds?)

Returning our attention to the January 31 meeting, Dr. Amouzegar said the Gulf states would give the industry their rock bottom terms for a take it or leave it response by 10:00, February 3. If no response were forthcoming, the Shah would tell the OPEC representatives that Iran was immediately enacting "an entirely new system" which all of OPEC would endorse and support with concerted action. The Team interpreted this to mean Venezuelan terms.

In addition to having to worry about what was being done to the Libyan producer by the "assurances committee" a Gulf "freight committee" also went to work on a "possible future freight escalator for Gulf postings" indicating that "we have to discuss outline of such a formula tomorrow morning." The implications of any freight discussions for the Libyan producer were too much, and the LPG expressed concern asking for a "clearer explanation of your intentions."

In response to the deteriorating assurances, the LPG tried once again to fix Eastern Mediterranean postings, suggesting that Howard Page or George Parkhurst contact Yamani.

The LPG also advised that the so-called "agreed assurances" were "far short" of those approved in London and urged tabling of the London draft.

In response, Mr. Tavoulareas drafted a cable which outlined the successes achieved on assurances regarding inter-Gulf disparities and foreclosing leap-frog from East Mediterranean to the Gulf. However, he expressed considerable despair at the Team's inability to set Eastern Mediterranean terms or to obtain assurances against an Eastern Mediterranean embargo. He stated his belief that Saudi Arabia and Iraq would permit increased liftings from the Gulf to make up for a Mediterranean short-fall and his conviction that they wanted a final settlement in the Mediterranean which had "a rationale and structure consistent with the Persian Gulf," and emphasized that "We must consider our posture with Iran or with Japan if a final break comes over this point." (Comment: the Libyan producer was more concerned about his posture in Libya than with Iran where he had no production or Japan which was too far away to be a market.)

The "Chiefs" met in London on February 1 to consider the deteriorating situation in Teheran. With the benefit of detachment it was obvious by this time that the Gulf states had no intention of providing really meaningful assurances so there were three possible courses of action: (1) give in and accept lack of assurances; (2) refuse to give any more and break over assurances (industry view) or insufficient money (OPEC view); or (3) offer to consider increasing the ante provided they obtained authority to negotiate for the Mediterranean. While this last approach had several dangers and was unlikely to succeed at this late stage in the game, it had the considerable merit of reverting to the Mediterranean "hinge." Furthermore, it apparently had the full support of the U. S. Government. A cable from New York reports that "The quote higher echelons unquote in the State Department" had advised Mr. McCloy of the hope that, prior to breaking off, the negotiators would release a statement that the companies wanted to continue negotiations but that they were running into difficulty because:

> it seemed that the OPEC negotiators for the Gulf countries asserted they lacked authority to widen those assurances which the companies felt were essential to accomplish the objectives of the discussions: that the company negotiators had limited authority with respect to increasing the amount of government take as long as these assurances were not available: that it was hoped that each side at this stage could seek fuller authority in their respective areas on the basis of which the negotiations could continue and any break off on procedural grounds be avoided.

In line with this approach, the "Chiefs" agreed a message to the OPEC countries which Mr. Piercy hand-carried to Teheran. It asked the Gulf states to seek new authority to settle the Eastern Mediterranean in the following terms:

> At the moment we are apart. Apparently the financial terms offered by us are not sufficient and we do not at present have authority to increase these. You tell us that you do not have authority to settle the East Mediterranean position or to give assurances which will prevent the leapfrogging from the Mediterranean into the Gulf, and leapfrogging within the Mediterranean. Will you please go back to OPEC and get authority to negotiate for your oil in the East Mediterranean and to widen the assurances to cover the points that we need covering. In this case we will go back to our principals and ask for authority to enhance the financial terms.

Except for some work by the technical groups on the Gulf producers' problem of inter-Gulf gravity disparities, the Team in Teheran spent most of the day trying frantically to obtain better assurances. A formal 1½ hour meeting with the Gulf states at 14:30 was opened by the companies with what had become for them the most important issue: avoidance of a Gulf increase if Libya refused to permit the temporary freight to come off when conditions normalized. The Gulf states caucused and proposed three solutions:

"A. Resolving disparity (Med and PG) resulting from lower freight element by paying equivalent amount to PG countries according to formula.

"B. A one year deal in lieu of a five year deal wherein the freight element would not be applicable.

"C. . . . only the PG companies submitting to legislation must pay the PG countries the equivalent amount." (Comment: the Gulf states are effectively giving the Gulf companies the alternative to abandon their Libyan operations at some future date.)

Iraq and Saudi Arabia refused to discuss an Eastern Mediterranean settlement but agreed to the following assurances:

"A. The Persian Gulf agreement is a reasonable settlement of OPEC Resolution 120.

"B. Iraq would not take part in concerted action to support the demands of any other country outside of Resolution 120 or demands under 120 which are unreasonable."

The Team concluded that they could not do any better on assurances since Iraq now seemed to be prepared to avoid an East Mediterranean embargo, and they raised the suggestion that Gulf companies could rely on their "concessionary arrangements" to accomplish the production increase required to satisfy the Sharing Agreement. They recommended acceptance of alternative "C" regarding the unjustified Libyan freight premium. Subsequently they received the Gulf state lawyers' draft which did not even provide what the ministers agreed.

At a 1900 meeting with the Gulf ministers, it became re-apparent that there had been no agreement regarding Eastern Mediterranean embargos. The Gulf states would agree only that "without limiting any existing rights it is agreed that the countries around the Gulf shall not take *concerted* action *in the Gulf* to support any OPEC member country which may demand terms *beyond the scope* of our agreement concerning *Resolution 120*. . . ." (Emphasis supplied to demonstrate the holes in this assurance. Various members of the Team admitted that "a favorable sign from them no longer existed" and described it as "disappointing.")

Even with well-organized hind-sight, the picture portrayed is difficult to follow, but this is nothing compared to the confusion that existed in London at the time with phone calls coming in from Teheran to particular "Chiefs" superseding cables which arrived later in time, etc. Out of this confusion, the "Chiefs" determined that the Team should elicit the Gulf states' final position on substantive terms and assurances, and if these were unsatisfactory, the Team were to use the approach agreed earlier in the morning and hand-carried by Mr. Piercy to Teheran.

Unfortunately, an incident took place on the evening of February 1 which was to put the companies at a tremendous psychological disadvantage. A copy of the key January 30 cable, with full terms of reference found its way into the hands of the Teheran press corps. Although no official explanation was ever sought, it was speculated that it was lost or stolen at a press conference given by the Team's public relations man who also subsequently accompanied the other half of the Team to Tripoli for a brief period. In any event the damage was done.

This cable, like all others, had been sent via the secure channels of the Foreign Office to the British Embassy and, therefore, carried the nominal signature of the Foreign Secretary. The Iranian Government invoked censorship to eliminate Sir Alex Douglas-Home's name at the bottom but otherwise permitted publication. It was reproduced verbatim in Teheran's morning papers on February 2 accompanied by bitter attacks because its terms of reference offered far less than the Iranian people had been led by the press to expect. Its publication was expected to embarrass the Team and stiffen the Minister's demands.

Against this background the Team (minus Lord Strathalmond who remained in the office) went to an extremely critical meeting with the ministers at 1000, February 2.

The Team opened with an explanation that Lord Strathalmond was busy elsewhere and with apologies for the leak which they assured was "accidental." The Team were then treated to a harangue including Dr. Amouzegar's pointed comment that removal of censorship would make clear "that the British Government was running negotiations." He then noted that the Team had not tabled all the authority they had and asked for the rest which was promptly given by the Team.

The report of this meeting says that the word "assurances" now makes the ministers "absolutely furious," and there is an implication that part of this unhappiness is over a difference between the assurances required by the "Chiefs" and the modified assurances presented earlier by the Team, but it is not really clear who had earlier agreed what with whom. Perhaps as a result of their embarrassment over the "leak," the Team then digresses in its report to explain the background in order to avoid condemnation of the minister's view on assurances. Similarly, one of the Team members reported that he was now convinced that the previous Gulf retreat on assurances was a "genuine misunderstanding" and not a renege. At the meeting, the Team tried out a new version of the assurance which it had drafted in Teheran although admitted to be without London authority:

> The parties to the agreement agree the terms are reasonable under the meaning of OPEC Resolution 120. The Gulf countries are obliged to support OPEC members through concerted action only when such member countries are pursuing reasonable demands under OPEC Resolution 120.

The Gulf ministers agreed to accept this provided the words "on Gulf production" were included after "concerted action." (Comment: In other words they want freedom to embargo Mediterranean exports to obtain stiffer terms than obtained in the Gulf.)

The ministers then offered their rock-bottom demands for 5 and 1 year deals and said the Shah had decided to recommend OPEC adoption of the Venezuelan pattern if the companies would not accept. The ministers then indicated their unwillingness to settle *intra-Gulf* posting disparities at this Teheran meeting but promised no leapfrogging on later individual settlements. At 0945, February 2, the specific demands were telephoned to the "Chiefs" ' meeting in London and later received by cable.

It may be noted that Mr. Hamadi suggested inside conversations with the BP and Mobil representatives that because of the "atmosphere of mutual trust" that was apparent during these Teheran negotiations, there was hope for an Iraqi settlement with IPC over the Law 80 dispute. Having offered the carrot, he also offered the stick saying, "I don't want to destroy that atmosphere." (Comment: this is noted because it is part of the atmosphere against which some companies very appropriately considered their position vis-à-vis the Teheran negotiations. IPC was in fact nationalized 16 months later.)

The "Chiefs" spent the day of February 2 considering the reports coming in from Teheran. During the morning session they rejected the form of assurance tabled by the Team with Amouzegar at 1000. The "final" language of the assurances was forwarded from Teheran and was found to fall "far short" of what was needed.

The Gulf companies were particularly disturbed to find that the compensating element if Libya failed to lower its freight premium was now described as being "to the same extent" which means a barrel-for-barrel increase of the same amount whereas the earlier language described it as "an appropriate amount" which the companies had taken to mean total excess premium given Libya by a company which, if divided by that company's total production in the Gulf, would result in a much lower per barrel increase.

The Teheran Team must have known that the assurances were entirely inadequate but that afternoon recommended it be given full authority so as to avoid legislation and even suggested accepting a one year deal on the understanding that negotiations for a five year deal would commence. The "Chiefs" rejected both recommendations and instructed them to make the approach hand-carried by Mr. Piercy. The "Chiefs" also approved a message to be delivered to Mr. Nadim Pachachi, the Secretary General of OPEC, in the event that the ministers did not agree to seek additional authority as requested in the Piercy route. This message recited the facts in a very moderate tone and urged that "no immediate and irrevocable action be taken by OPEC member countries."

Late in the evening of February 2, Lord Strathalmond and Mr. Piercy saw Dr. Amouzegar and advised him that his terms for either a one or a five year deal were unacceptable. They then read the so-called final message which had been modified as follows:

> We believe the best way to remove the problems . . . is to urge that somehow the procedures of OPEC are modified. If you could negotiate for your oil in the Eastern Mediterranean and if other negotiations in the Mediterranean could also move forward we believe progress can be made.

Dr. Amouzegar contended that the assurances were adequate since they had accepted the language tabled by the Team and he had "little interest in the rest (since) . . . it was impossible to bring Libya in." He suggested that the companies should have gotten OPEC to form a Persian Gulf Committee without Saudi Arabia and Iraq and an Eastern Mediterranean Committee with Saudi Arabia and Iraq. Dr. Amouzegar advised that the Shah would announce that there would be legislation and pending its being drafted, the terms of the one year deal would apply. A company which didn't accept would be shut down.

The negotiators released a statement that read in part:

> the critical point of assuring an uninterrupted flow of oil in the face of threats to restrict oil remains a major problem. The problem of spiralling increases in financial demands between some of the major producing countries could not be resolved in these discussions (because) the assurances necessary to make this realistic could not be reached. . . .

Dr. Amouzegar also released a statement which included the now familiar claim that assurances against disruption of supplies by areas outside "the Persian Gulf region were beyond the authority of the committee."

At 0745 on February 3, the letter was delivered in Teheran to the Secretary General of OPEC. Mr. Angus Beckett, Head of the Oil Section at the British Department of Trade and Industry, briefed the OECD countries and a background note was provided to consumer governments.

At 1600, February 3, the Shah addressed the OPEC Conference as did the heads of other delegations.

With regard to the message to OPEC and the global approach at the Conference, the Shah said merely, "We therefore *recommended* that negotiations should take place on regional basis instead." With regard to legislation, he said: "I now suggest that the countries of this region should adopt a system which would be *rational and reasonable. . . .*" At the press conference, he implied that acceptance by the companies would avoid legislation and that *there would have to be further co-ordination and consultation with other Gulf countries.* He also said *it would not necessarily follow the Venezuelan pattern.* In reply to a question about Western government attitudes, the Shah said, "The major governments happily, after my warning two weeks ago . . . have shown not the slightest sign of any interference or support for the companies." (Comment: while governments apparently did not *support* the companies, we are told by Lord Strathalmond that "virtually every Ambassador in this town" had been pressing for a delay in legislation so that the companies could finalize a deal.)

The OPEC Conference continued for the remainder of the day and into the next. On February 4, they reached agreement on two resolutions. Publication was delayed until February 8, but a copy of 131 was given privately by Dr. Amouzegar to Lord Strathalmond.

Resolution 131 resolved that each member country in the Gulf would introduce legislation on February 15 to implement Caracas Resolution 120 unless the companies accepted the terms prior thereto. If the companies did not accept by February 22, all OPEC countries would take "appropriate measures including total embargo. . . ." The resolution also supported legislation in Libya and Algeria and threatened an embargo if a company did not accept Gulf terms "plus an additional premium reflecting a reasonably justified short-haul freight advantage." (Comment: Amouzegar contended that he had great difficulty with Libya because the resolution was too limited, but it still left plenty of scope for embargo.)

On February 8, we also learned that there was a Resolution 132 which "gives full support to measures taken or to be taken . . . for safeguarding the legitimate interests of the Libyan people against any collective act that might be exercised by oil companies. . . ." (Comment: it was clear that this could create grave problems for implementation of the Sharing Agreement which might be described as "a collective act." If Libya were to shut a company in, the Gulf countries might feel bound to support Libya by refusing to increase production if not by outright embargo. This danger was far from unrealistic, for, no matter what assurances we had, it is undeniable that Iraq and Saudi Arabia would benefit from any Libyan demands through their Eastern Mediterranean postings which were as yet unresolved.)

The Team returned to London late on the 4th and the "Chiefs" met with the Team at 1000 on February 5. Based upon private conversations with Dr. Amouzegar and Mr. Pachachi, the Team provided its assessment of what was required to make a deal in the Gulf. The financial terms were not significantly more onerous than what had been tabled already, but the absence of a "hinge" to the Mediterranean and the appearance of capitulating in the face of threatened legislation raised very serious problems. It was still possible to cast the OPEC resolution in a very unfavorable light and to distinguish away the legal basis for the Venezuelan legislation but it was decided to keep a low posture and try to achieve a settlement.

Throughout the first week of February, much of the formal and corridor conversation focused on the question of legislation versus capitulation. An assessment of risk involved two questions: firstly, what was the probability that all of OPEC would legislate, and, secondly, were the consequences of legislation so horrendous as to justify avoidance *at any cost*? The OPEC governments would have to consider certain risks:

1. Although OPEC were reported to believe that home governments would accept legislation, they could not be certain that this was true or that such things as arms supplies would be secure in the future.

2. The blame for any cost increases to the consumer would fall clearly upon the producing government if they legislated.

3. Unilateral abrogation of existing contracts would discourage the foreign investment and credit which some still desperately needed at that time (particularly Iran).

4. There would be a great deal of difficulty in drafting legislation which could apply uniformly to all companies.

5. They had to fear that the legislative approach might get out of hand when the opposition got hold of it in the legislature (e.g., Kuwait or Venezuela).

Although the people with firsthand contact in Teheran thought legislation a 96% probability, it was not a foregone conclusion throughout *all* of OPEC. As noted, an appraisal of risk involves investigating consequences as well as probability. Although no one welcomed legislation, it could be argued that it was not so horrendous that industry should avoid it *at all costs*. One could find advantages in legislation over capitulation:

1. It would eliminate accusations that companies were conniving to increase prices and this would increase company credibility with all concerned.

2. It would clearly indicate to the consumers that producing governments rather than industry were responsible for increased prices.

3. It would weaken the assumption of consuming governments that they could negotiate better direct deals because there would be *no negotiation* whatsoever.

4. It would eliminate the constant crises and deadline atmosphere which debilitated the operating people.

5. It would set up the vehicle for industry to continue producing while paying the increase into escrow pending arbitration which might produce a compromise.

6. Actual legislation would leave us no more vulnerable to constant change than the threat of legislation and capitulation does. "If they believe they can legislate and if they believe our governments agree to this approach, then why do we expect they will accept anything less than they can get through legislation and why do we expect them to honor any commitment to put off legislation?"

7. It might be possible to achieve harmonious OPEC-wide "government take" if industry could guide the legislation.

8. It might be possible to build some guarantees of stability/duration into legislation which cannot be built into commercial contractual arrangements.

9. It would better preserve industry unity. Contrary views

were very effectively expressed in a paper presented by CFP on February 7 but it is fair to say that reasonable men could conclude that there was a viable alternative to capitulation. The real problem arose from the fact that the definition of "capitulation" was largely subjective or psychological. Although one had to look through the eyes of the consumer and of home governments, the most important, and potentially dangerous view was through the eyes of the producing governments. Industry had to ask itself what sequence of events and what set of terms and conditions could be accepted without OPEC viewing it as "capitulation"? Some people thought that point had already been passed.

On February 7, a small group of lawyers met to draft assurances, and their output included some very specific efforts to preclude the Gulf supporting unreasonable Libyan claims.

On February 8, the "Chiefs" met to consider the previous days' efforts by the Teheran Team to develop terms of reference and assurances which would be acceptable to the Gulf ministers in place of legislation. During the morning session a draft "Memorandum of Agreement," Terms of Reference and a paper listing alternative approaches regarding "No support for unreasonable claims" were distributed by the Team. The existence of three separate but over-lapping papers raised considerable confusion but the essence of the approach was as follows:

1. The "no embargo" position was so generalized as to be essentially meaningless. Because of the new knowledge of Teheran Resolution 132, an unsuccessful effort was made by Hunt to insert language which would indicate that this provision superseded all prior and future OPEC Resolutions.

2. There were two alternative approaches designed to avoid the "reverse hinge" or "play back" whereby Gulf postings would increase if and when Libya refused to eliminate the "temporary freight premium." One approach was based on the total cost concept and the other on a freight formula. Although the provision was labeled "Libyan freight allowance," it had no direct bearing on the Libyan producer; however, it was of immense importance to the Gulf producer and Lord

Strathalmond insisted that sale of one or the other was a "breakpoint."

3. There were five alternatives for the "No support for unreasonable claims." The first represented a toughening up of the "No embargo provision" and was struck as already covered but in fact it was a far preferable version. The second (relabelled A) characterized the freight formula incorporated in one version of the "reverse hinge" as "a reasonably justified short-haul freight advantage" and precluded embargo if Libya demanded more. Although A was entirely satisfactory, Lord Strathalmond described it as a "non-starter." The third (relabelled B) was a general statement which failed to define what was a "reasonably justified" freight premium. The fourth didn't even mention freight premiums and the fifth alternative was to exclude any assurances at all.

The "Chiefs" agreed that the negotiators "would break" if they didn't get either A or B. The trouble was the chief negotiator said A was a "non-starter" and B was worth little or nothing. Therefore, I made a last ditch effort to stop the slide. My original "talking points" paper reads:

1) We were willing very reluctantly to accept the 10 cent hedge on the safety net because, in our weighing of all the considerations, we arrived at the conclusion that if we took the global approach where all the OPEC demands were laid on the table, then the chances were slim that we would ever have to collect on the net.
2) We reluctantly backed-off the global approach into two halves of one team.
3) We reluctantly backed-off the two halves of one team approach into an agreement whereby eastern Med postings would be fixed.
4) We reluctantly backed-off the approach which required the fixing of east Med postings into an approach which required assurances that we could implement our safety net.
5) NOW: we find great holes in the assurances and therefore no longer have assurance we can implement net.

The safety net has become more and more important to us as we have backed successively farther off the unified global approach . . . we have to import the PG deal to Libya—if we had never joined up we had at least some slim chance of avoiding—we have increased the demands of

Libya, e.g., Shah's point, over even those the Libyans demand so we are more likely to need the safety net.

The plea was respectfully listened to and received the support of the Aminoil representatives but the meeting was in a "do-something-anything!" mood, and only I felt that we had already done enough to meet the Gulf ministers' demands.

The meeting moved on to discuss the Terms of Reference, including an increase to $0.30 for OPEC Resolution 120 (2) and (3) claims. The Moratorium Factor (Shah's point) was stated as $0.03 starting January 1, 1972 but "authority may be required for $0.04 to $0.05/Year." The effective date was to be February 3, but "authority may be required for January 15th" in which case a lump sum back payment would be avoided by moving up the "moratorium factor" of $0.03–$0.05 from January 1, 1972 to February 3,′1971. (Comment: this was a very dangerous precedent. Both the amount and the precedent were sure to be imported by Libya.)

With respect to Teheran Resolution 132 which was published that morning, the Team reported that Amouzegar described it as "lip service."

The morning meeting broke up without a poll of the "Chiefs" having been taken. The Team were to spend the day revising their position and return with a final position for the evening meeting.

Apparently because of my recalcitrance, contact was made directly with Mr. Hunt in Dallas. During the afternoon, I was handed the text of a statement which Mr. Hunt gave to Mr. J. K. Jamieson at 1300, February 8. It is such a clear exposition of the Hunt position that it is quoted in its entirety:

It is my feeling that the producing companies have little chance of isolating the demands of one producing country from the demands of other producing countries. Ultimately, each producing country will demand and get the most generous terms which are extended to any other producing country.

It seems to me that once you leave a legally binding concession agreement and permit one party to this agreement to unilaterally disregard it, there only remains the question of how far such party wishes to go. It seems to me that the only chance the producing companies have, in view of the above situation, is to receive meaningful support from the large consuming countries who ultimately must pay the bill. Failing to get this support, one must soon expect the producing countries will exact a price for crude oil in the neighborhood of $4–$5/barrel.

Personally, I take little stock in the theory that certain so-called moderate producing countries desire to isolate certain more radical countries in their demands for excessive increases. To the contrary, it would seem that the so-called moderates and radicals are now playing a rather unmelodious duet. It is my feeling that, to paraphrase Benjamin Franklin, all of the producing companies will either hang together or hang separately—maybe both. As long as there is some meaningful joint support among the producing oil companies, I wholeheartedly agree to go along.

An evening meeting was held by the "Chiefs" on February 8 to make a decision whether to accept legislation or to make "one last effort" to create the semblance of a negotiated deal. The Team presented their redraft of the morning proposals. The "no embargo" provision was no more satisfactory than in the morning and the "no support for unreasonable claims" alternatives remained unchanged. The so-called "Libyan freight allowance" which called for a formula "tentatively" included World Scale 65 as a base and $0.10–$0.15 as the maximum allowable adjustment. The terms of reference were described merely as what the Team thought they could obtain, and there was no formal vote on them as such. What was voted on was the basic question of whether industry should make a final effort to head off legislation. A number of arguments were offered to convince the Libyan producer that acceptance of the Gulf terms would strengthen his ability to resist unreasonable Libyan demands:

1. A deal would keep CFP in line thereby disabusing Libyans of the idea that they could count on the French.

2. A deal in the Gulf would make it easier to fight unreasonable legislation in Libya because there would be no principle of accepting legislation.

3. A deal would secure alternative oil supplies from the Gulf and the Eastern Mediterranean.

4. A deal would identify what was "reasonable" thereby isolating Libya.

These all depended upon "good faith" which had not been displayed so they seemed a little hollow. Even among the Gulf producing companies the expression of opinion ranged from approval of what the Team has presented on the 8th to refusal to make a deal which would save a mere $0.06 versus legislation and which would not in any event be honored. Nonetheless, the consensus called for continuing informal discussions with the ministers while reserving all options until the *final* "final terms" were obtained.

On February 9, the "Chiefs" met again in the morning to hear that Lord Strathalmond and Mr. Piercy would meet that evening with Dr. Amouzegar in Paris. The papers circulated at the meeting were "Strathalmond Note for Principals," a paper called "Five Year Agreement," a "Memorandum of Agreement" and a paper labelled "Fall Back on Assurances". These papers were the same as those distributed on the 8th. With respect to the "no embargo" provision, Lord Strathalmond indicated that it might become necessary to limit it even further by applying it only to Gulf terminal exports. Depending upon the current World Scale assessment, the base point in the freight formula might need to be increased from W65 to W72.5 but this was entirely satisfactory to the Libyan producer even though we were told by the proponent of the freight formula approach that this formula was "separate from Libya."

At 1030, February 10, Lord Strathalmond reported to the "Chiefs" on his meeting with Dr. Amouzegar. He reported that the $1.40–$1.60/ton freight in our proposal was "in the ballpark" and Dr. Amouzegar was willing for us to quote him in Libya. With respect to the "reverse hinge," Dr. Amouzegar agreed to the total cost concept rather than the barrel-for-barrel increase. This was a major victory for the Gulf producing companies because their comparatively small Libyan production would mean extra payments in the Gulf of only 10% of what they would be on a barrel-for-barrel basis (at $1.40/ton, $44,000,000 vs. $485,000,000; at $2.00/ton, $77,000,000 vs. $700,000,000). Because Dr. Amouzegar had been so reasonable on this point, Lord Strathalmond felt it would be desirable to meet his insistence on $0.33 rather than $0.30 under OPEC Resolution 120. At another point, it was proposed that the $1.40–$1.60 range be increased to $2.00 per ton (about $0.26 per barrel) "as we may have to go up to keep off the barrel-for-barrel basis and on the total amount basis." The Shah's point was political and immovable from $0.05. Dr. Amouzegar would use his influence with Yamani and Hamadi to assure that there would be no embargo *even in the Eastern Mediterranean* if Libya asked for more than the Gulf settlement plus what Dr. Amouzegar considered "reasonable freight." (Comment: he must have had a lot of influence since Yamani and Hamadi had both rejected any such assurance and they would both benefit from exorbitant Libyan demands. Not to mention that Iran and Iraq were at swords point.) The agreement was to be effective January 1, but the 6 weeks' retroactivity could be buried in the overall package.

The meeting broke for lunch and resumed in the afternoon to review the "Final Terms of Reference." At this and other meetings a number of comments and questions were raised to protect the Libyan producer:

1. Clarify the words "concerted" and "embargo" so as to avoid production restrictions.

2. Make sure that no more than $0.15 of the $0.33 is labelled "general increase."

3. State inflation escalation as $0.06 per barrel rather than 2½% which would produce $0.07 in Libya due to higher postings; consider burying the Shah's point.

4. Make sure Shah's point of $0.05 is not under Resolution 120 and therefore exportable to Libya; preferably describe it as something which fits in the package already demanded by the Libyans.

5. How was the retroactivity to be "spread out." The negotiators should try to avoid export to Libya.

6. In exercising the discretion to move from $1.40 to $2.00, the Team will be taking a step which will necessarily affect the Libyan producer. The employment of a formula is useful *provided* the assurances describe it as "reasonable," but, if there is no such description, then the alternative more general-

ized approach based upon total cost might be preferable for the following reasons:

a. The $2.00 maximum equates to $0.26 per barrel which is within $0.04 of Jallud's opening demand and leaves little room for negotiation in Libya.

b. There is inadequate Libyan independent representation on the Teheran Team to leave unlimited discretion.

c. Because the formula approach could conceivably cost the Gulf companies a great deal more than the total cost approach, there is less incentive on their part to see freight rates lowered. (Note: apparently no such distinction was intended but the limitation had been inadvertently left from the draft so confusion reigned.)

d. The formula provides for termination of the supplement in the Gulf when the Suez Canal opens so Iraq and Saudi Arabia have no incentive to open the Canal if they are collecting a premium because freight rates fell due to increased tankers or the SUMED pipeline. So long as Suez is closed, Jallud demanded an additional $0.13 so he also had no particular incentive to open it.

e. The formula would not apply to all companies operating in the Gulf because several companies, e.g., CFP and Gulf, had no production in Libya.

In view of these concerns several possibilities were considered for proposal: firstly, limit discretion by requiring the Team to move off the formula approach before going past $1.80 per ton; secondly, devise new formula that splits any fall in freight rates between the Gulf and Libya, thereby giving Gulf incentive to push Libya to reduce their premium instead of to keep the full premium on; thirdly, increase the Libyan independent representation on the Teheran Team.

The meeting recessed for the Teheran Team to draw up new documents reflecting the morning's discussions. The final documents labelled "Power of Attorney copy" were then presented to the "Chiefs" at 2000. As previously, there was considerable confusion resulting from a proliferation of documents. A document labelled "Five Year Agreement" contained a generalized statement against *production* as well as export limitations and referred to a *maximum* of $2.00 a ton as "a reasonably justified shorthaul freight advantage."

Furthermore it said that the money offers "can be split any way we want that will help us in Libya." The "play-back" or "reverse hinge" provision reflected the total cost approach and included a maximum of $2.00/ton.

Similarly, the "Memorandum of Agreement" contained a satisfactory "no embargo" provision in that it limited Libya's short-haul premium to "the allowance calculated according to the freight index formula attached hereto . . ." which called for a base of W72.5; it even pledged no embargo in the East Mediterranean but it did not specifically mention no production limitations. Unfortunately, there was also a Power of Attorney copy of the old document entitled "Fall Back on Assurances" which emasculated all foregoing without limitation or guidance on its employment. I repeated the requests for caution and consideration but it was too late in the day to scream "Stop." The "Chiefs" approved.

Later that evening the LPG met with the Teheran Team to go over some of the gaps left by the "Chiefs," and it was agreed that the Team would have discretion to decide how to break out the "general increase" and whether to state the inflation escalator as a flat sum per barrel.

On February 11, Hunt and the other companies executed a Letter of Endorsement, but there still remained problems to be sorted out. Specifically, there had been a great deal of confusion about the so-called "Libyan freight factor" at the previous day's meetings of "Chiefs" and a Freight Committee provided an analysis of this very complicated problem.

It is highly significant that concern about the potential implementation of the "Sharing Agreement" began to grow among many of the Libyan independents with the departure of "solidarity," the deterioration of "assurances" and the concession of a Gulf deal which would be very costly on top of the Libyan demands. For example, the representative of Gelsenberg read a statement to the "Chiefs" meeting on February 10 which stated "the continuing intention of the Gulf Producing Companies to provide oil. . . ." There was no denial among the "Chiefs" that this was their intention. Similarly, on February 12, the representative of Occidental called a meeting of the members of the Sharing Agreement specifically to investigate certain matters. Certain questions were answered but then no one took a position on the application of the "safety net" in an instance involving legislation.

Team returned to Teheran, and the Shah returned to television with a BBC interview on February 10. He suggested the companies reach agreement because legislation "is a process or a project which could be repeated continuously." He also reiterated his view on home government representations and his desire to deal directly with consumer governments. Not much else changed either—at a private meeting on February 12, Lord Strathalmond discovered that he and Dr. Amouzegar had had a "mutual misunderstanding" in Paris about the "playback" or "reverse hinge."

Amouzegar would not now accept a freight formula which was applicable to the Mediterranean as well as the Gulf nor could he accept the total cost rationale on existing terms. However, in order to prove that he was not unreasonable, he would reinstate the total cost approach so vitally wanted by the Gulf companies provided that they would increase their offer from $0.33 to $0.35 with the $0.02 put somewhere that it would not be exported to Libya. He also thought the base point should increase from $1.40/ton ($0.18/barrel) to $1.90/ton ($0.25/barrel). This was necessary as "the only way for the Shah and he to avoid criticism later if Libya retains its per barrel freight premium is to say we got something from the beginning."

We were subsequently told at the Team debriefing on February 16 that the additional $0.02 was used to satisfy all the countries in the Gulf because the reverse hinge freight premium would not be paid by all companies, i.e., it was "the price that had to be paid to get paragraph 3(d)." (Comment: Amouzegar is leapfrogging before the terms are even set in Libya.) Unfortunately, there had been another "mutual misunderstanding" in Paris about the "no embargo" assurance applying to the Eastern Mediterranean and the characterization of the freight premium as being "reasonable."

Neither existed in the Minister's draft. (We were told at the subsequent Team debriefing that Hamadi refused to accept the "reasonable" characterization, but that Dr. Amouzegar had explained that Hamadi had "always reserved" on this.) The negotiators agreed to increase the maximum freight factor from $0.18 to $0.215. (Comment: this was a mere "horse-trade" splitting the difference between 18 and 25. It was of only hypothetical future importance to Gulf postings and it would have no restraining influence on Libya; but Libya producers would be stuck with it as a starting point.)

Relative to other matters of interest to Libya, Dr. Amouzegar recommended a flat [percentage increase] but the Team recommended against this because 2½% produced a lower weighted average. (Comment: the percentage of course produced more than $0.06 in Libya.) Dr. Amouzegar also sought to split the $0.33 into $0.15 general increase and $0.18 disparity, but the Team refused to do so. (Comment: this also had Libyan implications.) Amouzegar also sought and obtained retroactivity to January 1 by moving up the first year escalator and moratorium. The Team also drew up for the Teheran Agreement a schedule which for illustrative purposes "showed a Libyan freight premium of $0.30. The LPG noted that this was "dangerously rich in its implications" and asked that the format be revised to show less than $0.215.

However, the Teheran Team did not agree. It was not only the Libyan producer who took a back seat in the rush to make a deal; the Japanese-owned Arabian Oil Company had sought relief from a special problem in the Neutral Zone, but Yamani resisted so the Japanese would not sign the Teheran Agreement. Much of the final days' work was spent on IPC problems with Iraq, and at the last minute, Hamadi insisted upon and obtained a side letter which read inter alia:

The abovementioned agreement is applicable solely and exclusively to crude oil exported from Gulf terminals, and contains *no obligation or commitment whatsoever* on Iraq or any of the said companies in respect of crude oil exported from Mediterranean terminals. (Emphasis supplied.)

The Agreement was signed on February 14 but before we leave Teheran, we should note that there were several conversations with Yamani and Hamadi about the next round in

Libya. Hamadi told the IPC representatives on the morning of February 13 that a Mediterranean Committee of Iraq, Libya, Saudi Arabia and Algeria would be formed and would hold its first meeting on January 16 in Tripoli. Yamani also confirmed that he and Hamadi would join the Libyan negotiations.

On February 16, a Teheran newspaper reported Dr. Amouzegar was also going to Tripoli before the end of the week "to advise the Libyan Government on its negotiations with the oil companies." Apparently, any such move was not enthusiastically endorsed, for we are told that the Shah ordered Dr. Amouzegar to take a 10 day holiday in Germany and that Yamani would be represented by a deputy.

When the Teheran Team returned to London, they advised that although the Libyans had invited Yamani and Hamadi, the question of a Mediterranean Committee was still very much up in the air as Yamani was still reserving his position. (Comment: it is not clear how or why the plans changed, but the Gulf producing companies may have discouraged a Mediterranean Committee for fear of having to associate "moderate" Yamani with all the "radicals." The U. S. Government may have had similar views.)

On February 16, the Shah issued a statement in Zurich expressing "satisfaction" with the Teheran Agreement. He was also reported to have cautioned Libya to be "reasonable." He was quoted as saying: "We wish them success if they get better terms but we aren't bound to support them if they ask for more than we have achieved in the Gulf." (Comment: when the Libyan deal was made he was reportedly "furious" about the amount of money given.) He also pledged to honor the agreement regardless of what should happen in Libya; "Whatever happens, there will be no leapfrogging."

He also said Iran would respect its present contracts with the Consortium. OPEC solidarity came in for praise and he urged countries exporting other primary products, specifically copper and cotton, to form similar groupings to achieve fair prices from the consumers.

About the same time, the vice president of the EEC Commission, Wilhelm Haferkamp, expressed similar satisfaction with the Teheran Agreement and suggested that any Mediterranean Agreement should "take account not only of the special situation of the producing countries, but also of the great importance of Mediterranean oil for the Community.' This and other comments were interpreted as a warning to Libya to be "reasonable."

On February 26, the British Government gave its official blessing in a statement by the Foreign Secretary to Parliament. He specifically noted the Shah's statements of the oil countries' readiness "to eschew price 'leapfrogging' as between the Persian Gulf and other areas."

CONCLUSIONS TO BE DRAWN FROM ROUND 7

1. Because of a seeming lack of resolve on the part of the companies and their governments, in one month, the elation over the solidarity which arose out of the message to OPEC turned into the humiliation of a side letter from Esso, Mobil, BP, CFP and Shell to Iraq expressly denying that the Teheran Agreement had any bearing on the as yet unsettled Mediterranean terms.

2. Before the abandonment of the Eastern Mediterranean "hinge" on January 30, the major emphasis was upon somehow assuring that a reasonable deal would be made in Libya. After January 30, it was recognized that an *unreasonable* deal was inevitable in Libya, and the major emphasis shifted to assuring that the unreasonable terms did not "leap-frog" back into the much larger volume of exports from the Gulf. Thus meaningful Gulf Country assurances against supporting Libya by limitations on production in the Gulf or on exports from the Eastern Mediterranean were sacrificed for general assurances against leapfrogging into or within the Gulf and assurances which would limit the freight premium "leap" to a maximum exposure of $0.215 multiplied by the number of barrels produced by an individual company in Libya.

3. Once the Eastern Mediterranean link was removed, it was incumbent upon each company to pursue its legitimate self interests which would also be in the short-term interests of the consumer. Thus, it was a major victory for Gulf companies to limit the "playback" or "reverse hinge" to $0.215 multiplied by their Libyan production because this would cost less than 10% of the "full reverse hinge" based upon a barrel-for

barrel increase. It was good economics to increase posted price by $0.05 and to raise the maximum freight from $0.18 to $0.215 in consideration for the limitation.

4. Unfortunately, once we had begun with a "global approach" and "global offer," there was no way to avoid importing the full Gulf terms into Libya as a base upon which Major Jallud would build his own demands. This included the cost of buying out of the "full reverse hinge" so the Libyan producer paid twice.

5. The entire approach in Teheran after the split-up was based upon the assumption that Libya would not honor any reductions in the freight premium and this was *expressly recognized in the Teheran Agreement*. This was a far cry from the much-vaunted five year "stability of price." It should be noted that Libya has, in fact, honored its commitment to fluctuate with a formula.

6. The threat to call an OPEC Conference which would demand legislation on the Venezuelan pattern proved to be an all-powerful weapon of coercion in the Gulf, but it is hard to understand why. It was as clear then as it is now that this threat would be used repeatedly until all OPEC countries got the same "take" in one form or another. At the first sign of real resistance, OPEC would legislate posted prices just as they did in October 1973. The message to OPEC had, after all, called for OPEC-wide negotiations and had invited OPEC to lay all its demands on the table: surely, no one expected the Venezuelan delegate to demand something less than he already had. In fact, it can be argued that implementation of legislation would at least fix the highest common denominator at a given point in time whereas individual threats of legislation keep the highest common denominator moving out ahead.

7. Possibly because of incomplete understanding of the commercial and financial implications, consumer and "home" governments put too much emphasis on pledges which were clearly contrary to commercial logic. It was clear that Iraq and Saudi Arabia had great interest in maximizing the Libyan terms because these would also be the terms for their Eastern Mediterranean exports; therefore, they would be unwilling or politically unable to deliver on any promises. Possibly because they took the view that these were political matters better un-

derstood by diplomats, the companies let themselves be persuaded to settle for "assurances" even though they knew better from experience.

8. As pointed out by the Shah, the success of OPEC in forcing industry and consumer governments to capitulate was a sign-post that other developing country exports of raw material were sure to follow.

9. In 1971, OPEC suddenly discovered that Western companies and governments were unwilling or unable to organize resistance to illogical and unreasonable demands. This started a momentum of price demands that has accelerated at a fantastic pace to a level that endangers the economy and financial framework of the entire World.

10. With the abandonment of the Eastern Mediterranean hinge and of meaningful assurances, the "Sharing Agreement" becomes a great deal more important because it is now the *only alternative* to capitulation to even more unreasonable demands in Libya. This, of course, would lead to a whole new round which may be exactly what OPEC wanted.

### ROUND 8—TRIPOLI, JANUARY 30—APRIL 2, 1971

The result in Tripoli was inevitable after the debacle in Teheran, but it is worth covering rather more briefly to demonstrate the gathering momentum. After the Team returned to London on January 30, the local representative of Esso was summoned to meet the Minister. The familiar record was played about the joint approach being a challenge to Libyan sovereignty, but the Minister agreed a single company could establish a pattern for all companies. It was clear that nothing would be done until after the Teheran settlement and this was confirmed by another meeting on February 9.

During this period there was very close liaison with the Algerians on oil policy: on February 11, the Algerian Oil Minister came to Tripoli to obtain Libya's support for its dispute with France; on February 17, another Algerian oil delegation arrived.

On February 18, Major Jallud put the next round in an unmistakable context with a speech saying, "The Teheran oil agreement did not fulfill the aspirations of the Gulf peoples but

he joint stand of the producing countries against the indus-
rialized countries and their monopolistic companies was a vic-
ory." The local representative of BP was promptly summoned
and given the 5 point demand with a February 23 deadline for
acceptance. The Minister was warned that the reply would be
an industry position to which he raised no objection. Mr.
Mabruk also said that the Oil Ministers of Algeria, Iraq and
Saudi Arabia would meet in Tripoli to "rubber-stamp" Libya's
demands.

Although it was still possible to contemplate the legislation
alternative, not many people had any confidence left. The
LPG met in London on February 19 to approve Terms of
Reference. Work on these had started as early as February 8
and the group went through many drafts including one
presented to the "Chiefs" on February 9; however little could
be done before the Gulf was settled. The major questions from
the outset were:

1. How to handle the freight element?—this involved questions of total amount and of distribution between: "permanent" (would never come off and a disparity would upset the
Gulf); "fluctuating temporary" (having obtained the total
cost limitation on the "reverse hinge," there was no particular
"leap-frog" reason for Gulf companies to want to hold this
down); and "Suez temporary" (this was sought by Jallud for
political purposes to hurt the U.S. which allegedly permitted
the Israelis to sit on the East Bank of the Canal and keep it
closed; however, the Gulf companies did not like it because it
was not covered by the "total cost limitation" on the "reverse
hinge"). Another major problem was to develop a rationale to
make the various numbers jibe without upsetting the Gulf settlement.

2. How to handle the claimed sulfur premium?—This also
involved questions of not upsetting the Eastern Mediterranean
(which also had "quality" claims) or creating claims for Abu
Dhabi (which had slightly higher sulfur content than Libya).

3. How to present the offer?—Should we build on a Gulf
posting (this always raised Libyan objections that they were a
republic not a Sheikdom); on pre-September Libyan postings
this was a means to wipe out the over-posting in September
and to incorporate the old $0.02/year escalation into the new

$0.05/year); or on current Libyan postings (this raised th specter of having to incorporate the entire Gulf deal on top o September's over-posting).

4. How to handle the buy-out of retroactivity so as to hol tax rate at 55% as agreed in Teheran? There was a genera desire to correct the mistake we had made in September. In ad dition, the Gulf states had insisted that only $0.10 of the $0.3 September increase had been really justified by a disparity wit Sidon. Therefore, with the impending Eastern Mediterranea negotiations in mind, the Gulf companies were very anxious t clarify that the amount of retroactivity agreed reflected the ta owed on the number of barrels produced prior to Septembe 1970 multiplied by the $0.10 per barrel disparity with th Eastern Mediterranean (Comment: if $0.10 transportatio was justified for Gulf of Sirte terminals, only $0.08 wa justified for Tobruk which was 1 day's steaming closer t Sidon). The Gulf companies also wanted to keep the "buy out" out of posted price so as to avoid a leap-frog into th Gulf.

5. How to avoid the compounding effect of applying th 2½% inflation factor agreed in the Gulf.

The discussions were long and often heated, with the in dependent companies generally trying to hold down the size o the increase, and the Gulf companies willing to make offers o very large increases if characterized as fluctuating freight. Th first approved terms of reference were settled on February 1 and called for a maximum freight, inflation and moratoriun ("Shah's point"). The rationale could not be agreed in Lon don so was left to the Team to agree in Tripoli. In addition th companies would pay $0.05625 per barrel on future produc tion until retroactivity was settled (this represents $0.1 under posting on Sidon times old 50% tax rate and 12½ ' expensed royalty).

On February 22, the Team flew to Tripoli. On the same da Yamani and the Iraqi Minister Hamadi arrived for consulta tions on the Mediterranean settlement. Major Jallud welcome them with another speech to a mass rally at Homs, calling fo more than Teheran or Caracas and saying the oil battle ha "political implications." The Team met to settle the rationa of the approach and immediately the problem of the "Suez a lowance" arose. Several of the independents argued that we had to put part of the total freight in a "Suez factor" because it was a politically-motivated demand and because failure to do so would result in a rationale which lead inevitably to a greater "permanent" freight, thereby increasing the differential with the Gulf. The opposing argument of the Gulf companies included a lot of freight double-talk but was based upon the expectation (then current) that Suez would open.

It was feared that Libya would not remove the Suez premium and the full effect would go into the Gulf on a barrel-for-barrel basis. In any event we never had to make an offer because the BP meeting was cancelled.

The Mediterranean ministers met for 6 hours on the 23rd, and a joint communique was issued the next day declaring unanimous support for Libya and threatening a Mediterranean embargo if the companies refused to accept the agreed upon "minimum demands." The Team met that day, and the Chairman expressed the view that, contrary to earlier hopes that Yamani was morally committed to Gulf terms for the Mediterranean, it was now certain that both Saudi Arabia and Iraq would support the embargo. We were told that the earlier hope had proved unjustified because Saudi Arabia was afraid the Libyans would pay Palestinian fedayeen to blow up Tapline and the Iraqis had secured Libyan financial aid to cover any short-falls created by an embargo.

The Chairman suggested, therefore, that we and the principals would have to reevaluate our decision to stand and fight now; perhaps it would be better to give in and fight another time. (Comment: we had been sold on the idea that the Teheran Agreement would secure Western Europe's oil supplies and our "back-up" oil so as to let us resist unreasonable Libyan demands, but before it was 10 days old we were having to reevaluate!)

That evening, the local representatives of all companies were summoned to a meeting with Major Jallud where they were treated to the usual speech about "cartels" violating national sovereignty and international law, and they were handed a written sheet of demands. It called for a posting of $3.75, including a "fixed" freight premium of $0.41 retroactive to

1967, a 5% increase in tax rate and $0.25 per barrel reinvest ment undertaking. The method by which the Libyans built on the Teheran Agreement is particularly noteworthy; instead of asking for $0.35 (which Amouzegar had said included $0.2 to correct the excess given to Libya in September 1970), the Libyans calculated that the figure represented 19.5% of old Gulf postings and asked for $0.50 which is 19.5% of higher Libyan postings. (Comment: this demonstrates the problems that are created by undertaking a global settlement and then abandoning the global negotiations.) The representatives were given 3 days to start negotiations and 2 weeks to finish. The Team promptly left for London the next day without even trying its offer.

In a not-unrelated development, on February 24 Algeria an nounced that it was nationalizing 51% of all remaining oil production, 100% of all pipelines and 100% of all gas pro duction. Thus, the French were also a victim of the gathering momentum.

The LPG convened on February 26 to consider new terms of reference. Once again those independent oil companies without Gulf production favored lower terms than the major oil companies. This attitude was influenced by several factors: (1) remaining competitive with Gulf Oil was of vital im portance to those non-integrated or partially-integrated compa nies who sold oil in the "third party market": (2) the Oc cidental representative had reported to the Team that the Undersecretary had said that Libya would be back for 51% participation as soon as prices were settled: (3) we felt that we had been dragged along into approving a Gulf deal which would prompt the Gulf states to urge Libya to hold on to "temporary freight"; and (4) some of the people with the greatest experience in Libya felt that Jallud was in no position to carry through with his threats if we showed a will to resist

There was agreement on a posting of $3.41, and most peo ple agreed we were not going to get by with the $0.05625 buy out but had to go to the equivalent of what the Libyans cur rently received from us for the 4–5% tax increase given in Sep tember (about $0.10). Most of the independents thought that the $3.41 should *include* a notional $0.18 for buy-out whereas the major companies thought the buy-out should come on top of $3.41. (Comment: part of this problem was a fear that the buy-out would get into postings and into the Eastern Mediterranean if not into the Gulf, and part of the problem was a seeming certain knowledge that this was not sufficient to make a deal. Some of the Gulf company representatives began to talk of a "magic number" of $0.80 plus moving up the $0.12 escalator and plus buy-out. At the time these figures were thought to be educated hunches, but, in hindsight, they probably came from Yamani and/or Hamadi.)

This basic dispute continued through the next day as well and eventually settled on $3.31 including first year escalation plus a notional $0.10 for buy-out with some vague understanding that the Team could come back and ask the LPG for the full notional $0.18 for buy-out. It was recognized that negotiations on a team basis would be impossible so we chose Gelsenberg and BP to represent the Team since they reflected "major" and "independent" view-points and both were from European consuming countries. The Team returned to Tripoli on February 28.

BP and Gelsenberg had separate appointments with the Minister on March 1, but those produced little real negotiating. The Libyans seemed to be setting up Suez retroactivity and a five year deal as their main trading points. On March 2, the "magic number" approach was revived with all the old disagreements about where to put the freight element, and whether to make the "buy-out" additive. The Team eventually agreed to ask the "Chiefs" who were meeting in New York on March 5 to give the LPG authority to raise the $3.31 to $3.36 with the additional $0.05 "preferably put into . . . temporary freight factor but authority should be given if necessary for the five cents to be in . . . sulfur and basic freight" and also asked to raise the buy-out from $0.05625 to "the financial equivalent of the September agreed surtax increase for each company." Comment: throughout the negotiations there was much discussion about obtaining "maximum flexibility" for the Team and about a largely artificial distinction between "strategy" and "tactics." This arose out of the understandable desire for each company to have a voice in the settlement in order to avoid being "rail-roaded" but it also reflected the confused chain-of-command that existed. For example the *"Chiefs" in*

*New York* were asked to "agree" that the *LPG in London*
should have additional authority which they could give the
*Team in Tripoli* and which the Team could, in turn, use at its
discretion. It was pretty clear that a single "Chief" could exer
cise a blocking veto, but there was no reason for the "Chiefs"
to be able to follow the full ramifications of complicate
freight arguments so they would be reluctant to do so; it wa
also pretty clear that a member of the LPG could veto, but he
was unlikely to do so in the face of his "Chief" having agreed
so he would pass the buck to the Team; unfortunately, it wa
far from clear that an individual Team member could veto the
tabling of an offer which he considered excessive.)

Later in the day BP, Occidental and Marathon were sum
moned to meetings with Major Jallud. Although Jallud threat
ened unspecified "action" it was clear that the Libyans wanted
to negotiate a deal so the three companies went back in the
evening with an offer of $3.095 (including escalation o
$0.06 derived from the Gulf and $0.05 moratorium) bu
excluding buy-out. Because it was built-up from a Gulf post
ing, Jallud threw the companies out with a harangue abou
feudal countries in the Gulf. On March 3, seven companie
including Hunt were summoned but only BP was called in fo
a 5 hour meeting. This time the harangue against the "join
front" was accompanied by threats to legislate U.S. postee
prices and to institute a Mediterranean embargo if the compa
nies did not submit written acceptance by March 7.

On March 4, the BP and Gelsenberg representatives flew t
New York to brief the "Chiefs" on the Team's request fo
$3.36. The Team had also agreed that an agreement throug
December 1972 was preferable to a five year deal which Liby
would not honor. Furthermore, the Team identified th
requirement of "fluctuating freight" as a "breakpoint" an
probably meant it because it was necessary to avoid the ful
"reverse hinge." The "Chiefs" agreed our requests but insiste
on a five year deal so as to avoid repercussions in the Gulf
The written proposals were prepared on March 6 and wer
standard for everyone except Occidental which, at the las
minute, sought Team approval for a special clause covering it
extra 3% tax.

The proposal offered to raise postings by $0.72 to $3.2

(including $0.10 for sulfur, $0.11 for Suez closure, $0.27 for fluctuating freight based on W60 and $0.12 for the first year's escalator in lieu of new retroactivity) plus $0.0506 for buy-out (56.25% of $0.09 industry average cost since September). It also met some of the other Libyan demands including elimination of marketing allowance, provision of oil and gas for internal consumption, monthly payment of taxes and royalties and an exploration commitment. The proposals were presented by Occidental and BP on March 7. Jallud never even read through the proposal and pressed for the final numbers "at which we would walk out of Libya." The Under-secretary made clear to Occidental that he believed the company would stay as long as it received *a small positive cash flow.* Jallud said that if the companies' final offer was too low, Libya would nationalize the companies and pay compensation. He again threatened an embargo, stating that Libya did not care what effect this would have on Europe, and something even more drastic if the companies did not accept by 1000, March 9.

On March 8 all the other companies submitted identical offers to demonstrate their support for BP and Occidental. On March 8 and 9, Texaco and Socal met with Jallud and Mabruk in an effort to demonstrate how generous the industry offer was, but they were told to improve it. During this period, the company experts on freight and sulfur attempted to educate the Libyan "experts," but it was clear that all decisions would be political rather than technical. On March 10, Texaco and Socal presented the same proposal in abbreviated form, showing an increase of $0.82 to $3.27 plus notional $0.10 posting for buy-out.

At this stage the OPEC solidarity reemerged and was strengthened. On March 11, the Deputy Prime Minister of Syria flew to Tripoli and pledged his support for joint action against the oil companies (possibly a hint to nationalize the IPC and Aramco pipeline). On March 12, Nigeria announced its intention to join OPEC and sent a delegation to Tripoli to "co-ordinate respective positions in the face of foreign oil companies." On March 13, the Algerian Oil Minister and Hamadi arrived to be joined by Yamani on the 15th.

On March 13, with Team approval, Texaco and Socal raised

the offer from $3.27 to $3.31 plus $0.10 notional buy-out for an $0.86 increase. Major Jallud threw the proposal at their feet and threatened action if no change by midnight. The Libyans demanded $3.38 (with no fluctuating freight) or $3.40 (with $0.20 fluctuating freight) plus first years' escalation plus full buy-out, i.e., a notional posting of $3.68–$3.70. (Comment: in hindsight, it is interesting that Jallud sought $0.02 more to incorporate a fluctuating freight clause because this is the same amount that was sought by Amouzegar in the Gulf in order to justify the incorporation of the fluctuating freight protection against the "reverse hinge.") On March 14, Jallud and Mabruk met with the Chairman of the Team and Jallud was extremely rude.

He threatened more than a production stoppage and harangued that "You've tied the hand of the independents." The Team met at 1730 to consider a new idea proposed by Texaco which attempted to be "responsive" to Jallud's demand for something more in the "permanent" element by establishing a "guaranteed minimum" or floor of $0.07 (later $0.10) in the so-called "fluctuating freight." This was bitterly fought by Hunt because, call it what you will, it was an unjustified increase of $0.10 in the permanent disparity with the Gulf. It was unanimously rejected by the Team at the 1730 meeting but revived by our Chairman at 2000 over dinner. He required an immediate response because he had an appointment with Yamani and wanted to try it out. Hunt reluctantly agreed that it be floated without commitment provided the buy-out was limited to $0.05625. As it turned out, Yamani had not yet reached Tripoli so it was floated with his deputy, Joukhdar. (Comment: this was the first admitted instance of the "clear-it-with-Yamani" approach which had undoubtedly been practiced for some time.)

On March 15, Yamani arrived for the first meeting of the 4 Ministers which lasted from 1200 to 1430. During the afternoon, our Chairman had a meeting alone with Yamani where he was advised that the Libyan demands for the permanent posting were "way above $3.05." The Libyans were purportedly insisting upon a 48 hour deadline after which Saudi Arabia, Iraq and Algeria would join in an embargo. Jallud was also talking about nationalization, with compensation to be set-off by retroactive claims. Mr. Piercy met again at 2100 with both Yamani and Hamadi who rejected the "guaranteed minimum" scheme and suggested adding full Teheran general increase of $0.35 plus $0.10 for sulfur plus $0.05–$0.10 more permanent freight (on the rationale that VLCC's could not use the Suez Canal even if it opened) to the existing posting of $2.55. If you added to this what we had already offered for fluctuating freight ($0.27), Suez premium ($0.11), first year's escalator ($0.12) and notional buy-out ($0.10–$0.18), you would set Libyan postings at $3.65 (minimum) or $3.78 (maximum). Mr. Piercy described the Yamani/Hamadi proposal as "leapfrogging in the biggest way" and pleaded for more time.

The meeting of the Ministers resumed and lasted until midnight on the 15th when they issued a joint communique saying:

> they agreed on the lower limits of the posted prices in crude produced from their territories, which will be shut in if the companies do not agree to them and to apply them within the periods of time which the Government of Libya fixes for the shut in.

The next morning, March 16, Yamani told Mr. Piercy that he had had to make direct appeal to Col. Qaddafi who was sick in bed to overrule Major Jallud's desire to nationalize all companies on the Algerian pattern.

Later on March 16, Occidental met with the Minister and received indications which confirmed the Yamani/Hamadi suggestion although there was no firm indication that $0.05 was enough more for permanent freight. There was also talk of nationalizing Esso's Zelten Field as an example and imposing an embargo if there was no acceptance of the Libyan demands by March 18. (Comment: the Libyans were not interested in Esso's gas plant because they were convinced that they could not hire people to operate this prestige project which was said to be of marginal profitability in any event.) The Team flew to London on the 16th.

On March 17, the Team met to consider the situation. They listed on the blackboard the pros and cons of making a settlement as follows:

1. Pro settlement:
   a. Defers nationalization and makes it less tempestuous.
   b. Helps to maintain the industry as the middle man.
   c. Keeps the oil flowing.

2. Con settlement:
   a. Puts strains on Teheran.
   b. Makes Libyan oil uncompetitive.
   c. Whets appetite in Libya and elsewhere.
   d. Possibly difficult to convince Europe of its necessity.
   e. Strengthens appeal of Libyan type approach.
   f. Could keep Canal closed because Libya will finance Egypt. (Comment: there were some indications that Libya would give the $0.12 per barrel Suez allowance to Egypt to compensate for its loss of Canal tariffs.)

It was, however, too late and the entire Team except myself agreed to recommend a settlement to the "Chiefs." The Team then proceeded to outline what it considered to be the minimum and maximum terms required to make a deal; these ranged from a notional $3.40 to a notional $3.72 which represented a $0.09 to $0.41 increase over the $3.31 then on the table in Tripoli. The "Chiefs" met in the afternoon and agreed to increase the Terms of Reference to a notional posting of $3.58 which included full Teheran general increase ($0.35), sulfur premium ($0.10 to $0.02 each year), additional permanent freight ($0.07), full Teheran first year escalation ($0.12 composed of $0.05 "Shah's point" and $0.07 for 2½% on higher Libyan postings), notional buy-out ($0.16 which was the industry average $0.09 grossed-up to postings) and $0.23 for inclusion in temporary freight (Suez and/or fluctuating). Hunt objected strenuously to this arrangement because:

1. Total freight in the posting would range from $0.79 (minimum) to $1.02 (maximum).

2. The old $0.50 limit on permanent freight was eliminated, leaving the distribution of the $0.23 additional freight to the Team.

3. The tax paid cost of Libyan crude would increase to a maximum $2.40 versus $1.36 for an equivalent crude in the Gulf.

4. Every year the gap with the Gulf would widen due to the $0.02 annual increase for sulfur on top of the effect of the 2½% inflation factor.

As with the Teheran negotiations, it was too late to stop the momentum.

The Team returned to Tripoli on March 18 and Occidental sought a meeting with the Minister who indicated that their figure was $3.47 plus buy-out (a notional $3.65). He also kept alive the Suez retroactivity threat. They met again on the 19th and established the same figure. The Minister reportedly asked to meet the Gelsenberg representative and the Team agreed that he and his major oil company partner, Mobil, would make the proposal.

On March 20, Mobil and Gelsenberg met with Major Jallud for 7 hours. The final outcome of this meeting was that the company negotiators were forced to use the full authority in their terms of reference to go to $3.40 excluding the notional $0.16 or $0.18 buy-out. It consisted of general increase $0.35, sulfur ($0.10), "something special" ($0.05), temporary freight ($0.23) and first year escalation ($0.12).

Although the negotiators had gone to the limits of their authority, there was some satisfaction that the permanent "something special" had been limited to $0.05 rather than the authorized $0.07 for permanent freight. At the conclusion of the meeting Jallud indicated agreement except he wanted an additional $0.02 for temporary freight. The negotiations recessed during which the Team agreed to give the additional $0.02 with "temporary freight" split $0.12 for Suez and $0.13 fluctuating. The offer was made in meetings which lasted from 2030 to 2400 and which now included the lawyers and freight experts. On the 21st, there were further meetings which hung-up over our willingness to make only a one-year exploration commitment with the remaining 4 years contingent upon developing drillable prospects. On the 22nd, the problem was joined by a problem over the sulfur cut-off point of 0.5%. Meetings to sort these out took place on the 23rd. . . .

On March 25, Occidental met with Jallud and Alhuni, another member of the RCC. There were several points raised but the biggest hang-up was alleged RCC reluctance to accept a 5 year deal. Later that day, the Team (minus its Chairman who stayed behind on Esso business) left Tripoli to await developments. Local company representatives had limited contact and the LPG agreed on March 28 to extend the 5 year exploration commitment to gas utilization or secondary recovery in the event that a company had no drillable prospects. Again on the 29th, Jallud told the local Esso representative that the RCC was unhappy with the lack of formal recognition of Suez retroactivity and the 5 year duration. At the very last minute, Jallud told the Esso man that there could be no signing unless Libya got an additional $0.02 in permanent freight and a March 20 operative date. (Comment: it can be surmised that Jallud somehow found out that the negotiators had held out $0.02 from the permanent freight on March 20 although it was put in the "temporary freight" at that time.) The "Chiefs" granted this final indignity.

On April 2, 1971, 15 companies signed the Tripoli Agreement (Murphy and Hispanoil signed on April 19) which would increase posted prices to $3.44 plus a buy-out of September 1970 retroactivity which costs an additional $0.09 per barrel. The notional posting including buy-out was $3.62. Depending upon operating costs, the tax paid cost was some $0.80–$0.90 higher than the tax paid cost of Iranian Light crude which is comparable in yield.

One final post script: Dr. Amouzegar told the Consortium shortly after the Tripoli Agreement that the Shah was "incensed" that the industry had given Libya so much more than they gave the Gulf and threatened to lend Iranian support to the "radical" members of OPEC if the Consortium would not concede more in Iran. Here we go again . . .

### CONCLUSIONS TO BE DRAWN FROM ROUND 8

Rather than go through the previous description to pick out high points, it is only necessary to go through one document, a reconstruction of the long March 20 meeting as put together by two of the participants later. The following conclusions are apparent:

1. Jallud expressed repeated concern that Libya must get more than the Eastern Mediterranean or Nigeria, i.e., Libya's demands are *politically motivated.*

2. One of the Libyans said they would accept the exploration commitment for the moment but would be back for reinvestment later, i.e., we were warned that we were *not* getting a *meaningful "quit claim."*

3. The companies admitted that they were building in an unjustifiably high permanent freight differential with the Gulf, i.e., *we didn't stand on principle or logic.*

4. In response to the companies' complaint that the so-called debt recognition in 1970 was a shotgun-signing, Jallud said, tough luck, you signed, i.e., *pieces of paper should be honored by everyone except us sovereign nations.*

5. Jallud said the 1970 agreement was not intended to bind Libya for five years because "we are against the five year principle then (1970) and now," i.e., we knew we were *not* getting a *real commitment for five years* no matter how much we were prepared to give.

6. When companies refused to identify Suez retroactivity, Jallud very obligingly agreed to call it "something special" so long as it was made permanent, i.e., we repeatedly adopt *expediencies* which come back on us later.

7. Jallud asked why the companies made such a big deal of giving Libya the full $0.35 increase when in "your cable to OPEC the oil companies said that they would give everybody the general increase."

8. *The joint approach was used to hurt the Libyan producers* after it had floundered. This comment also demonstrated that the much proclaimed *consideration of "sovereignty"* did *not inhibit Jallud from recognizing the global approach when it was to his advantage.*

# 2. UP FOR AUCTION: MALTA BARGAINS WITH GREAT BRITAIN, 1971

*W. Howard Wriggins, Columbia University*

Most studies of international bargaining have been concerned with encounters between major powers (see, for instance, Ikle 1964, Schelling 1960, Kecskemeti 1964). Bargaining, however, can be just as useful a frame of reference for considering encounters between small, weak, and poor on one hand, and major industrialized countries on the other. Even where relative political or economic power positions are highly asymmetrical, this approach can help one to understand what the respective parties are attempting to accomplish (see Zartman 1971). Moreover, the preference of many students of international politics for system-type analysis often leads to ignoring the room for maneuver that statesmen in fact can sometimes create for themselves if their strategies are shrewdly designed and carefully implemented. Indeed, even states with few perceivable assets, apart from location, can gain major benefits if the fault lines of the international system are favorable and their bargaining strategies make the most of their circumstances. The elements of power at the disposal of a bargaining party define certain outside limits to the outcome. But it is the ingenuity and skill with which these elements are deployed or withheld that actually shape the outcome. It is as much a matter of bargaining strategy as it is of pre-existing elements of power.

The bargaining encounter between Malta and Great Britain in 1971 is a case in point. It underlines how much Malta was able to gain under what appeared to be rather unpromising circumstances. It also demonstrates a number of bargaining strategies that small countries situated in certain circumstances can in fact pursue. Classic ploys of attempting to withhold assets coveted by outsiders were combined with gradually intensifying the pain the outsiders experienced during the haggling to remind them that many conveniences taken for granted in the past could not be taken for granted any more. A number of outside players were drawn in, transforming what hitherto had been a limited bilateral negotiation between a large country and a small country into a multipartite bargaining game with the smaller finding allies among the newer participants. Saying "no, but . . ." or "yes, but . . ." for much longer than most reasonable men could stand almost led to a final rupture more than once. But as Dom Mintoff himself was reputed to have said, "Each time we came back we were offered more." In the end, the island's cash income was dramatically increased as a result of the nine months of haggling. Malta's short-run interests were well served. Whether they will prove to have been as well served in the longer run remains to be seen.

## MALTA'S REMARKABLE GAINS

In this process, the tiny island, with only 350,000 inhabitants, unilaterally abrogated a treaty of mutual defense and assistance with Great Britain that should have run until 1974, and induced the British to begin dismantling major electronics installations. The British reduced their forces on the island from some 3,500 troops and 7,000 dependents to a handful of 30 men. As a result of the negotiations, NATO and Great Britain together agreed to pay £14 million annually (or three times the annual rent before the negotiations began) for the use of port, air, and electronics facilities, and the use to which these facilities could be put was narrowed. Additional cash grants of £4 million were obtained from Italy and Libya, a fur-

ther increase of some £2.5 million resulted from back-dating
the start of the new arrangement, and the island received
concessional development loans of some £7 million in addition.

These gains were all the more remarkable because Great
Britain and other NATO strategists were clear that Malta was
"important but by no means indispensable" to NATO's military activities in the Mediterranean. During the century and a
half after the British gained possession of the island following
the defeat of Napoleon, Malta has been a critical naval base on
the route of empire. Its heroic role during World War II had
dramatized its position in the narrow waist of the Mediterranean, separating the western from the eastern basins. In the
1970s, however, it was manifestly less important. NATO's
major navies all had cruising ranges unknown in the days of
sailing ships; Grand Harbor itself was so small as to be unable
to safely accommodate NATO's American aircraft carriers. To
be sure, two RAF squadrons were stationed on the island, and
used it for air surveillance of Soviet naval activity in the eastern Mediterranean; a major radar installation also kept watch.
But NATO had comparable alternatives in Cyprus, Greece,
Italy, and France, permitting antisubmarine reconnaissance
over the whole area, and surface surveillance posed few
difficulties.

How then was it possible for the Prime Minister of Malta to
do as well as he did? What were the factors that led to this remarkable outcome?


THREE LEVELS OF ANALYSIS

The following analysis will suggest that variables at three
levels of international politics were at play, and the Prime
Minister showed himself adroit at using all three to his advantage. In terms of the world state system, he rightly perceived
that changes in the overall world strategic balance, particularly the changing balance of naval forces in the Mediterranean region, gave a certain plausibility to ploys that would
not have been taken seriously ten years earlier. In his bilateral
relations with Great Britain, he showed the utility, in the short
run, at least, of certain negotiating tactics which, while greatly

annoying the British, managed to draw Russia and Libya into the game. Their obvious interest brought in Britain's NATO partners in their train. Third, in domestic politics, despite only a one-vote margin of parliamentary safety at home, he succeeded in holding his majority and so confusing his opposition that he ended the nine months of uncertainty with substantially more popular support than he had had immediately following his election.

BACKGROUND: INTERDEPENDENCE AND
ECONOMIC CONSTRAINTS

Although Malta gained its formal political independence in 1964, it faced sharpening domestic economic problems and continued to be intimately linked with Great Britain for its economic well-being. The Maltese had become used to a standard of living considerably above their neighbors' in either Sicily, Tunisia, or Libya. Its "fortress economy" had been comparatively prosperous. Substantial British maintenance payments for facilities and expenditures by its men and their families accounted for nearly one fifth of the total annual GNP of some £100 million in 1971, the year of these negotiations.[1] At the time, these transfers met nearly half of Malta's deficit in its balance of trade.[2] Malta itself possessed no raw materials useful for helping to pay for imports, except cement and sunshine. At the time of independence, both Maltese and British officials recognized that the British official and service presence was likely to decline considerably over the next decade. Malta could no longer depend for the longer run on British service expenditures to help meet its deficit on current account.

Concurrently with the 1964 mutual assistance treaty signed at the time of independence, a financial agreement was entered into that committed the British to provide annually some £5 million sterling of "development assistance," as the British called it (while the Maltese came to consider it "rent for the use of facilities"). For its part, Malta agreed to remain in the sterling area and to keep its reserves in sterling. Specific conditions were then defined to slow the pace at which workers in the dockyards and in the base facilities would be fired as British activities on the island declined. It was hoped that the "economic assistance," plus investment incentives and promotional activities designed to lure capital and tourists, would render the economy much less dependent on Britain by 1974.[3]

The run up to the election in June of 1971 revealed contrasting approaches to the island's economic future and to the relationship with Great Britain. The government, headed by Dr. Borg Olivier of the Nationalist party, generally took an optimistic view of Malta's future. He argued that under his regime, Malta had moved from economic stagnation in the late fifties to a fairly steady annual growth of 6–7 per cent since the midsixties. His policy of promoting industry, construction, and tourism had worked with notable success. If the country held to a steady course, his followers maintained, it would be able to cope with the stresses of fuller economic independence when the ten-year mutual defense agreement should expire in 1974. As no industry could flourish if limited to such a tiny island market, Malta had pressed for and been given access to the EEC, and expected to gain advantages for new Maltese consumer and other light industries.

The year 1969 had been an important one, giving many Maltese confidence that they did not need the British as much as they had always assumed. In that year, protracted haggling over the proportion of loans to grants in the second *tranche* of Britain's ten-year contribution had led to a temporary suspension of British "aid" transfers. This hiatus had not slowed the pace of economic growth appreciably, for the Maltese Government's efforts to raise funds locally had been more successful than had been foreseen, demonstrating unexpected strengths in the local economy. At the same time, Britain's efforts to bring economic pressure to bear by stopping the transfers had underlined Malta's persisting economic vulnerability to decisions made in London.[4]

Economic difficulties were apparent, nevertheless. Unemployment was already in the neighborhood of 7–8 per cent of the labor force. Ever since the closure of the Suez Canal in 1967, the work at the Malta dockyards—the single largest employer—had declined, its revenue dropping by nearly 20 per cent instead of growing by an anticipated 10 per cent. Effective labor organization under the leadership of Mr.

Mintoff had forced wages up and protected many of the redundant workers. But from the government's point of view, deficits were yearly growing and came to represent a considerable drain on government resources after the dockyards were nationalized in 1959. The boom in housing for retired British families and hotel construction for transient but free-spending tourists had brought foreign exchange. However, these developments had inflated property values and construction costs out of reach of the average Maltese. Before the election, the opposition charged the government with inducing widespread inflation, tolerating inadequate low-cost housing, and drifting into administrative lethargy.

More important, however, Dom Mintoff attacked the whole concept of economic policy pursued by the previous government. Instead of the government's apparent bland confidence, Dom Mintoff dramatized Malta's economic weaknesses. Instead of sharing the government's view that Malta would be economically independent by 1974, he seemed "obsessed" by Malta's desperate economic plight—its continued dependence on the British economy, its vulnerability to the "whims" of British governmental decisions or the changing tastes of British tourists.[5] He argued that only if the annual grants from the outside were sharply increased could Malta hope to make the transition from a fortress economy to an open, equitable, and growing economy. Only by diversifying its industry, its economic links with outside economies, its markets, and its sources of tourism and investment could Malta be reinsured against future discriminating decisions in any one capital (i.e., London).

With this background, it will now be possible to turn to a more analytical discussion of how Malta improved its bargaining position.

## MALTA'S ASSETS SOUGHT BY OUTSIDERS

Malta had few economically useful resources; its population of less than half a million could not be expected to make a contribution to international politics or the world economy, either as military forces or as a source of inexpensive or unusually skilled labor, although its level of skills is unusually high for the area. Malta's only international political assets were its location and whatever military facilities are there or might be placed there by someone else. In the Mediterranean narrows, 60 miles south of Sardinia and 200 miles north of Libya, Malta has traditionally commanded the narrow link between the eastern and western Mediterranean. NATO had its naval headquarters there; it was a site for air control over North Africa, stretching across Libya and Egypt and reaching as far south as the Sudan. Two RAF squadrons stationed at Luqa Airport provided air and radar surveillance of naval activity in the Mediterranean and for NATO-related ASW roles. The dockyards had been convenient for ship repairs.

While on balance these facilities were useful, both the British Government—and Dom Mintoff—could expect that they would be less needed in the future. They were not likely to be critical in an age of nuclear weapons and ICBMs. Possible Soviet initiatives in the Mediterranean might as likely be countered from the Sea of Japan or off the shores of Norway as from Malta itself. The range of air surveillance planes was now so great that flights from France, Italy, or even Gibraltar or Cyprus could cover the same sea areas. Satellite photography was rendering even this function less urgent in normal times, however convenient such flights might still be in moments of impending international crisis. The British had come to believe that the dockyards, invaluable as they had been in the past, were now more of a burden for them to maintain than an asset. They were, however, crucial to the government of Malta in its fight against growing unemployment.

The location, then, had had great historical importance. But the island played only a moderate strategically active role in contemporary defense within the Mediterranean area. There was more than one substitute easily available to the British and to NATO for whatever activities they were then mounting from Malta.

### CHANGE IN THE STATE SYSTEM:
#### SHIFTS IN THE REGIONAL STRATEGIC BALANCE

Changes in the contours of the world state system were also significant for Malta. Until the late 1960s, Malta had been clearly within the geopolitical sphere of the Western powers. The Borg Olivier government had even been seeking closer links with NATO, although Scandinavian countries had opposed the move, and NATO had dropped the idea. But by the later 1960s, major changes were under way. Open Arab resistance to Western influence became more active—and effective—during President Nasser's rule, and intensified when Colonel Qaddafi seized political control in Libya in September 1969. In June 1970 America's major communications and Air Force base in Libya was withdrawn at Libyan insistence.

As the American presence disappeared from the North African shore, Malta found itself in closer proximity to influences from an increasingly dynamic Arab world. In the eyes of some of Malta's leaders, including Dom Mintoff, Libyan wealth so near at hand might mean that Malta would have an alternative source of economic support if Britain did not assist sufficiently in the future. Indeed, Colonel Qaddafi had implied as much on a number of occasions. Libya's ejection of the Italians in the summer of 1970 awakened hopes that some of Malta's skilled manpower could find remunerative and influential positions in Libya if the unemployed became too numerous in Malta. However, in return for such assistance, Colonel Qaddafi was likely to require a policy of complete neutrality in Mediterranean affairs, a position hard to square with continued use of the island by the British, NATO, or other naval powers.

But the Mediterranean basin was experiencing a more fundamental sea change. Russian naval activity gradually increased in the Mediterranean during the 1960s. Indeed, its regular patrol strength went up from an average of eight vessels at one time, with a maximum of 13 in 1964, to some 50 on the average and a maximum of 66 on one day in 1971.[6] Occasionally Soviet cargo vessels sought repairs, and the Soviet ambassador to London, also accredited to Malta, paid periodic visits, seeking to establish at least a legation on the island. These military/strategic changes and diplomatic initiatives ran parallel with increasingly obvious Soviet political influence in Egypt, Syria, and Iraq.

These new sources of political influence and of possible economic assistance presented opportunities that the Maltese had not had since World War II. But these new possibilities involved unfamiliar risks that many Maltese believed were not worth running.

## DOM MINTOFF'S STAKES AND BARGAINING LIMITS

Within this strategic context, Dom Mintoff's narrow electoral victory in July 1971 placed in his hands full constitutional powers. His stakes and bargaining limits were defined by a number of considerations.

His domestic political position was strong, and he took prompt steps to consolidate it further. Although he had a parliamentary majority of only one, his elected followers were devoted and disciplined, while his opposition in Parliament was in disarray. Electoral defeat opened serious divisions among them and sharply reduced the political influence of the defeated Borg Olivier. Outside Parliament Mintoff's solid support among organized labor was periodically dramatized by rallies and street demonstrations, inducing anxious critics of his foreign-policy initiatives to keep quiet. He appointed a "hawkish" Cabinet and guaranteed himself a free hand by dismissing the British governor general and appointing a Maltese in his place who would be unlikely to invoke emergency powers no matter what difficulties should arise. Mintoff also ensured himself initial room for maneuver by postponing calling Parliament until toward the end of August, by which time his confrontation with Britain was well advanced. Anyone who then voiced sharp criticism of the Prime Minister could be charged with weakening the country in its critical confrontation with Great Britain.

## FOREIGN-POLICY OBJECTIVES

As Mintoff approached reopening discussions of the ten-year mutual defense agreement three years before its expiration, it seems likely that he saw his problem in the following terms: In addition to ensuring his own position within domestic politics, he set three foreign policy objectives: (1) to increase the cash return Malta would receive for the use of its naval and air facilities; (2) to broaden Malta's options and its security in the Mediterranean by improving relations with its Arab neighbors and the Soviet Union; and (3) to develop in the Maltese a sense of self-respect and self-reliance that would induce them to be psychologically less dependent on London.[7]

These goals were in part mutually re-enforcing. If he could induce the Arabs or Soviets to come near to or at least appear ready to come near to paying what the British laid out for rent and spent in the form of service maintenance and expenses, Mintoff might be able to play these two potential new friends off against the more familiar Great Britain. In this way he might induce the British to pay substantially more than he could expect if he had to face the British in an exclusive, bilateral bargain. While out of office Mintoff had visited Nasser several times and had probably heard him discuss such an approach to relations with both the Western powers and the Soviet Union.[8]

The Arab and Soviet options could be played simultaneously for a certain time, since both preferred to see a diminished Western presence. Unfortunately for Malta, however, these two sources of support had contrasting interests which, at some point, would probably lead to incompatible demands being made upon Malta. Colonel Qaddafi wanted Malta to join the "neutralists" and prevent both Moscow and the NATO powers from using Malta. The Russians would be unlikely to subscribe to such a proposition, except as a significant first step on the way to transforming Malta into an island directly useful to their growing Mediterranean interests.

These two, then, might be useful in providing a credible alternative to the British. But a cool analysis must have led the new Maltese Prime Minister to the conclusion that not for some time would either or even both of the alternative sources of support provide equivalent economic resources to match Britain's annual rent of £5 million plus some £15 to £17 million expenditures by the servicemen and their families. The problem then became not one of substituting Libya and the Soviet Union for the British, but of persuading the British and their NATO associates to contribute substantially more.

## PATTERN OF INTERDEPENDENCE

In considering this problem, Mintoff had to recognize that Malta and Great Britain were linked in an intricate and intimate pattern of interdependence. As already pointed out, Britain was still a critical factor in both the balance of payments and in maintaining employment at a politically bearable level. If the haggling between the two was to become intense, Mintoff had one major card to play. He could threaten to disrupt that relationship by requesting the British to leave. Given London's mood of 1971, it was unlikely that Britain would remain against his express request for her to go. To maximize pressure on the British if they didn't meet his terms, he would have to demand that they evacuate the base. But such a gambit had dangers, since if they did take him at his word and withdrew, unemployment would rise in lock step with their departure, and his domestic political support would erode. On the other hand, if he did not press hard in some dramatic way, it seemed unlikely that he could either extract more from the British alone or so broaden the bargaining that Britain's NATO partners would be drawn in. As will be seen, he chose a high-stakes strategy, and was prepared to risk all on behalf of very high gains. Such a policy would call on all his political talents to sustain the solidarity of his followers, as the possibility of growing misery resulting from his tactics seemed ever more likely.

## BRITISH STAKES AND BARGAINING LIMITS

Assessing the stakes on the British side was more difficult. The British had already shown a certain nervousness about Malta. Prior to Edward Heath's electoral victory in 1970, the Ministry of Overseas Development (MOD) had been negotiating with the Maltese, seeking to reduce the proportion of grants to loans in the second *tranche* of the 10-year British subsidy of £5 million per year. Understandably enough, the Maltese wanted to continue the present arrangement of 75 per cent grant, 25 per cent loan; the MOD sought to shift to the reverse proportions, and discussions were deadlocked. Once

Edward Heath came in in 1970, the Maltese position was quickly acceded to, demonstrating the fact that despite London's apparent nonchalance about Malta, the island still counted for something in British calculations, at least in the eyes of the Tories.[9] On the other hand, all commentators expected a decline in British activities on Malta. Even if the Suez Canal should reopen, British interest in the island was bound to diminish further, since Britain had given up a continued role east of Suez.[10]

At the same time Britain, whose declining interest in Malta was evident, was not an entirely free agent. Off the northern shore of Western Europe, Britain might no longer have a direct interest in the Mediterranean that could be credibly supported by British power alone. But other NATO countries did believe they still had a major stake. After all, Malta was close to France, and only some 60 miles from Sicily. The Americans took more seriously than did Great Britain the growing presence of the Soviet fleet in the Mediterranean, and were directly involved in Middle Eastern responsibilities through their concern for continued supplies of oil to Western Europe and the United States and for their link with Israel. Great Britain could not let NATO down, and Dom Mintoff must have perceived this limitation on Britain's freedom of action. As will be seen below, the Maltese Prime Minister took several steps that were (1) to make clear his own determination to draw these NATO partners of Britain into the negotiations and (2) to underline the interest these countries had in assuring that Britain's efforts to keep Mintoff's demands "within reason" did not risk the loss of continued Western access to the island's facilities. The British press accurately summed up the situation when *The Times* of London observed, "what is important . . . is not that [the facilities] are badly needed in an age of nuclear war, but that they should not on the other hand be possessed by Russia."[11]

## PERSONALITY

The British recognized that when he returned to power Dom Mintoff would be a difficult negotiating partner. They recalled that during negotiations in the mid-1950s looking toward a new status for Malta, Mintoff, who was then Prime Minister, abruptly changed course in quite unpredictable ways. At first he sought to integrate Malta with Great Britain, rather along the lines of Northern Ireland. When the very advantageous economic terms he demanded were not forthcoming, he then threatened independence and resigned. He had so effectively agitated opinion and sharpened divisions within Malta that the then existing constitutional arrangements had to be temporarily suspended and governor's rule installed. Only two years later had a new constitution been finally steered through to acceptance. Elections brought in the Borg Olivier government, which ruled for eight years before its 1971 defeat at Dom Mintoff's hands. In considering the new Prime Minister's likely approach to negotiations, the *Financial Times* of London commented that Dom Mintoff's tactics "often appear slightly nutty to the outsider and there is no point in evading it." "Nutty" or not, they proved remarkably effective in the end.[12]

It was therefore no surprise to British officials that while Dom Mintoff talked of neutralism, detachment from Cold War blocs, and the liabilities of depending upon Great Britain for the future, he kept his lines open for a renewal of the defense agreement, although at a much higher price. Indeed, it is even possible to argue that his reputation for unpredictability and for the rash gesture added to his bargaining strength, since outside observers could have some reasonable expectation that he just might decide to throw the British out in the hopes that between Libya and Soviet Russia he could gain greater support.[13]

## ANGLO-MALTESE BARGAINING, JUNE TO DECEMBER 1971

It would be tedious to reconstruct in detail the prolonged and, for the British, exasperating negotiations that stretched from late June 1971, shortly after the new government was formed, until late March 1972, when a new agreement was finally signed. However, there were certain characteristic patterns to the negotiations that are worth identifying.

In the first place, Dom Mintoff had obviously assigned highest priority to this enterprise. He devoted all his energies to it from the time his government was formed until the agreement was signed nine months later. Moreover, even before he came to power he had laid the general lines for a position that he held to subsequently and that provided him substantial room for maneuver.

There were at least four components to his position in principle:

1. The rent the British paid for the use of facilities on the island had to be very much higher than it had been. No precise figure had been stated prior to the start of negotiations, but he had tried to make clear that it would have to be of a different order of magnitude. Figures ranging from £14 million to £30 million were bruited, perhaps on the basis of inspired leaks. Compared to the present £5 million annual rent, they were astonishing. But nothing precise was known, at least publicly. That ambiguity served him well, for he could test the market without setting an upper price prematurely.

2. More particularly, the dockyard was to be available to the highest bidder. Since there were other countries with a growing marine interest in the Mediterranean, this ploy was not entirely unreal. Russian freighter traffic as well as naval vessels had become more prominent; occasionally Soviet cargo vessels entered for routine repairs and restocking. The Arab countries, for which Libya was the spokesman, dropped hints of new tanker fleets to handle petroleum shipments on behalf of the Arab oil producers. If Malta were their home port, they could keep the dockyard busy, even should the British withdraw completely.[14]

3. Powers other than Britain who did use the facilities would have to pay. Hitherto, NATO's vessels had used Malta's facilities without paying additional rent apart from normal docking and facilities charges. Dom Mintoff made clear that that could no longer continue. If there should be an eventual agreement with Great Britain, other NATO partners would have to contribute, too.

4. In order to reassure the British and to ensure that they found his strident tactics at least bearable, Dom Mintoff made two other points. In the coming auction, Britain was to have first refusal.[15] In this way he underlined his own desire to offer the British a position consistent with past preferences. Second,

he held out the hope of a long-term agreement, even mentioning a twenty-year period, if a satisfactory new agreement could be reached. This position did something to weaken the British perception that he was essentially an opportunist who, on the basis of past performance, would use the slightest excuse to go back on any agreement. He may not have been taken seriously within Whitehall, but at the very least, it would be a useful approach to parliamentary opinion.

These general positions remained essential to his bargaining effort from the time he came to power. Shortly thereafter he declared that the mutual defense treaty was no longer valid and required a thorough recasting, if, indeed, an Anglo-Maltese agreement were to be renewed at all.

### NUISANCE VALUE TO GAIN ATTENTION
#### OF OTHER MAJOR POWERS

Two other operating principles appear to have guided his activities. If small powers are to be listened to by major powers, the former must find ways to make a sufficient nuisance of themselves to claim the attention of already hard-pressed policymakers within the major powers. Dom Mintoff showed himself a skilled artisan of this delicate and sometimes dangerous craft.

In one of his early steps he declared that "it would not be in the interest of Malta for the time being" for American-flag naval vessels to visit the island.[16] This prohibition against American ships, he argued, was to save Malta from becoming an instrument of American foreign policy. It was also in line with his stated aspiration to be neutralist, particularly in regard to issues where Israel and the United States might be associated together against the Arab states. His refusal to allow American vessels to enter brought Malta's position quickly to the attention of top policymakers in the United States; within days of his taking office, a number of American newspapers ran articles on Malta's change of course.[17] The substance of the articles would have shown him, if he had not known this already, that however calm the British might be about a run-down—and perhaps even a closing—of the Malta facilities, the Americans were not likely to be so detached. His "nuisance value" steps had produced unambiguous signals that the Americans would be more willing to raise the stakes than the British seemed likely to be.

A parallel move had similar results in Italy. The commander of the combined NATO naval headquarters located on Malta was an Italian, Admiral Birindelli. Dom Mintoff had often been anti-Italian in his foreign-policy statements, and in domestic politics, too, at least until his "concordat" with the Church prior to the election. And his socialist orientation in domestic politics had led him to be particularly critical of the wealthier Maltese who, he argued, were drawn toward Italian economic interests and upper-class life styles. In line with a populist position he often took in domestic politics, Mintoff accused the admiral of being a creature of Italy's upper classes and too closely associated in the past with Fascist elements for him to be acceptable to the government of Malta. As a result, the NATO commander was replaced and the naval headquarters were subsequently transferred to Naples in mid-August. As a by-product of this initiative, the Italian Government began to look with greater care at how the negotiations between Britain and Malta were going.

### DRAMATIZE ALTERNATIVES

A second major approach was to dramatize Malta's alternatives. Both the Russians and Arabs appear to have been very ready to assist in this. Shortly after the elections, the Libyans were reported to have made a considerable contribution, of perhaps £1 to £1.5 million.[18] This helped tide over the Mintoff government, then short of cash because grants-in-aid from London had been stopped when the Prime Minister had abrogated the defense agreement. He needed to pay civil-servant salaries, for the civil servants could not be expected to wait patiently until agreement was reached with London.

In line with this strategy, on several occasions after a British offer was communicated to Valetta, Dom Mintoff would highlight the possibility of alternative sources of support by confabulation with Russian or Libyan representatives.

The following example is typical. In mid-August, the British

Government offered Malta £8.5 million annually—£5 million for rent and £3.5 million for development assistance—to be shared by Britain and its NATO partners. Within 48 hours, Dom Mintoff received Ambassador Smirnovsky, who publicly indicated that Russia would "sympathetically consider" any request for economic aid to Malta. A few hours later, Prime Minister Mintoff flew to Libya, where he reportedly received generous (though indefinite) offers of aid, provided he didn't allow either Russian or Western facilities on Malta (this was in fact the Maltese Prime Minister's second visit to Libya in as many weeks). All this consultation was sandwiched between his learning the specifics of the British offer and his receiving Lord Carrington, the British negotiator, a few days later.[19]

More generally, both Russian and Libyan emissaries were welcomed in Valetta. In July, Colonel Qaddafi's government agreed to release to Maltese businessmen some £600,000 impounded at the time of the Six-day War in retaliation for Malta's alleged lack of sympathy for the Arab cause.[20] The Libyan Prime Minister visited briefly and publicly recommended that Malta should follow a neutralist policy, in effect ejecting the British base and facilities entirely. Rumors were circulated from Beirut and Tangier that the Arab states would more than match the British offer of £8.5 million.[21] The Russian ambassador visited the island the day before the opening of the Maltese Parliament in mid-August. These together helped to maintain the impression that Malta had genuine and comparable alternatives.

### NUISANCE VALUE, NATO, AND THE BRITISH

Third, during the negotiations, Malta periodically complicated the tasks of British forces and the NATO headquarters. The request for the NATO naval commander to leave has already been mentioned. Perhaps to Dom Mintoff's surprise, the British authorities and NATO agreed without hesitation, and the small headquarters staff was transferred to Naples. In August, the two RAF squadrons were deprived of the right to receive their fuel free of Maltese import taxes, one condition specifically subscribed to in the mutual defense agreement of 1964.

These steps were annoying, and they served to remind British and NATO officials that the Maltese facilities could not be taken for granted indefinitely. In themselves, however, they did not materially affect the functioning of the limited defense activities still based on Malta.

Dom Mintoff had a rather original negotiating style. He was prepared to make himself personally quite intolerable to his British counterparts by protracting the negotiations interminably and by the "yes, but" tactic. In all, nine months were consumed in the negotiations, involving more than nine substantive meetings between British and Maltese negotiators. His frequent use of the "yes, but" tactic was particularly infuriating. At the very moment when a number of additional concessions to his views had been laboriously negotiated and differences apparently eliminated once and for all, he would say, in effect, "yes, agreed, but there is one more problem," such as a request for a £10 million cash advance or a new condition guaranteeing the dockyard and base workers their jobs for the life of the agreement just reached. Each such step resulted in postponing the settlement once again, extending still further the period of uncertainty—and leading his negotiating counterparts to raise the ante once more prior to the next round of talks.

For their part, the British made it apparent that they were in no hurry to conclude the negotiations. They acted as if they thought time was on their side. Since Dom Mintoff had himself abrogated the mutual defense pact, the British were under no obligation to continue the rent-*cum*-aid subsidies, and the longer the negotiations dragged on, the more the pressure of cash scarcity would beset the Maltese Government. Libya's £1.5 million grant following the election had brought temporary relief to the government's cash flow difficulties. But would Libya prove to be a serious alternative beyond the emergency grant? Russia's talk of trade negotiations could not be expected to bring resources to the island in any way to match what the British connection provided. At the same time, the British showed their growing disinterest in the island by slowing down and then halting altogether the transfer of fresh troops to Malta, although rotation schedules would have called for substantial replacements in July. New contracts were not being let for base improvements and investment; stocks were not being replenished.[22] Moreover, Dom Mintoff's dramatic negotiating tactics led to a prompt decline in the number of British tourists, and possible investors were holding back until the results of the negotiations were known.

By mid-September pressures had built up sufficiently so that it was agreed that Prime Minister Heath and Dom Mintoff should meet at Chequers. At the mid-September meeting, the British upped their offer by £1 million to £9.5 million, plus some £4.8 million for development assistance. Mintoff appeared to accept this on condition that he should be free to open separate bilateral negotiations with Britain's NATO partners in the search for additional assistance. Britain also agreed to make an immediate cash transfer of £4.75 million as the first payment on the basis of the new £9.5 million figure. This eased Dom Mintoff's immediate cash position and was presumed to indicate a firm agreement on the level of annual rental payments. There now seemed to remain only the details of the force agreement—the use of land, the status of forces, and the pace at which the work force on the base should be reduced. These "details" could easily be worked out by technical staffs.

Having succeeded at Chequers in broadening his reach into direct contact and negotiations with Britain's NATO partners, Mr. Mintoff's first stop on the way home was Rome. No specific commitments were made by Italian officials, but he received a warm reception. He must have read this, in such contrast to his own earlier strong public criticism of the Italians for alleged interference in Malta's domestic affairs, as a sure sign of Rome's worry about the future of the island and its facilities.

As a result of the Chequers agreement, the British decided to send to Malta the 900 men of the British Marine Commandos who had been held back in Britain pending some visible progress, and these arrived in mid-October, suggesting that relationships were returning to normal. A series of defense talks was held during September and October on the remaining technical details. However, by late November there was a serious hitch. Talks were abruptly suspended, though there was still no full public explanation.[23]

It turned out that the "Chequers agreement" had not met Dom Mintoff's requirements after all. He now argued that Britain's down payment had been for only three months, instead of the six (i.e., to March 31) that the British had assumed, and he now demanded that a second payment of £4.75 million should be made before December 31. To have accepted Mintoff's new proposition would have meant in fact a doubling of the agreed "rent" to an annual total of £19 million, nearly four times what it had been in the spring. The British were not prepared to agree to this.

In the meantime, Malta had not succeeded in reaching supplementary agreements with NATO members, as Dom Mintoff had hoped would promptly occur following the Chequers meeting. The budgeting cycle within the NATO machinery could not meet Mintoff's urgencies. Moreover, once a settlement with Britain seemed near, as it did following the Chequers meeting, the Brussels officials were less inclined to force innovative additional costs through their complex budgeting systems, however small the actual contributions of any one NATO member might be.

In early December the Maltese Prime Minister declared that if the British were not prepared to meet his demand that an additional payment of £4.75 million be made by the end of the month, the British would have to evacuate all their forces by January 15, 1972. Prime Minister Heath, whose recollection of the Chequers agreement was perfectly clear, refused to meet Dom Mintoff's changed terms. Instead, he agreed that British forces should evacuate the island not by January 15 but by the end of March, when Britain's lease arrangement would have expired. He ordered service families to begin packing up, and a gradual but fully visible rundown of the British military presence got under way.

### BARGAINING—JANUARY TO MARCH 1972

There now began a complex game played at several levels. The British-Maltese game involved a visible British withdrawal. British expenditures and Maltese employment declined. The British trusted to the economic facts of deepening unemployment and worsening future economic prospects to undermine the Prime Minister's public support should he persist. They also believed that growing Catholic anxiety about increased Russian or Arab Muslim influences would build up pressure for accommodation with London. And the British press reported increasing signs of economic anxieties among all levels of Maltese society, including the trade unions organized under Mintoff's leadership.

For his part, Mintoff counted on the rundown of British facilities to bring Britain's NATO allies into the game. Already in December the Americans had sent their NATO ambassador to Malta for a short visit, signaling American concern. The Italian interest had been manifested in a number of ways. It was not unexpected to the Maltese that representatives of the British, Italians, NATO, and Malta were invited by the Italians to meet in Rome in early January. At the first meeting, Dom Mintoff surprised a number of the participants, and confirmed Britain's worst expectations, by making agreement conditional on a further cash payment of £10 million, over and above the £9.5 million rent Britain and NATO had by now agreed to. The British angrily refused to respond to this abrupt increase in the demand, but Mintoff insisted, and the meeting broke up without agreement. The British withdrawals continued.

But the Italians and Americans were unwilling to see the end of the British facilities. The British believed that if their tactics were allowed to run their course, Malta would give in at the last moment and settle for "reasonable" terms. But the Italians, who were geographically much nearer to Malta than the British, and the Americans, with less experience of Mintoff, were not prepared to run that risk. They feared that as the Russians had "bought their way" into Egypt, they might do the same in Malta once the British had left. As the *Guardian* put it, Mintoff says he wants to remain independent of both blocs, "but under pressure, his attitude toward the Soviet Union could prove as unpredictable as his negotiating tactics with Whitehall."[24]

In sum, Dom Mintoff had persuaded enough people in the military and national security bureaucracies of the United

States and Italy that he might not agree to a settlement acceptable to Great Britain, and that he just might open the Maltese gates to the Russians.[25] Anxious American and Italian officials came in with urgent suggestions. Together, they proposed to the NATO Council that the offer to Mintoff be raised to £14 million rent, on condition that Warsaw Pact ships or planes not be allowed to use the island.[26] The archbishop of Malta was enlisted to visit London and Rome to persuade both governments that the Prime Minister simply had to have £18 million to £20 million if the fortress economy was to be transformed by 1979, when the defense agreement would terminate.

Italian and American encouragement lay behind another concession to Malta. Since the British were firm that £14 million was sufficient annual rent, and Malta was insisting that it needed more before agreement could be reached, it was proposed that the £14 million annually should begin as of October 1971 instead of March 31, 1972 or even January 1972, when the British thought it should begin. In this way Dom Mintoff received an additional £2.4 million or more.[27]

Other issues were brought forward. Secure employment for Malta's work force had been a recurrent problem. As British activities declined, fewer workers would be needed at the base. Dom Mintoff sought guarantees that all workers presently employed would have guaranteed jobs over the period of the agreement. The British, however, were firm that since there would be a decline in need for workers, the British had to have the right to release members of the work force as they became redundant. Discussions on this and related issues, as well as on the major point of defining how the facilities should be used, again broke down in early February. British servicemen started to dismantle the main radar reflector in late February. And the British indicated that by the end of February they would issue termination notices to the 6,100 local employees at the base.

As this critical date approached, Mintoff sought a further conversation with Heath. But Heath did not wish to involve himself personally in any further negotiations with the elusive Mintoff. The Maltese Prime Minister attempted to down play the significance of the impending redundancy notices and organized a large public demonstration to show that the workers of Malta were behind his risky policy. But his desire to have further discussions with Heath suggested that he might be ready to settle. He first hoped for resumed discussions in Rome, where he no doubt expected Italian sympathies to work in his favor. But he did visit London in the first week in March, with only three weeks to go before the British installations would have been completely dismantled and the personnel fully evacuated.

In London, the £14 million rent was confirmed; and the NATO governments had agreed together to add £7 million in development assistance in various grants and loans over the next seven years. But agreement could not be reached on what proportion of the labor force would be retained over the next two to five years. And Dom Mintoff went away without a settlement.

Familiar with the Mintoff tactic of adding new issues at the last minute, Heath made clear that once the British forces were off the island, a "new situation would have arisen"; the proposal then under discussion would not stand once all the troops were gone. There were rumors that Mintoff kept delaying because he was hopeful till the last of being able to obtain a very large cash commitment from Libya if he would dispense with the British bases altogether.[28]

As the last critical point of full British withdrawal approached, the tension mounted. The British themselves recognized that if Dom Mintoff did not yield and they fulfilled their threat of total withdrawal, they would have no further influence on his future actions. A threat of that kind is its own wasting asset once a critical point is passed. For his part, Dom Mintoff must have known that once the British had left, Malta and its people would have been worse off. He publicly acknowledged that his course was risky, but "only if we risk all" can we obtain the resources we need.

On March 17 the press reported that 1,000 British servicemen would be airlifted from Malta, and Maltese officials met with Defense Ministry specialists to work out details of the final evacuation. At the same time, Monsignor Ginzi of Malta went to Rome to seek the support of NATO Secretary General Luns and the government of Italy for further compensation.[29]

The Maltese Prime Minister was reported ready to accept the figure of £14 million for rent and £7 million in bilateral aid over seven years. But he was now demanding another £4 million interest-free loan to assist in the transformation of the economy. Italy appeared sympathetic to this latest request, and was reportedly prepared to contribute £2.5 million.

In the end, the Italian ambassador in London played a critical role as go-between. He is credited with having persuaded the Italian Government to contribute the additional £2.5 million cash grant. He also devoted his full persuasive powers in a nine-hour interview with Dom Mintoff in Valetta, succeeding in persuading him that the British would not be budged and that other NATO members had contributed all they were going to. Further efforts to gain more would be futile. The base was now practically evacuated, and once the British had completed that withdrawal, they would not return.[30]

Accordingly, on March 21, with all but 30 of the British forces evacuated and 50,000 tons of equipment withdrawn, agreement was finally reached.[31]

### THE AGREEMENT

The agreement represented substantial gains for the government of Malta. The NATO powers retained important interests, but at a sharply increased cash cost. Their use of the island was also restricted in specific ways.

As pointed out at the outset, Dom Mintoff trebled the annual rent, from £5 million to £14.5 million; he also gained during the negotiations additional outright cash payments from Italy and Libya over and above rent amounting to two thirds of the previous annual rent (£2.5 million from Italy and £1.5 million from Libya). By backdating the start of the new level of rent payments, he gained £2.5 million to £3 million more. Furthermore, he obtained £7 million in development loans from Britain and other NATO members over the next seven years.

The new agreement implied a lesser security link to Great Britain and NATO, for it was not a "treaty of mutual defense and assistance" but a treaty "with respect to the use of facilities in Malta." The facilities were to be used for defense purposes of the United Kingdom and NATO, but the forces of other countries in NATO could use the facilities only after bilateral agreements between Malta and each interested party. The forces of any Warsaw Pact country were expressly excluded (Article 2), except in case of emergency or distress. To make unambiguously clear the size of the transfer payments, a schedule of payments with dates due was included.[32]

In addition, the British made commitments on the pace at which men on the base would be declared redundant as the activities of the base declined. Malta obtained a reversion of all real estate hitherto occupied by the British, except those properties specifically designated as appropriate for present British purposes. The air-traffic control facilities at Luqa Airport were to be operated by the British, but the latter agreed to step up the training of Maltese traffic controllers so that, should Britain withdraw from the base, the operation could be handled up to ICAO standards by Maltese.

Apart from the cost to the British and NATO of the increased rent and other cash and loan payments, the cost of withdrawing the families, troops, and equipment and of re-establishing the facilities once the agreement was signed reportedly was in the order of £6 million.[33]

It may turn out that rotation of British troops will be more rapid than before, sharply reducing the numbers of dependents who will be living on Malta. This, in turn, would reduce the cost of maintaining dependents to below the £17 million annual payments the island had become accustomed to. The uncertainty generated by Dom Mintoff's negotiating tactics discouraged new investment and seemed likely to reduce the numbers of British who retire to Malta.

On balance, however, this represents an example of a highly successful bargaining by a small, physically "helpless" country in dealing with a major industrialized power. Changing power relations in the Mediterranean brought new alternatives within reach. The possibility that others might use Malta if the negotiations broke down was an important threat. While the British were dubious, the American and Italian governments and NATO were more credulous. Mintoff's reputation for unpredictability and for irresponsible actions, and the size of the stakes as the NATO countries understood them led the latter to take seriously his implicit threat.

But his approach to negotiations was also critical. By dragging out the negotiations, by rejecting successive offers at the last moment, he upped the ante at nearly each one of nine negotiating encounters. By emphasizing his potential alternatives and by taking high nuisance-value steps toward Washington and Rome, he enlisted on his own behalf the anxieties and resources of two of Britain's most concerned allies. For nine nerve-wracking months, during three of which the British ostentatiously reduced their presence on the island, thus threatening the island's employment balance, he managed to hold his trade-union followers in line and keep his political opponents divided.

If all states dealt with each other in this way, a viable comity of nations would be impossible to maintain. It would truly be a Hobbesian world. But for the small maverick like Malta, such an approach proved highly rewarding this time.

## NOTES

1. *Economist* (Jan. 8, 1972).
2. Government of Malta, Office of the Prime Minister, *Outline of a Development Plan for Malta 1975–1980* (Valetta: Aug. 1973), p. 37.
3. For a detailed discussion, see *Financial Times* of London (Dec. 15, 1970).
4. For a discussion, see *Financial Times* of London (Mar. 10, 1970).
5. *Sunday Times* of London (June 22, 1971).
6. NATO, *Fifteen Nations* (Apr.–May 1972), Supplement 129, p. 51.
7. For a discussion, see *Financial Times* of London (Oct. 27, 1971).
8. See Miles Copeland, *The Game of Nations* (New York: College Notes and Texts, 1969), p. 143; but also see Anthony Nutting, *Nasser* (London: Constable, 1972), p. 271.
9. For an analytical discussion, see *The Guardian* (Sept. 1971).
10. For a discussion of British policy, see Phillip Darby, *British Defense Policy East of Suez 1947–1968* (London: Oxford University Press, 1973).
11. *The Times* of London (July 2, 1971).

12. *Financial Times* of London (July 19, 1971).

13. Thomas Schelling has discussed the short-run advantages of having a reputation of irrational behavior (Schelling 1960, pp. 16–20).

14. *Christian Science Monitor* (London) (Aug. 26, 1971).

15. *The Guardian* (June 26, 1971).

16. *The Guardian* (July 1, 1973).

17. See, for instance, *Herald Tribune* (Paris) (July 1, 1971).

18. *Financial Times* of London (Oct. 27, 1971).

19. For details, see the London *Daily Telegraph* and *The Times* of London (Aug. 18, 1971). A similar round of visits occurred after Lord Carrington's first visit in mid-July and before a reply went to London, *Daily Telegraph* (July 23, 1971).

20. *Financial Times* of London (July 6, 1971).

21. *The Times* of London, quoting ABC from Madrid (Aug. 18, 1971).

22. London *Daily Express* (July 8 and 9, 1971).

23. *The Times* of London (Nov. 21, 1971).

24. *Guardian* (Dec. 31, 1971).

25. For a discussion of this type of tactic, see Schelling 1960, p. 22, on "burning bridges."

26. *The Times* of London (Jan. 15, 1972).

27. *Financial Times* of London (Feb. 1, 1972).

28. *Sunday Times* of London (Mar. 12, 1972).

29. *The Times* of London (Mar. 13, 1972).

30. For press report, see *Guardian* (Mar. 29, 1972).

31. *Economist* (London) (Sept. 16, 1972), p. 44.

32. On signing, Britain would pay £12.75 million; on January 1, 1973, £3.5 million; and on April 1 and October 1, each year, £7 million, until March 31, 1979. *Treaty Series No. 44 (1972)*, *Cmd. 4943*, London (Mar. 26, 1972).

33. *Guardian* (Mar. 25, 1972); *Economist* (London) (Sept. 16, 1972), p. 44.

# 3. RACIAL STRATIFICATION AND BARGAINING: THE KENYA EXPERIENCE*

*Donald Rothchild, University of California, Davis*

An interracial bargaining situation prevails when the leaders of two or more collectives are prepared to engage in tacit or direct negotiations to achieve certain joint objectives. These collectives employ various bargaining techniques which further unity under conditions of enduring conflict (Simmel 1955, p. 13). Divergent interests—not values—are apparent; yet intergroup reciprocity is dictated by the common need to avoid mutual damage and to secure convergent goals.

Implicit in the bargaining situation is sufficient goodwill on all sides to provide an incentive to negotiate as well as an adequate dispersion of power to necessitate compromise. Without moral links there is no framework within which to reconcile divergent interests. Moreover, where one section boasts overwhelming power, it is in a position to impose its will on others. "But when each side is powerful enough to inflict considerable damage on the other, unilateral dictation is no longer possible and bargaining becomes necessary" (Diesing 1965, p. 406).

* Reprinted with permission from *Canadian Journal of African Studies* VII (1973), No. 3, pp. 419-31.

Each contending group must maintain sufficient strength to sustain the ongoing bargaining process. Nevertheless, the resort to bargaining does exhibit an inner momentum of its own, creating new relationships, practices and expectations which are "likely to broaden in the long run the area of common values and common sentiments" (Coser 1967, p. 264). Consequently, bargaining appears as an asymmetrical means of conflict management which can be of help in fostering harmony and integration in multiethnic communities.[1]

Intergroup bargaining affects social stratification in certain circumstances only. It is of limited relevance where racial rankings are frozen, and political and economic power is lodged firmly in the hands of a small racially exclusive elite (i.e., colonial East Africa). However, various forms of bargaining encounter are possible where group power is sufficiently dispersed to make exchange mutually beneficial (i.e., East African societies during the terminal stages of colonialism or immediately after). Such encounters can speed the process of restratification, allowing adjustments to occur swiftly with increases and decreases in community strength. Bargaining, then, is both a reflection of the existing configuration of group power as well as a means of effecting changes in the societal structures at hand.

In this respect, the Kenya experience is instructive. During the colonial period, Kenya's society was rigidly compartmentalized and stratified. A three-tier economic and social structure was discernible: The Europeans held the most prominent places in the public and private sectors of the economy; the Asians[2] predominated in the middle-level positions, as artisans, clerks, professionals, merchants and tradesmen; and the Africans filled out the picture by performing unskilled tasks on the farms and in the homes and factories. Such a racially-based stratification system entrenched a thoroughgoing structure of group inequality. The various strata had different rights and opportunities, prestige, educations, amenities, access to administrators and courts, and freedom of movement. In the Kenya colonial context, racial rankings remained largely frozen; with few exceptions, people were "sentenced for life to a social cell shared by others of like birth, separated from and ranked relative to all other social cells."[3]

Such an unbalanced power situation left little scope for interracial bargaining encounters. Even so, it is important to recognize that some limited interaction did occur between the two racially-privileged strata at the top of the colonial hierarchy. These intermittent encounters, which we would characterize as *hegemonial bargaining*, reflect the fact that group power is, to some extent at least, relational. As one sociologist puts the matter, "Since power is a property of social relations, of the nature and type of social interdependencies, it follows that it is a question of dynamic balances and not, in some static manner, of absolute possession and absolute deprivation."[4] Europeans had an overwhelming power advantage, but not a power monopoly; hence, on specific issues (i.e., representation in the legislative council and closer union in East Africa), they had no choice but to compete with the Asians, their closest ranking rivals.

In the somewhat unique and transitory hegemonial bargaining situation, interracial reciprocity occurs under the aegis of third party (governmental) control. Such bargaining is aptly described as "conduct between or among groups to affect the authoritative allocation of rewards and costs, as determined by governmental decision, when the government has a series of alternative distributions from which to choose" (Curry and Wade 1968, p. 37). Interethnic conflicts of interest are ever present; yet the determination of policies regarding the distribution of resources is largely vested in administrative hands —and therefore outside the reach of the contending collectivities. Although the first two decades of Kenya colonial experience were marked primarily by unacknowledged transactions between the dominant European community and the less politically organized Asian and African collectives, the next decades of British rule witnessed increasing conflict between the racial sections at the top of the hierarchy.[5] As the Asians achieved better organization, they competed more and more effectively with the powerful European community for the favor of the administration (both in Kenya and in Britain). At all times, therefore, non-official European power remained circumscribed. Not only was the local administration (under pressure from London) careful to deny a monopoly of influence to any one racial collective, but the other main group of immigrants, the Asians, were to compete (although unequally) for governmental favor. Although the protracted Asian-European encounter of the 1920s demonstrated the great strength of the resident European community, it nonetheless revealed the outer limits of their influence. Lacking the capacity to carry off a Rhodesian-type Unilateral Declaration of Independence, the European settlers were compelled in a showdown to accept an externally-imposed exchange. Such a manifestation of bureaucratic hegemony did not go unnoticed on any side, and it left the settlers vulnerable to any policy shifts on the part of British officialdom.

As African spokesmen evinced increasing dissatisfaction with the structure of Kenya society in the 1950s (shown by the call for greater political representation and the Mau Mau Emergency), the rigid political, economic and social stratification system gradually underwent a process of change. To be sure, the three-tier racial structure remained very much in evidence. Nevertheless, the dominant Europeans began to lose some of the moral certainty required to keep these racial rankings intact, and the Asian and African sections, increasingly indignant over their status, powerlessness, and lack of benefits, competed with ever greater effectiveness for an egalitarian system based upon achievement criteria. The politically conscious elements among the majority Africans would no longer accept the assumptions legitimatizing a hierarchy of color. And once the mystique of racial mastery had lost its hold, race relations seemed inevitably to move from a "paternalistic" to a "competitive" model.[6]

Thus shifts in group political power became the cause of intensified interethnic conflict and, over a longer time span, of restratification. As Leo Kuper notes, the process of group confrontation and accommodation in white settler societies initially involved "an increasing reliance on the collective organization of racially defined groups, a heightened awareness of racial identity, and a more intense hostility."[7] Such organization and consciousness became manifest in Kenya by the late 1950s, first altering the old balance of political power and subsequently affecting the dominant groups' economic and social advantages. The move from a white dominance system to "undiluted democracy" (i.e., the one man, one vote principle) acted as a catalyst of change. The old hierarchy of symbolic and substantive rewards did carry over temporarily into the decades following independence, but, with political relations profoundly altered, social status was necessarily affected. To some extent the possession of essential capital or skills or the maintenance of links with multinational firms buttressed the economic position of a select number of resident Europeans, and to a lesser extent, Asians; even here, however, political transformation was not without impact upon old-established patterns of privilege and prestige.

It is possible to view this larger interactional process as a new, or second, stage in race relations. As African power achieved near parity with the entrenched Europeans, Kenya entered what we would depict as a *direct bargaining* stage in interethnic encounters. Such a direct bargaining situation exists when the spokesmen for the various racial collectivities communicate openly with each other for the purpose of reaching a mutually beneficial agreement. Group leaders negotiate out of self-interest, but their concessions may represent a triumph for enlightened self-interest. As Robert Dahl and Charles Lindblom (1963, p. 326) maintain, "bargaining takes place because it is necessary, possible, and thought to be profitable." Although the convergence point varies largely according to the configurations of power in each bargaining encounter, all parties must in some sense see themselves as beneficiaries for the exchange to be significant.

The direct bargaining phenomenon reached its high point in Kenya in the 1950s and early 1960s when the spokesmen for the three major races jockeyed for a meaningful say in, even control of, the main political institutions as well as for future guarantees of property and civil liberties.[8] In this protracted power play, the non-African sections slowly and hesitantly gave in to majority African demands, securing what concessions they could from African leaders primarily bent upon wresting the right to national self-rule from metropolitan authorities. A trade-off occurred between legal and constitutional concessions to non-African interests on the one hand and the acceptance, with certain limitations, of African self-determination on the other. Such a trade-off reflected the distribution of group power on the local scene at that moment, but it inevitably lost some relevance as European and Asian bargaining capacity declined after *uhuru* (freedom).

Since Kenya remained under colonial control throughout this stage, the administration participated actively in the interrelations of groups by providing a framework through which diplomatic action would proceed. Once the colonizer had begun to lose what Frantz Fanon describes as his sense of assurance, he had little alternative, save a costly policy of repression, to opening a meaningful dialogue with local leaders. Britain chose the political course in Kenya and, responding to various local demands, supervised the search for interracial accommodation. British leaders were in a strong position to influence the course of the proceedings by dint of their capacity to delay independence, devolve powers upon the territorial authorities, and provide aid and support for British nationals overseas. Nevertheless, despite these very significant external influences at hand, clear evidence remains of a direct bargaining encounter in the negotiations that preceded independence. A close examination of the dates set for self-government and independence, constitutional protections, and the racial composition of the executive and legislative organs points up the configuration of interethnic bargaining power at each phase of the constitutional deliberations.

But with the transfer of power to African hands, the Kenya bargaining situation was fundamentally redefined. The colonial stratification system crumbled, losing its meaning first in the political sphere and then moving on more slowly to the economic and social sectors. Accelerated by local demands for a rapid Africanization of positions held by non-citizen Europeans and Asians (a survey of Kenya African attitudes we conducted in 1966 showed that 70 percent of the 653 respondents felt that big businesses in their country should employ Africans rather than Asians or Europeans) (Rothchild 1973, table 5, Chap. 7), the programs set up to replace expatriates with African citizens demonstrated substantial results by the 1970s. During the decade following *uhuru*, the civil service had become 96 percent Kenyanized and Kenyans of African origin had made significant inroads into small shopkeeping as well as into such larger industrial and commercial enterprises as banking, insurance, manufacturing, and industrial sales.[9]

Moreover, in the once "white" highlands a profound change in the farming sector had taken place. The government's various settlement schemes, aimed at reducing political pressures by alleviating landlessness and unemployment, resulted in the establishment of several hundred thousand Africans on former European-owned estates. The consequences of this Africanization of commercial agricultural activities are apparent to any observer of the scene. Indicative of the extent of the changeover was the fact that wheat, an almost exclusively European-raised crop in the 1950s, was 22 percent African-raised in 1967; that by 1967, Africans secured control over two-thirds of the 3,000,000 acres of mixed farming land; and that Africans supplied over half the milk to the organized dairy industry by 1968 (Rothchild 1973, p. 218).

Certainly it would be unwise to see this restratification process as in anything but a transitional stage. The Europeans, as a result largely of their linkage with international capitalist enterprises, remain powerful, but somewhat less visible, factors in the larger decisions affecting the economy. The highly-skilled Asians retain an indispensability which is tied to current manpower shortages. Even so, Kenyans have gone a considerable distance toward righting some of the most pronounced imbalances of the past, and there is no reason, in light of expanding educational opportunities, to doubt that accelerated progress in this direction will take place in the future.

The further change in intergroup power relationships leads, we feel, to a third or *tacit bargaining* stage in interracial encounters. A tacit bargaining situation exists when a powerful racial section (in this case, the Africans) and its less and less effective racial rivals achieve reciprocity primarily by means of quiet transactions. No longer does an alien administration act as a balancing force among collectives; instead, the overwhelming nature of majority African political control, unimpeded by constraints from a higher administration, leaves little scope for anything but tacit exchanges among racial sections on the local scene. For a tacit bargaining situation to be availing, all parties must come to recognize the mutuality of benefit from a reconciliatory course. Agreements need not be stated or explicit. What is essential, however, is that the collectives accept a given line of action in order to maximize convergent interests.

In colonial Kenya unacknowledged transactions were evident where relatively unorganized aggregates worked for minimal rewards within the externally-imposed white dominance system; unless the dominant European community acceded to crucial African demands, the African majority might have attempted, as in the Mau Mau Emergency, to force structural transformation through violence. And in the period after independence, unacknowledged transactions again became evident in the relations between the politically dominant African majority and the economically-significant non-African minorities. An unspoken agreement to tolerate these affluent strangers existed, provided they contributed to economic well-being and acquiesced, in good faith, in their own demise when their services were no longer deemed essential. Tacit bargains over property rights, citizenship, resource allocation and Africanization programs have been important. Certainly in all the instances of tacit bargaining just noted, a conflict of interest is apparent; yet direct bargaining is precluded by the disparity of group power inherent in each situation. Therefore, tacit bargaining becomes the means of ensuring the persistence of the existing structure through an implicit recognition of reciprocal interests under present time-place circumstances.

Several propositions about the bargaining situation in Kenya are suggested by the foregoing discussion of changing stratification systems and bargaining styles:

(1) Hegemonial bargaining was distorted in the colonial situation by the rigid stratification of political and economic power.

In colonial Kenya, the striking disparity in group power militated against the employment of direct bargaining techniques to manage interethnic conflict. The combination of European control of capital and high-level skills and their easy access to bureaucratic decision-makers insulated them temporarily from the need to engage in explicit transactions with the indigenous aggregates in their midst. Since many officials regarded the settlers' contribution to economic development as indispensable to Britain's "civilizing" mission in the area, it is not surprising, at the outset at least, that the settlers acted highhandedly when confronted with divergent claims from other communities. Most dramatically, the Vigilance Committee of the Convention of Associations planned an uprising in 1923 aimed at forcing the government to abandon the Wood-Winterton proposals regarding Indian immigration, residence, and franchise rights in Kenya. Less sensational, but equally haughty, was the colonists' fervent opposition to fingerprinting and the income tax and their demands for large land alienations, a European unofficial majority on the Legislative Council, and policies on resource allocation that favored their need for roads, railroad lines, and educational facilities. The Convention of Associations, which united various farmer organizations in 1910, long spearheaded an effective drive by the colonists to influence the sometimes reluctant officials. The authorities' concurrence with many of these claims is a measure of this sectional interest group's success. Reluctant to undertake economic development primarily on the basis of publicly sponsored capital and cadres, the colonial government came to rely essentially on private sources of initiative, expertise and wealth.[10] Such dependency made them vulnerable to European settler influence, thereby distorting the hegemonial bargaining process by an open favoring of a single community's interest.

Nevertheless rival interests were not long in making an appearance upon this colonial scene. The Kenya Asians, stronger in numbers and resources than their Uganda and Tanganyika counterparts, were soon to pose a basic challenge to settler designs. The Convention of Associations' record of accomplishments in pressing forward European interests clearly had a demonstration effect, for in 1914 the Indians organized into an East African Indian National Congress. From that point onward, the Congress demanded full equality as British subjects in the activities of the Colony. "The object of our association or Congress," remarked T. M. Jeevanjee in his Presidential Address to the first session, "is primarily to defend against attacks on the rights and interests of our people in British East Africa; to maintain a watchful regard upon and to combat legislation which in our opinion may constitute an encroachment upon or derogation of the rights enjoyed in this Country from time immemorial."[11] Congress bitterly criticized the doctrine of "European paramountcy" and differentiating practices in such areas as immigration, franchise, the purchase of farms in the highlands, and residence in choice urban areas. In place of existing discriminatory patterns and practices, its spokesmen urged a policy of legal equity which would enable enterprising Indians to compete on equal terms with the favored Europeans. In addition, Congress leaders sought to protect and promote the interests of their community through political participation in the legislative and executive branches of government. They argued that "the Government obviously is primarily and exclusively . . . run, for the benefit of the Europeans, Indians do not count." Because of unofficial European hostility and official European indifference, it was essential that Indians "have sufficient political rights and strong voice in Central and Municipal Governments to protect their own interests."[12]

In the following years the Indians were to press their claims on the issues of the franchise, segregation, land occupancy, immigration, and, above all, political power. Although the Colonial Secretary finally decided the European-Indian dispute of the 1920s substantially in favor of settler interests (preserving communal representation, maintaining the highlands as an exclusive European area, and continuing strict immigration controls), he was forced to state explicitly the principle of African "paramountcy."[13] In this sense the political initiative of the Indian community had forced the imperial government's hand, for the latter was now revealed as the key balancing element in Kenya interethnic conflicts. Thus if hegemonial bargaining had not proved particularly productive of immediate Indian goals, it did have significant long-term effects in redefining the political system in favor of majority African interests.

Only gradually did the Africans organize for effective political action. Up to the time of the European thrust into the Kenya heartland, these African aggregates had lived a largely compartmentalized, rural, and communalistic existence. The European advent, however, meant a thoroughgoing disruption of old patterns, substituting a money economy, legal contracts party systems, urbanization, norms of achievement, and a high level of specialization for the natural ties of a rural folk society. For good or ill, the twin thrusts of colonialism and capitalism forced many Africans from the intimate small world of the traditional system into the wider and more cosmopolitan context of the modern state.

African leaders, recognizing the strength of the new political and economic order, began increasingly to assert sectional interests within the externally imposed structure. Continued tacit bargaining held out prospects of minimal advantage, and a more direct mechanism of influence was patently necessary. Hence during the early 1920s, African political spokesmen began organizing their own constituents and making demands upon the political system. Several rural and urban-based political organizations sprang up for the purpose of securing a rectification of African grievances. These organizations did not challenge the legitimacy of the colonial system so much as they made known deep-felt dissatisfaction on certain issues: land alienation, the *kipande* (registration certificate), hut taxes, and forced labor. Employing a variety of means (delegations, mass meetings, petitions, cables, letters to newspapers, demonstrations, strikes), they strove to make the bureaucracy and expatriate communities aware of their frustrations. Some of these initiatives, such as Harry Thuku's East African Association, were doubtlessly more productive of long-term than immediate consequences; nevertheless, it would be wrong to overlook the concrete results stemming from early African political activity. Following political protests on the part of the Young Kavirondo Association in Nyanza Province in 1922, General Sir Edward Northey, appeared in the region and announced measures to abolish labor camps, reduce hut and poll taxes, and demarcate the boundary of the Luo Reserve.[14] Subsequent opposition on the part of the Kikuyu Central Association to the establishment of an unofficial European majority on the Kenya Legislative Council as well as to East African unification contributed to the ultimate decision by British policy formers to abandon these proposals.[15] Thus while it is necessary not to overstate the African role in the hegemonial bargaining process of early nationalist times, it is nonetheless important to keep in mind the genesis of the interactional

process as well as the growth of the political mechanisms for
future direct bargaining. A trend toward more direct competition was apparent in African nationalist politics.

(2) Direct bargaining was only a temporary phenomenon
which reached its zenith during the pre-independence
negotiations. Its brief duration was a product of an ex-
ternally-inspired diplomatic sitting in which a convergence occurred between majority aspirations for independence and development and minority goals of
stability, property rights and, possibly, political representation. Reciprocity involved a short-term trade-off
of interests between the leaders of powerful sections to
achieve convergent needs.

As African cohesion and political power increased after
World War II, interethnic bargaining moved from the
hegemonial to the direct bargaining stage. The narrowing of
the power disparity among groups made interethnic bargaining
more essential than ever. Unless sectional leaders could
manage to negotiate their main differences, a mutually disadvantageous economic and political crisis might become un-
avoidable. In this regard, the role of sectional leadership was
of the essence. It was the leaders of the collectives who engaged in the give-and-take process of exchanging interests.
Like diplomats on the international scene, they played the key
roles in the interethnic negotiating process.

During the 1950s direct intergroup bargaining took place in
respect to both economic and political matters. At the time
that the East Africa Royal Commission urged an end to "the
racial reserve principle" prevailing in the highlands in 1955, it
commented on an instance of exchange which involved the
release of 19,000 acres of land in the Ithanga hills for African
use in return for making 1,800 acres of national forest available for European use.[16] Sectional leaders also concluded a
series of group bargains over ethnic representation in the
legislative and executive councils and over constitutional guarantees for the minority communities. In these transactions, the
growth of African power had to be accommodated by a continuing process of negotiations. Thus group representation was
modified periodically in order to reflect the changing nature of

sectional power on the territorial scene. The pre-Emergency parity of European/non-European unofficial representation on the Legislative Council was replaced in 1957 by African-European parity, and then, in 1960, by an effective African majority. In a parallel development, an African was first assigned a ministerial post in 1954; by 1960, following protracted negotiations at Lancaster House on the part of British leaders and representatives of all major communities in Kenya, a compromise formula was hammered out which provided for a Council of Ministers composed of four officials and three European, one Asian, and four African unofficial members. The formula eventually presented by Colonial Secretary Iain Macleod in 1960, involving maximal minority concessions and minimal majority expectations, represented something of a high point in Kenya's direct interethnic bargaining encounter.

If the 1960 conference was the culmination in Kenya's direct bargaining process, it was also somewhat unique as an exchange of interests. Its short duration can be attributed to a quick passing of the interethnic power balance and to the eclipse, with the grant of independence, of the colonial authority's intermediary role. Once effective power had been transferred to majority African hands, a process was set in motion which would result in the creation of a new internal power disparity, one which was most favorable to African objectives.

What had in fact promoted this unusual and fleeting opportunity for interethnic transaction was a once-ever convergence of interests on the part of the major racial groups in the country. In its essentials, the exchange involved a trade-off between the African need for smooth and continuing progress toward *uhuru* and the minorities' need for a stable and secure political and economic environment. African leaders, keenly aware of the important contribution which non-African skills, capital and enterprise contributed to the country's economic development, were prepared to make limited concessions (fundamental rights, property guarantees, parliamentary representation) to secure minority goodwill. It was an explicit exchange of communal interests.[17] Convergent expectations had led to a temporary agreement which was instrumental in nature. But because the moral linkages between role partners lacked enduring historical roots (Evan 1962, p. 349), new initiatives and new forms of reciprocity became inevitable in the changing circumstances of the post-independence period.

(3) Tacit bargaining occurs most pronouncedly when great disparities of power exist between groups in the political sphere. At the same time, interethnic reciprocity is made necessary by a mutuality of economic interests.

Great disparities in interethnic power relations became evident soon after the transfer of effective authority to African hands. Africanization occurred rapidly in the legislature and in the civil service, to be followed in due course in other walks of life. The consequences of this changed minority position upon the interethnic bargaining process were highly significant. Europeans and Asians, dislodged from many decision-making posts, were no longer able actively to shape policies affecting their interests. Moreover, as their numbers, cohesiveness, and economic indispensability declined, their effectiveness as a political force diminished considerably (Blalock 1967, p. 91). Obviously leaders are more effective bargainers when backed up by a sufficient "critical mass" of constituents. Thus their decline in numbers as well as cohesiveness and economic indispensability led to a drastic reduction in political effectiveness. This reduced effectiveness brought on a change in bargaining techniques from direct to tacit bargaining. The immigrant communities, attempting to compensate for their increasingly apparent political insignificance, stressed, in interest group fashion, the less visible mechanisms of tacit bargaining.[18]

Post-independence tacit bargaining surfaced in a variety of ways. In the broadest sense, government's willingness to create an environment favorable to Western capitalism and the acceptance by expatriate businessmen of the need to pursue reformist policies on such questions as Africanization, exchange controls, taxation, and so forth represents an exchange of interests between the different elites. Kenyans have at times made reference to this implicit transaction. On independence day, notes Iconoclastes in the *East Africa Journal,*

status and wealth still remained in the hands of expatriates, with only one new exception: a handful of Africans mainly politicians and civil servants, were now allowed to share in the wealth. These few, in their turn, promised to protect the property and the rights of the expatriates. . . . In his turn, the European behaved himself so well that Kenya leaders were persuaded to proclaim, at the top of their voices, that Kenya was to be emulated by the rest of the world as a racial sanctuary. Accordingly, a definite business alliance was formed between the immigrant communities and an ever growing local bourgeoisie.[19]

More explicitly, however, quiet behind-the-scenes negotiations have occurred between the government on the one hand and such organizations as the Kenya National Farmers' Union (KNFU), the Kenya Chamber of Commerce and Industry, and the Federation of Kenya Employers (FKE) on the other. In February 1970, Sir Colin Campbell, the out-going president of FKE, referred in a speech in Mombasa to consultations his organization had been having with the government on an apprentice levy scheme;[20] his successor, Christopher Malavu, asserted later in the year that the "present satisfactory Kenyanization progress is largely due to the close contact the Federation has maintained with the Government . . .", and he urged still more consultations with governmental authorities in months to come.[21] Delegations from these interest groups have also met with government officials on such questions as trade licensing, staff housing, and the anticipated future role of expatriate farmers and businessmen.[22] Such direct connections have received official encouragement and have done much to clear the air of misunderstanding and needless anxiety.[23] Therefore, some opinion leaders have come to prefer a quiet exchange of differences to a public airing of complaints. For example, an editorial in the *East African Standard* discussed the way in which former Minister for Agriculture Bruce McKenzie's assurances to a KNFU meeting helped to restore the confidence of expatriate farmers and urged a policy of quiet diplomacy: "The trouble is, in farming and other sectors of the economy, that too often a dialogue is carried on in public between Government leaders and businessmen (or farmers), through conference speeches or Press statements, but without sufficient hard bargaining and thrashing out of problems behind closed doors."[24]

A striking example of an exchange of interests between government and employers in the post-independence period is the Tripartite Agreements of 1964 and 1970. The 1964 agreement involved the close collaboration of governmental, management and labor leaders for the purpose of creating 34,000 new jobs. In a trade-off of interests, public and private employers established the new positions and labor cooperated by refraining temporarily from strike actions and by accepting a moratorium on wage increases. Then in February 1970, Sir Colin Campbell, when responding to a government suggestion that urgent action be taken to put together 50,000 new jobs, declared that FKE would welcome negotiations with the government and the trade unions on another tripartite agreement and wages policy.[25] Despite the reservations of labor leader Denis Akumu that such agreements would not go to the heart of the unemployment problem, the government did go ahead and negotiate the 1970 compact.[26] Progress in recruiting a ten percent increase of staff under the 1970 plan was indeed slow. Employers insisted upon the right to hire experienced personnel—a right upheld by government but criticized by labor as a pretext for sabotaging the objectives of the plan.[27] By October 1970, both FKE and the Central Organization of Trade Unions found it necessary to grant a request by the Minister for Labour for an extra month's period in which employers could recruit their full quota of employees under the Tripartite Agreement.

Thus convergent economic interests did lead to an exchange of interests among Kenya communities in post-*uhuru* times. The employers' need for a favorable climate in which to do business overlapped the government's and unions' need for equity goals and for steadily increasing work opportunities. The upshot was a pragmatic and reformist government policy on Africanization, citizenship, repatriation of profits, nationalization of industries, and so forth. Government paid a price in terms of equity aspirations to secure certain economic objectives requiring full expatriate cooperation. The spirit of Kenya pragmatism is reflected in its assessment of the tripartite agreements. "Aside from the direct benefits which have resulted from tripartite cooperation," observed the *Development Plan 1970–1974*, "the close working relationship which has evolved between the three parties has resulted in an enhanced mutual appreciation of their economic interdependence."[28] The existence of such moral bonds meant that a tacit bargaining process might be productive of significant results.

(4) A functionally-inspired bargaining process will endure only so long as a sufficient dispersion of power persists to make reciprocity essential.

Since a low power disparity among collectives facilitates conflict management through some form of the bargaining process, it follows that a reversal of these factors will reduce the usefulness of this general approach. Groups engage in some form of bargaining to maximize their own self-interest; their willingness to negotiate and compromise is often more sociational in its consequences than in the initial motives that brought men around the bargaining table.

But it is precisely because the linkages are functionally rather than organically inspired that they prove fragile and lacking in endurance. Sigmund Freud's remark that "the interest of work in common would not hold (civilized society) together" may overstate the case.[29] Yet Freud's comment is quite meaningful when applied to the specific case of pluralistic societies, for in such societies one sometimes finds the most pronounced resistance to economic cross-cutting ties of a transsectional nature.

The implications of fragile functional linkage for the future of interracial reciprocity can be significant whenever the status quo is altered in any fundamental way. For example, should restratification cause one of the parties to suffer a severe power loss, the necessity for continuing the difficult search for mutual accommodations would diminish, and the dominant group would find itself at a vantage point at which it could seek to achieve its expectations unilaterally. Bargaining can abet the process of conflict management only so long as a dispersion of power prevails. Consequently, the momentary opportunity to engage in a bargaining encounter must be seized in order to deal with divergent interests at hand as well as to widen the sphere of social communications for the future. Unless the expediency of the present contributes to the learned sense of intersectional solidarity for times to come, the weaker collectivities may well find themselves unwelcome guests in the African polities.

Kenyan leaders have shown themselves to be quite aware of the critical importance of intersectional cooperation. As President Kenyatta states, it would be a pity if long time expatriate residents were reduced to the status of technical mercenaries, for they would be unlikely to develop any sense of identity with Kenya's course.[30] In brief, then, a bond of empathy and understanding must emerge or one can anticipate a decline of minority group presence paralleling the decline in minority group power. Some well-trained persons with low visibility might stay on as individuals in the burgeoning industrial state, but a larger presence requires a transition from what Aristotle described as friendship of kinsmen (based on blood ties) to a friendship of association (based on compact).[31] Group transactions must give way to individual transactions, or racial interaction, based on sectional power and functional contributions, may come to a halt over the long term.

## NOTES

1. In this essay, the term ethnicity is used broadly to cover a variety of kinship clusters based upon race, language, culture, religion, or region. On the basic similarities of systems of "birth-ascribed stratifications," see Gerald D. Berreman, "Race, Caste, and Other Invidious Distinctions in Social Stratification," *Race* XIII, No. 4 (Apr. 1972), pp. 388, 392.
2. The term Asians (or "Indians") refers to peoples from the Indian sub-continent (now India, Pakistan, and Bangladesh).
3. Berreman, op. cit., p. 386.
4. Eric Dunning, "Dynamics of Racial Stratification: Some Preliminary Observations," *Race* XIII, No. 4 (Apr. 1972), p. 421.
5. On the distinction between unacknowledged and acknowledged transactions, see Donald Rothchild, "Ethnicity and Conflict Resolution," *World Politics* XXII, No. 4 (July 1970), p. 602. Also see Schelling 1960, pp. 21, 53; and William C. Mitchell, *The American Polity: A Social and Cultural Interpretation* (New York: Free Press, 1970), pp. 295–96.
6. Philip Mason, *Patterns of Dominance* (London: Oxford University Press for the Institute of Race Relations, 1970), pp. 60–65.
7. Leo Kuper, "Political Change in White Settler Societies: The

Possibility of Peaceful Democratization," in Leo Kuper and M. G. Smith, eds., *Pluralism in Africa* (Berkeley: University of California Press, 1969), p. 170.

8. During this period a paralleling bargaining process was also taking place among the indigenous African ethnic groups of Kenya. These negotiations are described in Donald Rothchild, "Majimbo Schemes in Kenya and Uganda," in Jeffrey Butler and A. A. Castagno (eds.), *Boston University Papers on Africa: Transition in African Politics* (New York: Praeger, 1967), pp. 291–313.

9. J. A. Gethenji, the Director of Personnel and Permanent Secretary in the Office of the President, observed in late 1971 that out of about 90,000 personnel in the civil service, some 4,000 were expatriates. *Daily Nation* (Nairobi), November 29, 1971, p. 14.

10. ". . . Where white settlement is firmly established," observed M. F. Hill, "the Crown Colony system of Government only functions tolerably under a Governor who is prepared to 'govern by agreement' with the elected representation of the European Community." *The Dual Policy in Kenya* (Nairobi: The Highland Printing Press, 1944), p. 35.

11. Presidential Address, T. M. Jeevanjee, First Session, East African Indian National Congress, Mombasa, 1914, p. 1. (Typescript copy.)

12. East African Indian National Congress, "Review of Indian Political Question in Eastern Africa: An Up-to-date Summary, Contained in a Memorandum to the Rt. Hon. David Lloyd George by the Standing Committee of the East African Indian National Congress, 1919, sect. 45. (Typescript copy.)

13. *Indians in Kenya*, Cmd. 1922 (London: His Majesty's Stationery Office, 1923), pp. 6–10.

14. Carl G. Rosberg, Jr. and John Nottingham, *The Myth of "Mau Mau": Nationalism in Kenya* (New York: Praeger, 1966), p. 63.

15. The Memorandum of the Kikuyu Central Association, Fort Hall, to the Hilton Young Commission in 1928 is reprinted in part in Donald Rothchild (ed.), *Politics of Integration: An East African Documentary* (Nairobi: East African Publishing House, 1968), p. 25.

16. Great Britain Colonial Office, *East Africa Royal Commission 1953–1955 Report*, Cmd. 9475 (London: Her Majesty's Stationery Office, 1955), pp. 381–82.

17. A. Oginga Odinga, *Not Yet Uhuru* (London: Heinemann, 1967), pp. 179–80.

18. The importance of "numericalism" in intergroup relations is discussed in David B. Truman, *The Governmental Process* (New York: Alfred A. Knopf, 1953), pp. 506–7; and Ali A. Mazrui,

"Numerical Strength and Nuclear Status in the Politics of the Third World," *Journal of Politics*, XXIX, No. 4 (Nov. 1967), p. 793.

19. Vol. V, 4 (Apr. 1968), p. 6.

20. *Daily Nation* (Nairobi), Feb. 20, 1970, pp. 1, 32.

21. *East African Standard* (Nairobi), Mar. 27, 1970, p. 9 and Aug. 13, 1970, p. 5.

22. Ibid., Feb. 15, 1968, p. 4, Jan. 5, 1970, p. 4 and May 5, 1970, p. 5.

23. Ibid., Feb. 15, 1968, p. 4; and *East African Report on Trade and Industry* (Nairobi) I, 6 (June 1970), p. 3.

24. Editorial, *East African Standard* (Nairobi), Feb. 15, 1968, p. 4.

25. *Daily Nation* (Nairobi), Feb. 20, 1970, p. 1. In parliament, Maina Wanjigi, the Assistant Minister for Agriculture, called for the immediate "negotiation" of another Tripartite Agreement. *National Assembly Debates* (Kenya), XIX, First Session (Feb. 17, 1970), col. 318.

26. *East African Standard* (Nairobi), Aug. 19, 1970, pp. 1, 8.

27. "While it is true that most employers are doing their best to make the agreement a success, it is equally true," claimed Akumu, "that certain employers are demanding unnecessarily high qualifications for certain jobs." Ibid., p. 1.

28. Republic of Kenya, *Development Plan 1970–1974* (Nairobi: Government Printer, 1969), p. 109.

29. *Civilization and Its Discontents* (London: Hogarth Press, 1963), p. 49.

30. *East African Standard* (Nairobi), Feb. 19, 1968, p. 5.

31. *Ethica Nicomachea*, in The Works of Aristotle, Vol. IX, trans. by W. D. Ross (London: Oxford University Press, 1915), Vol. VIII, ch. 13, sects. 1161b–1162a.

# PART IV
## Communications Analysis and Related Approaches

# INTRODUCTION

The chapters in this section all deal with the study of negotiations as an exchange of messages, in which outcomes depend on a sense of balance or of appropriateness in that exchange. In this view, *the chances of a successful outcome vary directly with the responsiveness of the communications exchange*, expressed in various measures. The underlying notion is a common-sense idea of mutual understanding, and the more scientific background of the proposition lies in psychological studies of stimulus and response and in cybernetics. The approach also emphasizes the assumption that outcomes and the negotiating process itself are matters of volition and decision-making, and not simply accidents of predetermined relations or external forces. Communications analysis of negotiations is therefore quite antithetical to structural analysis (although the additions and correctives to structural explanation work to bring the two approaches closer together), and indeed it takes little account of differences in power resources. It may be no accident that communications analyses, as represented by the selection of chapters in this section, focus on bilateral negotiations between approximate equals, whereas structural analysis was a response to the intriguing questions raised by multilateral negotiations or those with high-power-resource differentials. One advantage that communications analysis has over structural analysis and allied approaches is that it permits an explanation of failure as well as success, of breakdown as well as of agreement, distinctions that are not particularly stressed in discussions of structure and tactics.

The Cuban Missile Crisis of 1962 has furnished material for a number of analyses (Abel 1963, Horelick 1964, Hilsman 1967, Larson 1963, Pachter 1963, Scheinman and Wilkinson 1968, Schlesinger 1965, Wright 1964, Forward 1971, O. Young 1968), although it was scarcely a typical negotiation. Although somewhat overstated, the convergence point was always known and present; the crisis involved efforts to get there rather than attempts to define an unknown point. Yet so many other aspects—notably the bare simplicity of the interaction between essentially two counterbalancing parties—makes it an attractive model for study. The analysis by Holsti, Brody, and North has the additional advantage of being based only on publicly available documents, subjected to content analysis with the aid of a computer, showing that insightful study does not have to await some fifty-year declassification rule. The success of the outcome is ascribed to the fact that both sides tended to perceive rather accurately the nature of the other's actions and then acted on a corresponding level. Efforts by either party to delay or reverse the escalation of the conflict were perceived correctly and responded to in kind. This mechanism was not mechanical, however; it reflected a clear will to communicate, to remain flexible, to save the other fellow's face —in a word, to arrive at a successfully negotiated outcome.

Such characteristics were not always present in the seventeen years of disarmament negotiations that preceded the partial nuclear test-ban treaty of 1963. Running through many regimes and many phases of the Cold War, these negotiations permit the analysis of different types of behavior, with relational and motivational inferences based on them. Jensen's thorough study deals with concessions rather than all types of communications, but it examines the stimulus-and-response relation between the two parties' behavior, dealing empirically with the matter of concession rates that others (Coddington 1968, Cross 1969) have handled theoretically. Thus negotiators, like generals, seem always to be fighting the last war, and *concession rate behavior is a direct function of the other party's concession rate behavior in the immediately preceding round.* This has led to a lot of unrequited conceding or inversely responsive bargaining, quite a different pattern than during the Cuban crisis (although the latter was admittedly much shorter in duration). In terms of one of the lessons of the Maltese encounter, Russians seemed to be engaging in deadline bargaining and Americans in nondeadline negotiations. Another characteristic of the earlier part of the negotiations is approach-avoidance bargaining, which represents a third type of concession rate—mixed stable and unstable. The fact that such behavior can be assigned concession rates does not necessarily put it in the category of "cataclysmic," beyond the control of human hands. To the contrary, during the last year of the negotiations, the pattern was changed, consciously and deliberately, for reasons related to the changed value of the substance under discussion, but also because of an overall phasing in the negotiations, by which the parties had backed into near agreement that it would have been impolitic to back out of.

Like the Cuban crisis but almost for inverse reasons (length of time and complexity of interaction), disarmament has been the subject of many negotiations analyses (Nogee 1960, Nogee and Spanier 1962, Wadsworth 1962, Lall 1964, Jacobson and Stein 1966, Dean 1966, Schelling 1966, Stone 1967). As befitting the phasing, many of the earlier studies have focused on the propaganda aspect of the encounter, frequently to prove a charge of bad faith because the right kind of game was not being played. Nogee's analysis too emphasizes the propaganda or nonresponsive communications aspect but examines it as a type of communications behavior similar to that found in negotiations with successful outcomes. The establishment of the fact, principle, logic, and legitimacy of one's means of persuasion (as noted in Schuler's chapter) and of the reality and justice of one's goals and proposals (as brought out in Wriggins' chapter) are important ways of bringing outcomes close to one's positions, especially when vital interests are at stake; and the division of the opposing team is a tactic right out of structural analysis. Indeed, if anything, it is striking that a study of appropriate means of persuasion has come from a case of unsuccessful rather than successful outcomes.

Unsuccessful outcomes and communications analysis can provide other lessons for the study of negotiations as well. Spector subjects the Aswan High Dam negotiations of 1955–56 to content and cybernetic analysis to find out the correlates of breakdown, and he finds that neither side was listening to the other. Unlike most studies of this type, the analysis focuses both on positions and on persuasion, to determine not merely the characteristic patterns of each but also the relationship between them. By building a model based on these relationships, the author is able to determine the point of breakdown or disjunction in the mechanism of communications flow. Again, like the other cases studied in this section, the analysis was conducted on the basis of public statements. Tapes of the closed-door discussions might have provided more juicy detail, but the results appear to indicate that sound interpretations of events can also be early, as long as the conceptual tools are at hand. In the process, the study also shows that *goal behavior is related to—and hence can be inferred from—strategy, an intent to agree being reflected in co-operative strategy and an intent to avoid agreement being expressed in hostile strategies.* At a broader level of generalization, these findings suggest that responsive behavior is a correlate only of intent to seek agreement; when there is no interest in seeking agreement, the hearing aid is turned off and behavior is determined by internal processes, not by any responsiveness to the other party's stimuli.

But it then becomes important to keep the hearing aid on and open, since communications may well have an important effect on the internal processes that decide whether agreement is worth it or not. Among many other things, the analysis of the Vietnam negotiations shows the immense difficulties that two parties, deafened by their ideologies and stammering through the noise of their past history, have in getting their message across to each other. The length of time it took between the initial suggestion of a new proposition and its final inclusion among the points under consideration will surprise laymen but makes up much of the daily history of the Paris (and other) exchanges. The type of analysis with which the events fit most comfortably, however, is a further refinement of the earlier communications approaches. Although the author initially set out to analyze the encounter in terms of concessions and concession rates, this approach was proven quite inapplicable. On one hand, it was manifestly difficult to force the many items of negotiation into a single comparable scale of concession behavior. On the other, the negotiations themselves clearly fit into a different pattern, one of long efforts to establish a concordant image of the subject and solution under discussion, which then led to a suspicious but joint-discovery venture into applicable details. Thus, *responsive behavior is more likely when the image of negotiations has been established than before,* an important paradox because it explains why it is often so difficult to establish that very image. Along the way, the parties to the Vietnam negotiations also engaged in behavior related to the third aspect of their encounter, efforts to change the ambient reality. These negotiations, in addition to bringing out these three aspects of any bargaining encounter, also show one use of strategic analysis as expressed in a matrix of choices. Although game theoretic portrayals take no account of skill, power, or process, the matrix can be used in this type of situation to portray succinctly the dynamic elements of the encounter.

# 1. MEASURING AFFECT AND ACTION: THE 1962 CUBAN CRISIS*

*Ole R. Holsti, Richard A. Brody, and Robert C. North, Stanford University*

## THE BACKGROUND—THE CUBAN CRISIS

In October 1962 the first nuclear confrontation in history was precipitated by the establishment of Soviet missile sites in Cuba. For a period of approximately one week, the probability of a full-scale nuclear exchange between the United States and the Soviet Union was exceedingly high. Speaking of the events of the week of October 22, Attorney General Robert Kennedy recalled: "We all agreed in the end that if the Russians were ready to go to nuclear war over Cuba, they were ready to go to nuclear war, and that was that. So we might as well have the showdown then as six months later."[1]

An examination of the events immediately surrounding the crisis, analyzed in four rather distinct periods, offers the clear-cut case history of a conflict that escalated to the brink of

* Reprinted with permission from *Journal of Peace Research* I (1964), Nos. 3–4, pp. 170–89. This study was supported by the United States Naval Ordnance Test Station, China Lake, California, Contract N60530–8929. The authors wish to express their gratitude to Mrs. Marian Payne for her research assistance in collecting the financial data analyzed in this paper.

war—and then de-escalated. This presents a useful contrast with another great crisis in history—which spiralled into major war. The two are almost classic patterns of international conflict.

During the 1962 pre-crisis period President Kennedy had been under considerable domestic pressure to take action against Cuba. In addition to attacks on Administration policy by Senators Capehart,[2] Bush, Goldwater, and Keating,[3] the Republican Senatorial and Congressional campaign committees had announced that Cuba would be "the dominant issue of the 1962 campaign. . . . Past mistakes toward Cuba could be forgotten if the Administration now showed itself willing to face reality. But there is little evidence of willingness to recognize the developing danger and to move resolutely to cope with it."[4] Public opinion polls revealed an increasing impatience with American policy toward Communist influence in the Caribbean (Wright 1964, p. 184). When the President arrived in Chicago on a campaign tour in mid-October, one "welcoming" sign read: "Less Profile—More Courage" (ibid., p. 186).

There had been a number of rumors regarding the emplacement of Soviet missiles and troops in Cuba, but "hard" evidence was lacking; those most critical of administration policy were not, in fact, willing to reveal their sources of information. Although Cuba had been under surveillance for some time, the first active phase of the crisis, from October 14 to October 21, began with the development of photographic evidence that Soviet missiles had indeed been located in Cuba. It was during this period that—according to President Kennedy—"15 people, more or less, who were directly consulted" developed "a general consensus" regarding the major decision to invoke a limited blockade.[5] Unfortunately for the purposes of this analysis, there are no publicly-available documents from either Soviet or American decision-makers for the period.

The second and third periods—October 22–25 and October 26–31 respectively—might be described as the "period of greatest danger of escalation" and the "bargaining period." The present paper is confined to this time span, and is not concerned with the final period, during which the agreements reached between President Kennedy and Premier Khrushchev were assertedly carried out and in which further questions regarding verification were raised.

The period of most acute danger of escalation began with President Kennedy's address to the nation on October 22 regarding recent events in Cuba and announcing the institution of certain policies designed to compel the withdrawal of Soviet missiles from the Caribbean. The President announced:

> Within the past week unmistakable evidence has established the fact that a series of offensive missile sites is now in preparation on that imprisoned island. The purpose of these bases can be none other than to provide a nuclear strike capability against the Western Hemisphere.
>
> Additional sites not yet completed appear to be designed for intermediate-range ballistic missiles capable . . . of striking most of the major cities in the Western Hemisphere.
>
> This urgent transformation of Cuba into an important strategic base—by the presence of these large, long-range, and clearly offensive weapons of mass destruction—constitutes an explicit threat to the peace and security of all the Americas, in flagrant and deliberate defiance of the Rio Pact of 1947, the traditions of this nation and hemisphere, the Joint Resolution of the 87th Congress, the Charter of the United Nations, and my own public warning to the Soviets on September 4 and 13.

The United States would, according to the President: (1) impose a "strict quarantine" around Cuba to halt the offensive Soviet build-up; (2) continue and increase the close surveillance of Cuba; (3) answer any nuclear missile attack launched from Cuba against any nation in the Western Hemisphere with "a full retaliatory response upon the Soviet Union"; (4) reinforce the naval base at Guantanamo; (5) call for a meeting of the Organization of American States to invoke the Rio Treaty; and (6) call for an emergency meeting of the United Nations. At the same time he stated that additional military forces had been alerted for "any eventuality." James Reston[6] reported "on highest authority" that,

> Ships carrying additional offensive weapons to Cuba must either turn back or submit to search and seizure, or fight. If

they try to run the blockade, a warning shot will be fired across their bows; if they still do not submit, they will be attacked.

In accordance with the Joint Congressional Resolution passed three weeks earlier, the President signed an executive order on October 23 mobilizing reserves. It has been reported that decision-makers in Washington also wanted the North Atlantic Treaty forces placed on a maximum missile alert, which meant putting American-controlled nuclear warheads on the NATO-controlled missiles aimed at the Soviet Union. This would prepare them for instant firing. General Lauris Norstad, Supreme Commander of NATO, is reported to have objected successfully, arguing that in the absence of secrecy, such preparations could bring war when neither side wanted it, by way of "the self-fulfilling prophecy" (Bagdikian 1963, p. 6).

In its initial response the Soviet Government denied the offensive character of the weapons, condemned the blockade as "piracy," and warned that Soviet ships would not honor it.[7] It was also reported that Defense Minister Malinovsky had been instructed to postpone planned demobilization, to cancel furloughs, and to alert all troops. Although the issue was immediately brought before the United Nations and the Organization of American States, the events of October 22–25 pointed to a possibly violent showdown in the Atlantic, in Cuba, or perhaps in other areas of the world. President Kennedy apparently expected some form of retaliation in Berlin. In his October 22 address he specifically warned the Soviet Union against any such move: "Any hostile move anywhere in the world against the safety and freedom of people to whom we are committed—including in particular the brave people of West Berlin—will be met by whatever action is needed."

The blockade went into effect at 10 a.m. Eastern Standard Time on October 24. At that time a fleet of 25 Soviet ships nearing Cuba was expected to test the American policy within hours. Statements from Moscow and Washington gave no immediate evidence that either side would retreat, although the Soviet Premier dispatched a letter to Bertrand Russell in which he called for a summit conference. The next day rumors of an American invasion of Cuba were strengthened by the announcement by Representative Hale Boggs that if the Soviet missiles were not removed the United States would destroy them: "if these missiles are not dismantled, the United States has the power to destroy them, and I assure you that this will be done."[8] At the same time American intelligence sources revealed that work on the erection of missile sites was proceeding at full speed.

The first real break in the chain of events leading to an apparently imminent confrontation came on October 25 when twelve Soviet vessels turned back in mid-Atlantic. It was at this point that Secretary of State Dean Rusk remarked, "We're eyeball to eyeball, and I think the other fellow just blinked."[9] Shortly thereafter the first Soviet ship to reach the blockade area—the tanker *Bucharest*—was allowed to proceed to Cuba without boarding and search.

By the following day the crisis appeared to be receding somewhat from its most dangerous level. The Soviet-chartered freighter, *Marucla* (ironically, a former American Liberty ship now under Lebanese registry), was searched without incident and, when no contraband was discovered, allowed to proceed to Cuba. In answer to an appeal from Secretary General U Thant, Soviet Premier Khrushchev had agreed to keep Soviet ships away from the blockade area for the time being. President Kennedy's reply to the Secretary stated that he would try to avoid any direct confrontation at sea "in the next few days." At the same time, however, the White House issued a statement which said: "The development of ballistic missile sites in Cuba continues at a rapid pace . . . The activity at these sites apparently is directed at achieving a full operational capability as soon as possible." The State Department added that "further action would be justified" if work on the missile sites continued. Photographic evidence revealed that such work was continuing at an increased rate and that the missile sites would be operational in five days.

The "bargaining phase" of the crisis opened later in the evening of October 26. A secret letter from Premier Khrushchev acknowledged the presence of Soviet missiles in Cuba for the first time.[10] He is reported to have argued they were defensive in nature but that he understood the President's feeling about them. According to one source, "Never explicitly stated, but embedded in the letter was an offer to withdraw the offensive weapons under United Nations supervision in return for a guarantee that the United States would not invade Cuba."[11] A second message from Premier Khrushchev, dispatched twelve hours later, proposed a trade of Soviet missiles in Cuba for NATO missile bases in Turkey; the United Nations Security Council was to verify fulfillment of both operations, contingent upon the approval of the Cuban and Turkish governments.

In his reply to Khrushchev's secret letter of Friday evening, the President all but ignored the later proposal to trade bases in Turkey for those in Cuba. At the Attorney General's suggestion, the President simply interpreted Premier Khrushchev's letter as a bid for an acceptable settlement.[12]

> As I read your letter, the key elements of your proposal—which seems generally acceptable as I understand them—are as follows:
> 1) You would agree to remove these weapons systems from Cuba under appropriate United Nations observation and supervision; and undertake, with suitable safeguards, to halt the further introduction of such weapons systems into Cuba.
> 2) We, on our part, would agree—upon the establishment of adequate arrangements through the United Nations to ensure the carrying out and continuation of these commitments—(a) to remove promptly the quarantine measures now in effect and (b) to give assurance against an invasion of Cuba.

He added, however, that,

> . . . the first ingredient, let me emphasize, . . . is the cessation of work on missile sites in Cuba and measures to render such weapons inoperable, under effective international guarantees. The continuation of this threat, or a prolonging of this discussion concerning Cuba by linking these problems to the broader questions of European and world security, would surely lead to an intensification of the Cuban crisis and a grave risk to the peace of the world.

In responding to Khrushchev's proposal to trade missile bases in Turkey for those in Cuba, a White House statement rejected that offer: "Several inconsistent and conflicting proposals have been made by the U.S.S.R. within the last 24 hours, including the one just made public in Moscow. . . . The first imperative must be to deal with this immediate threat, under which no sensible negotiation can proceed."

Despite the advent of negotiations, the probabilities of violence remained high. On October 27 an American U-2 reconnaissance plane had been shot down over Cuba, and several other planes had been fired upon. The Defense Department warned that measures would be taken to "insure that such missions are effective and protected." At the same time it was announced that twenty-four troop-carrier squadrons—14,000 men—were being recalled to active duty. The continued building of missile sites, which would be operational by the following Tuesday, was of even more concern. Theodore Sorensen, speaking of the events of October 27, said, "Obviously these developments could not be tolerated very long, and we were preparing for a meeting on Sunday [October 28] which would have been the most serious meeting ever to take place at the White House."[13]

On the following morning, however, Moscow Radio stated that the Soviet Premier would shortly make an important announcement. The message was broadcast in the clear to shortcut the time required by normal channels of communication.[14] Premier Khrushchev declared that,

> I regard with great understanding your concern and the concern of the United States people in connection with the fact that the weapons you describe as offensive are formidable indeed . . . The Soviet Government, in addition to earlier instruction on the discontinuation of further work on weapons construction sites, has given a new order to dismantle the arms which you describe as offensive, and to crate and return them to the Soviet Union.

The statement made no reference to the withdrawal of American missiles from Turkey.

In reply, President Kennedy issued a statement welcoming Premier Khrushchev's "statesmanlike decision." He added that the Cuban blockade would be removed as soon as the United Nations had taken "necessary measures," and further, that the United States would not invade Cuba. Kennedy said that he attached great importance to a rapid settlement of the Cuban crisis, because "developments were approaching a point where events could have become unmanageable." According to one source, all agreed that the Soviet missiles had to be removed or destroyed before they were operational; thus, an air strike against the missile sites was planned by no later than Tuesday, October 30.[15]

Although Khrushchev stated that the Soviet Union was prepared to reach an agreement on United Nations verification of the dismantling operation in Cuba, Fidel Castro announced on the same day that Cuba would not accept the Kennedy-Khrushchev agreement unless the United States accepted further conditions, including the abandonment of the naval base at Guantanamo. But the critical phases of the Soviet-American confrontation seemed to be over. Despite the inability to carry out on-site inspection, photographic surveillance of Cuba confirmed the dismantling of the missile sites. The quarantine was lifted on November 21, at which time the Pentagon announced that the missiles had indeed left Cuba aboard Soviet ships.

## THE INTERACTION MODEL

What research questions does the Cuban crisis suggest? The analyst of international relations may examine the events of October 1962 in such a manner as to permit relevant comparisons with other crisis situations, both those resolved by war and those eventually resolved by non-violent means. Are there, for example, patterns of behavior that distinguish the situation which escalates into general war—as in 1914—from those in which the process of escalation is reversed? This concern for comparable, replicable, and cumulative studies requires a model and research techniques which permit the student to investigate international transactions, examine how they were initiated and received, and compare those of October 1962 with others as widely separated in time and circumstance as the events leading to world war in 1914, and the continuing Arab Israeli conflict.

A conceptual framework developed for such analysis is a

two-step mediated stimulus-response model; S–r:s–R. Within the model the acts of one nation are considered as inputs to other nations. The nations are information processing and decision-making units whose output behavior (responses), in turn, can become inputs to other nations (Figure 1). The basic problem is this: given some action by Nation B, what addi-

FIGURE 1.
*The Interaction Model*

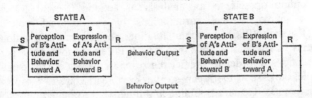

tional information is needed to account for Nation A's foreign policy response?

Within the model a stimulus (S) is an event in the environment which may or may not be perceived by a given actor, and which two or more actors may perceive and evaluate differently. A stimulus may be either a physical or a verbal act.

A response (R) is an action of an actor, without respect to his intent or how either he or other actors may perceive it. Both S's and R's are non-evaluative and non-affective. For example, during the early autumn of 1962, the Soviet Union began erecting launching sites for medium range ballistic missiles in Cuba (R). Regardless of the Soviet motives or intent behind this act, it served as an input or stimulus (S) to the United States, which responded by a series of steps, including the blockade of Cuba (R).

In the model the perception (r) of the stimulus (S) within the national decision system corresponds to the "definition of the situation" in the decision-making literature. (See Snyder et al. 1962, March and Simon 1958). For example, the Soviet missile sites in Cuba (S) were perceived by President Kennedy as a threat to the security of the Americas (r). Finally, the "s" stage in the model represents the actor's expression of his own intentions, plans, actions or attitudes toward another actor, which becomes an action response (R) when carried out. Both "r" and "s" carry evaluative and affective loadings.[16] Thus, irrespective of Russian intent, the Cuban missiles were perceived as a threat (r) by President Kennedy, who expressed American intent (s) to remove them from Cuba. This plan was put into effect by the blockade (r), which then served as an input (S) to the Soviet decision-makers.

Operationally it would be much simpler, of course, to confine oneself to an analysis of actions (S and R) as do many classical formulations of international politics (Rosenau 1966). In some situations the one nation's actions may be so unambiguous that there is little need to analyze perceptions in order to predict the response; consider, for example, the case of the Japanese attack on Pearl Harbor. Unfortunately, as Kenneth Boulding and others have pointed out, it is less clear that rewarding actions will lead to reciprocation.

In any case, not all—or even most—foreign policy behavior is consistent or unambiguous. For political behavior, what is "real" is what men perceive to be real. Boulding (1959, p. 120) has summarized this point succinctly:

We must recognize that the people whose decisions determine the policies and actions of nations do not respond to the "objective" facts of the situation, whatever that may mean, but to their "image" of the situation. It is what we think the world is like, not what it is really like, that determines our behavior.

At this point one might protest that surely well-trained statesmen will find little difficulty in interpreting the facts as they pertain to foreign policy. Yet one can cite example after example to the contrary. Consider, for example, the various interpretations—even among foreign policy professionals—which in the U.S.A. and other NATO countries almost inevitably follow nearly every turn in Soviet policy. Such problems of interpretations are encountered at every point in the stream of decisions which constitute foreign policy, and *mis*perceptions may have behavioral consequences as "real" as more accurate perceptions do.

If the real world for a President, Prime Minister or Foreign Secretary—and for their counterparts in friendly and hostile nations—is the world as they perceive it, perceptual variables are crucial in a conflict situation (North 1962). Thus, since all decision-making is rooted in the perceptions of individuals, our model attempts to assess both objective and subjective factors. Our research indicates the necessity of accounting for perceptual variables (North, Brody and Holsti 1964).

There have been serious doubts about the feasibility of quantifying perceptual and affective data, and the inclination, until recently, has been to emphasize "hard" variables and aggregate data; to measure gross national products and populations, or to count troops or planes or ships or megatons and assume that decision-makers respond to the "objective" value assigned to these capabilities by the investigator.

As important as these "objective" data are, they may fail to take into sufficient account how human beings react to these factors. Moreover, objective data are usually compiled on an annual, quarterly, or monthly basis. Thus, while these indices may well be relied upon to reveal the existence of an environment conducive to crisis (Richardson 1960, Wright 1957, Holsti 1963) such as Europe in 1914 or the Cold War since 1945—they may prove less useful for the intensive study of a short time period and for identifying human factors giving rise to conflict. Thus it is particularly important for the investigator who seeks to analyze short term changes in the international system—such as the crisis situation—to incorporate subjective data into his model.

Some objective indices—such as commodity futures, exchange rates and securities prices—are available on a day-to-day basis. A study of the 1914 data had revealed a striking correlation between fluctuations of the economic indices and such psycho-political variables as perceptions and expressions of hostility (Holsti and North 1965). These indices are particularly useful as an independent check on the validity of one's techniques of measurement, and will be incorporated into this analysis of the Cuban crisis.

## METHODOLOGY AND DATA

The premise that the analysis of political behavior is enriched by the incorporation of perceptual data poses special problems for the student of international relations. Clearly the standard method of attitude measurement—the personal interview, the questionnaire, or the direct observation of decision-makers in action—can rarely be used by the social scientist who seeks to study human behavior at the international level. What he needs are instruments for measuring attitudes and actions "at a distance." This is perhaps the primary rationale for settling upon the content analysis of the messages of key decision-makers—those who have the power to commit the resources of state to the pursuit of policy goals at the international level—as an important research tool.

Source materials used for the analysis of perceptions (s and r in the model) consist of 15 United States, 10 Soviet, and 10 Chinese documents, a total of approximately fifty thousand words, from the ten-day period opening on October 22—the day of President Kennedy's address on the Cuban crisis—and closing on October 31.[17] Whereas all Soviet and American documents focus on the situation in Cuba, five of the Chinese documents are concerned solely with the border fighting in India. After relevant decision-makers had been selected, *all publicly-available documents,* rather than a sample, were used. For example, President Kennedy, Secretaries Rusk and McNamara, Ambassador Stevenson, and Attorney General Kennedy were selected as the key American decision-makers. *The entire verbatim text of every available document* authored by these five persons during the ten-day period was included.

These documents were subjected to analysis by means of the General Inquirer system of automated content analysis via the IBM 7090 Computer (Stone et al. 1962). The Stanford version of the General Inquirer includes a dictionary which can be used to measure changes in verbalized perceptions—the "r" and the "s" sectors in the basic model—in terms of both frequency and intensity.

The Stanford General Inquirer is programmed to measure perceptions—as found in written documents—along three dimensions: strength—weakness, activity—passivity, positive affect—negative affect. These dichotomized dimensions correspond to the evaluative, potency, and activity dimensions which have been found to be primary in human cognition in a variety of cultures (Osgood et al. 1957, Suci 1957, Osgood

1962). The dictionary thus reflects the assumption that when decision-makers perceive themselves, other nations, events—or any stimulus—the most relevant discriminations are made in a space defined by these three factors. The computer can be used to analyze perceptual units defined in terms of the following elements: the *perceiver;* the perceived *agent* of action; the *action* or *attitude;* and the *target* of action. The components may be illustrated in a statement by President Kennedy (perceiver): "Soviet missiles [agent] threaten [action] all the Americas [target]." For the present analysis the computer has been instructed to measure the *action-attitude* component within a specified set of agent-target relationships involving the United States, Soviet Union, China and Cuba.

The scaling of action data (S and R in the model) was accomplished by the following technique. Three judges were given a set of cards concerning Soviet and American actions for the ten-day period October 22–31—the same period which encompasses all the publicly-available documents by key Soviet and American decision-makers. Each action was typed on a separate card and these were then aggregated on a day-to-day basis. Thus each judge was given a set of cards for both United States and Soviet actions, each set being subdivided into ten periods. The judges were instructed to rank order the events—using the day as the unit of analysis—for the degree of violence or potential violence. The Soviet and American actions were scaled separately largely because of the disparity of available data; published chronologies of American actions during the crisis period are detailed to almost an hourly basis, whereas the action data for the Soviet Union are relatively sparse.

The level of agreement between each pair of judges for scaling both Soviet and American actions was:

| Judge | A | B |
|-------|------|------|
| C | .800 | .883 |
|   | .891 | .842 |
|   |      |      |
| B | .967 |      |
|   | .939 |      |

The top figure is level of agreement for the scaling of Soviet action; the bottom figure is that for the scaling of United States action. All figures are significant at beyond the .01 level.

The scaling of action data (S and R in the model) resulted in the following ratings (1 is the highest level and 10 is the lowest level of violence or potential violence):[18]

### TABLE 1

*Scaling of Action Data*

| | October | | | | | | | | | |
|---|---|---|---|---|---|---|---|---|---|---|
| | 22 | 23 | 24 | 25 | 26 | 27 | 28 | 29 | 30 | 31 |
| United States | 2 | 3 | 1 | 4 | 5 | 6 | 7 | 9 | 10 | 8 |
| Soviet Union | 3 | 1 | 2 | 5 | 6 | 4 | 7 | 8 | 9 | 10 |

The perceptual data generated by the General Inquirer are combined with the scaled action data into the S–r:s–R model for the United States and the Soviet Union in Tables 2 and 3. It is apparent that Soviet and American actions during the period are closely correlated; that is, the actions for both sides are most violent or potentially violent in the first three days, followed by a relatively steady decline through October 31. The Spearman rank-order correlation between Soviet and American actions ($r = .89$) is significant at the .01 level.[19] The correlation coefficient should not be interpreted to indicate that the level of violence in the actions of each of the two parties was of equal magnitude; the separate scaling of Soviet and American actions precludes such an inference. Rather, it indicates that as the level of violence in the actions of one party increased or decreased, the actions of the other party tended to follow a similar pattern.

The input (S) and output (R) action may also be compared with the perceptual General Inquirer data (r and s). The pattern of perceptions was relatively consistent with the course of events surrounding the Cuban crisis.[20] In each case October 25–26—previously identified as the point dividing two phases of the crisis—was the point at which mutual perceptions appeared to change. The rigidly negative-strong-active perceptions of the period of highest danger became somewhat

## TABLE 2.
### Action and Perceptual Data—The United States

| Oct. 1962 | S | r | | | | | | s | | | | | | R |
|---|---|---|---|---|---|---|---|---|---|---|---|---|---|---|
| | | Positive | Negative | Strong | Weak | Active | Passive | Positive | Negative | Strong | Weak | Active | Passive | |
| 22 | 3* | 1.3‡ | 33.5 | 37.2 | 5.5 | 16.2 | 6.3 | 11.9 | 11.2 | 29.5 | 4.4 | 31.8 | 11.2 | 2 |
| 23 | 1 | 0.3 | 30.3 | 26.1 | 3.6 | 32.3 | 7.4 | 11.6 | 9.7 | 35.7 | 2.0 | 35.7 | 5.3 | 3 |
| 24 | 2 | | | | | | | | | | | | | 1 |
| 25 | 5 | 17.8 | 15.6 | 31.1 | 0.0 | 24.4 | 11.1 | 16.0 | 9.0 | 21.0 | 5.0 | 32.0 | 17.0 | 4 |
| 26 | 6 | 13.5 | 8.1 | 21.6 | 2.7 | 35.2 | 18.9 | 30.3 | 0.0 | 30.3 | 3.0 | 12.1 | 24.3 | 5 |
| 27 | 4 | 10.7 | 16.4 | 21.4 | 8.9 | 19.6 | 23.3 | 24.3 | 1.7 | 28.6 | 6.7 | 22.7 | 16.0 | 6 |
| 28 | 7 | 25.3 | 13.4 | 33.3 | 2.7 | 18.6 | 6.7 | 16.4 | 21.7 | 23.1 | 3.7 | 21.7 | 13.4 | 7 |
| 29 | 8 | | | | | | | | | | | | | 9 |
| 30 | 9 | | | | | | | | | | | | | 10 |
| 31 | 10 | | | | | | | | | | | | | 8 |

S — Soviet action
r — U.S. perceptions of Soviet action
s — U.S. statements of intent
R — U.S. action
\* The values for S and R are rank-order figures.
‡ The values for r and s are percentages of the total loading on the three dimensions.

## TABLE 3.
### Action and Perceptual Data—The Soviet Union

| Oct. 1962 | S | r | | | | | | s | | | | | | R |
|---|---|---|---|---|---|---|---|---|---|---|---|---|---|---|
| | | Positive | Negative | Strong | Weak | Active | Passive | Positive | Negative | Strong | Weak | Active | Passive | |
| 22 | 2* | | | | | | | | | | | | | 3 |
| 23 | 3 | 3.4‡ | 27.2 | 28.8 | 1.6 | 34.0 | 5.0 | 17.7 | 13.6 | 31.2 | 6.4 | 22.8 | 8.3 | 1 |
| 24 | 1 | 5.9 | 19.6 | 21.6 | 3.9 | 31.4 | 17.6 | 24.5 | 10.5 | 27.8 | 3.5 | 15.4 | 18.6 | 2 |
| 25 | 4 | 0.0 | 16.7 | 22.2 | 2.8 | 30.5 | 27.8 | 22.2 | 7.4 | 22.2 | 3.7 | 7.4 | 37.1 | 5 |
| 26 | 5 | 0.0 | 29.7 | 21.6 | 0.0 | 48.7 | 0.0 | 21.2 | 1.9 | 26.9 | 0.0 | 32.7 | 17.3 | 6 |
| 27 | 6 | 15.9 | 12.9 | 22.1 | 9.8 | 27.0 | 12.3 | 24.7 | 6.9 | 20.1 | 9.2 | 20.7 | 18.4 | 4 |
| 28 | 7 | 12.6 | 16.6 | 23.4 | 4.0 | 30.3 | 13.0 | 24.6 | 8.1 | 25.9 | 4.5 | 21.4 | 15.5 | 7 |
| 29 | 9 | | | | | | | | | | | | | 8 |
| 30 | 10 | | | | | | | | | | | | | 9 |
| 31 | 8 | | | | | | | | | | | | | 10 |

S — U.S. action
r — Soviet perceptions of U.S. actions
s — Soviet statements of intent
R — Soviet actions
\* The values for S and R are rank-order figures.
‡ The values for r and s are percentages of the total loading on the three dimensions.

modified at this point. Perceptions along the evaluative dimension became more neutral and, in some cases, actually became positive. As one would expect, during the latter days of the crisis there was also an increase in perceptions of passivity. The potency dimension, on the other hand, remained predominantly on the strong side throughout the crisis period.

Spearman rank-order correlation coefficients across various steps in the model are presented in Table 4.[21] The evaluative dimension is the most sensitive to behavioral changes; the highest correlation coefficients are consistently those for positive affect (positive correlation with decreasing violence).

Table 4 also reveals that there is a relatively close correspondence between the actions of the other party (S) and perceptions of the adversary's actions (r). By themselves these findings are hardly conclusive. When compared with a similar analysis of the crisis which escalated into World War I (Holsti, Brody, and North 1964), however, one interesting point emerges. The members of the Dual Alliance (Germany and Austria-Hungary) consistently reacted at a higher level of violence than did the members of the Triple Entente (Britain, France and Russia). At the same time, they also consistently overperceived (r) the level of violence in actions (S) taken by members of the Triple Entente. British, French and Russian decision-makers, on the other hand, underperceived (r) the level of violence in the actions of the Dual Alliance. In terms of the S–r:s–R model, this relationship between one coalition's actions (S), the other coalition's perceptions of those actions (r), and the resulting policies (R) was apparently the crucial one.

In the Cuban crisis, however, both sides tended to perceive (r) rather accurately the nature of the adversary's actions (S), and then proceeded to act (R) at an "appropriate" level; that is, as the level of violence or potential violence in the adversary's actions (S) diminished, perceptions of those actions (r) increased in positive affect and decreased in negative affect, and the level of violence in the resulting policies (R) also decreased. Thus, unlike the situation in 1914, efforts by either party to delay or reverse the escalation were generally perceived as such, and responded to in a like manner. Whether the different patterns of action and perception found in the

## TABLE 4
### Rank-Order Correlations Across S − r : s − R Model

| | SOVIET UNION (n=6) | | UNITED STATES (n=7) | |
|---|---|---|---|---|
| | U.S. Action (S) | Soviet Action (R) | Soviet Action (S) | U.S. Action (R) |
| **Perceptions of Other State (r)** | | | | |
| Positive | +.70 | −.07 | +.93 | +.71 |
| Negative | −.43 | −.20 | −.82 | −.79 |
| Strong | −.13 | −.13 | +.11 | −.25 |
| Weak | +.54 | +.09 | −.24 | +.17 |
| Active | −.43 | −.20 | −.18 | −.14 |
| Passive | −.31 | +.03 | +.18 | +.32 |
| **Self-Perceptions (s)** | | | | |
| Positive | +.66 | +.32 | +.79 | +.71 |
| Negative | −.31 | −.60 | −.11 | −.11 |
| Strong | −.31 | −.49 | +.46 | +.21 |
| Weak | +.20 | −.32 | +.29 | +.29 |
| Active | +.37 | +.14 | −.86 | −.71 |
| Passive | −.37 | +.03 | +.79 | +.54 |

1914 and Cuban cases will be found consistently to distinguish
crises that escalate and de-escalate, of course, can only be
determined through continuing research. . . .

However some further indirect analyses are possible. For
the purposes of comparison, all documents have been divided
into two periods—October 22–25 and October 26–31. The data
are further divided to distinguish between perceptions of one's
own actions toward others (s in the model), and the actions
of others toward oneself (r in the model). From the General
Inquirer output it was determined whether these actions were
perceived as positive or negative, strong or weak, and active or
passive, together with the intensity level of each. The results
yielded a series of fourfold contingency Tables.[22] Tables 6a
and 6b reinforce the earlier finding that both the United States
and the Soviet Union regarded *each other* as significantly less
negative during the latter stage of the crisis period. They also
regarded *themselves* as less negative toward the adversary
than during the first four days of the crisis. . . .[23]

TABLE 5

*Frequency of Appearance of Actors in Documents
Relating to Cuban Crisis*

| Date | UNITED STATES DOCUMENTS | | | SOVIET DOCUMENTS | | |
|---|---|---|---|---|---|---|
| | United States | Soviet Union | Cuba | United States | Soviet Union | Cuba |
| Oct. 22 | 54.5% | 37.2% | 8.3% | — | — | — |
| Oct. 23 | 45.8% | 34.6% | 19.6% | 59.6% | 29.8% | 10.5% |
| Oct. 24 | — | — | — | 27.5% | 71.0% | 1.5% |
| Oct. 25 | 61.1% | 38.9% | 0.0% | 60.5% | 39.5% | 0.0% |
| Oct. 26 | 40.9% | 59.1% | 0.0% | 53.9% | 46.1% | 0.0% |
| Oct. 27 | 41.0% | 59.0% | 0.0% | 41.8% | 48.2% | 10.0% |
| Oct. 28 | 57.8% | 41.4% | 0.8% | 30.8% | 65.7% | 3.5% |

DISCUSSION

Having utilized the S–r:s–R model to examine the pattern of Soviet and American interaction, it may be useful to attempt at least a partial explanation for the patterns with some
comparisons with the 1914 crisis. Such an analysis will be con-

## TABLE 6a

### United States Perceptions in the Early and Later Periods of the Crisis
### United States Perceptions of Soviet Actions

|  | October 22–25 | 26–31 |  | October 22–25 | 26–31 |  | October 22–25 | 26–31 |
|---|---|---|---|---|---|---|---|---|
| Positive Affect | 13* | 40 | Strong | 153 | 57 | Active | 153 | 47 |
| Negative Affect | 203 | 36 | Weak | 28 | 13 | Passive | 39 | 38 |
| $X^2 = 80.3$ | P = .001 |  | $X^2 = 0.1$ | P = n.s. |  | $X^2 = 15.7$ | P = .001 |  |

### United States Perceptions of United States Actions

|  | October 22–25 | 26–31 |  | October 22–25 | 26–31 |  | October 22–25 | 26–31 |
|---|---|---|---|---|---|---|---|---|
| Positive Affect | 106 | 61 | Strong | 149 | 75 | Active | 280 | 60 |
| Negative Affect | 90 | 31 | Weak | 31 | 14 | Passive | 79 | 45 |
| $X^2 = 4.2$ | P = .05 |  | $X^2 = 0.1$ | P = n.s. |  | $X^2 = 15.9$ | P = .001 |  |

*Figures are weighted (frequency × intensity) total.

## TABLE 6b

### Soviet Perceptions in the Early and Later Periods of the Crisis

#### Soviet Perceptions of United States Actions

| | October 22–25 | October 26–31 | | October 22–25 | October 26–31 | | October 22–25 | October 26–31 |
|---|---|---|---|---|---|---|---|---|
| Positive Affect | 16* | 50 | Strong | 176 | 85 | Active | 216 | 115 |
| Negative Affect | 163 | 61 | Weak | 12 | 23 | Passive | 46 | 43 |
| | $X^2 = 52.1$ | P = .001 | | $X^2 = 14.4$ | P = .001 | | $X^2 = 5.2$ | P = .05 |

#### Soviet Perceptions of Soviet Actions

| | October 22–25 | October 26–31 | | October 22–25 | October 26–31 | | October 22–25 | October 26–31 |
|---|---|---|---|---|---|---|---|---|
| Positive Affect | 76 | 128 | Strong | 127 | 127 | Active | 92 | 117 |
| Negative Affect | 56 | 35 | Weak | 21 | 29 | Passive | 46 | 85 |
| | $X^2 = 18.5$ P = .001 | | | $X^2 = 0.6$ P = n.s. | | | $X^2 = 2.6$ P = n.s. | |

*Figures are weighted (frequency × intensity) total.

cerned primarily with what might be called "styles of decision-making," and must of necessity be based on incomplete data. Although there are several accounts of the process by which American policy was formulated, such data with respect to the Soviet Union are much more fragmentary and inferential (Kolkowicz 1963, Horelick 1964).

One major characteristic of Soviet policy during this period is clear. Unlike German leaders in 1914, Premier Khrushchev did not irrevocably tie his policy to that of a weaker—and perhaps less responsible—ally. The Cuban response to President Kennedy's address of October 22 was stronger and more unyielding than that of the Soviet Union. Premier Castro in fact ordered a general war mobilization *prior to* the delivery of the President's speech. The following day Premier Castro in effect left no room for either Cuba or the Soviet Union to maneuver: "Whoever tries to inspect Cuba must come in battle array! This is our final reply to illusions and proposals for carrying out inspections on our territory." Premier Khrushchev, on the other hand, like President Kennedy, almost immediately chose to interpret the crisis as one involving the United States and the Soviet Union alone. In his correspondence with President Kennedy during October 26–28, it is also apparent that the Soviet Premier was unwilling to let the intransigence of Dr. Castro stand in the way of a possible solution of the crisis. In his letter of October 28, in which Khrushchev offered to withdraw the missiles, there was, in fact, no acknowledgment of the necessity to obtain Cuban agreement on the terms of the settlement.

American decision-making in regard to the missiles in Cuba was characterized by a concern for action based on adequate information. The resistance of the Administration against action—despite public pressure—until photographic evidence of the missile sites was available, has already been noted.[24] As late as Thursday, October 18, a series of alternatives was being considered pending more accurate information, and while the decision to institute a blockade was being hammered out, open discussion of the alternatives was encouraged. The President recalled that "though at the beginning there was a much sharper division . . . this was very valuable, because the people involved had particular responsibilities of their own."[25]

Another participant in the decision-making at the highest level wrote: "President Kennedy, learning on his return from a mid-week trip in October 1962, that the deliberation of the NSC [National Security Council] executive committee had been more spirited and frank in his absence, asked the committee to hold other preliminary sessions without him" (Sorensen 1963, p. 60). Thus despite the very real pressure of time —the missile sites would be operational by the end of the month—the eventual decision was reached by relatively open discussion. Group decision-making does not ensure the emergence of sound policy, of course, but it does limit the probability of a decision performing a personality-oriented function.[26]

Actually, it was not until Saturday, October 20—almost a week after the photographic evidence became available—that the general consensus developed. The President himself acknowledged that the interim period was crucial to the content of the final decision: "If we had had to act on Wednesday [October 17], in the first 24 hours, I don't think probably we would have chosen as prudently as we finally did, the quarantine against the use of offensive weapons."[27]

Another characteristic of the decision process in October 1962 was the very conscious concern for action at the very lowest level of violence—or potential violence—necessary to achieve the goals. J. William Fulbright and Richard B. Russell, both Democratic policy leaders in the Senate, were among those who urged immediate invasion of Cuba, a suggestion against which the President stood firm.[28] According to Kennedy, the decision to impose a blockade was based on the reasoning that "the course we finally adopted had the advantage of permitting other steps, if this one was unsuccessful. In other words, we were starting, in a sense, at a minimum place. Then, if that were unsuccessful, we could have gradually stepped it up until we had gone into a much more massive action which might have become necessary if the first step had been unsuccessful."[29] By this step, no irrevocable decisions had been made—a number of options remained.

The concern of the President and his advisers with maintaining a number of options was based at least in part on an explicit differentiation between a violent "bid" or threat (such as the blockade), and a violent commission. The use of threats has become a more or less accepted tool of international politics in the nearly two decades of cold warring. The United States and the Soviet Union, on the other hand, had systematically abstained from direct violent action against each other. The desire to avoid killing Soviet troops was an important factor in the decision to refrain from an air strike against Cuba.[30] Instead the blockade shifted the immediate burden of decision concerning the use of violence to Premier Khrushchev. Even if Soviet ships refused to honor the blockade, the initial American plan was to disable the rudders of the vessels, rather than to sink them (Bagdikian 1963, p. 6). . . .

American decision-makers also displayed a considerable concern and sensitivity for the position and perspective of the adversary as a vital variable in the development of the crisis. Unlike some of the key decision-makers in the 1914 crisis, those in October 1962 thought in terms of linked interactions —closely tied reciprocations—rather than two sides, each acting independently, *in vacuo*. Theodore Sorensen described the deliberation as follows: "We discussed what the Soviet reaction would be to any possible move by the United States, what our reaction with them would have to be to that Soviet reaction and so on, trying to follow each of those roads to their ultimate conclusion."[31]

This sensitivity for the position of the adversary was apparent in a number of important areas. There was a concern that Premier Khrushchev should not be rushed into an irrevocable decision; it was agreed among members of the decision group that "we should slow down the escalation of the crisis to give Khrushchev time to consider his next move."[32] There was, in addition, a conscious effort not to reduce the alternatives of *either* side to two—total surrender or total war. According to one participant, "President Kennedy, aware of the enormous hazards in the confrontation with the Soviets over Cuba in October 1962, made certain that his first move did not close out either all his options or all of theirs" (Sorensen 1963, pp. 20–21).

Sorensen (ibid., p. 22) added that:

The air strike or an invasion automatically meant a military attack upon a communist power and required almost cer-

tainly either a military response to the Soviet Union or an
even more humiliating surrender . . . The blockade on the
other hand had the advantage of giving Mr. Khrushchev a
choice, an option, so to speak, he did not have to have his
ships approach the blockade and be stopped and searched.
He could turn them around. So that was the first obvious advantage it had. It left a way open to Mr. Khrushchev. In this
age of nuclear weapons that is very important.

Thus, unlike the 1914 situation, in which at least one ultimatum was worded so as to be incapable of execution, there
was no demand which the Soviet Premier could not understand, none that he could not carry out, and none calculated to
humiliate him unduly. During the summer of 1914, by way of
contrast, there were numerous instances of failure on all three
of these important points. The Austro-Hungarian ultimatum
was deliberately worded in such a manner as to humiliate Ser-
bia and to provoke rejection. The policy of the other powers,
on the other hand, was hardly characterized by clarity. Russian decision-makers failed to communicate their initial desire
to deter Vienna rather than to provoke Berlin. This was
matched by England's inability to convey to German leaders
their intention to intervene should the local conflict engulf the
major continental powers.[33] And, in the culminating stages of
the crisis, decision-makers in the various capitals of Europe
made the very types of demands upon their adversaries—notably in regard to mobilizations—which they admitted they
could not reciprocate.[34]

NOTES

1. Stewart Alsop and Charles Bartlett, "In Time of Crisis," *Satur-day Evening Post* (Dec. 8, 1962), p. 16.
2. "He [President Kennedy] said to Mr. Khrushchev you go ahead and do whatever you want to in Cuba, you arm in any way you wish, and do anything you want to. We'll do nothing about it . . . ," NBC, "Cuba: The Missile Crisis" (Feb. 9, 1963), p. 8.
3. "I am sure the administration must have been fully aware of what has been going on for the past month and yet they have remained silent on the threat to our security now festering in Cuba," ibid.

4. "Cuban Crisis," *Data Digest,* p. 35.

5. CBS News, "A Conversation with President Kennedy" (Dec. 17, 1962), p. 2.

6. New York *Times* (Oct. 22, 1962).

7. William Knox, Chairman of Westinghouse Electric International, was told by Premier Khrushchev on October 24—the day the blockade went into effect—that "as the Soviet vessels were not armed the United States could undoubtedly stop one or two or more but then he, Chairman Khrushchev, would give instructions to the Soviet submarines to sink the American vessels," NBC, op. cit., p. 36.

8. New York *Times* (Nov. 3, 1962).

9. Alsop and Bartlett, op. cit., p. 16.

10. Subsequent to the original publication of this article, this communication from Khrushchev, along with all of his and Kennedy's correspondence on the crisis, was published in *Department of State Bulletin* LXIX, No. 1795 (Nov. 19, 1973), pp. 635–55.

11. New York *Times* (Nov. 3, 1962).

12. Alsop and Bartlett, op. cit., p. 18.

13. NBC, op. cit., p. 42.

14. "During the Cuban crisis, it took four hours, with luck, for a formal message to pass between Kennedy and Khrushchev. Any such message had to be carried physically from the head of state to the local embassy, translated, coded, transmitted, decoded on the other side, and carried to the other leader" (Bagdikian 1963, p. 6).

15. Alsop and Bartlett, op. cit., p. 18.

16. A number of factors—including those of personality, role, organization and system—will affect the perceptual variables in the model. A further elaboration may be found in (Holsti, Brody, and North 1964, Chs. 1–2).

17. The present analysis is concerned primarily with Soviet-American interactions. Chinese data briefly analyzed in the original article has been left out here.

18. A more complete description of the research techniques may be found in Holsti 1964.

19. Sidney Spiegel, *Non-Parametric Statistics for Behavioral Sciences* (New York: McGraw-Hill, 1956), Table P.

20. The reader may wonder why, in Table 2, the highest level of negative affect in the "s" sector of the model is found on October 28, the day of the Kennedy-Khrushchev agreement. This result is due primarily to President Kennedy's expressions of regret about an American weather airplane straying over Soviet territory; many of the words used by the President are "tagged" for negative affect in the General Inquirer dictionary.

21. Because there are no United States perceptual data for October 24, the average of the values of October 23 and 25 has been used for the purpose of calculating the correlation coefficients in Table 4.

22. The cell entries, which are based on a weighted (frequency × intensity) total, are independent of each other. The frequency and intensity of positive actions, for example, have no bearing on the number of actions which are rated negative. Nor can a single action word be entered in both the positive and negative cells; no dictionary entry is tagged for both ends of a single dimension.

23. The figures on Tables 6a and 6b support other studies which have found the evaluative dimension of cognition to be the most important (Osgood et al. 1957). It is also true, however, that the activity dimension provides rather consistent discrimination between the early and later periods of the crisis. Inasmuch as there was little, if any, actual change in Soviet and American capabilities during the short period under investigation, it is not surprising that perceptions of potency show little variation.

24. McGeorge Bundy recalled that upon receiving the first news of the photographic evidence, "his [President Kennedy's] first reaction was that we must make sure, and were we making sure? And would there be evidence on which he could decide that this was in fact really the case" (NBC, op. cit., p. 14).

25. CBS, op. cit., p. 4.

26. Verba 1961, p. 103. In this respect the contrast to many of the crucial decisions made in 1914 is striking. That the German Kaiser underwent an almost total collapse at the time he made a series of key decisions—the night of July 29–30—is evident from a reading of his marginal notes. Max Montgelas and Walter Schücking, *Outbreak of the World War,* New York: Oxford University Press, 1924.

27. CBS, op. cit., pp. 2–3. Despite the relative lack of speed—with the possible exception of the German army—with which European weapons systems could be mobilized in 1914, decision-makers in the various capitals of Europe perceived that time was of crucial importance—and they acted on that assumption. The Kaiser, for example, immediately upon learning of Russia's mobilization (which had been intended only to deter Austria-Hungary), ordered: "In view of the colossal war preparations of Russia now discovered, this is all too late, I fear. Begin! Now!" (Montgelas and Schücking 1924, p. 368). One can only speculate on the outcome had there been some delay in the making of such decisions in 1914.

28. NBC, op. cit., p. 30. According to one top official, "invasion was hardly ever seriously considered," New York *Times* (Nov. 3, 1962).

29. CBS, op. cit., p. 4.

30. NBC, op. cit., p. 22.

31. NBC, op. cit., p. 20. President Kennedy and others were aware of the possibility of misperception by their counterparts in the Kremlin, "Well now, if you look at the history of this century where World War I really came through a series of misjudgments of the intentions of others . . . it's very difficult to always make judgments here about what the effect will be of our decisions on other countries" (CBS, op. cit., p. 3).

32. NBC, op. cit., p. 19.

33. The failure of communication was not, of course, solely attributable to the sender. The Kaiser, for example, consistently dismissed the warnings of his able ambassador in London, Prince Lichnowsky.

34. For example, both the Kaiser and the Tsar demanded that the other stop mobilizing. Nicholas replied that, "it is technically impossible to stop our military preparations" (Montgelas and Schücking 1924, p. 402). At the same time Wilhelm wrote: "On technical grounds my mobilization which has already been proclaimed this afternoon must proceed against two fronts, east and west" (ibid., p. 451).

# 2. SOVIET-AMERICAN BEHAVIOR IN DISARMAMENT NEGOTIATIONS*

## Lloyd Jensen, Temple University[1]

To begin an analysis of the meandering course of the postwar disarmament negotiations with a bargaining model is perhaps the height of optimism. Some would doubt the utility of such a model because they regard the negotiations primarily as parallel monologues in which the basic appeals are made to the galleries of world public opinion rather than across the table to the opposition. It further has been asserted that the negotiations have been "utilized as diplomatic weapons to achieve certain aims that are not primarily concerned with a reduction of armaments" (Nogee and Spanier 1962, p. 6). Without denying that both the United States and the Soviet Union have used the negotiations for many different purposes, I want specifically to concentrate upon the negotiations in terms of what I consider to be the most important goal of all—the reaching of agreement on disarmament.

* "Soviet-American Bargaining Behavior in Postwar Disarmament Negotiations" by Lloyd Jensen is reprinted from *Journal of Conflict Resolution* VI (Sept. 1963), No. 3, pp. 522–41, and "Approach-Avoidance Bargaining in the Test-Ban Negotiations" by Lloyd Jensen is reprinted from *International Studies Quarterly* XII (June 1968), No. 2, pp. 152–60, by permission of the publisher (of both journals), Sage Publications, Inc.

### THE PROPENSITY TO COMPROMISE ON DISARMAMENT

The essence of effective bargaining is a willingness to make concessions in order to enhance agreement. Concessions thus provide one possible indicator of the propensity of a nation to negotiate seriously on disarmament, and as such they furnish a means for analyzing bargaining in the postwar disarmament negotiations.

In an effort to compare the two sides' propensities to compromise, I attempted to collect all concessions and their counterparts, retractions, which were made during the postwar negotiations. The technique used was to abstract and to study all disarmament proposals sponsored or co-sponsored by either the United States or the Soviet Union in order to detect any fundamental changes of position on the various issues of disarmament. Such a change might be in the direction of a concession to the position of the opposition, or it might be a retraction in the form of a reversal from a more acceptable position to a less acceptable one as far as the other side was concerned. The search, however, was not confined to formal proposals, since many reversals in bargaining positions were found in the debates themselves. These changes also were included, provided that they were not merely a slip of the tongue or a negotiator exceeding his instructions. To guard against this danger, the concession or retraction must have been repeated several times during a round of negotiations. Although every attempt was made to be all-inclusive, it was decided at the outset to restrict the list to changes of a substantive nature directly related to the proposed disarmament treaty. Procedural concessions and retractions, such as those which might change the size or debating rules of the negotiating body, were not included. The results of this listing will be found in Tables 1 and 2.

It would have been misleading to have measured a nation's propensity to compromise simply by counting the number of concessions and subtracting from that the number of retractions from previously held positions which that nation made during a particular round of negotiations. There are obviously important qualitative differences as well. To take account of

# TABLE 1

## U.S.S.R. Propensity to Compromise — All Postwar Disarmament Negotiations (1946-60)

| U.S.S.R. Concessions and Retractions | Document | Date | Mag. |
|---|---|---|---|
| Drops insistence on national legislation as main inspection device. | p. 42* | 11-29-46 | 5 |
| Agrees to policy of submitting information on own armed forces at home as well as in foreign countries. | p. 42 | 11-29-46 | 2 |
| Day-to-day decisions of control agency to be made by majority. | A/C.1/SR38 p. 257 | 12- 4-46 | 5 |
| Agrees to periodic inspection. | pp. 61-64 | 2-18-47 | 4 |
| Ban on possession doesn't include destruction in 3 months. | pp. 61-64 | 2-18-47 | 3 |
| Agrees to "inspection, supervision, and *management*" of all atomic plants. | p. 61 | 2-18-47 | 2 |
| Delete word "management" (retraction) | p. 73 | 3- 5-47 | −2 |
| Inspection system to include mining facilities. | p. 86 | 6-11-47 | 2 |
| Inspection personnel selected on an international basis. | p. 86 | 6-11-47 | 3 |
| International Control Commission to conduct peaceful atomic research. | p. 88 | 6-11-47 | 2 |
| Special investigation permitted in cases of suspicious events. | p. 87 | 6-11-47 | 3 |
| Simultaneous conclusion of prohibition and control treaties. | p. 178 | 10- 2-48 | 4 |
| Continuous inspection. | AEC/C.1 PV. 46 | 6- 3-49 | 5 |
| 3-month limit to destroy atomic weapons (retraction). | p. 225 | 10-25-49 | −3 |
| Drops reference to 3-month limit for destroying atomic bombs. | pp. 248-50 | 10-23-50 | 3 |
| First proposal envisaging one control organ for both nuclear and conventional weapons. | pp. 332-33 | 12-11-51 | 3 |
| Agrees to control provisions and atomic disarmament in same resolution. | A/C.1/ SR. 464 | 12-12-51 | 4 |

TABLE 1 *(Cont.)*

## U.S.R. Propensity to Compromise — All Postwar Disarmament Negotiations (1946-60)

| U.S.S.R. Concessions and Retractions | Document | Date | Mag. |
|---|---|---|---|
| Agrees to use Anglo-French proposal of June 11, 1954, as basis for discussion. | p. 431 | 9-30-54 | 1 |
| First time for stages. | pp. 431-33 | 9-30-54 | 5 |
| Agrees to continuous inspection but without reference to domestic jurisdiction. | p. 432 | 9-30-54 | 3 |
| Reduction of armed forces without specifying ⅓ reductions—hint of acceptance of fixed ceilings. | p. 432 | 9-30-54 | 2 |
| 50% reduction of agreed conventional force reductions before nuclear prohibition. | p. 432 | 9-30-54 | 3 |
| Instructs Disarmament Commission to study proposal of U.K. and France banning the use of atomic weapons but with the right to use them in self-defense against aggression. | pp. 432-33 | 9-30-54 | 1 |
| Separate control organs for conventional and nuclear arms—former to be temporary (retraction). | p. 432 | 9-30-54 | −3 |
| Calls for immediate agreement on destruction of nuclear weapons (retraction). | DC/SC.1 PV. 23 | 3- 1-55 | −3 |
| Returns to proposing ⅓ reduction for convention and armed forces (retraction). | DC/SC.1 PV. 31, 175 | 3-22-55 | −2 |
| Signed convention providing for use ban no longer a precondition for disarmament. | DC/SC.1 PV. 36, 291 | 3-30-55 | 3 |
| Nuclear possession ban after 75% of the conventional reductions complete. | p. 463 | 5-10-55 | 3 |
| Agrees to force level of 1—1.5 million for U.S.-U.S.S.R.-China. | p. 461 | 5-10-55 | 3 |
| Stresses need for political settlement. | p. 465 | 5-10-55 | 2 |
| Nuclear production ban begins before possession ban, i.e., at very beginning of second stage. | p. 463 | 5-10-55 | 3 |

# TABLE 1 *(Cont.)*

### U.S.S.R. Propensity to Compromise — All Postwar Disarmament Negotiations (1946-60)

| U.S.S.R. Concessions and Retractions | Document | Date | Mag. |
|---|---|---|---|
| Ground inspection control posts. | pp. 464-67 | 5-10-55 | 5 |
| Access to budgetary records. | p. 467 | 5-10-55 | 2 |
| No longer insists upon separate control organs for nuclear and conventional weapons. | pp. 464-67 | 5-10-55 | 3 |
| Admits difficulties of preventing clandestine production and detecting hidden nuclear stockpiles. | p. 464 | 5-10-55 | 2 |
| Nuclear weapons may be used for defensive purposes with permission of Security Council. | p. 485 | 7-21-55 | 3 |
| Will consider aerial inspection for final stage. | p. 516 | 9-19-55 | 1 |
| Agrees to establishment of control system pending the initiation of arms reduction. | p. 606 | 3-27-56 | 4 |
| Accepts 2.5 million and 750,000 level for first-stage forces (non-Big Five limited to 150-200,000 men). | DC/PV. 57 p. 14 | 7-12-56 | 2 |
| Officially accepts aerial inspection: 800 kilometers each side of line dividing east and west. | p. 727 | 11-17-56 | 4 |
| Agrees to unilateral obligations not to use nuclear weapons (no convention needed). | p. 754 | 3-18-57 | 3 |
| Drops insistence on 200,000 level for forces of lesser powers. | p. 781 | 4-30-57 | 3 |
| Aerial inspection extended to include eastern Siberia for Alaska and western U.S., also a little beyond 800 kilometers to the east. | pp. 784-85 | 4-30-57 | 2 |
| Control posts at airfields only in second stage, along with nuclear disarmament (retraction). | p. 783 | 4-30-57 | −2 |
| Accepts 2.5—2.1—1.7 million armed force levels (but with no conditions such as political settlement). | p. 822 | 7-19-57 | 3 |

TABLE 1 *(Cont.)*

## U.S.S.R. Propensity to Compromise — All Postwar Disarmament Negotiations (1946-60)

| U.S.S.R. Concessions and Retractions | Document | Date | Mag. |
|---|---|---|---|
| Five-year nuclear weapons use ban pending agreement (retraction). | pp. 877-78 | 9-20-57 | —3 |
| Agrees to reduce armaments according to mutual lists. | p. 877 | 9-20-57 | 2 |
| Fails to stress ban on foreign bases, would discuss possibility of *limiting*. | p. 882 | 9-20-57 | 1 |
| Indicated acceptance of idea of international disarmament depots for the storage of arms. | Cited by Lodge, p. 895 | N.S. | 2 |
| Aerial inspection of all of U.S.S.R. after abolition of atomic weapons and substantial conventional reductions. | p. 1025 | 5- 5-58 | 2 |
| Aerial inspection to include Turkey, Iran, Japan in addition to territories of 4-30-57 (also back to 800-kilometer extensions—retraction). | p. 1598 | 11-28-58 | —1 |
| First commitment on numbers of control posts: Warsaw, 28; West, 54 (includes 6 each for U.S. and U.S.S.R.) | p. 1267 | 11-28-58 | 2 |
| NATO and Warsaw aerial inspection groups to photograph own side, but must include representatives of the other side (retraction). | p. 1301 | 12-12-58 | —2 |
| Equal representation of sides in the International Supervisory Body and the Control Posts (retraction). | pp. 1298-1302 | 12-12-58 | —2 |
| If West doesn't agree to comprehensive measures, may accept partial measures, including those suggested 5-10-55. | p. 1474 | 9-19-59 | 2 |
| Four-year time limit for GCD (retraction). | p. 1471 | 9-19-59 | —3 |
| Extensive conventional disarmament in first stage, i.e., 1.7 million level (retraction). | p. 1471 | 9-19-59 | —2 |
| Aerial inspection relegated to third stage (retraction). | p. 1473 | 9-19-59 | —3 |

## TABLE 1 *(Cont.)*

### U.S.S.R. Propensity to Compromise — All Postwar Disarmament Negotiations (1946-60)

| U.S.S.R. Concessions and Retractions | Document | Date | Mag. |
|---|---|---|---|
| Cut-off in nuclear production in second stage instead of third. | p. 109 | 6- 2-60 | 3 |
| More flexible on four-year timetable but limit must be specified. | p. 104 | 6- 2-60 | 3 |
| Place militia at disposal of Security Council where necessary. | p. 111 | 6- 2-60 | 3 |
| Moves production-possession ban on delivery systems from third to first stage. | p. 107 | 6- 2-60 | 0 |
| Moves ban on foreign bases from second to first stage (retraction). | p. 107 | 6- 2-60 | -3 |
| Permanent control teams at some plants. | p. 108 | 6- 2-60 | 3 |
| On-site inspection over disbanding of troops and destruction of armaments. | pp. 108 ff. | 6- 2-60 | 3 |
| 1.7 million level moved to second stage. | p. 109 | 6- 2-60 | 2 |
| Period between signature and ratification should be used for taking practical steps to establish control organ. | TNCD PV. 38 | 6-14-60 | 3 |
| Khrushchev: "As for control over the destruction of armaments and disarmament, let the United States propose a system of such control. We shall accept whatever proposals the U.S. will make. . . ." | Cited by Zorin, A/C.1/ PV. 1089 p. 62 | 9- 9-60 | 3 |
| 1.7 million level moved back to first stage (retraction). | p. 244 | 9-23-60 | -2 |
| Proposes troika for U.N. Secretariat and Security Council. The agents of enforcement in Soviet plans (retraction). | p. 298 | 10-13-60 | -3 |

*Unless otherwise noted, page numbers refer to pages in U.S. Department of State, <u>Documents on Disarmament 1945-59</u>, publication 7008 (1960), and ibid, <u>1960</u>, publication 7172 (1961).

## TABLE 2

### U.S. Propensity to Make Concessions — All Postwar Disarmament Negotiations (1946-60)

| U.S. Concessions and Retractions | Document | Date | Mag. |
|---|---|---|---|
| International control system may operate in framework of Security Council. Unless otherwise specified, no sanctions without agreement of permanent members. | p. 49* | 12-14-46 | 4 |
| Ownership and management of large-scale mining and industrial operations *re* thorium and uranium unnecessary. | pp. 52-53 | 12-31-46 | 4 |
| Quotas *re* ownership of nuclear materials will be put into Treaty rather than left to discretion of International Agency. | p. 97 | 9-11-47 | 4 |
| Production of nuclear fuels to be restricted to that required for plants actually entering into construction. | p. 98 | 9-11-47 | 3 |
| Controls limiting powers of the Agency, e.g., procedure for warrants, restrictions on inspector's behavior, etc. | pp. 140-47 | 9-11-47 | 2 |
| Less emphasis upon punishment of violators and more upon establishing effective warning system in case of violations. | pp. 93-152 | 9-11-47 | 2 |
| Security Council to be primarily responsible for sanctions involving violation of conventional arms agreement. | p. 235 | 5-18-50 | 3 |
| Disclosure in each stage of both nuclear and conventional weapons. | pp. 346-56 | 4- 5-52 | 2 |
| Staging made more specific, making clearer how it would lead to atomic disarmament. | pp. 346-56 | 4- 5-52 | 2 |
| Not as adamant about U.N. Plan— will support only until better plan devised (or as good). | pp. 346-56 | 4- 5-52 | 2 |
| Softens meaning of "ownership," suggesting several restraints on ownership powers. | DC/C.1/ PV. 6 | 5-14-52 | 3 |

## TABLE 2 *(Cont.)*

### *U.S. Propensity to Make Concessions — All Postwar Disarmament Negotiations (1946-60)*

| U.S. Concessions and Retractions | Document | Date | Mag. |
|---|---|---|---|
| Commits self on reduction levels, e.g., 1—1.5 million, 700 to 800 thousand for U.K. and France (conditional on political settlement, e.g., Korea). | p. 366 | 5-28-52 | 2 |
| Accepts veto with regard to conventional and atomic reductions—physical sanctions only in accordance with Chapter VII of Charter. | DC/SC.1/ PV. 4 | 5-17-54 | 5 |
| Abandoned procedure of getting General Assembly approval of Western resolutions—worked out compromise with Soviets—first unanimous disarmament resolution since 1946. | GA Res. 808 (IX) pp. 444-46 | 11- 4-54 | 3 |
| Nuclear *possession* ban may begin before conventional arms reduced (i.e., after 75% of agreed conventional reductions) | p. 454 | 4-19-55 | 3 |
| Eisenhower's departure from disarmament to open skies (retraction). | pp. 486-88 | 7-21-55 | −5 |
| Reservation placed on all past United States proposals (retraction). | p. 513 | 9- 6-55 | −5 |
| Opposes nuclear-production-possession ban unless better inspection techniques can be developed (clearly didn't expect much in this regard—retraction). | pp. 523-25 | 10- 7-55 | −4 |
| Agrees to production ban if satisfactory progress on effective inspection system. | p. 594 | 3-19-56 | 3 |
| Calls for limited inspection zones, demonstration test area. | pp. 600-01 | 3-21-56 | 2 |
| Devises plan for first phase of a comprehensive plan: forces 2.5 million and 750 thousand. | pp. 608-13 | 4- 3-56 | 1 |
| Proposes limits on nuclear possession by transferring to peaceful uses. | p. 613 | 4- 3-56 | 2 |
| 10% expenditure reduction in first stage. 15% for second stage. | DC/SC.1/ PV. 99 | 4- 8-57 | 1 |

## TABLE 2 *(Cont.)*

### U.S. Propensity to Make Concessions — All Postwar Disarmament Negotiations (1946-60)

| U.S. Concessions and Retractions | Document | Date | Mag. |
|---|---|---|---|
| Proposes second stage reductions of 2.1 million level for armed forces. | DC/SC.1/ PV. 124 | 6-20-57 | 2 |
| Third stage force reduction—1.7 million level (conditional on political settlement). | p. 798 | 6-25-57 | 2 |
| Will transfer 53% of nuclear materials to peaceful uses compared to Soviets' 47%. | DC/SC.1/ PV. 130 | 7- 5-57 | 1· |
| Package proposal made inseparable (retraction). | p. 874 | 8-29-57 | −3 |
| Alternative aerial inspection zones: (1) All U.S.-Canada for U.S.S.R. (2) Arctic inspection zone. (3) Linked with one of the above would be an all-European and significant amount of western Russia. | pp. 872-3 | 8-29-57 | 2 |
| First GCD plan. | pp. 68-71 | 3-16-60 | 4 |
| First unequivocal statement on possession ban since 1955 reservation. | pp. 81-82 | 4-26-60 | 3 |
| Agrees to reduce forces as low as 1.7 million for second stage—third stage to internal security level. | p. 130 | 6-27-60 | 3 |

*Unless otherwise noted, page numbers refer to pages in U.S. Department of State, <u>Documents on Disarmament 1945-59</u>, publication 7008 (1960), and ibid, <u>1960</u>, publication 7172 (1961).

these differences I have weighted concessions from 1 to 5 in which a magnitude of 5 would be a very important concession and 1 would be quite insignificant. Retractions were also ranked from −1 to −5 in which the −5 would be the most severe retraction. In those cases where a concession was made conditional upon a retraction, the procedure used was to weight the two as if separate, then to calculate the difference. If the difference was a minus, it would be a retraction; if a plus, it would be a concession. This left the possibility of the two cancelling each other out at 0. After developing certain guidelines for ranking the importance of concessions and retractions, I decided upon the magnitudes shown in the right-hand columns of the two tables. These in turn were checked for reliability by an independent coder.[2]

The lines separating the various concessions in the two tables were added to denote different rounds of negotiations in order that a weighted score of compromising behavior might be established. Table 3 then represents the final results of this tabulation. The choice point is the month in which the negotiations ended, and includes all concessions and retractions made since the previous round of negotiations. Thus, for example, in the period ending December, 1946, the Soviet Union scored a total magnitude of 12 on concessions as compared to the United States 8. These data have been represented graphically in Figure 1.

## TABLE 3

### The Propensity of Compromise — All Postwar Disarmament Negotiations* (1945-60)

| Date Ending | U.S.S.R. | U.S. | Date Ending | U.S.S.R. | U.S. |
|---|---|---|---|---|---|
| December 1946 | 12 | 8 | May 1955 | 21 | 3 |
| September 1947 | 17 | 11 | October 1955 | 4 | −14 |
| October 1948 | 4 | 0 | January 1956 | 0 | 0 |
| July 1949 | 5 | 0 | May 1956 | 4 | 8 |
| November 1950 | 0 | 3 | January 1957 | 6 | 0 |
| December 1951 | 7 | 0 | September 1957 | 11 | 5 |
| August 1952 | 0 | 11 | December 1957 | 0 | 0 |
| April 1953 | 0 | 0 | December 1958 | −1 | 0 |
| November 1953 | 0 | 0 | November 1959 | −6 | 0 |
| July 1954 | 0 | 5 | June 1960 | 14 | 10 |
| October 1954 | 12 | 3 | November 1960 | −2 | 0 |

*Weighted Concession Score per negotiating round.

One should be careful not to read too much into these figures, which seem to indicate that the Soviet Union has a greater propensity to negotiate seriously on disarmament, since its concession score is frequently higher than that of the United States. This situation may be due only to the tendency of the Soviet Union to begin a round of negotiations with a more extreme bargaining position than it is willing to accept, later making concessions to show public opinion that it is negotiating seriously.

Two major patterns of concession-making appear to predominate, as illustrated in Figure 1. The first of these is the

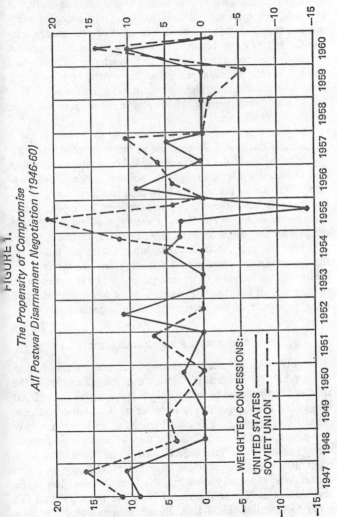

FIGURE 1.
The Propensity of Compromise
All Postwar Disarmament Negotiation (1946-60)

WEIGHTED CONCESSIONS:
UNITED STATES ———
SOVIET UNION — — —

tendency for concessions to be reciprocated during the same round, as occurred during 1946 through 1948 and in 1957 and 1960. The second pattern shows a delayed reaction of one round before concessions were reciprocated, as in 1949 through 1952. A general proposition would seem to be that if concessions are not reciprocated during a given round of negotiations, then a nation will reduce its level of concessions during the next round—hence the tendency to show an inverse correlation in concession scores. But whichever of these two patterns is followed, it appears that the making of concessions plays a very important role in terms of inducing the opposition to be more compromising, whether within that same round or in the following one.

The year 1955, however, is more difficult to explain. It looks almost as if the Soviet Union made so many concessions in the spring meetings of the Disarmament Subcommittee in London that the United States thought its position needed re-evaluation. If the Soviet Union were beginning to accept some of the Western proposals, then these proposals must have been disadvantageous to the West. Such is the type of reasoning that exists only too often on both sides of the Iron Curtain. But whatever the motivations of the United States on this issue, this reversal casts some doubt upon the seriousness that the United States attached to its own proposals, or it represents a serious lack of homework in analyzing the full implications of those proposals before they were officially presented.

## THE POLITICS OF COMPROMISE

Having charted the propensity of the two sides to compromise on disarmament, let us examine more closely the role that compromise has played in their respective operational bargaining codes, specifically in terms of the timing and purposes of concessions. Effective bargaining requires not only that concessions be made, but that they be made at a strategic time. The two sides have differed sharply in terms of at what point in a set of negotiations they are most likely to make concessions. Generally speaking, the United States has made concessions earlier in the round than the Soviet Union. In order to calculate this, I took all concessions and retractions

## TABLE 4

*Percentage of Concessions Made During Each Third of
Seven Select Rounds of Postwar Negotiations*

| | First Third | | Second Third | | Final Third | |
|---|---|---|---|---|---|---|
| | U.S. | U.S.S.R. | U.S. | U.S.S.R. | U.S. | U.S.S.R. |
| Number of Concessions | 58%* | 15% | 25% | 15% | 17% | 70% |
| Weighted Concession Score | 82% | 14% | 14% | 12% | 5% | 75% |

*After compensating for retractions, N = 12 concessions for U.S.
and 22 for U.S.S.R. When weighted, concession scores were 20 for U.S.
and 51 for the Soviets.

made during seven select rounds of negotiations which
included meetings of the Disarmament Subcommittee, the
Surprise Attack Conference, and the Ten-Nation Disarmament
Conference. Other negotiating bodies were excluded from this
analysis because they usually did not extend over a long
enough period to justify breaking concessions into the time
units in which they occurred or they were interrupted by
debates on other subjects.

To ascertain whether a nation tended to present its concessions early or late during a debating round, I divided each of
the seven rounds chronologically into thirds. For example, if
the round lasted 45 days, each third would be 15 days. The
next step was to divide both the number of concessions and
their weighted concession scores according to whether they
were presented in the first, second, or third period of the
round. The results showed that in the seven negotiating rounds
analyzed, the United States made a net total (adjusted for retractions) of 12 concessions compared to 22 for the Soviet
Union. When weighted, the net scores showed a total magnitude of 20 for the United States and 51 for the U.S.S.R. In
Table 4, I have converted these figures into percentages for
each of the three periods.

Thus the United States made 58 per cent of its concessions
during the first one-third of the negotiating round as contrasted with the Soviets' 15 per cent. In terms of a weighted
concession score, the figures were even more remarkable with
the United States making 82 per cent of its total concession

score during the *first* third of the seven rounds of negotiation compared with the Soviet score of 75 per cent of the *last* third of these same negotiations.

The question naturally arises as to why such extreme differences between the two sides have persisted with regard to the times at which they make concessions. One explanation might be that the United States is more predisposed than the Soviet Union toward making concessions, but after a time, when these concessions have not been reciprocated, it becomes disillusioned with the bargaining process and wants to terminate it. The Soviets, on the other hand, in an effort to have the debate continued, and particularly to prevent others from placing the blame for the breakdown of the negotiations upon the Soviet Union, have tended to make a number of last-minute compromises.

Concession-making of this nature is hardly conducive to good bargaining. When concessions are widely separated time-wise in the negotiations, the side which is making the bulk of the concessions without much reciprocation, other than hostility, is likely to become rapidly disillusioned with the negotiations. Far more effective bargaining could be established if concessions by both sides were staggered throughout the negotiations.

Another important aspect of effective compromise is a demonstrated willingness to react favorably to conciliatory moves on the part of the opposition. I chose in this case to examine the modes of reactions to concessions in the Geneva Test Ban Negotiations since it was impossible to do a similar analysis of the regular postwar disarmament negotiations due to the diffuse and sporadic nature of concession-making in the latter.

It is possible for a nation to react at least three ways to a concession: it may reject it because it does not go far enough; it may offer its own compromise without entirely accepting the position of the opposition; or it may accept the concession in its entirety. The results showed that out of 42 Soviet concessions made during the course of the Test Ban Conference, the United States agreed to 18 without modification, rejected 5, and compromised with regard to 19 of them. The Soviet record was somewhat less impressive, for out of a total of 44 American concessions the Soviets accepted only 14, while rejecting 20 concessions without qualification. The remaining 10 concessions led to compromise proposals by the Soviet Union. Translating this into percentages, we find that the Soviets rejected unconditionally 45 per cent of all United States concessions made during the Test Ban Conference as contrasted with United States rejection of only 12 per cent of the Soviet concessions. Thus it has been the United States which has been the more likely to reward compromising behavior either by accepting the compromise *in toto* or by offering to bridge the gap further with a concession of its own on the particular issue at stake.

A recent study has suggested that the major reason for rejecting compromise proposals of the other side has been due to the tendency of both sides to combine concessions with a "joker" which is known in advance to be completely unacceptable to the one rejecting the proposal (Nogee and Spanier 1962, p. 52). This form of "gamesmanship" enables the proposing side to claim that the rejector was opposed not only to that part of the plan, but to the whole concept of disarmament. My findings, however, indicate that the use of "new jokers" to offset each concession has been minimal, for the majority of the proposals involving concessions have not included retractions from a previous position. Thus of a total of 28 separate Soviet proposals involving changes important enough to merit a concession score, only 6 included retractions. The United States showed even less gamesmanship in this respect as only one of its 20 proposals incorporating concessions included a retraction. Instead, most retractions have been made separately from concessions, and consequently may not be regarded as the cause for rejecting concessions. Furthermore, even when retractions have been included in the same proposal with concessions, the latter usually predominated. For example, the six Soviet proposals containing both concessions and retractions showed a weighted concession score of 46 as contrasted to 23 for retractions, indicating an over-all bridging of differences.

Modifying to a certain extent Nogee's earlier conception (Nogee 1960, pp. 277–89) which emphasized the use of jokers as an indicator of bargaining in bad faith, Spanier and Nogee now distinguish between two types of jokers: "those which are riveted into disarmament proposals with the full knowledge that the other side will be compelled to reject them" and those "considered to be a necessary safeguard of national security" (Nogee and Spanier 1962, pp. 53–54). However, I believe it is quite erroneous to refer to the latter as jokers because in order to prove the predominance of gamesmanship in the negotiations, it has to be shown that these jokers are presented mainly for the purpose of prohibiting agreement. In other words, to claim that a nation is bargaining in bad faith requires more evidence than simply referring to provisions in a disarmament proposal that "the other could not possibly accept" (ibid., p. 5). Obviously, if there were no differences, we would now have disarmament. What I am suggesting then is that "gamesmanship" can be substantiated for the most part only when retractions accompany concessions in the same proposal or another proposal presented at about the same time. Other unacceptable positions might simply be dictated by what a nation perceives to be its valid security interests, and not *a priori* bargaining in bad faith. . . .

## APPROACH-AVOIDANCE BARGAINING IN THE TEST BAN NEGOTIATIONS

The partial nuclear test ban agreement of 1963 has frequently been cited as the most significant outcome of over twenty years of negotiating disarmament with the Soviet Union, but the agreement was reached only after several years of negotiation of the most intensive sort ever entered into by nation-states. During the five-year period in which the negotiations took place, over 400 formal meetings were devoted specifically to the nuclear test ban question, exclusive of frequent references to the problem in larger international bodies concerned with questions of disarmament.

In view of the effort expended, it would seem that agreement ought to have been achieved earlier than it was. Significant technical consensus had been reached as early as the summer of 1958 at the Conference of Experts held in Geneva, and by October 1960, 17 articles and the annex had been agreed upon.

# TABLE 5

## USSR Propensity to Compromise —
## Test Ban Negotiations (1957-63)

| USSR Concessions and Retractions | Document | Date | Mag. |
|---|---|---|---|
| Agrees to reciprocal control posts for policing test ban (2 or 3 year moratorium). | Doc. Dis. 11, p. 791 | 6-14-57 | 5 |
| One convention for both control and cessation measures. | p. 23 | 11-29-57 | 3 |
| Proposes Commission of 3 Founder States. Will accept 7 providing the 3 have a veto. | DNT 19 | 12- 8-58 | 2 |
| Agrees to a single administrator. | p. 29 | 12-12-58 | 4 |
| Headquarters staffing: East-West parity in key positions. | p. 46 | 1-30-59 | 2 |
| 4 or 5 out of 10 or 11 specialists at control posts to be foreigners. (Total at each post to be 30.) | p. 39 | 2- 2-59 | 3 |
| Control Commission: 3 Soviet, 3 West, and 1 neutral. | p. 45 | 2-11-59 | 1 |
| Responsible duties for foreigners at control posts (not to be just observers). | p. 40 | 2-20-59 | 3 |
| Agrees to peaceful detonations (if able to see internal design). | p. 47 | 2-23-59 | 4 |
| Proposes amendment article requiring 2/3 rather than unanimity (but must be ratified by the Three). | PV. 72 p. 11-12 | 3-19-59 | 2 |
| Agrees to US duration article allowing withdrawal under specified circumstances. | PV. 72 p. 4 | 3-19-59 | 3 |
| Agrees to US proposal for periodic review of the inspection system. | PV. 72 p. 4 | 3-19-59 | 2 |
| Accepts concept of quota for on-site inspection. | p. 356-7 | 4-23-59 | 4 |
| No veto for on-site inspection if within bounds of quota. | PV. 83 p. 10 | 4-27-59 | 3 |
| Agrees to technical discussion of methods for detecting high-altitude tests. | | 5-14-59 | 2 |

## TABLE 5 *(Cont.)*

### USSR Propensity to Compromise —
### Test Ban Negotiations (1957-63)

| USSR Concessions and Retractions | Document | Date | Mag. |
|---|---|---|---|
| Agrees to consider creation of a permanent corps of inspectors at Headquarters. | PV. 91 p. 19 | 6- 9-59 | 2 |
| Veto not to be used in regard to on-site inspection at any stage. | PV. 93 p. 11-12 | 6-11-59 | 3 |
| Raises foreign inspectors at control post to 6 or 7. | PV. 100 p. 14 | 6-22-59 | 2 |
| Drops veto re Treaty violations. | p. 64 | 6-30-59 | 4 |
| Will drop veto on staffing when agreement is reached on that subject. | p. 74 | 6-30-59 | 2 |
| Drops item veto on budget. | | 6-30-59 | 2 |
| Will delete veto on control posts and aircraft routes if these matters will be defined in advance with the host country (host country would have right to propose alternative routes). | p. 64 | 7-16-59 | 3 |
| Proposes that 10 of 30 specialists at each control post be foreign. | PV. 114 p. 9 | 7-24-59 | 2 |
| Agrees to technical study re Berkner findings. | PV. 137 p. 3 | 11-24-59 | 2 |
| Administrator may recommend inspection sites, patterns for air sampling flights and equipment. | PV. 142 p. 31-32 | 12- 3-59 | 2 |
| Will accept control posts of thirds (last third divided again into thirds) if West agrees to 3-3-1 Commission. | p. 74 | 12-14-59 | 1 |
| If 3-3-1 proposal accepted, Soviets will allow 2/3 vote on budget: Each state's share must be inserted in Treaty. | PV. 148 p. 11 | 12-14-59 | 1 |
| Parity between two sides of observers on air flights. | PV. 166 p. 3 | 2- 4-60 | 2 |
| Accept British idea for criteria for inspection of suspicious events (e.g., localization in 200 sq. kilometers, etc.). | p. 87 | 2-16-60 | 2 |
| Joint research could begin immediately after signature, but need use only chemical explosives. | p. 87 | 2-17-60 | 1 |

## TABLE 5 *(Cont.)*

### *USSR Propensity to Compromise —*
### *Test Ban Negotiations (1957-63)*

| USSR Concessions and Retractions | Document | Date | Mag. |
|---|---|---|---|
| Agrees to a ban above 4.75 magnitude with a *moratorium* below that level. | p. 89-90 | 3-19-60 | 4 |
| Agrees to unilateral moratorium on tests below threshold (to last 4-5 years). | PV. 202 p. 4 | 5- 3-60 | 2 |
| Will allow limited number of underground tests to verify detection effectiveness, but no decoupling experiments. | PV. 202 p. 6 | 5- 3-60 | 2 |
| No research on Soviet territory; USSR to have a veto over US research (retraction). | 1960 Doc. p. 257 | 6- 3-60 | −3 |
| Proposes 3 Deputy Administrators including one neutral who would succeed Administrator if latter unable to fulfill functions. | PV. 216 p. 10-11 | 6-21-60 | 2 |
| Soviets accept 5 Deputies, but object to Administrator appointing 4. | PV. 224 p. 3 | 7- 5-60 | 2 |
| Proposes 3 on-site inspections annually, including events both above and below 4.75 magnitude (retraction). | PV. 234 p. 15 | 7-26-60 | −2 |
| It will take four years to construct the control system and on-site inspection is to be postponed for that long (retraction). | p. 244 | 8-11-60 | −1 |
| Soviet demand for troika in administrative office (retraction). | p. 127-8 | 3-21-61 | −5 |
| Soviets insist on linking test ban with disarmament (retraction). | p. 538-42 | 6- 4-61 | −5 |
| Not to be any controls for test ban "while the arms race and intensified military preparations continue . . ." (retraction). | PV. 337 p. 20 | 8-28-61 | −5 |
| Soviets resume testing (retraction). | p. 171 | 8-30-61 | −3 |

## TABLE 5 (Cont.)

### USSR Propensity to Compromise — Test Ban Negotiations (1957-63)

| USSR Concessions and Retractions | Document | Date | Mag. |
|---|---|---|---|
| Proposes treaty with national systems of detection for atmospheric explosions and a moratorium on underground tests while adequate internal detection procedures are devised. | (1961) Doc. Dis. p. 703 | 12- 5-61 | 1 |
| Accepts neutral nation suggestion that nation allow visits to "suspicious and significant events upon invitation". | Doc. Dis. (1962) p. 447 | 4-24-62 | 2 |
| Suggests creation of an international scientific organ to examine the data of national observation posts. | Doc. Dis. (1962) p. 447 | 4-24-62 | 2 |
| Accepts notion of automatic seismo-logical instruments (black box). | Doc. Dis. (1962) p. 1149 | 12- 3-62 | 4 |
| Proposes three automatic seismic stations with international teams to remove recording device. | Doc. Dis. (1962) p. 1184 | 12-10-62 | 1 |
| Accepts notion of two or three on-site inspections. | Doc. Dis. (1960) p. 1241 | 12-19-62 | 2 |
| Agrees to relocate proposed auto-matic seismic stations if US desires. | Doc. Dis. (1963) p. 2-3 | 1- 7-63 | 1 |
| Khrushchev proposes ban on tests in atmosphere, outer space, and under-water without controls; not to include underground tests. | Doc. Dis. (1963) p. 245 | 7- 2-63 | 5 |

Sources: "Doc. Dis." refers to the collection of *Documents on Disarmament* compiled annually since 1959 by the Department of State. A page number alone refers to the State Department publication *Geneva Conference on the Discontinuance of Nuclear Weapons Tests* (Washington: Government Printing Office, 1962). PV. indicates meetings of the Geneva Test Ban Conference (GEN/DNT/PV).

## TABLE 6

*US Propensity to Compromise —*
*Test Ban Negotiations (1957-63)*

| US Concessions and Retractions | Document | Date | Mag. |
|---|---|---|---|
| Offers not only limitation of tests but ultimate elimination (linked to nuclear production cut-off). | p. 7 | 1-12-57 | 3 |
| Agrees to place nuclear test ban in first stage of disarmament program. | DC/SC. 1/ PV. 130, p. 11 | 7- 5-57 | 3 |
| Dulles proposes 10 month test suspension. | p. 10 | 7-22-57 | 2 |
| Agrees to 12 month suspension and 12 month extension if satisfactory progress toward nuclear production cut-off. | p. 11 | 8-21-57 | 2 |
| Hardtack data presented. Desires Commission to discuss (retraction). | PV. 29 | 1- 5-59 | −2 |
| Drops link between test ban and disarmament. | p. 29 | 1-19-59 | 5 |
| Control post staff in USSR: one-half Anglo-American, one-half "international," and no nationals in key positions. | PV. 42 | 1-26-59 | 1 |
| Accepts qualified veto re revision of Treaty, new detection methods, air routes, budgets. | p. 43-4 | 2- 5-59 | 3 |
| Control Commission-3 permanent, 1 Soviet, 1 West, and 2 neutrals (if Soviets drop veto). | p. 45-6 | 3- 2-59 | 2 |
| Staff-Headquarters: one-third each side: top positions parity. | p. 40 | 3- 5-59 | 3 |
| Agrees to unanimity in selecting Administrator. | PV. 67 p. 6 | 3- 4-59 | 3 |
| Treaty to remain indefinitely, subject to inherent right of withdrawal in case of violation or inadequate control. | DNT/45 | 3-10-59 | 2 |
| Eisenhower calls for atmospheric and underwater test ban instead of comprehensive one (retraction). | DNT/53 | 4-13-59 | −4 |
| Accepts Soviet proposal as modified by UK on amendments which would require ratification by all three. | PV. 74 | 4-14-59 | 2 |

TABLE 6 *(Cont.)*

### US Propensity to Compromise — Test Ban Negotiations (1957-63)

| US Concessions and Retractions | Document | Date | Mag. |
| --- | --- | --- | --- |
| Agrees to quota for on-site inspections but with no veto. | p. 360-62 | 5- 5-59 | 4 |
| Agrees to concept of a limited number of nationals having technical functions at control posts. | PV. 89 p. 11 | 5- 8-59 | 3 |
| Specified the number of 4 or 5 nationals for control posts. | PV. 100 | 6-22-59 | 1 |
| Staffing of control posts by thirds (Administrator and 10 technical personnel may come from host country). | PV. 113 p. 5 | 7-20-59 | 3 |
| The Deputy Administrator, or some other individual chosen by the Control Commission will be acting Administrator in case of no agreement on successor. | DNT/79 | 1-29-60 | 2 |
| Phased comprehensive treaty: 4.75 level but no moratorium below. | p. 85-6 | 2-11-60 | 1 |
| Qualified acceptance of Soviet criteria for suspicious events. Regards localization in 200 sq. kilometers as too small. | PV. 180 p. 7 | 3- 2-60 | 2 |
| A representative of the host nation may accompany international observers on aerial flights. | DNT/81 | 3-14-60 | 2 |
| Proposes *unilaterally* declared moratorium for tests below 4.75 (Contingent on treaty signature and research provisions). | p. 423-4 | 3-29-60 | 4 |
| Proposes to stagger terms of Administrator and Deputy (to minimize succession problem). | p. 94 | 4- 8-60 | 1 |
| Agrees to permanent flight routes if Soviet Union accepts proposal for selection of 2 technical observers for each flight by the Administrator. | p. 196 | 4-13-60 | 2 |
| Third-third of control staff to be proportioned so as not to prejudice the legitimate interests of both sides. | p. 111 | 5- 9-60 | 2 |

TABLE 6 *(Cont.)*

*US Propensity to Compromise —*
*Test Ban Negotiations (1957-63)*

| US Concessions and Retractions | Document | Date | Mag. |
|---|---|---|---|
| Agree to localization of 200 sq. kilom. except where insufficient control posts around event — in such a case area would be 500 sq. kilom. | p. 107 | 5-12-60 | 2 |
| Proposes two Assistant Administrators just below Deputy Administrator. | | 6-28-60 | 1 |
| Agrees to British proposal for 5 Deputy Admin. (East-West parity plus 1). | PV. 225 p. 3 | 7- 6-60 | 2 |
| Pool old nuclear weapons for research purposes (if Soviets agree US will get Congress to OK showing of internal design of these old weapons). | p. 102-3 | 7-12-60 | 3 |
| Finally specifies length for underground test moratorium (2 years or as long as research progresses plus 3 months to evaluate). | PV. 247 p. 8 | 9-27-60 | 2 |
| Five deputies-appointed by Administrator and confirmed by the Commission. | p. 120 | 10-20-60 | 2 |
| Agrees to 3 year moratorium for underground tests. | p. 126 | 3-21-61 | 2 |
| Agrees to *total* ban on high altitude tests. | p. 126 | 3-21-61 | 3 |
| Agrees to accept Soviet safeguards for nuclear devices used in research. | p. 126 | 3-21-61 | 1 |
| Will reduce control posts in USSR from 21 to 19 (Reduce one in US). | p. 126 | 3-21-61 | 1 |
| Will allow Soviets to have twice as many annual inspections as West. | p. 126-7 | 3-21-61 | 2 |
| Proposes parity for Control Commission (4 West, 4 Soviet, and 3 neutrals). | p. 127 | 3-21-61 | 4 |
| Right to veto budget as whole, but not an item veto. | PV. 274 | 3-21-61 | 3 |
| Makes it mandatory that third-third (control posts) be divided equally between East, West and neutrals. | PV. 279 | 3-28-61 | 3 |

TABLE 6 *(Cont.)*

## *US Propensity to Compromise —*
## *Test Ban Negotiations (1957-63)*

| US Concessions and Retractions | Document | Date | Mag. |
|---|---|---|---|
| Proposes sliding scale on inspections — 12 to 20 annually. | p. 154 | 5-29-61 | 2 |
| With more manned or unmanned control posts, US will agree to reduce or even abolish threshold. | p. 164 | 8-28-61 | 3 |
| Control Commission by majority vote may recommend control system to be used for reduced threshold 6 months before moratorium on underground tests ends. | p. 164 | 8-28-61 | 2 |
| On-site inspection teams may consist of 50% from non-aligned countries. | p. 169 | 8-30-61 | 2 |
| Atmospheric test ban with no controls. | p. 620 | 9- 3-61 | 3 |
| Refuses test moratorium during procedural talks (retraction). | Doc. Dis. (1961) p. 697 | 12- 5-61 | −1 |
| Expresses acceptance of nationally owned and operated detection networks. | Doc. Dis. (1962) p. 34 | 2-12-62 | 3 |
| Proposes to shorten time before beginning of inspection process (retraction). | Doc. Dis. (1962) p. 150 | 2-12-62 | −2 |
| Agrees to allocate limited number of inspections to areas of low seismic activity. | Doc. Dis. (1962) p. 150 | 3-15-62 | 1 |
| Reduces seismic threshold to 0. | Doc. Dis. (1962) p. 150 | 3-15-62 | 2 |
| Accepts eight nation plan if it is read to mean nations "must" accept the control commissions inspection parties. | Doc. Dis. (1962) p. 559 | 5-29-62 | 1 |
| Will reduce number of on-site inspections subject to acceptance of recognition procedures for international control of seismic events. | Doc. Dis. (1962) p. 716 | 8- 6-62 | 2 |

## TABLE 6 *(Cont.)*

*US Propensity to Compromise —*
*Test Ban Negotiations (1957-63)*

| US Concessions and Retractions | Document | Date | Mag. |
|---|---|---|---|
| Hints reduction of in-country permanent stations subject to international control of their technical adequacy. | Doc. Dis. (1962) p. 717 | 8- 6-62 | 2 |
| Uninspected treaty to be extended to all but underground tests. | Doc. Dis. (1962) p. 861 | 8-31-62 | 2 |
| Proposes that the number of automatic seismic stations be in three figures. | Doc. Dis. (1962) p. 1211 | 12-11-62 | 0 |
| Suggests 8-10 on-site inspections per year. | Doc. Dis. (1962) p. 1278 | 12-28-82 | 2 |
| 7-10 automatic seismic stations on Soviet territory. | Doc. Dis. (1963) p. 37 | 2-12-62 | 2 |
| Lowers on site inspection to six annually. | Doc. Dis. (1963) p. 193 | 5-22-63 | 1 |

Sources: "Doc. Dis." refers to the collection of *Documents on Disarmament* compiled annually since 1959 by the Department of State. A page number alone refers to the State Department publication *Geneva Conference on the Discontinuance of Nuclear Weapons Tests* (Washington: Government Printing Office, 1962). PV. indicates meetings of the Geneva Test Ban Conference (GEN/DNT/PV).

The delay in reaching agreement is difficult to explain if one assumes that the two sides were serious about a comprehensive test ban. Rather than approaching each other at the point of agreement, the two states in their relations with one another appear to have exhibited approach-avoidance tendencies.

The theory of approach-avoidance, which is usually applied to individual motivation, suggests that if one is ambivalent about a goal when he is at a distance from that goal, there is a tendency to approach; near the goal the tendency to avoid is greater. The result is a self-sustaining conflict at the point where approach and avoidance tendencies cross (Berelson and Steiner 1964, p. 272). When applied to a bargaining situation this theory would suggest that as long as the goal of agreement appears to be remote, concessions can be made at minimal cost. As agreement is approached, concessions become more costly, particularly if there are strong predispositions toward avoidance of agreement. When agreement is imminent, concessions are unlikely, and retractions become the basic mode of bargaining. . . .

The pattern of approaching agreement is effectively represented by the early tendency of the two nations to reciprocate concessions. In fact, the two weighted concession scores show a positive correlation of .60 which is significant at the .01 level for the various rounds up to and including the one ending in December 1960. It was at the point when agreement appeared imminent that the tendency to avoid became pronounced, for the Soviets made several retractions. In a final effort to reach agreement the Kennedy administration in March 1961 made a number of concessions to the Soviet position which failed to affect Soviet bargaining behavior. Yet even the latter moves are compatible with the approach-avoidance notion. Since agreement was no longer imminent, given the Soviet retractions, a state not serious about reaching a test ban agreement could make a number of "cheap" concessions which were not likely to be accepted or at least would not fulfill the demands of the adversary.

In view of the increasing recalcitrance of the Soviet Union on the test ban issue, it is remarkable that the United States was caught off guard by the Soviet resumption of testing in

## TABLE 7

### Weighted Concession Scores in the Nuclear Test Ban Negotiations (1958-63)

| Date Ending | USSR | US | Date Ending | USSR | US |
|---|---|---|---|---|---|
| December 1958 | 14 | 10 | May 1961 | −5 | 25 |
| May 1959 | 27 | 22 | September 1961 | −13 | 10 |
| August 1959 | 22 | 4 | January 1962 | 1 | −1 |
| December 1959 | 6 | 0 | June 1962 | 4 | 5 |
| April 1960 | 9 | 14 | September 1962 | 0 | 6 |
| August 1960 | 2 | 10 | January 1963 | 8 | 2 |
| December 1960 | 0 | 4 | July 1963 | 5 | 3 |

FIGURE 2.
Concession-Making in the Test Ban Negotiations

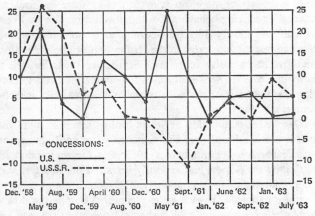

September 1961. The Soviets bargained vigorously during the early years of the test ban negotiations, scoring their first retraction in June 1960, but they failed to make any concessions during the year immediately preceding their resumption of testing. Mysteriously Soviet disarmament proposals and speeches also paid less attention to the testing issue, perhaps in anticipation of their plans to resume nuclear testing.

The infrequency of concessions carried over into the post-September 1961 period, as each side bargained from incompatible positions. As a starting point, the Soviets demanded a comprehensive test ban without controls, and the United States offered the option of a partial test ban without controls or a comprehensive one with controls. Never again did the United States seem willing to agree to a moratorium on testing which would depend upon Soviet good faith alone. Either position was equally unacceptable to the Soviet Union. Because of the completely changed circumstances between the pre- and post-1961 negotiations, no effort is made to link them in terms of concession-making behavior. To do so would require that one virtually take every Soviet concession score made during the test ban negotiations prior to the resumption of nuclear testing and give it a negative score after September 1961. Instead, a new time referent was established for concessions and retractions on the basis of positions taken by the two sides in September 1961.

Despite the resumption of Soviet testing, discussions on test ban issues continued over the next two years until agreement was reached in the summer of 1963. But the resumption of testing by the Soviets had seriously impaired the debates, and concessions came most grudgingly. The momentum of the earlier negotiations was never quite recaptured despite the divergence between the two which should have made concessions appear "cheap."

A number of indicators demonstrating avoidance tendencies on the part of one or the other of the negotiators can be found during the negotiations following the Soviet resumption of testing. Among these were the insistence upon linking agreement on a test ban with some improbable achievement such as general disarmament, the presentation of less specific proposals, and the tendency to support a test ban only when it was specifically to a state's advantage to do so, e.g., either immediately after completing a testing series or during the tests of one's opponent in an effort to get the opponent to desist.

In June 1961, prior to its resumption of testing, the Soviet Union introduced a severe impediment into the negotiations with its proposal for linking a test ban treaty with agreement on more general disarmament. With this proposal the test ban negotiations had made a complete circle since it was the United States which had insisted upon such a linkage at the beginning of the talks. Such a move had the effect of making an agreement on a nuclear test ban virtually impossible or at least highly improbable.

Proposals were also much less specific following Soviet resumption of testing. The Soviet Union began to emphasize a treaty without controls, reminiscent of its earlier proposals for "banning the bomb." Since controls were viewed as an unacceptable option, Soviet proposals did not include reference to such issues as inspection techniques and staffing problems.

Further evidence suggesting the lack of seriousness in the quest for a test ban agreement is illustrated by the tendencies of each side to support a ban only after completing its own series or in an effort to disrupt imminent or ongoing tests by the adversary. If one favored avoiding an undesired agreement, no move would be wiser in terms of ensuring rejection by the other side. Organizing for successful testing takes time, as indeed does the subsequent analysis of the results. Consequently, there is real incentive to complete a test series and then to commit the other side to a ban on further testing in the hopes of gaining a scientific advantage in nuclear development. The U.S. proposal in September 1961 for an immediate atmospheric test ban would have required that the Soviets cease testing within six days. This was unacceptable given the extensive planning which must have gone into the preparation of the test series. After completing the series, it was time for the Soviets to call for an immediate test ban. They proposed a ban on testing in all environments with the exception of underground testing which would be covered by a moratorium. Since the moratorium of 1958–61 had been broken there was a clash as to who should test last. The Soviet Union argued that it should be allowed to do so since it was the United States which first developed and tested atomic weapons.

To break the vicious cycle of testing in which neither side wanted to be disadvantaged appeared to be an insurmountable task. But following the 1962 test series "both sides appeared to be losing interest in testing nuclear weapons in the atmosphere, at high altitudes, and in outer space" (Jacobson and Stein 1966, p. 423). The general feeling that perhaps not that much could be learned from continued testing in these environments was indeed a factor in reaching agreement on a partial test ban.

The fact that approach-avoidance tendencies were finally surmounted in 1963 must be attributed to several additional factors. Chief among these was the fact that a partial test ban applying to the environments of the atmosphere, outer space, and underwater would placate the major concerns of the United States and the Soviet Union. The United States would no longer need to fear possible evasion of the treaty, for scientific advances appeared to guarantee that national inspection systems would be capable of detecting any violation of the Treaty. Since national devices were adequate in all environments but underground, the Soviets did not need to feel threatened by an international inspection system capable of penetrating their relatively closed society. Both sides could continue testing under the Treaty since it did not apply to underground testing.

Although it is easy to document the notion that a partial test ban was less risky as far as both sides were concerned, it is less persuasive to prove that real benefits would be gained. Since the Treaty would not eliminate all testing, its effectiveness in restricting the size of the nuclear club was reduced. These difficulties were only underscored by French and Chinese insistence upon continued nuclear development. The Soviet Union must likewise have felt that it had little to gain in a test ban treaty when the United States was involved in discussions on nuclear sharing with its NATO allies. Furthermore, the

United States failed to gain another objective of some of the advocates of a test ban, namely the hope that the ban would provide a pilot control system which might then be expanded to broader disarmament efforts.

In addition to the fact that a partial test ban could be viewed as less threatening to national interest, agreement was also spurred by pressures external to the major actors involved. World public opinion, despite the vagueness of the concept, was an apparent factor in reaching agreement. The dangers of radioactive fallout had been heavily publicized, and nations like India and Japan became intensively involved in the movement for a ban on atmospheric nuclear testing. The structure of the Eighteen Nation Disarmament Conference, representing as it did East, West, and Neutrals, provided a useful framework for pressure as well as for serious negotiation. The primacy of the powers directly involved was epitomized in the utilization of subcommittee meetings composed of the United States, the Soviet Union, and the United Kingdom. Pressure could be exerted upon the three members of the subcommittee by the larger conference since the subcommittee was required to report its progress to the Eighteen Nation Conference. Arthur Lall (1964, pp. 22–23), who represented India in these debates, argues that the eight neutral nations' memo presented in 1962 was "one of the factors" prompting the Soviet Union to accept 2 to 3 on-sight inspections per year. It also influenced the United States to accept the notion of an uncontrolled ban on outer space and under-water tests. These moves, though limited, had the effect of breaking through a serious deadlock in the negotiations.

A final factor in eventual agreement despite earlier approach-avoidance tendencies might be attributed to the momentum of concession-making. Given earlier tendencies toward concession, considerable progress had been made in the test ban negotiations. This had generated expectations and hopes, both internal and external to the major actors. It may be that the two sides were not that serious about agreement on a test ban except on their own terms. They in effect may have become victims of their own earlier performance, creating an environment in which some kind of agreement had become essential. Perhaps a partial test ban was a reasonable way out. It would represent some success but not impinge upon Soviet fears of an invasion of sovereignty. Nor would the U.S. need to fear evasion. In this sense, reciprocation of concessions may be viewed as an important forerunner of agreement even though the preference of the actors was avoidance of agreement.

It is difficult to ascertain the motivations of individuals and even more precarious to determine them for nations. Nevertheless, the tendency to make frequent concessions while agreement was remote, followed by limited concession-making and even retractions, suggests a pattern of approach-avoidance on the part of the United States and the Soviet Union. Moreover, the insistence of the two states upon linking a test ban to other disarmament measures, the presentation of less specific proposals, and attempts to accept the notion of a test ban only when it was decidedly to a state's advantage provide further evidence of avoidance tendencies.

The fact that agreement was finally reached might be attributed to the momentum created by earlier concession-making and pressures of world public opinion. The limited test ban agreement was an obvious "saddle-point" in game theoretic terms, for it minimized U.S. fears of evasion and Soviet concern over opening its relatively closed society for minimal gain. Perhaps there is some truth in the old adage, "as long as they negotiate," for out of long, arduous negotiations, the pressures for agreement are born.

## NOTES

1. The research for the study on which this paper is based was made possible by a generous grant from the Center for Research on Conflict Resolution. For this I am grateful, as well as for the constant help and encouragement provided by Professor J. David Singer. The more extended study will be found in the author's unpublished doctoral thesis.
2. The check for reliability showed 31 cases where I agreed with the independent coder; 47 rankings were off by one magnitude; 17, by 2; and the remaining 6 cases showed a discrepancy of a magni-

tude of 3. The check for statistical reliability showed a probability of occurring by chance of less than one in ten thousand. My special thanks go to Professor J. David Singer for serving as the independent coder, and to Dr. Kendall O. Price for helping compute the statistical significance of this data.

# 3. PROPAGANDA AND NEGOTIATION: THE TEN-NATION DISARMAMENT COMMITTEE*

*Joseph L. Nogee, University of Houston*

One of the requisites for assessing the meaning and direction of disarmament negotiations is to distinguish between proposals, statements, and negotiating postures that are primarily propagandistic in nature and those designed to reach an agreement. It is hardly deniable today that propaganda has been an integral feature of much of the disarmament negotiations since 1946. Elements of propaganda have probably been a constant—though not exclusive—feature of all postwar disarmament negotiations, but it is by no means clear exactly what role propaganda has played in all of these negotiations.[1] There are considerable differences of opinion as to whether propaganda has been a primary or secondary factor in the timing and content of Soviet and American proposals. Then there are distinctions made between specific negotiating efforts at different periods of time. Some negotiations such as those carried on in the United Nations in the late 1940's and early 1950's are widely viewed as exercises in propaganda

* "Propaganda and Negotiation: The Case of the Ten-Nation Disarmament Committee" by Joseph L. Nogee is reprinted from *Journal of Conflict Resolution* VII (Sept. 1963), No. 3, pp. 510–21, by permission of the publisher, Sage Publications, Inc.

maneuvering and little more;[2] others, e.g., the two Geneva test ban conferences, seem to have been guided by a genuine effort to reach some sort of an agreement through traditional diplomatic bargaining.

## THE FUNCTION OF PROPAGANDA

"Propaganda" can be defined as any activity designed to influence the attitudes and values of individuals and groups for the ultimate purpose of influencing actions. Although the term has a negative connotation in the popular mind, propaganda is a politically neutral tool which may be used for any end, good or bad. Properly speaking, a particular use of propaganda should be judged by evaluating the ends it seeks to attain. With respect to disarmament or arms control negotiations, propaganda is usually thought of as an alternative to serious bargaining and thus essentially negative. We speak of a particular proposal as a bona fide effort to reach agreement or "just propaganda." In a large number of instances this attitude is justified, but not necessarily so. Propaganda itself can be an important instrument for the attainment of arms control. The Ten-Nation Disarmament Committee of 1960 is a classic example of the skillful use of propaganda as an alternative to serious bargaining. Yet one can find even in these negotiations propagandistic elements favorable to disarmament. For example, both sides frequently spoke of the horror of a nuclear war. This attitude in itself, if it accomplishes nothing specific, is conducive to continuing negotiations.[3]

The objectives of propagandistic behavior in disarmament negotiations can be classified into two general categories: (1) those designed to bring about an agreement along lines favorable to one party, and (2) those designed to discredit or weaken the other party without an agreement. In the first category the objectives of propagandistic and diplomatic behavior coincide; in the second diplomacy is subverted toward strictly propagandistic objectives. Indeed it is not always clear into which of these two categories a particular proposal belongs. One might well question whether the Baruch Plan was proposed in order to secure internationalization of atomic production or to discredit the Soviet Union and justify the American monopoly. Similar questions could be asked about the Soviet proposals to ban nuclear weapons tests.

Where there is a sufficient mutuality of interests, agreement can be reached.[4] Unfortunately the political and ideological hostility between the Soviet Union and the West has been so great as to preclude any major disarmament agreement. In spite of the destructiveness of modern weapons and the appalling prospects of nuclear war, each side has looked to its own armaments rather than disarmament as the key to national security. Even a limited agreement on some measure of arms control has so far been impossible because neither East nor West has come up with a proposal that the other side did not consider, on balance, to be disadvantageous.

Whatever the prospects of agreement, the element of propaganda must be considered. The extent and characteristics of propagandistic behavior will vary according to the expectations of reaching an agreement. That is to say, the tone of the negotiations, the techniques of debate, and the quality of concessions will differ depending upon whether one or both of the parties are seeking their ends through agreement or nonagreement.

### DEADLOCK IN THE TEN-NATION COMMITTEE

The Ten-Nation Disarmament Committee which met from March 15 through June 27, 1960, illustrates the techniques of debate and propaganda maneuvering when neither side is prepared to negotiate seriously and expectations of agreement are low. These meetings took place in a period of tension between the Soviet Union and the West and between the Soviet Union and its Chinese ally. They were the first to consider comprehensive disarmament since the ill-fated sessions of the Disarmament Subcommittee in the spring of 1957. The Committee's membership consisted of five Eastern European nations and five Western powers, thus according the Soviet Union its long sought after parity of membership in a body negotiating general disarmament.[5] Each side began with a set of proposals fundamentally objectionable to the other side, and neither side in the course of discussions altered the substance of its position. The verbatim records reveal an almost total lack of genuine bargaining in the lack of give and take and compromise. Where policy positions become deadlocked and hardened such as in the Ten-Nation Disarmament Committee, propagandistic debate and "extranegotiatory tactics" become particularly important.

The irreconcilable points of conflict between East and West at this conference can be noted without going into the details of each plan. The Soviet Union proposed a treaty providing for "general and complete" disarmament to be effected within a four-year period. It would be carried out in three stages and include every instrument of modern warfare. At the conclusion of the four-year period only internal police forces would remain. An international control organ would supervise the disarmament process and insure its maintenance. Several features of the program met with strong objections, the most fundamental of which were (1) the refusal of the West to commit itself to any disarmament—even in principle—without prior assurances that the disarmament measure was controllable and that the Soviet Union would accept adequate control, and (2) the Western refusal to commit itself to a time limit for disarmament.[6] A single problem will illustrate the deadlock. In the third stage of the Soviet plan was a provision for the destruction of all types of nuclear weapons. Such a measure was then (and still is) virtually uncontrollable because no method existed for detecting past production of these weapons.[7] Yet the Soviets were insisting upon a commitment for their destruction. Some of the measures in Khrushchev's plan were controllable but the Soviets would not discuss the specifics of a control plan until *after* the treaty was signed. The United States responded that:

. . . it would be futile and dangerously misleading to the peoples of the world to agree to accept any disarmament measure or measures until we knew that agreement was possible as to verification. People everywhere would be led to believe that a serious disarmament programme had been agreed and was about to be carried out, when in fact the verification system essential to the programme had not yet been agreed. This would be a cruel deception and my Government will not be a party to it. [TNCD/PV. 36, pp. 480–81].

For their part the Western powers stressed control provisions rather than disarmament as such. The Western plan was divided into the popular three stages but no time limit was established, and the third stage was made conditional upon the completion of the first and second stages. Stage 1 would consist essentially of control measures. First there would be a joint study leading to the formation of an international control organization; then the establishment of the organization; to be followed by a collection of information by the organization for a reduction of force levels and conventional armaments. While this was being done, joint studies would be undertaken to determine control measures for a number of specific disarmament measures. No commitment to any disarmament was provided until measures for a verification were established. Finally, before any comprehensive disarmament could be *completed* there would have to be established an international military force to enforce international law and preserve world peace.[8] Of the many Soviet objections to this plan the most fundamental were (1) its failure to provide for the complete liquidation of all armed forces and armaments within a specified time period; (2) the provisions for control studies before any commitment to disarmament; and (3) the extensiveness of control stated and implied in the Western plan.[9] Again a single issue will illustrate the deadlock. The Western powers insisted that verification of a manpower reduction must include inspection not only of the number of troops demobilized but also of those under arms after the reduction—i.e., of the retained forces as well. This the Soviets would not accept. "We are," said Zorin, "realists. We understand that if inspectors are sent to verify armed forces and armaments which are not subject to reduction or abolition, this can only be attributed to a desire to learn what those armed forces are, and that cannot be regarded as other than military intelligence or, to use a coarser word, spying" (ibid., 7, p. 141).

In short, the Ten-Nation Disarmament Committee could not agree on a priority of subjects to negotiate, let alone the substance of the issues. The West would not commit itself to any disarmament until the Soviets had worked out with them and accepted an adequate system of verification; the Soviets would not even discuss the details of a control system until the West committed itself to disarmament.

It is difficult to determine from the verbatim records at what point each side abandoned hope for a breakthrough, if indeed either party entertained any such expectations from the start. In any event both sides were prepared to utilize the negotiations for whatever propaganda value they had. The tactics in this contest were many—logic, invectiveness, sarcasm, appeals to reason, threats, appeals to common values, quoting statements out of context, repetition, judicious timing of remarks and proposals, and selective questioning, to name a few.[10] Some of the tactics were subtle, some gross. Of the many varied objectives in this propaganda duel, the following were the most important:

1. To maneuver the other side into a public recognition of the necessity and legitimacy of its principal position. For the Soviet bloc that meant getting the Western powers to endorse general and complete disarmament. For the Western powers that involved obtaining a recognition from the Soviets of the necessity for adequate control.

2. To portray its own plan as realistic and concrete; and conversely to expose the unreasonableness and unfairness of the opposition proposals.

3. To divide or reinforce divisions within the opposing team.

EFFORTS TO SECURE RECOGNITION OF PRINCIPLE

Valerian Zorin and his Eastern European team doggedly attempted to elicit from the West an acknowledgment, either tacit or open, of the necessity of general and complete disarmament. Such an acknowledgment would not necessarily bring the two sides closer to agreement, but it would lend support to the Soviet program and make easier its justification in the United Nations and throughout the world. It would furthermore tend to undermine the Western plan which was not so all-embracing and inclusive as implied in the meaning of general and complete disarmament. Since the Western delegates would not directly accept the Soviet plan as a basis for negotiations, the Soviet diplomats sought to attain that end indirectly. What they could not obtain *de jure* they sought *de facto*. One of the most common methods utilized was to focus the discussions on the Soviet plan itself, i.e., to get the Committee to talk about the Soviet plan rather than the Western plan. They invited Western comments on their plan and asked for amendments to it. When the desired response was not forthcoming, the Soviet diplomats accused the West of "ignoring" or "evading" their proposals. As early as the second session Zorin was complaining of Western delay in responding to the Soviet plan and asking the Western delegates to express themselves "very soon" on Khrushchev's proposal (ibid., 2, p. 35). From the first week on, the Soviet delegates alternated between requests for comments on the Soviet proposals and charges that the Western delegates were evading discussing them (ibid., 1, p. 21; 4, p. 71; 5, p. 94; 15, p. 281; 17, p. 328; 20, p. 382; 38, p. 738).

A somewhat different approach to the same end was the Soviet effort to focus discussion upon goals of a disarmament treaty rather than the means to enforce or verify them. In principle both sets of proposals provided for controlled disarmament. Before they would even begin discussions on the details of any control plan the Soviets wanted agreement on the disarmament measures to be controlled; and they insisted that these measures be total. "I am instructed to declare," Zorin insisted, "that . . . it is necessary to formulate the basic principles of general and complete disarmament . . ." (ibid., 19, pp. 368–69). When reminded by the Western representatives that they would not accept disarmament without a prior consideration of its control, Zorin asked, "Why must we begin with control?" (Ibid., 9, p. 178.) Mr. Nazkowski, the Polish representative, defended this position logically:

> Seeing that control is only a means to an end and not the end itself . . . what would be the point of embarking on a detailed discussion of means before we had agreed on the end to be served by those means? Would that not, as the proverb says, be putting the cart before the horse? [Ibid., 13, p. 243.]

Zorin similarly opposed discussing a verification system for a hypothetically assumed reduction of arms.

> Why should we discuss some verification system or other suitable [*sic*] for verifying a figure which has not yet been adopted? We do not think that would be productive work; it would be a waste of time, because we might consider a verification system in relation to some given figure and then not happen to accept that particular figure. What then would be the good of our considering this verification system, especially in all its details? [Ibid., 26, p. 485.]

This position was confirmed by the four other Eastern representatives. Mr. Nazkowski (Poland) accused the Western representatives of seeking "to sidetrack the Committee into minute speculations on technical matters" (ibid., 40, p. 761). Mr. Mezincescu (Rumania) branded technical studies as "premature, if not sterile" (ibid., 45, p. 849; 9, p. 174; 12, p. 236; 46, p. 854).

Specifically the Eastern bloc wanted the Western powers to acknowledge that general and complete disarmament was the Committee's goal. Those four words—general and complete disarmament—were repeated endlessly. Frederick Eaton complained at the fourth session that in just three days "those noble words" had been "mouthed 135 times in a lesser number of minutes" (ibid., 4, p. 70). In Soviet hands, general and complete disarmament acquired a twofold meaning: as the essence of the Soviet plan and as the goal of the conference. Zorin insistently challenged his opponents either to accept general and complete disarmament as the official purpose of the conference or openly to repudiate it (ibid., 5, p. 87; 10, p. 193; 15, p. 284; 23, p. 422). Every favorable use of these words by any of the Western representatives was applauded by the Soviet members and hailed as a sign of a rapprochement. Mr. Nosek (Czechoslovakia) at the third session warmly welcomed the relatively simple and innocent statement of Frederick Eaton that, "I, for one, am willing to assume that we are all desirous of achieving the goal of general and complete disarmament" (ibid., 3, p. 45) with the remark, "It is very encouraging, I think, to hear the words 'general and complete disarmament' from the representative of the United States" (ibid., 3, p. 49). As the conference wore on such gratuities from the West diminished. In response to Western pressures for discussion of partial or first-step measures, Zorin on April 28 flatly informed Eaton that they would support partial measures "only if and when you reject general and complete disarmament" (ibid., 31, p. 615).[11]

One of the tactics designed to induce Western acceptance of general and complete disarmament—even if only verbally— was to call upon the authority of the United Nations as endorsing general and complete disarmament. In the fall of 1959 the General Assembly had unanimously passed a resolution which contained the phrase, *"considering* that the question of general and complete disarmament is the most important one facing the world today."[12] This resolution was interpreted by the Soviet bloc as an endorsement of its position. Mr. Nazkowski even went so far as to assert that the United Nations "recommended the Soviet plan to our Committee" (ibid., 18, p. 340; 3, pp. 56, 59–60; 5, p. 73; 10, p. 200; 11, p. 204; 13, p. 242; 15, p. 281; 16, p. 311; 18, p. 352; 20, p. 380; 30, p. 576).

We approach our work [said Zorin] in accordance with resolution 1378 (XIV) of the General Assembly of the United Nations, and I believe that it is our duty, the duty of all of us, to strive for the accomplishment of the provisions of resolution 1378 in the shortest possible time.

We fully agree with the point of view . . . that the fundamental task of our Committee rests on the clear wording of the first operative paragraph of resolution 1378 adopted unanimously on November 20, 1959, by the delegations of all Member States of the United Nations during the fourteenth session of the General Assembly. In this paragraph the General Assembly of the United Nations "Calls upon Governments to make every effort to achieve a constructive solution of this problem;"—that is, the problem of general and complete disarmament. As has already been stressed here, the representatives of the governments of all countries participating in this Conference voted for this paragraph.

Thus the obligation which has been assumed is clear, and we can hardly imagine any delegation abandoning it. Should that be the case, however, we must be told so quite clearly and publicly. Then world public opinion will be able to judge who is in favor of and who is against an accelerated working out of proposals on general and complete disarmament—the early achievement of which is being awaited with great hope by peoples all over the world [ibid., 5, p. 87].

A simple syllogistic theme permeated the Soviet speeches: the General Assembly set general and complete disarmament as a mandate for the Committee; only the Soviet plan provided for general and complete disarmament; therefore, the Committee should consider only the Soviet plan.

In April the Committee recessed to await the anticipated summit conference. Just before adjourning Zorin proposed a brief communiqué which summarized the Committee's activities. It concluded with the sentence, "The members of the Committee recognized the need to continue, after the recess, negotiations on the working out of the basic principles and a programme of general and complete disarmament under effective international control in accordance with the United Nations General Assembly resolution of November 20, 1959 on general and complete disarmament" (ibid., 31, p. 593). Jules Moch (France) pointedly expressed the Western reaction to that sentence:

> . . . I again recall how, with diabolical skill, the terms of the United Nations resolution transmitting all the documents and suggestions to our Conference have been interpreted and distorted, and how for the last six weeks that resolution has been represented as obliging us to approve all the Soviet proposals exactly as they stand. We have fallen into that trap once and . . . we shall not fall into it again [ibid., 32, p. 625].[13]

No communiqué was adopted.

The principal Western effort in the Committee was to obtain from the Soviets a recognition of the necessity and feasibility of controls. To obtain this in principle was not difficult because the Soviet proposals already contained broad general references to control. What disturbed the West were the limited powers of inspection and verification the Soviet plan would accord to a control agency. They accordingly attempted to draw the Soviet delegations into a discussion of the specifics so as to expose the inadequacies. Philip Farley, then Special Assistant for Disarmament, revealed to a Senate investigating committee one of the approaches Frederick Eaton and his colleagues followed in the Committee.

> *Senator Green.* Then your criticism is they don't answer your proposal?
>
> *Mr. Farley.* That is correct, and we think that one of the points in their latest plan, if I can shift to what one might call the propagandistic or public relations side, is that the provisions do make it pretty clear that they have this limited conception of what an inspector's rights should be, which I think is an unsound and a vulnerable point.
>
> *Senator Green.* Have you attempted to make it sound?
>
> *Mr. Farley.* Yes, this is a point which became clear as part of their position during the course of the arguments in the first thirty meetings in March and April of this year, and we hammered pretty hard on it [United States Senate, 1960, pp. 6–7].

Operating as a team, the five Western delegations tried continuously to keep the discussions focused on control. First one representative would discuss one aspect of control, then another would tackle a different aspect. During the first two weeks, most of the debate was general and rather aimless. On March 25 Frederick Eaton made a determined effort to focus the discussion on the proposed international control organization. His suggestion was immediately rebuffed by the Soviets, but the Western powers—almost as though carrying on a monologue—continued to discuss control. Mr. Cavalletti (Italy) delivered on the following day a lengthy speech outlining the functions of a control agency. The next day Jules Moch proposed the appointment of committees of experts to study in detail techniques of control (TNCD/PV. 9, p. 171; ibid., 10, pp. 186–87; 11, pp. 226–27).

Although rebuffed in every effort to isolate the subject of control and discuss its specifics, the Western team persisted. They remained united in their demand for control as a prerequisite for disarmament. They welcomed every Soviet acknowledgment of the necessity for control. They argued the logic of arms control. They cited previous Soviet statements (such as the May 10, 1955, Soviet proposals) justifying control. They invited amendments to the Western proposals (ibid., 6, p. 128; 8, p. 149; 9, pp. 155, 182; 13, p. 251; 16, pp. 305–6; 23, p. 430; 26, pp. 482–84; 38, p. 709). Not the least of their efforts was a continuous peppering of questions to expose the Soviet weaknesses and compel them to talk about control. Jules Moch, the most experienced of the Western negotiators, pressed his Eastern colleagues the hardest. The following excerpt from a speech made on June 23 will illustrate his tenacity:

I had asked two questions. I will repeat the first one exactly as I asked it:

"Will the control authorities be able to ascertain not only what equipment has been eliminated, but also the quantities remaining after such elimination, to the full extent necessary to verify their conformity with treaty obligations?"

The answer I received to this was as follows—and I quote:

"[Control] must offer every possible guarantee that no State will be able to evade its responsibilities for carrying out disarmament measures within the time-limit fixed or circumvent the treaty on general and complete disarmament in any way whatsoever."

My question was quite precise and concrete; but the reply is couched in terms so general that I am obliged to ask whether, to ensure that no State will be able to evade carrying out disarmament measures, the control authorities will, or will not, have the right to verify the equipment on hand as well as the equipment eliminated. I do not know at all. Quite frankly, after reading the reply, I am no wiser than before, and the question is so important that I must press for an equally precise answer [ibid., 45, p. 836].

Since the gulf between both sides' policies on control of major disarmament measures was too wide to bridge without major compromises, the West also pressed for consideration of limited first-stage agreements. The practical advantage of a small first step was the minimal amount of control involved. "We must design a plan," said Eaton, ". . . which moves by measured, safeguarded steps toward an attainable goal" (ibid., 1, p. 24). On April 1, after several weeks of Committee wrangling, Eaton attempted to discuss a plan for prohibiting weapons of mass destruction in outer space which could be implemented apart from any larger disarmament measure. His inducement to the Russians was that verification would not require many men. Other Western spokesmen stressed the mutual advantages of such a step. Jules Moch warned of the future difficulty of control after weapons-bearing satellites were put in orbit. Mr. Cavalletti stressed the "favorable psychological effects" of a first-step agreement. Even during the waning days of the conference, Canada vainly suggested that perhaps an initial limited agreement could be made on the basis of some "package deal" (ibid., 14, pp. 267–73; 28, p. 526; 46, p. 860).

## WHOSE PLAN IS MORE REALISTIC?

A second major objective of the negotiators was to defend their own proposals and to indict those of the opposition. It is interesting that both sides justified their proposals principally by the same criterion: realism. Such expressions as "clear, definite, and realistic," and "constructive, realistic, and practical" typified the Soviet description of Khrushchev's program. Mr. Tarabanov (Bulgaria) asserted that only the Soviet plan was realistic. As defined by Valerian Zorin, a realistic plan was one that: (1) provided for concrete measures insuring the liquidation of all armed forces and armaments; (2) included a time limit for the completion of the plan; (3) conferred no military advantage to any state during implementation; and (4) established effective control but only over manpower disbanded or material destroyed (ibid., 2, pp. 38–40; 5, pp. 26–27; 4, p. 63). Another adjective frequently applied by the Soviets to their plan was "concrete." Their plan was "concrete" because it included a specific time period (four years) and provided for the abolition of all armaments. According to the Bulgarian representative, the West found the Soviet plan objectionable just because it was concrete.

Yet [said Mr. Tarabanov] there is every reason to believe—and there can be no mistake about it—that what renders the Soviet plan unacceptable to the Western delegations is precisely the concrete disarmament measures it contains, the fixed time-limits for their implementation, and the abolition of all armed forces and of all armaments, both conventional and nuclear, within fixed time-limits agreed between the Powers—namely the features which make the plan a real plan for general and complete disarmament [ibid., 17, p. 321].[14]

In seeking to discredit the Western plan the Soviets stressed three ideas: (1) the West desired extensive control for espionage reasons; (2) the Western plan conferred a military advantage to the NATO powers, and (3) the West was fundamentally opposed to disarmament. Mr. Zorin, in a long speech at the beginning of the conference, set the tone for all subsequent Soviet pronouncements on control when he warned that "It would be . . . unrealistic . . . to endow the control organ with powers for controlling armaments which still remain at the disposal of States . . . for these powers could be used for intelligence purposes and could, naturally, not be accepted by States jealous of their own security" (ibid., 2, p. 40; 3, p. 43; 6, p. 114; 7, p. 141; 8, p. 152; 13, p. 257; 27, p. 508). Later as the debate became more heated, the Soviet bloc asserted that indeed espionage was the Western motive. One of their tactics was to cite statements of Allied military leaders to the effect that Western military strategy required more precise information about Soviet military establishments.[15]

One of the most bitterly condemned features of the Western plan was its insistence upon the destruction of intercontinental ballistic missiles (in the first stages) without providing for the disbandment of any overseas bases. The Soviets saw in this evidence of a United States desire to secure a military advantage through its plan.

Is that not proved [said Zorin] by constant emphasis in this plan on establishing control first of all over those types of armaments in the development of which the Western Powers, as they themselves admit, are lagging behind the Soviet Union? It cannot very well be regarded as accidental that the Western plan provides for measures to set up control over the possible use of outer space for military purposes and over long-range missiles, but says nothing about the liquidation of military bases on foreign territory [ibid., 15, pp. 283–84].

This criticism complemented the oft-repeated theme that fundamentally the United States opposed disarmament and was using the negotiations to support its military program. Proof of this was found in the fact that the United States would not commit itself to any significant disarmament measures. The studies demanded by the West in Stage 1 were denounced as "theoretical dissertations" whose real purpose was to delay action on disarmament (ibid., 2, pp. 40–44; 6, p. 119; 14, p. 276).

As did the Soviets, the Western powers justified their plan principally on the basis of its realism. On introducing the Five Power plan to the Committee, David Ormsby-Gore stated that the

. . . basic principle of this plan is realism. It is a practical plan. We do not ask that in the present state of international relations countries should make a great act of faith and subscribe to far-reaching commitments before there is some practical demonstration of good will on all sides [ibid., 2, p. 30].

Out of the debate as to which plan was more realistic emerged two different conceptions of international politics and the Cold War. In contrast to the utopian assumptions of the Soviet bloc, the West stressed the role of power in national security. Mr. Martino expressed this view most directly in a speech on April 6.

International politics is and must always remain, for everyone, something firmly anchored in realism, in other words *Realpolitik*. It is the policy that every people must pursue in order to safeguard and, if possible, to improve its living conditions and opportunities for development within the international community. It is always borne, and will always bear, a typical stamp of realism, without which it would never have been possible and would never be possible for any people to make its own way of life and ensure its own security. To this end every people needs to know and to assess its own strength and qualities precisely, and to know just as precisely on whom and on what it can rely in carrying out the programme of its national life. If this realism has often manifested itself in a brutal manner, that is due to the nature and organization of the international community, in which might has prevailed over the rule of the law. For hundreds and thousands of years nations have confronted one another just as individuals did before the birth of States. *Bellum omnium contra omnes*—War by all against all. This is why international politics have so often been characterized by brutal realism [ibid., 17, p. 327].

Where the Soviets saw the Cold War as a result of the arms race, the United States saw the arms race as a result of "the lack of confidence in each other" and "the political differences which divide us." Where Zorin envisioned disarmament as basically a simple question, Jules Moch saw it as an "infinitely complex" problem (ibid., 1, p. 22; 25, p. 468; 2, pp. 31, 35; 22, p. 419).

The West continuously hammered at the unrealism of the Soviet plan. David Ormsby-Gore labeled it a "blueprint for an unrealizable Utopia." Frederick Eaton referred to the Soviet arguments as "sweeping, meaningless, age-worn slogans" (ibid., 13, p. 251; 14, p. 271). They attacked as unrealistic the limited powers of inspection in the Soviet control plan, the demand for abolition of weapons when no known control existed, and particularly Soviet insistence upon stipulating total disarmament in four years.

Contrary to the practice of their Soviet opponents, the Western representatives avoided a direct assault upon the motives of the opposition. Throughout the conference the Western representatives affirmed the importance of reasonableness and patience and stressed the sincerity of their desire to negotiate. Recriminations upon the motives of the Eastern delegates would have tainted the image the West sought to create. However, as the conference wore on the Western delegates began to insinuate that the Soviets were interested in little more than propaganda. On April 20, Mr. Martino (Italy) openly, but without violating the canons of diplomatic finesse, pressed the charge.

> What [he asked] are we to believe? Even in Mr. Zorin's own words doubt is raised in the mind of any reasonable person whether the Soviet four-year plan is a practical plan, but again this morning we are told that unless we accept this unrealistic timetable we indicate no desire for disarmament. I wonder whether any of us here at this table really believe that. I fear that the only conclusion to be drawn from this is that the Soviet plan for disarmament, although undoubtedly not so intended, can only be a deceptive propaganda device to lead the mass of people to believe that complete disarmament is possible overnight, and this is a tragic deception [ibid., 31, p. 600].

As the stalemate deepened the Western delegates increased their attacks on Soviet motives—never, however, totally closing the door to further negotiations. Even during the bitter speeches of early June, Mr. Burns (Canada) went no further than to suggest.

> One might [said Burns] also say that to propose general principles without preliminary investigation to see if they were practical and could be put into effect could also be attacked as insincere and intended more to mislead uninformed public opinion than to facilitate serious and effective discussions on the attainment of disarmament [ibid., 45, p. 833].

Only after the dramatic departure of the Soviet delegates, ending the conference, did Eaton in anger condemn the Soviet proposals as "propaganda, pure propaganda" (ibid., 47, p. 888).

### TO DIVIDE THE OPPOSITION

A third objective of East-West maneuvering was to divide the opposition. Obviously the opportunities available to the West were considerably more limited than those of the Soviets. Where possible the West sought to find contradictions between statements of different Communist delegates although there were very few to find. Occasionally a Western delegate would chide one of the "satellite" representatives for his close adherence to Zorin's line, suggesting a puppet relationship. Jules Moch, for example, accused Mr. Tarabanov of taking his cues from the Soviet delegate and suggested that the four non-Russians were incapable of reasoning for themselves (ibid., 11, pp. 219–20).[16]

Valerian Zorin resorted to similar tactics with about the same lack of success. He too sought to find contradictions among the Western positions. Likewise he attempted to pit the smaller powers against the United States. His most trenchant comments were directed to the Italian delegate whom he on occasion dismissed as an American satellite. In one speech Zorin speculated that "perhaps, Mr. Martino is expressing the view of the United States, and not of Italy." He suggested that United States armed forces in Italy limited her freedom of action and commented, "I do not know—perhaps Italy is content with this situation, but it seems to be the victimized part" (ibid., 38, p. 729; 5, p. 94; 9, p. 177; 11, pp. 230–31; 46, p. 870).

A more direct effort to split the Western allies was made following the May recess. Zorin tabled a revised plan which featured one change that had been expressly sought by France. The French, who themselves were on the threshold of developing a nuclear weapon, were particularly concerned that a disarmament program begin with provisions for the destruction of the means of delivering nuclear weapons—i.e., intercontinental missiles—rather than the weapon itself. In its revised plan of June 7, the Soviet Union moved the destruction of missiles from the third stage to the first. Zorin explained that the change was effected to comply with France's views. Whatever hopes the Soviets may have had were dashed by Jules Moch's comment on June 13 that "If . . . the authors of the [revised Soviet] plan had devised it with the ulterior motive of using it to weaken or even to dislocate the Western alliance, they would have been making a grave mistake, for nothing will shake our solidarity" (ibid., 37, p. 690).[17]

These three objectives of Soviet-American propaganda by no means exhaust the list. Nor do the techniques described cover the full range of propagandistic behavior in this conference. However barren the formal results may have been, the negotiations were characterized by a richness of maneuver that was at times crass and at times extremely subtle. The effects and consequences of such maneuvering are difficult to assess or measure. Though propagandistic behavior dominated this particular conference, it was not the propaganda that stood in the way of agreement. The failure was the product of incompatible national policies. Where such incompatibility of policies exists, propaganda will play an important role in any disarmament negotiations. The propaganda front is only one of many in the Cold War. It needs to be recognized to be won.

## NOTES

1. For a general analysis of the role of propaganda in postwar disarmament negotiations, see Nogee and Spanier 1962.

2. Frye 1961, p. 25, notes, for example, that "In late 1953, the U.N. General Assembly asked the Disarmament Commission to set up a subcommittee consisting of the 'powers principally concerned' . . . in the hope that confrontation in private in a restricted circle would help exploit the new atmosphere and turn disarmament from propaganda to negotiation."

3. For an analysis of the role of debating technique and propaganda in pressuring the United States into separate negotiations for a nuclear test ban, see Zoppo 1961. On propaganda, see Evron Kirkpatrick, *Target: The World*. New York: Macmillan, 1956, and Ithiel Pool, "Public Opinion and the Control of Armaments," *Daedalus* LXXXIX, pp. 984–99, 1960.

4. One exception to the generally barren record of post World War II disarmament negotiations is the Antarctic Treaty signed December 1, 1959, by the U.S.S.R., the United States, and ten other nations. Article 1 provides: "Antarctica shall be used for peaceful purposes only. There shall be prohibited, inter alia, any measures of a military nature, such as the establishment of military bases and fortifications, the carrying out of military maneuvers, as well as the testing of any type of weapons." The treaty further provides for an inspection system to guarantee observance.

5. This Committee was agreed upon by the Foreign Ministers of France, the United Kingdom, the United States, and the U.S.S.R. in Geneva in August 1959. It included representatives from Bulgaria, Canada, Czechoslovakia, France, Italy, Poland, Rumania, United Kingdom, United States, and U.S.S.R. For a concise summary and

alysis of its work, see Bechhoefer (1961, pp. 536–57). See Wads-
orth (1962, pp. 56–59) for a discussion of the effects of parity on
e negotiations.

See the initial speech of Frederick Eaton in Command, 1152,
*erbatim Records of Meetings of the Ten-Power Disarmament
ommittee*, TNCD/PV. 1, pp. 24–27. Henceforth verbatim sources
ll be cited by document symbol (TNCD/PV.–) and the page in
e Command paper.

These fundamental objections remained even after the revised So-
et plan introduced on June 7, 1960. See, for example, Eaton's
eech of June 10 (TNCD/PV. 36, p. 681).

Some of the implications of the nondetectability of existing
clear weapons are considered by Singer (1962, pp. 226–29)
d Nogee (1961, pp. 191–93, 203–5).

TNCD. 3. Annex 7 of Command 1152. In explaining the
quences of the Western plan, Eaton noted that Stages 1 and 2
re in effect one large stage (TNCD/PV. 3, p. 48).

See, for example, Valerian Zorin's speech of March 16 (ibid., 2,
. 35–40).

. I am not concerned here with the clever use of press releases
d the publicity made outside of the conference. For a perceptive
porter's view, see the articles by A. M. Rosenthal in the New
ork *Times* of March 22, 26, 27, and 30 and April 5 and 10, 1960.

. Just before the Committee adjourned Zorin complained: "This
andpoint also shows the two-faced attitude of the United States
elegation in our Committee, which—apparently with an eye on
orld public opinion—does not yet consider it advisable openly to
pandon the idea of general and complete disarmament but, acting
pon the instructions of its Government, is trying its utmost to frus-
ate constructive discussion of this question in our Committee"
TNCD/PV. 46, p. 855).

. General Assembly Resolution 1378 (XIV), November 20,
959. The third operative paragraph reads: *"Expresses the hope
at measures leading towards the goal of general and complete
isarmament under effective international control will be worked
ut in details and agreed upon in the shortest possible time."*

. Mr. Mezincescu replied to Moch's comment with "I wish also
refer to an idea expressed just now by the representative of
rance. He told us—and I am more or less quoting his words,
erhaps not literally, but giving the sense correctly—'We have fallen
to the trap once, and we shall not fall into it again.' That means
at the Western Powers once fell into the trap of declaring them-
elves, before world opinion, to be in favour of general and

complete disarmament, and Mr. Moch wished to reassure us by making it clear that such was not the intention of the Western Powers, and that they would not again give world opinion the satisfaction of thinking that they might commit themselves a little further, or at least continue on the course to which they are committed by United Nations General Assembly resolution 1378 (XIV) which they proposed and adopted, like all the other Members of the United Nations" [ibid., 32, pp. 628–29].

14. Among the provisions of the Soviet plan that the West found most unrealistic was the four-year time period. Zorin's reaction to Western critics of the time period was that "A refusal to set a time limit for completing the disarmament programme and for the various measures envisaged as part of it would give the disarmament programme an entirely indeterminate character and would create favourable conditions for one State or another to evade carrying out the programme" (ibid., 2, p. 39).

15. Generals Genevey and Gavin were quoted (ibid., 6, p. 114; 27, p. 508).

16. Mr. Mezincescu immediately replied, "I can assure the representative of France that I am just as capable of thinking for myself as any other delegate here present" (ibid., 11, p. 221).

17. Zorin later remarked that "In one of his first statements in this Committee after the resumption of its work, Mr. Moch gave us to understand that on this question he would try to bring the position of the other Western Powers closer to the French position. We are now wondering whether the opposite has not occurred, and whether France's allies, and the United States in particular, have not induced the French Government to depart from its original position, which was that priority in the disarmament programme should be given to measures for destroying the means of delivering nuclear weapons" (ibid., 46, p. 868).

# 4. A SOCIAL-PSYCHOLOGICAL MODEL OF POSITION MODIFICATION: ASWAN

*Bertram I. Spector, New York University and Consolidated Analysis Centers, Inc.*

Power is a major factor contributing to the dynamics of the negotiation process. Defined as the ability to influence the behavior of another in an intended direction, power is a causative concept that can help explain behavior and attitude change. If the bargaining process is defined as the transformation or modification of various individual and divergent positions to reach common and group interests and agreements, the behavior and attitude changes that result can be credited, in large degree, to the use of power by one or all of the parties involved.

In this chapter, we will discuss the determinants of position and behavior modification in the context of the bargaining process. In doing so, we will inquire into the effects of power on bargaining participants, and the effectiveness of power as witnessed in the outcome.

We will pursue a phenomenological approach to enable us to analyze the intrapsychic factors that react to power attempts and that motivate negotiators to maintain or alter their position and behavior. Events and actions as they are perceived, experienced, interpreted, and responded to by individual negotiators will provide the basic framework for our inquiry. It is not the raw use of power that motivates position and behavior modification. Rather, change is determined by the way bargaining participants perceive influential communications and feedback. Our aim is to uncover the patterns of power relations in the bargaining process, the way in which these patterns are perceived, and the way in which they modify values, positions, and behavior to lead toward the convergence of previously divergent interests.

We will begin by examining certain social-psychological propositions concerned with the perception of environmental stimuli and responses to them. This perception-response paradigm will be related to our conception of the dynamics of the bargaining process. The suggested cybernetic model will then be applied to a particular historical case, the Aswan High Dam negotiations of 1955–56 among the United States, Great Britain, the World Bank, and Egypt. The analysis of this case indicates the utility of our approach to identify the determinants of position and behavior modification.

## THE SOCIAL-PSYCHOLOGICAL PARADIGM

### Behavior as a Function of Organism-environment Interaction

Social psychologists believe that behavior is a result of the interaction of the organism and the environment. Kurt Lewin conceptualized a vector psychology to describe the complex interaction between the inner-personal system (energy, tension, and needs) and valences and forces of the psychological environment. Locomotion is the outcome of this dynamic relationship. The arousal of a need causes the release of energy and thereby arouses tension within the inner-personal region. Need arousal also confers a valence on the needed objects and is responsible for the creation of a force acting upon a person. Barriers may exist in the environment that serve to frustrate needs and increase tensions, but a person may act to overcome environmental impediments by formulating alternate paths of behavior. The dynamics between personality and environment account for locomotion toward the achievement of need satisfaction and tension reduction.

Henry Murray also conceptualized the effects of personality nd situational stimuli on behavior. He felt that the organism ; not an inert body that merely responds to external stimula- .on; behavioral outcomes are the result of the dynamic in- :raction between the two. A person's needs are related to ten- ion creation and motivation within the individual to act. In Murray's own words (1938, pp. 123–24),

A need is a construct . . . which stands for a force . . . in the brain region, a force which organizes perception, ap- perception, intellection, conation and action in such a way as to transform in a certain direction an existing, unsatisfy- ing situation.

What arouses needs? They are sometimes provoked by inter- al conditions and processes, but are most often provoked by he occurrence or experience of environmental press. Press can e defined as a force in an object or situation that can facilitate r impede an individual's efforts to reach his goal; it can be atisfying or frustrating (ibid., pp. 118–22). Needs are nanifested when effective presses, impinging on an individual, re encountered or anticipated. The result of this interaction is he activation of overt behavior to alter the initial circum- tances in such a way as to provide a satisfying reduction of ension and drive (given that the individual possesses compe- ence, and external impediments are not insurmountable) ibid., p. 124).

Murray conceptualizes press in two different ways. Alpha ·ress is the press that actually exists based on objective deter- nination. Beta press is the subject's own interpretation of the ·henomena he perceives in the environment. The environment n individual responds to is very much influenced by the envi- onment that he perceives, whether it be a true or false image ·f reality. "An object may, in truth, be very well disposed to- vards the subject—press of Affiliation (*alpha* press)—but he subject may misinterpret the object's conduct and believe hat the object is trying to depreciate him—press of Aggres- ion: Belittlement (*beta* press). When there is wide diver- ·ence between *alpha* and *beta* press we speak of delusion" ibid., p. 122).

## Environments and Social Interaction

If the organism varies along certain dimensions of person ality, the environment also varies along certain dimensions The environment is a multidimensional phenomenon, whic can develop a "personality" or "climate" of its own in th mind of the perceiver and have definite effects on behavior an attitudes (Sells 1963).

One climate dimension of relevance to bargaining studie can be defined by the stressful and threatening atmosphere tha it creates. In experimental situations, it was found that th greater the induced psychological stress, the greater the anx ety and the greater the rigidity of response behavior (i.e., ad herence to past successful methods of problem-solving eve when they might be inappropriate) (Cowen 1952). Anothe study found that threat-induced anxiety increases perceptua rigidity and distortion (Moffitt and Stagner 1956). Janis an Terwilliger (1962) studied the effects of stressful and fearfu communications on an individual's willingness to change hi attitudes. They found that the stronger the threat, the greate the subject's defensiveness and resistance to attitude or behav ior modification. Searching for the influences of personalit and situation on bargaining behavior, Terhune (in Swingl 1970) found that the more threatening a situation appears t a subject, the greater his ego defensiveness and the smaller th effect of individual personality differences on behavior.

Another dimension of the environment can be defined as th emotional climate engendered by group identification. Th greater the identification with a group, the more hostile will b one's attitudes and behavior toward a competitive grou (Sherif 1966). The greater one's emotional commitment t an ingroup position, the greater one's distortion of reality an inability to comprehend the opposition's point of view. Thes effects hinder realistic interaction (Blake and Mouton 1961) Group loyalty and commitment is rationally reinforced by th threat of censure or ostracism by one's own group for devia tion from group objectives. But it has been proposed that suc intense partisanship is largely a result of ego defensivenes (Bass 1966, p. 2).

In summary, social psychologists have formulated a paradigm to explain behavior. The phenomenological approach posits perceptions of environmental stimuli as being subject to the interpretation and evaluation of one's belief system. A behavioral response is the outcome of the filtering and organizing process between environment and organism.

## THE PERCEPTION-RESPONSE PARADIGM
### AND THE BARGAINING PROCESS

### *A Definition of the Bargaining Process*

Bargaining is a process in which representatives of various individual and divergent positions interact to reach common interests and agreement (Ikle 1964, p. 34). If successful, this process involves a convergence of interests where previously there was a conflict of interests. Negotiators respond to their counterparts' actions such that their mutual constraint of interests results in an outcome in which there is a maximization of interests for both sides in a positive nonzero-sum agreement. The bargainers' gradual adjustment of their utilities enables this modification to occur. The pattern of demands and concessions, as well as the bargainers' mutual expectations of their opponents' utilities and strategies, contributes to this value change (Lall 1966, pp. 54, 311; Cross 1969, pp. 47–51).

Mutual interaction between parties, the essential element of the bargaining process, is based on the "mirror image" effect: "I am what I think you think I am." If agreement can be reached, it will happen in accordance with the perceptions and expectations each side has of the other side. Singer (1963) postulates that influential interaction depends on the mutual perceptions, predictions, and preferences of all the parties. In Sherif's (1966) Robbers Cave experiment, hostile interaction between two groups of campers was a result of the mutual attitudes, images, and expectations each group had of the other. It was not until the presentation of a series of superordinate goals that a climate of mutual trust and friendly perceptions developed between the members of the groups. Osgood (1962) also suggests that a spiral of threat and tension can be broken only by building a sense of mutual trust, and disarming stereotypes and prejudiced perceptions through a program of graduated reciprocation of co-operative measures. As we mentioned previously, the shifting of perceptions might result from the input of new information comprehended by an "open mind" under conditions that are neither threatening nor partisan (Bass 1966; Holsti 1969; Janis and Terwilliger 1962).

## Power Relations Between Negotiators

How do negotiators interacting with each other to maximize their group goals reach a convergence of interests? Power is a major force in the process toward convergence. The modification of bargainers' positions and expectations can be credited in large part to the use of power by one or both of the parties in negotiation.

Harsanyi's (in Bell, Edwards, and Wagner 1969, p. 227) redefinition of Dahl's conception of power is probably the most inclusive:

A's power over B should be defined not merely as an ability by A to get B to do X with a certain probability p, but rather as an ability by A to achieve this at a certain total cost u to himself, by convincing B that B would have to bear the total cost v if he did not do X.

But there are both operational and theoretical problems with the concept of power that have hindered its use as an explanatory factor of the negotiation process.

First, there are the operational problems. Many studies of bargaining use the term "power" but never really define it or use it to explain the convergence of positions. They typologize the bases or means of power, but don't proceed to correlate their taxonomies with bargaining outcomes. In any case, the power relation in bargaining interaction is more than the mere base or means of power that is used; these are only the instrumentalities. The ability to cause change in another's behavior in an intended direction involves a study of the expectations of the costs and strength of power. The human element of power interactions must not be forgotten or omitted.

Second, there are the theoretical problems. John Cross has pointed out the failure of scholars to distinguish sufficiently between power in the bargaining outcome and in the bargaining process (Cross 1969, p. 17). Does power determine the ability to win (is it involved in the *process?*), or does the ability to win determine who has the most power (is it involved in the *outcome?*)? (Zartman 1974, p. 395). What results from these conceptions of power is a problem of circularity. Is power to be conceived as the independent variable that causes the bargaining outcome, or is it the dependent variable, that which is obtained from the bargaining process?

Perhaps we are now led into a further and more difficult tautology. Zartman (1974, p. 397) points out that if power is a causative concept of behavior change, then a "theory of convergence in terms of power is thus merely a theory that explains the causes of convergence in terms of the causes of convergence."

To solve these problems we must conceptualize power so that it is not tautological or taxonomic, and in a way that we can define what it is about power that is causative. "A proper definition of 'power' should be directed at the determinants of the outcome and not the outcome itself" (Cross 1969, p. 17). I agree. Negotiation researchers are fundamentally interested in explaining how and why the *process* of bargaining results in various types of *outcomes*. Since bargaining is a process of position modification and convergence, and power is a concept covering the causes of change in attitudes and behavior, power can effectively be used as a means to explain the process.

What are the means of power? How are the resources at the disposal of the negotiator utilized so that he might attempt to alter the behavior of another in an intended direction? In addition to mutual perceptions and expectations, the bargaining process is a function of the use of persuasive and influential communications and feedback. Baldwin discussed the power of positive sanctions (actual or promised rewards) and negative sanctions (actual or threatened punishments). Positive sanctions might be conceived as improvements in the influencee's value position, while negative sanctions might be considered deprivations (Baldwin 1971b, pp. 23–24, 37). The outcome of the use of power is very much dependent on the influencee's utility and probability assigned to the possible out comes, and his behavior as a result of these two factor (Singer 1963, pp. 422–25). The success or effectiveness o various sanctions is also related to the costs involved to the influencer. "There is an asymmetry between promises and threats in that the former usually cost A (the influencer) more when they succeed while the latter usually cost A more when they fail. Thus A's incentive to use promises varies *inversely* with his perceptions of the probability of success while A's incentive to use threats varies *directly* with the per ceived probability of success" (Baldwin 1971a, p. 477).

Persuasive tactics are predictions of future events in which the other side becomes constrained as a result of the per suader's self-imposed commitment to constrain himself and the other (Schelling 1960, p. 160). Persuasion is communicated as conditional statements in which if a demand is not complied with under certain conditions, the commitment is threatened or promised to come into effect. Whether gratificational or deprivational in intent, the persuader's commitment is an exhibition of his potential strength and power—that he can do without or threaten sanctions. But ultimately, for a persuasive act to be effective and alter the other's behavior in the intended direction, it must be credible and convincing.

## Position and Behavior Modification in Bargaining

The aim of negotiation is to attain a convergence of interests between previously conflicting parties. Obviously, this process must entail a transformation or modification of the values and expectations of at least one of the bargainers involved.

The negotiator usually enters the bargaining situation with certain objectives or interests to fulfill for the group he repre sents. The negotiator's position can be conceived as the opera tionalization of his side's goals and interests. Often, a strong allegiance and loyalty to his group and its goals limits the various behaviors the negotiator might pursue in interacting with his counterparts in bargaining. The limits of his bargain ing strategies might have been worked out in advance with other leaders of his group. Or perhaps he was made to feel that the resolution he achieves must fall within certain guidelines that are acceptable to his group, or else he will face possible censure and ostracism (Bass 1966, p. 2). But, of course, if a convergence of interests is ever to occur, the negotiator's commitment to his group cannot be absolute. Positional and behavioral flexibility by both sides in negotiation is necessary to reach agreement.

A negotiator's position and bargaining behavior are interrelated. In pursuing certain goals, the negotiator will deem certain interactional strategies appropriate and others inappropriate. What behavior is appropriate can be "rationally" determined by specifying the tactics that will maximize his interests while imposing the least cost on himself (Sawyer and Guetzkow 1965, pp. 472–77). But as we mentioned earlier, to achieve a positive nonzero-sum agreement whereby both parties in negotiation profit, though not maximally, there must be a mutual constraint and modification of absolute and initial goals. Bargaining position modification is therefore a major phenomenon of the bargaining process.

A shift in bargaining position will probably be shadowed by a shift in bargaining behavior to attain the new and modified goals. Past behaviors might no longer be appropriate to present tasks, and under such changed conditions, adherence to old behaviors might indicate maladjustment and rigidity (Cowen 1952).

A change of position is a function of the communications network between negotiators and the constant shifting evaluations and expectations of the other party and one's own interests. A change of bargaining behavior may very well be a result of a change of bargaining position; it may be the means by which one side communicates to the other of its position change or it may be an indication of a new strategy to cope with new objectives. But this need not always be the case. A change in bargaining behavior may also signal the exercise of a new strategy toward old objectives (Ikle 1964, p. 177). Hence a change of bargaining position may affect a change of behavior, but a change of behavior does not necessarily indicate a change of position.

## The Feedback Model of the Bargaining Process

Using the propositions and relationships so far presented, we will formulate a model of the dynamics of the bargaining process. Our aim is to explain the process of negotiation that leads to a convergence of interests and common agreement. Toward this goal, we will attempt to identify the determinants of bargaining position and behavior modification and to distinguish these two phenomena from one another.

As an interactive process, bargaining involves influential and persuasive communications between the participants, with the objective of mutually influencing the other in an intended direction. But as we have seen, we must inquire into the intrapsychic dynamics, as well as the more apparent interpersonal interactions, to explain the communications and behavior that comprise the negotiation process. Researchers have not paid enough attention to the "black box" of motivation and personality that determine behavior. In our model, we attempt to unravel and demystify these "unknown" determinants by including the elements of perception, expectation, and strategic planning.

Specifically, we are interested in the effect of party A's persuasive communications on party B: What are B's expectations based on A's past behavior, how do the conflicts of interest between A and B affect B's present perceptions, what are B's perceptions of A's present influence attempts, and what are B's strategic plans for responding to A's attempts? B's experience of A's power attempt constitutes what has previously been left untouched by many researchers. But our interests go farther. How does B's response, based on its perceptual process, influence the position and behavior of A, such that a feedback loop of A's original power strategy is formed? The model depicted in Figure 1 provides a conceptual framework for the explanation of these relationships.

The bargaining process here is depicted as a system of reciprocal interaction and continuous feedback. The model is dynamic in that it views the influence of the past process on the immediate and ongoing process. The process is substantially motivated by the intervening "black box" of the negotiators'

## FIGURE 1.
*Feedback model of the bargaining process*

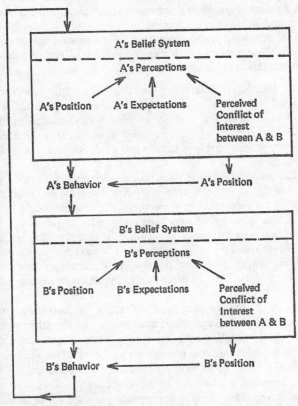

belief systems, the contents of which are often only partially known to the opposing side. The apparent process of bargaining exists only as far as the behavioral tactics used, modified by the bargaining position and interests of the negotiator. But we are primarily interested in the effects of inner, unconscious mechanisms on the manifest behavior and positions. It appears to be these latent elements of bargaining that are the true catalysts of the interaction process leading to behavior and position change and convergence of interests.

Thus, this model allows us to identify the effects of the use of different power strategies, some of the motivational elements behind behavior, and the operation of the feedback mechanism of persuasive communications in influencing position and behavior modification.

The following propositions describe the general linkages between the organism and his environment that are considered fundamental to this model.

1. Behavioral interaction in the bargaining process is typified by power relationships. Influential and persuasive communications are used to attempt a modification of the other party's position in an intended direction. In negotiation the power relationship is usually not unidirectional, but reciprocal.

2. A negotiating party's behavioral interaction with its opponent is influenced by its own objectives, interests, and position and by its perceptual interpretation of the situation.

3. The behavior of one bargaining party is perceived, interpreted, and evaluated by another in terms of the latter's belief system. This belief system itself is modified by the perceiving party's goals and position, its expectations based on past experience, and its perceptions of conflicts of interest with the opponent.

4. A party's position and objectives in bargaining are affected by its perceptions of the behavior of the other party.

5. A modification of bargaining position is a function of shifting evaluations and perceptions of the situation. Such perceptual change is, in turn, a function of the communication and feedback mechanisms of the interaction process between negotiators. Thus the bargaining process is a system of interaction that must be studied in a longitudinal fashion.

6. When bargaining positions change, bargaining behavior often changes in accordance with the new objectives. But a modification of behavior does not necessarily imply a modification of position.

7. Convergence of interests is basically a function of bargaining position modification, but bargaining behavior modification may be an important factor in implementing a change in position.

APPLICATION: THE ASWAN HIGH DAM NEGOTIATIONS

## *Historical Account of the Bargaining Process*

During 1955 and 1956, the United States, Great Britain, the World Bank, and Egypt negotiated an offer for financial aid to help build the Aswan High Dam. Few direct, face-to-face negotiating sessions occurred during eight months of bargaining. However, the positions, strategies, and reactions of the parties were communicated through diplomatic correspondence, statements, and visits.

By far the prime mover of the negotiating party for the West was John Foster Dulles, the U. S. Secretary of State. Because President Eisenhower was incapacitated by his second heart attack for the duration of these negotiations, Dulles had been given final decision-making power, as was the case during most of his tenure in the State Department. We can safely designate Dulles as the "decision-making negotiator" for the West.

The history of the negotiations can be divided into five stages. In the first, the intentions, positions, and possible reactions of both parties were identified and tested. On November 21, 1955, representatives of the United States, Great Britain, the World Bank, and Egypt met for the first time in Washington to discuss the possibility of the West providing aid to Egypt for the purpose of building a high dam at Aswan. Such a dam had been highly recommended by experts as an essential prerequisite for social and economic development in Egypt along the Nile River. The Egyptians were anxious to get this aid from the West to balance their September 1955 purchase of arms from Czechoslovakia and thereby maintain their neutral stance between the two great powers. To encourage Western aid, they promised greater order, stability, and progress within their own country, and friendship with the West. The Czech arms deal and Egypt's vehement campaign against the Baghdad Pact and Great Britain made the West especially sensitive to possible signs of Egyptian drift toward the Soviet camp.

However, the West did not respond to the Egyptian pledges

by providing aid immediately, directly, or freely. Dulles, with the consent of Eisenhower, decided to obtain more than a mere statement of friendship from Egypt in return for American help. Sending a secret emissary to Israel and Egypt at the beginning of December, Dulles attempted to tie a Middle East peace settlement to the West's financial backing of the dam. Despite an implicit threat by the United States to withdraw the promised aid if a peace agreement were not reached, Egypt decided that it could do without the aid under these conditions. The United States backed down from its threat, and on December 16, 1955, a joint offer of aid was made by the United States and Great Britain.

Attached to the offer, however, was an *aide-mémoire* containing certain unpublicized conditions that Egypt was required to comply with before the offer would go into effect. These entailed economic restraints and controls that the West wished to impose on Egypt. In addition to maintaining a stable economy in Egypt, the West intended these conditions to limit all new accords between Egypt and the Soviets, hopefully transforming Nasser into a pro-Western, anti-Communist ally.

In the second stage, Nasser reacted to these conditions by claiming that they were prejudicial to Egyptian sovereignty and were attempts by the West to obtain a voice in Egyptian foreign and domestic policy. He, in turn, threatened to seek aid from the Soviets if the West did not eliminate the conditions. (The Soviets had already offered financial aid for the dam.) Despite this threat, Nasser proceeded to impose on Egypt certain of the economic conditions that the West had demanded. Although these moves might be viewed as concessions to the West's demands, the West remained silent to these overtures and did not reply.

The third stage of the negotiations involved two major compromises on the part of Egypt, which could have transformed the outcome into positive sum payoffs for both participants. However, because of the development of internal and external pressures on the United States' negotiators at this time, no response was ever made to these Egyptian conciliatory initiatives. At the end of February 1956, Nasser sent letters to Washington and London indicating his willingness to accept the *aide-mémoire* if the West would alter the wording of the conditions so as to remove any hint of foreign domination of Egyptian policy. In effect, Nasser agreed to give the West economic assurances if the West would merely change the language of the agreement to divert potential domestic hostility.

In a second concession on April 3, Nasser promised the West that once the aid was given, there would no longer be any cause to fear a pro-Communist policy dominating Egypt. The West's acceptance of these Egyptian concessions would have made possible a maximization of interests and goals on both sides in the final outcome of the negotiations. However, the West did not reply at all to the concessions, in effect rejecting them.

The United States' decision-makers, around the end of February 1956, began to feel certain pressures building up domestically and externally against the aid offer. The Republican party feared a hostile reaction in the upcoming elections if the aid offer was implemented. The United States cotton lobby was afraid of a glut on the market, because the Western offer was to be repaid with sales of Egyptian cotton. The Senate, which was generally cold to the aid offer, was still wary of the Communist and neutralist leanings of the Egyptian Government. Great Britain, which had offered the aid as a joint venture with the United States, was quickly turning against the entire project in March, because of the Nasserite influence on the dismissal of the pro-British commander of the Jordanian Army, Glubb Pasha, and because of Egypt's generally hostile attitude against Britain. All of these factors apparently brought pressure on Dulles to alter his policy toward Egypt. In fact, historians Love (1969) and Deney (1962) feel that after February the State Department had totally capitulated to these outside influences. The very effective official Western silence to all of Nasser's attempts to create a compromise agreement points to the obvious Western reconsideration of its original offer of aid. Egypt's change of bargaining position was not matched by a similar counterconcession by the West, and therefore no convergence of interests occurred.

The fourth stage witnessed Egypt openly insulting the West by officially recognizing Red China in May 1956. Surprisingly, on May 24, the United States announced its continued support of Nasser and the offer of aid, despite Egypt's new diplomatic initiatives toward the Communists.

On June 19, during the final stage of the bargaining process, Secretary of State Dulles informed the Senate Appropriations Committee, and Egypt indirectly, that no United States aid for the High Dam would be available in the foreseeable future, and that Nasser might now seek aid if he wished from the Soviets. However, on July 13, Nasser suddenly and surprisingly announced that he now accepted all of the conditions originally set down by the West, and sent his ambassador to Washington to close the deal. Considering the tone of Dulles' remarks of June 19 and following, it appeared as though the West had irrevocably altered its position to provide aid. Nasser's eagerness to sign an agreement he originally found repugnant at this late date and in the aftermath of Dulles' recent public renunciation appears confusing. Finally, on July 19, Dulles officially withdrew the United States' aid offer for the High Dam. Some historians feel that Nasser wanted to be officially repudiated so as to appear morally justified in nationalizing the Suez Canal in retaliation.

The official explanation for the aid offer withdrawal revolved around the ability of the Egyptian economy to assure the project's success. All of the knowledgeable historians, and the World Bank, felt that such reasoning was unwarranted by the facts. They assert that the real reasons hinged on Dulles' Cold War ideology. Dulles was probably convinced that (a) Nasser had threatened to obtain Soviet aid for the dam in order to blackmail the West into meeting his terms, (b) Nasser had finally agreed to the West's conditions because the Soviets, during June, had refused to offer aid for the dam, and (c) Nasser had deliberately encouraged the withdrawal of the dam offer to obtain a pretext for nationalizing the canal. In addition, Dulles had a distinct dislike and distrust for neutrals and may have wanted to teach Nasser a lesson, cutting short the success of his "seesaw politics." Deney (1962) feels that Dulles' decision to renege was an attempt to appease the senators who opposed the dam offer. But above all, Dulles' fear of international communism, triggered by Egypt's recognition of Red China, was probably the most salient explanation of Dulles' decision to renege.

The five stages of the negotiations can be summarized in terms of the general bargaining positions taken by the two participants. Figure 2 illustrates the trends of the two positions. Acceptance of the available terms by both parties during the same stage would have resulted in a convergence of interests and agreement.

### FIGURE 2.
*The general bargaining positions of the West and Egypt during the five stages of the negotiations*

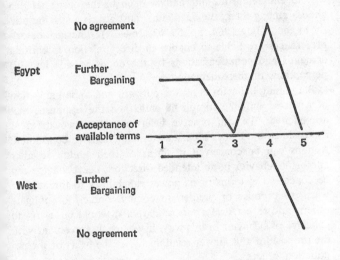

*Operationalization of Concepts*

In order to apply our feedback model to this or any historical case we must operationalize the theoretical concepts involved. The indicators we formulate should directly relate to the original theoretical considerations as well as to practical data-making procedures.

Operationalization of manifest bargaining behavior and stated position presents little problem. Variables attempting to tap the bargaining goals and objectives of a party—its bargaining position—must look to the party's choices and preferences. The range of alternatives open to the negotiator can be conceived of in terms of Ikle's "continual threefold choice"; his decision at any given moment indicates his preference and immediate priorities. The negotiator must constantly decide what are the immediate end states he hopes to attain for his side based on his perceptions and expectations of the other side's position and strategy, and his own calculations to achieve a joint maximization of interests. Ikle's choices—accept an agreement at the available terms, discontinue negotiations without an agreement, and bargain further—provide one way to enumerate the alternatives open to the bargainer. To choose among them, the negotiator must attach a specific utility to each (Ikle 1964, pp. 59–62, 164–70). The negotiator's preferences are liable to change in direct relation to shifting demands and communications by the opposing side and his perceptions of these demands.

Bargaining behavior is all the outward and apparent action of a participant—the stimuli he emits and the responses that are elicited. We can observe behavior along two different dimensions; the first is a persuasive-nonpersuasive continuum. Actions can be conceived in terms of their ability to alter another's behavior in an intended direction; i.e., behavior can be conceived in terms of its power capabilities to threaten or warn, to promise or predict, to commit oneself or obligate others, and to perform a *fait accompli*. It would be useful to conceive of behavior in this way, if we are in agreement with the proposition that power relations are at the heart of the negotiation process.

But does all bargaining behavior have to be persuasive to have an effect on the behavior of the other party? Perhaps not. Extremely hostile or co-operative behavior might cause a modification of the other side's behavior and position merely by changing the situation through the use of brute force or extravagant altruism. Such change should not be classified as a consequence of persuasive measures, because there are no power contingencies for the recipients of such action to respond to. Hence, we can alternatively conceive of behavior along a co-operative-hostile dimension (see Schelling 1966, pp. 1–34). In this study, we find it beneficial to view bargaining behavior from both perspectives.

The final category, perceptions, presents probably the most difficult operationalization decision for the researcher. Perceptions are constructs of the mind that are not apparent and obvious. Perceptions are a product of the operation of an individual's belief system. Without the benefit of psychoanalytic records or transcripts of the free associations of the negotiator at various points in the bargaining process, we are hard pressed for sources of data concerning his perceptions and expectations.

One method of empirically deriving a person's perceptions of the situation involves making educated inferences from the individual's behavior. Richard Snyder (1958, p. 31), discussing motivation in the decision-making process, argues that *real* motives can be inferred from the verbal behavior of decision-makers.

> Politics is a social realm where, par excellence, the participants pay a great deal of attention to the reasons they give for their actions and to arguing with others about the reasons for their action. . . . (I)t is in precisely those social situations in which purposes are vocalized and carried out with close reference to the speech and actions of others where motive avowals and imputations seem to arise most prominently.

As part of this internal motivation process, perceptions too can be inferred from behavior and statements through content analytic procedures.

But undoubtedly, an individual might rationalize his perceptions in his verbal behavior. How can we be sure that he really means what he says? Do we have a means of testing whether our inferences about perceptions from verbal acts are valid? Snyder suggests four criteria by which we justify our inferential assumption (ibid., p. 32):

1. Discrepancies between the alleged *real* perception and statements about perception might merely be a research problem of properly attributing verbal statements to intrapsychic phenomena.

2. Even if an individual's statements do not originally reflect his true perceptions of the situation, they may serve to influence a change in his perceptual viewpoint.

3. Even if an individual's statements are meant to mislead other actors, it must be taken into account that his statements, nevertheless, will affect them.

4. It seems unlikely that the constant falsification of statements would enable the survival of a decision unit.

Following is a list of the operational indicators of the model's theoretical concepts:

1. *Bargaining position*
   a. acceptance of agreement at available terms
   b. further bargaining
   c. acceptance of no agreement
2. *Conflict of positions between A and B*
   a. communality of positions
   b. conflict of positions
3. *Perceptions of the other party* ($t_1$)
   a. friendly
   b. mixture of friendliness and hostility
   c. hostile
4. *Expectations of the other party* (perceptions $t_0$)
   a. friendly
   b. mixture of friendliness and hostility
   c. hostile
5. *Total bargaining behavior*
   a. co-operative actions and statements
   b. mixture of co-operative and hostile actions and statements
   c. hostile actions and statements
6a. *Persuasive bargaining behavior only* (partial behavior, variable 5 minus variable 6b)
   a. gratificational persuasion (promise or prediction)
   b. mixture of gratificational and deprivational persuasion
   c. deprivational persuasion (threat or warning)
6b. *Nonpersuasive bargaining behavior only* (partial behavior, variable 5 minus variable 6a)
   a. co-operative actions and statements
   b. mixture of co-operative and hostile actions and statements
   c. hostile actions and statements

## Data-making Procedures

The data on these variables were collected from several sources in order to capture the most complete picture possible of the Aswan negotiation process. The New York *Times* Index, the London *Times Daily*, and the *Foreign Broadcast Information Service: Daily Report* were tapped to gather the positional, behavioral, and perceptual data needed. The *FBIS* daily reports were especially valuable in terms of obtaining direct quotations made by negotiators and their state-controlled press and radio stations. In addition, the detailed accounts of this bargaining process in Love (1969), Robertson (1965), and Deney (1962) aided in filling in the gaps during the eight-month period.

Once the data were collected and coded, it was observed that little information had been uncovered concerning the perceptions of the Western negotiators. The effective silence and ambiguity of the statements they made created impossible conditions within which we could validly infer their perceptions. Therefore, unfortunately, the "black box" for the West has been omitted from the subsequent analysis. Taking this into account, the version of the model that will be used is presented in Figure 3.

A decision had to be made concerning the time structure of the analysis. The model describes a continuous interaction process and calls for a time series or longitudinal approach, rather than a time point analysis. Since the model postulates action and reaction in terms of interactional units, equal time intervals (such as days or weeks) seemed not to be suitable. Instead, we have adapted Paul Smoker's time concepts of "interaction" and "reaction" (Smoker 1969, p. 180). Hence, each unit of observation is defined as a situation in which at least two behavioral entities respond to each other either at the same time or at a measurably later date (i.e., with a lag). Specifically, each observation describes a complete behavioral interaction sequence beginning with each manifestation of behavior by the West and ending with a response by Egypt. The eight-month period during which the negotiations took place yielded a total of eighteen time units. A listing of the interactional time period appears in the Appendix on page 371.

## Data Analysis and Discussion

Eleven variables over eighteen time periods were used to analyze the bargaining process of the Aswan High Dam negotiations. The specific list of variables follows:[1]

1. West's co-operative-hostile behavior
2. West's persuasive behavior
3. West's nonpersuasive behavior
4. West's position
5. Egypt's co-operative-hostile behavior
6. Egypt's persuasive behavior
7. Egypt's nonpersuasive behavior
8. Egypt's position
9. Egypt's perceptions
10. Egypt's expectations
11. Egypt's perceived conflict of interests between self and West

Before discussing the analysis of this bargaining process, one must be cautioned about the terminology applied to the actors. Although in the previous and subsequent accounts we refer to "Egypt" and "the West" as the two bargaining parties, these terms are merely used as a shorthand reference to the *individual* decision-making negotiators that lead each party (i.e., Dulles, Nasser, and their top aides). It is the individual negotiators whom we conceive to behave, perceive, and respond within the bargaining situation, not some anthropomorphized bargaining unit.

Figure 3 depicts the results of the correlational analysis along the lines of the feedback model. Only the statistically significant relationships have been indicated. Table 1 lists these and other important relationships uncovered in the analysis. Many high gammas between variables had to be discounted because they were found to be statistically insignificant. Largely, this was a function of a low number of observations coupled with a large amount of missing data.[2]

FIGURE 3.
*Model of the Aswan negotiation process (Gamma coefficients indicate the measure of association between variables, p< .10)*

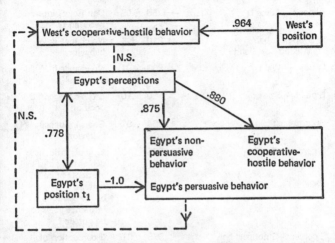

Overall, the conflicts of interest between the West and Egypt were high (−.75). Such a high negative correlation suggests what in fact we know of this bargaining process: A convergence of interests did not occur; there was no outcome. Was there movement by either side to reduce this conflict? There appears to have been no change of bargaining behavior by the West (.810), no change of bargaining position by the West (.838), and only little change in bargaining position by Egypt (.500). The fact that the tactics and objectives of both parties remained fairly constant and unmodified explains the bargainers' inability to reach convergence in the outcome.

How can we explain the flow of the bargaining process? We can divide the process into five steps:

*The West's position and behavior.* The results show a very high correlation between behavior by the West and its bargaining position (.964). The more the West leaned toward acceptance of an agreement, the greater was the probability it would use a co-operative strategy toward Egypt. The greater

TABLE 1.
*List of correlations*

| Variables | Gamma | Sign. level | Interpretation |
|---|---|---|---|
| W pos $t_1$—E pos $t_1$ | − .750 | .05 | Conflict of interest between W and E |
| W coop-host beh $t_1$— W coop-host beh $t_2$ | .810 | NS | No change in W behavior |
| W pos $t_1$—W pos $t_2$ | .838 | .01 | No change in W position |
| E pos $t_1$—E pos $t_2$ | .500 | .10 | Little change in E position |
| W coop-host beh $t_1$—W pos $t_1$ | .964 | .01 | Goals influence behavior |
| E percept—E pos $t_1$ | .778 | .10 | a. goals influence perceptions and elements of belief system. b. perceptions influence goals to be pursued. |
| E percept—E nonpers beh | .875 | .01 | E perception of situation influences behavior along a nonpersuasive, coop-hostile dimension |
| E percept—E coop-host beh | .880 | .05 | |
| E pos $t_1$—E pers beh | −1.00 | .02 | But E's goals influence persuasive behavior. |

the tendency to stop negotiating without agreement, the greater the use of a hostile strategy.

*Egypt's perceptions.* No relationship appears between the West's behavior toward Egypt and Egypt's perception of that behavior. No matter how the West's actions are conceived—whether along a co-operative-hostile or persuasive-nonpersuasive dimension—Egypt's perceptions seem to be independent of stimuli emitted by the West. The model had expected that one party would either clearly perceive the manifest behavior of the opposing side or systematically distort its perceptions in accordance with an internally consistent belief system. But neither appears to be the case in this bargaining process.

We might speculate that the absence of a relationship between the West's behavior and Egypt's perceptions is simply a function of our difficulty to infer perceptions from Egypt's behavior. Other than this methodological problem, the absence of association could have been influenced by Dulles' bargaining silence. Throughout the bargaining process, Dulles and his spokesmen released extremely few communications aimed at Egypt. (Our study revealed only eighteen manifestations of behavior by the West over an eight-month period.) Because of the paucity of cues, it was probably difficult for Nasser to comprehend the meanings of those few that were communicated; he did not enter the bargaining situation with a set of educated expectations. Hence, the type of strategy pursued by the West might explain the lack of correlation between the West's behavior and Egypt's perceptions.

What then did influence Egypt's perception of the situation? Because of the meager flow of information from the West, Egypt's expectations and its perceived degree of conflicts of interest with the West were not related to its perceptions of the situation. However, Egypt's bargaining position was positively associated with its perceptions (.778). The greater Egypt's tendency toward accepting an agreement, the friendlier its perceptions of the West, and vice versa. Egypt's bargaining position influenced its perceptions, and its perceptions also influenced the goals Egypt pursued.

*Egypt's behavior as a function of its perceptual process and position.* If behavior is a function of the organism interacting with its environment, we can conclude that Egypt's behavior in the bargaining process was largely a result of its inner perceptual dynamics. The more hostile Egypt's perceptions of the West, the more hostile its behavior. Egypt's perceptions of the situation were positively related to its behavior along a generally nonpersuasive dimension; its perceptions correlated highly only with its co-operative-hostile behavior (.880) and nonpersuasive behavior (.875).

This finding goes against the grain of most theories of negotiation as a process motivated by power. Decision-making by each bargaining participant usually entails the perception and evaluation of stimuli, followed by the planning of response behavior to modify the stimulator's position and future behavior.

Such power relationships in bargaining necessitate the use of persuasive strategies, but our findings indicate that Egypt's perceptual process was not associated with such strategies.

Egypt's use of power does relate highly with Egypt's bargaining position ($-1.00$). The greater Egypt's desire to come to agreement with the West, the greater its use of persuasive and threatening strategies. To achieve its goals and objectives, Egypt's negotiators continually threatened to turn to the Soviet camp for assistance if the West did not come through with its aid offer.

Although bargainers may utilize a combination of persuasive and nonpersuasive behaviors, persuasive acts can be identified as the major components of a strategy of power. Perhaps we can conclude from our findings that as far as its power strategy in the Aswan negotiations are concerned, Egypt's behavior was determined more by its objectives than by its perceptions of the situation.

*The West's behavior as a function of feedback.* Each interaction sequence in the model was structured so that it begins with a manifestation of behavior by the West and ends with a behavioral response by Egypt. The effect of Egypt's response on the subsequent behavior of the West in the next sequence has been identified as a feedback loop in the bargaining process.

The results indicate that no feedback indeed existed in this case. Egypt's behavior, no matter in what form it is conceived, varied independently of the West's strategy in the next time sequence. But as we noted earlier, we have omitted crucial intervening variables here: the West's belief system and perceptual structure. In fact, if we had found a strong correlation directly linking Egypt's behavior with the West's subsequent behavior, we would have invalidated one of our major assumptions—that negotiators do not simply respond to stimuli but perceive stimuli first and respond in relation to their interpretations of them.

*The determinants of position and behavior modification.* The Aswan negotiation process resulted in an outcome of no agreement. If both sides had modified their positions, lowered the conflicts of interest, and come to convergence, then agreement might have been reached. But positions and strategies basically remained the same and the conflicts of interest remained high throughout the bargaining process.

We noted earlier that behavior modification may be a function of a change of position or a change in tactics, while position modification is a function of shifting perceptions and evaluations of the environment. Position modification is the primary element contributing to the convergence of interests, but behavior modification is important in terms of manifesting and implementing the position change.

Why was there neither position nor behavior modification in the Aswan negotiations? Both Egypt and the West were using different power strategies aimed at each other, but neither responded to the other's influence attempts. Neither side's persuasive tactics appeared to be successful in achieving their intended effects.

Perhaps power was not effective in this situation because the means of influence were not appropriate or the goals not valued enough. Power attempts are effective when both sides desire something that only one has. But power loses its effectiveness if what is wanted can be obtained elsewhere at less cost or is not of high priority. In the Aswan case, Egypt felt it could always turn to the Soviets for aid if the West did not come through. Dulles, at first, was interested in trying to sway Egypt to a pro-Western stance, but quickly became disillusioned by his support of a regime that seemed to be drifting to the Communist camp. In addition, Egypt was not a necessary element of Dulles' Cold War program.

Too, perhaps power was not effective because the influential attempts were not credible. Trying to play the role of a neutral between the West and East, Nasser might have felt that despite Dulles' threats and promises concerning the aid offer, Dulles would eventually succumb to the Egyptian threat of moving to the Soviets for aid. Dulles, equally, might have felt that despite Nasser's threats, Nasser would have to accept the West's conditions because the Soviets would be unwilling actually to provide the financial assistance in the end.

We can conclude that neither side modified its position because of an inability to clearly perceive the other side's goals and strategies and act in relation to them. Egypt's perceptions were independent of the West's strategy, and the West's subsequent behavior was unrelated to previous Egyptian strategy. It was not so much a problem of misperception, but a total lack of comprehension of the other side's position and behavior. Similar to the experiments of Blake and Mouton, and Bass, this lack of comprehension resulted in a rigidity of position that could not be permeated and that led to deadlock and no outcome. Literally, we observed an extreme case of a problem in communications.

CONCLUSION

Analysis of the historical case study indicates the utility of applying the phenomenological approach to bargaining behavior. Certainly, the feedback model presented here greatly simplifies the actual process of bargaining. But it does offer some tangible explanations of the power relationships between bargaining participants based on motivational grounds. Perceptions and expectations though are not the only elements that motivate a negotiator to maintain or modify his position or attempt to influence the goals of others; a negotiator's needs and drives, defense mechanisms, level of moral judgment, and other aspects of personality also affect his motives. Perhaps our feedback model can be further elaborated to include more of these intrapsychic factors that influence the interpersonal dynamics of the bargaining process.

The empirical work of this study indicates that more insight is needed to heighten the sophistication of the operational measures. Snyder's criteria aside, I am not too sure that inferring perceptions from behavior is a completely safe or valid method. Also, since most of our measures are trichotomous over a range from extreme co-operativeness to extreme hostility, we cannot expect great sensitivity to the reality and complexity of events and perceptions.

As to our data-making procedures, the inaccessibility and ambiguity of information concerning the manifest behavior and communications of the bargaining process were largely overshadowed by the extreme difficulty of collecting data on the interests and perceptions of the negotiators. Better sources and improved-content analytic methods must be utilized so that the data we work with are more complete and reliable.

Despite its problems, theory and research along the lines suggested in this chapter will improve our ability to explain the bargaining process because they force us to focus on the human elements that are at the locus of bargaining dynamics. We must not only analyze the manifest interpersonal occurrences in the process, but also must search further into the forces motivating the negotiators themselves to explain why and when the bargaining process will yield successful agreements.

### Appendix: Interactional Time Periods

1. Nov. 21–Dec. 12, 1955
2. Dec. 8–10, 1955
3. Dec. 11–15, 1955
4. Dec. 16–19, 1955
5. Dec. 20–26, 1955
6. Dec. 27, 1955–Jan. 10, 1956
7. Jan. 11–22, 1956
8. Jan. 23–26, 1956
9. Jan. 27–Feb. 8, 1956
10. Feb. 9–11, 1956
11. Feb. 12–28, 1956
12. Mar. 1–Apr. 2, 1956
13. Apr. 3–May 23, 1956
14. May 24–June 18, 1956
15. June 19–July 8, 1956
16. July 9–12, 1956
17. July 13–18, 1956
18. July 19, 1956

### NOTES

1. "Black box" data for the West were unavailable, eliminating perception, expectation, and perceived conflict variables. Some of the West's variables were lagged forward one time unit in order to analyze the effects of Egypt's "black box" and feedback.

2. Since gamma measures both linear and curvilinear associations, there are several distributions of the data that will yield perfect correlations. See W. Buchanan, *Understanding Political Variables* (New York: Scribner's, 1969), pp. 221–26; M. Zelditch, *A Basic Course in Sociological Statistics* (New York: Holt, 1959), pp. 181–86; L. Freeman, *Elementary Applied Statistics* (New York: Wiley, 1965), pp. 79–88; H. Blalock, *Social Statistics* (New York: McGraw-Hill, 1960), pp. 225–28.

# 5. REALITY, IMAGE, AND DETAIL: THE PARIS NEGOTIATIONS, 1969–73

## I. William Zartman, New York University

No negotiations in recent times have aroused as much passion and controversy as the Vietnam negotiations. Yet several years later little is still known about what brought them about, what went on, what came out, and even who won. The "why" behind any of these simply descriptive questions is even further from a clear answer.

None of this is surprising. The issues are still very much alive, as are the participants in the negotiations. If the few accounts that are gradually appearing tend to reveal and deplore the variance between the carefully orchestrated public record and the equally delicate private assurances during the negotiations, few people would suggest that this convenant would have benefited from being openly arrived at. Furthermore, some of the above questions are more significant and legitimate than others: It is much more important to know what was really agreed to than to try to nail down precise findings about who won. As in many successful negotiations, some ambiguity about the latter question is part of the key to the success. "A lasting peace could come about only if neither side sought to achieve everything that it had wanted; indeed, that stability depended on the relative satisfaction, and therefore on the relative dissatisfaction, of all the parties concerned" (Kissinger 1973).

Journalists, functioning as an active press during the negotiations and producing some more concerted postmortems thereafter, including the work by Szulc (1974) and the Kalbs (1974), have helped pull the veils away from the train of events leading to the various Paris agreements. Their accounts, along with Secretary Kissinger's press statements and other news reports from both sides, will be used as the basis of the present study in its attempt to find the essence of the moves that lead to final convergence and agreement. Yet none of these accounts has gone beyond the point of historical description. The area of explanation, causality, and, ultimately, power is still totally unexplored. A preliminary reconnoiter in this terrain is the second purpose of this study.

## I

The war during the decade of the 1960s was an escalating stalemate. Although the fortunes of war had seemed to swing from one side to the other in comparison with previous moments, such changes were temporary and the advantages transient. Neither the United States nor North Vietnam could evict the other from South Vietnam. The mixture of guerrilla and conventional ingredients locked the stalemate more firmly into place. However significant the truth that "the guerrilla wins if he does not lose. The conventional army loses if it does not win" (Kissinger 1969, p. 214), it is only a partial truth. The rest of the truth is found in a further characteristic of guerrilla warfare, the need of the guerrilla to move on to a conventional phase to consolidate his guerrilla victory over the conventional army. But success is the guerrilla's biggest problem: It pushes him into a conventional war, where he is less well prepared to prevail. So a guerrilla army must clinch its victory diplomatically, if it is to avoid a conventional confrontation. On the other hand, failure is the biggest problem of the conventional army: It keeps it in a guerrilla war where it is less well prepared to prevail. In George's terms, the guerrilla uses coercion, the conventional army, force (George, Hall, and Simons 1971; Schelling 1960, pp. 174–80).

Thus the war was a dynamic stalemate, not simply a static one. The only way out is for one or both sides to get tired and turn stalemate into a negotiated outcome. Unfortunately, to become tired, both sides had first to exhaust the possibilities of victory and firmly establish the stalemate by fully escalating it (Ellsberg 1972). The road to that realization is the story of the negotiation. Ironically, when the negotiated outcome was established, in turn, the conditions which established the stalemate were removed, and Saigon fell within two years.

The diplomatic expression of the stalemate prior to 1970 has been well summarized by Neil Sheehan (New York Times, June 28, 1972) on the basis of the Pentagon Papers:

- The volumes do not indicate any missed opportunities for peace.
- While there may have been some misunderstanding, each side understood reasonably well what the other wanted. The problem was that neither side was willing to compromise on the basic substance of its position.
- What misunderstanding did exist seems to have been more on the part of Washington, which apparently could not believe that the Vietnamese Communists would adhere to their basic objective under the rising level of military punishment being inflicted by American power.
- Hanoi conducted relatively open diplomacy, saying virtually the same things in private that it did in public.
- Hanoi was willing to compromise only to the extent of giving Washington a face-saving method of withdrawal from the South and of postponing the achievement of its long-term objective for a few years by the formation of a supposedly neutralist regime in the South.
- When Washington spoke publicly of negotiations, it usually meant, in private, the evolution of similar face-saving means for Hanoi to halt the war in the South in exchange for an end to American bombing and ground intervention.
- Hanoi did not attempt to use the peace movement in the United States as a channel for negotiations. Rather, it seems to have regarded the peace movement as evidence of a fundamental political weakness in American policy that would tell against Washington at the end.
- Washington in turn tended not to take seriously non-Communist intermediaries, such as Swedish officials who were critical of American policy.

• The bombing in the North appears to have increased Hanoi's determination to achieve its basic objective of unifying Vietnam under its own leadership.

At the end of the decade, however, the escalation stopped, leaving the stalemate firmly in place. Three elements comprise the end of the trend of the 1960s: the end of the American bombing of the North on November 1, 1968; the subsequent beginning of the public Paris peace talks on January 25, 1969; and the first unilateral American troop reductions ordered on September 16, 1969. These events—some of which involve negotiations as well—were unilateral preconditions (in an analytical, not a diplomatic, sense) of the negotiations on the peace settlement in Vietnam. If mutual movement is the beginning of negotiation, however, negotiation did not take place until a year later, in the fall of 1970.

Succinctly, the position of Hanoi had been a demand for the immediate withdrawal of all American troops and of the incumbent Saigon government as well, with a cease-fire, release of prisoners, and a coalition government of peace parties to follow. Washington's position comprised a cease-fire and the release of prisoners, followed by withdrawal of North Vietnamese and American troops and then a government of all peace parties and internationally supervised elections. The first Communist move in more than 16 months came on September 17, 1970, in the third year of the Paris peace talks (New York *Times,* Sept. 18, 1970). Its new elements were not significant: It simply supplied two details on the same general proposition, calling for American withdrawal in about nine months by June 30, 1971, and for elimination of three specific figures from the incumbent Saigon government. More significant but more general elements in the proposal were the suggestions that cease-fire and prisoner exchange were to be discussed as concomitant items with withdrawal. "It may well be an invitation to further negotiating but it is not, of itself, much of a concession" was an official Washington reaction (New York *Times,* Oct. 2, 1970).

Washington, on the other hand, had coincidentally been working on a new proposal for four months, and it was announced by President Nixon on October 7 (New York

*Times*, Oct. 8, 1970). Its five points contained some new ele
ments: immediate cease-fire in place and exchange of military
prisoners, followed by a negotiated withdrawal timetable and
then a negotiated political settlement. Most notable was the
fact that "total withdrawal" was used only in regard to Ameri
can troops, with no specific reference to North Vietnam in tha
context. However, Washington continued to insist on the
maintenance of the Thieu government. In the other element
the two proposals differed not as much in their contents as in
the order and time of their proposed occurrence.

The American proposal of October 1970 marked a crucial
change in its image of settlement. Unlike the earlier American
proposals, and unlike the corresponding proposal of the other
side, it sought to transfer the military stalemate into a political
settlement rather than seeking either a military decision for po
litical problems or a political decision for unresolved military
problems. Its major new elements—immediate cease-fire in
place and total American withdrawal—created a differen
image than that set by the major elements of the Vietcong
proposal—removal of Thieu and total American withdrawal
Subsequent American efforts centered on changing the order
and time of the agreed elements and the elimination of the
removal of Thieu, as an expression of the underlying image. I
seems hard to maintain, as does Szulc (1974, pp. 29, 26)
that this was "a contradiction in terms" or "brinkmanship."
Subsequent efforts of the other side were expended in main
taining position and image until—for reasons to be explored—
an acceptable proposition came from Washington. Two
aspects therefore formed the process of the negotiation: the
basic image such as stalemate or victory, and the order and
content of the component elements. To these, a third must be
added: the ambient reality or relation of forces on the ground
that gave its meaning to the first aspect and that the two (or
more) sides tried to alter in their favor from time to time.

There was no favorable echo from Hanoi or the Vietcong to
the October proposals, and indeed it may well be that com
munications barriers between the two sides were so great tha
the implications of the proposals were not understood. Cer
tainly, there is much disagreement as to when between October
1970 and April 1972 the term "total withdrawal" came clearly

o refer only to American (and allied) troops and not to North Vietnam. Certainly too, this is not the first time in the following two and more years that one side's messages were not clear to the other, with the consequent loss of time, lives, and maneuvering room in the search for a solution. Understandably, such garbled communications are not surprising when one considers that the United States was emitting three different messages—through Nixon, through Kissinger, and through the chief Paris representative, notably William Porter—all of which were screened through Hanoi's ideological filters, and the Communists were issuing at least two messages—through Mrs. Nguyen Thi Binh of the Vietcong delegation and Le Duc Tho and Xuan Thuy from North Vietnam—not always in the clearest language.

In his secret parallel negotiations throughout the following year, notably during the eighth through the thirteenth meetings between May and September 1971, Kissinger sought to arrive at settlement by reshaping and arranging the elements on which agreement seemed possible in such a way as to win the Communists away from their demand for the removal of Thieu. On May 31, he specifically offered to set a deadline for total unilateral withdrawal in exchange for the immediate release of all POWs and a cease-fire in place. Whether a particular deadline was mentioned or not is a matter of dispute (New York *Times*, Feb. 1 and 6, 1972; Kalb 1974, p. 179). On June 26, at the ninth session, Hanoi countered with a nine-point plan that Kissinger accepted as a basis for negotiation. It called for a cease-fire in place, followed by concomitant American withdrawal and exchange of prisoners in six months or by the end of 1971; the United States "should stop supporting Thieu-Ky-Khiem," pay reparations to North and South Vietnam, and leave political matters to be solved by the Vietnamese themselves. Whether Hanoi at this time was willing to separate political from military aspects of a settlement while negotiating about the former is also something that has not been fully established (New York *Times*, Feb. 1 and 6, 1972; Szulc 1974, p. 27; Kalb 1974, p. 181). The tenth session on July 12 was apparently spent discussing whether to use the nine-point plan or the Vietcong's seven-point plan released in public session on July 1 as the basis for negotiations; when it was agreed to continue talking on the nine-point proposal, th eleventh session was scheduled for July 26. After a point-by point discussion during the twelfth session on August 16, Kis singer brought a new proposal for a cease-fire in place followed by an American withdrawal and release of prisoner in nine months (by Aug. 1, 1972), postwar aid, neutrality i the October 3 presidential election in South Vietnam, and a fu ture political settlement. A month later, in the last session, o September 13, 1971, North Vietnam turned down this pro posal while continuing to call for the removal of Thieu.

Attractive as these proposals may appear (especially in th light of the agreement that was finally reached and the inter vening costs), it was not unreasonable for the Communists t insist on the removal of Thieu given the current situation o 1971. This was the year of the contested and rigged presiden tial elections in South Vietnam in which Thieu's opponents ap peared so dangerous to him that he arranged their removal an in which the American ambassador, Ellsworth Bunker, the proposed to Washington that Thieu also be pressured t withdraw. As long as there was some real hope of eliminatin Thieu, Hanoi was scarcely interested in negotiating the lesse component elements of an agreement. In this light, one ma well doubt the North Vietnamese claim that, had the Unite States mentioned a withdrawal date before the October 3 elec tions, they would have accepted it along with the rest of th American proposal and Thieu would not have been elected; i would seem rather that such an acceptance would have mean very clearly giving in on the principle of Thieu's removal whil there was still hope for it. But whatever the fact or the strat egy, it is above all clear that communications—the accurat understanding of the other party's meaning—between two negotiating teams sitting face to face but wrapped tightly i their respective cultures and ideologies were awful.

When, on October 11, a week after Thieu's election, Wash ington sent a new eight-point proposal to Hanoi, it was clear to the latter that not only was the United States committed to leaving Thieu in place—which was true—but also that it wa no more seriously interested in a negotiated settlement tha was Saigon—which was not. The proposal called for a cease fire, concomitant American withdrawal and prisoner exchange within six months, reconstruction aid, and, as a strikingly new element (cf. Kalb 1974, pp. 179 f.), the resignation of the Thieu government one month before free elections, which would in turn be scheduled within six months of an agreement. There are two explanations for the absence of serious consideration of this proposal and the breakdown of negotiations for nearly half a year. One can variously be called disinterestedness, bad faith, or a desire to change the ambient reality. It may well be that one side or both had simply lost interest in negotiating because they felt that the military conditions should and could be altered in their favor. Vietnamization was anathema to the Communists—Porter told them on October 28 in Paris, with more accuracy than influence, "It is interesting to have indications from you that the Vietnamization program is developing well. Every time you declaim heatedly against that program, we realize that you find it bothersome" (New York *Times,* Nov. 12, 1971). A new military offensive was required to destroy both its reputation and its effectiveness, a conclusion that Hanoi reportedly reached sometime in October (Kalb 1974, p. 285). On the American side, Washington may have felt that it was making all the concessions without any reciprocity and that further negotiations would require some serious sign from Hanoi beforehand.

The other explanation goes back again to bad communications. When a thirteenth meeting was being set up to discuss the eight-point proposals, Le Duc Tho, the leading North Vietnamese negotiator, fell ill and Hanoi proposed to go on without him; Washington took this to be a signal that serious negotiations were not contemplated and so canceled the meeting until someone on Le's level was available (on Kissinger's experience with Xuan, see Kalb 1974, pp. 150, 174, 184). Hanoi later cited this as a U.S. signal to break off talks, which is what happened. On the other hand, there are some important discrepancies between the versions of the eight-point proposals released later by Washington and by Hanoi. Since there were also important discrepancies between public and secret negotiating stands of American negotiators and since the Washington version differed from Hanoi's by omission more than by divergence, it would not be surprising if Hanoi's version were correct. Even if it is not, it may well

represent a very accurate picture of Hanoi's understanding of
the proposal. Essentially, the major discrepancies bear on a
double meaning to the agreement date from which withdrawal,
elections, and Thieu's resignation would be calculated, so that
American troops would be present up till the moment of the
elections. In both cases, suspicious perception of intentions
and meanings may indeed have been the correct one, but it
may very well have not, and the meeting that might have
cleared up the suspicion and the misperception was not held.
In these cases, it was the first aspect, the basic nature or image
of the situation, that shaped the view of the second, the proposals' component elements, and left them unnegotiable.

In a situation where neither image nor details could be
changed through negotiation, the parties moved to "create a
new reality," in Kissinger's phrase on a different occasion
(Kalb 1974, p. 471). It was logical that North Vietnam take
the first move, since the current version of reality favored—or
was perceived to favor—the South Vietnamese and American
side, because of the presumed effectiveness of Vietnamization
supported by the effects of the Cambodia and Laos invasions
in May 1970 and February 1971. At the same time, however,
it was necessary in the context to justify this move by showing
how negotiations had broken down through the other side's
misdoings. Since either side would benefit from making this
revelation first, the element of diplomatic surprise was almost
as important as was military surprise (for further details, see
Szulc 1974, pp. 32–35). Thus, the United States put heavy
efforts into military supplies to the South Vietnamese armed
forces while pursuing its policy of unilateral withdrawal. But it
also began—after the perceived cancellation of the Kissinger-
Le talks in November—to consider "going public" about the
opposite conduct of the other side. The result of President
Nixon's dramatic revelation on January 25 of the past series of
secret talks was to produce—or register publicly—retreats on
the part of both sides on previously negotiated details, such as
the matter of an American withdrawal deadline, or a Vietnamese agreement to separate political from military matters, or a
Vietnamese commitment to POW release concomitant with
troop withdrawals and prior to any change in the Saigon government. The tone of the exchanges between Hanoi and Wash-

ington sharpened to accusations of lying. But the day after the public speech, Nixon asked Hanoi for a new meeting, and on February 14 Hanoi proposed another secret session a month later. When Washington agreed, however, Hanoi requested another month's postponement, arousing an angry response that brought the date back to March 31. In many ways, however, the situation was brought back to pre-January 1969, before the Paris talks—public or secret—ever began and before the first bombing halt.

The reality-changing exercise that began on March 30 and interrupted all negotiation was the North Vietnamese spring offensive, and it proceeded to show the clay feet of Vietnamization beyond Washington's deepest fears. An article at the time in the Vietcong magazine *Tien Phong* indicated that "our general offensive is designed to defeat the enemy's Vietnamization plan, force the enemy to acknowledge his defeat and accept a political settlement on our terms . . . a transitional government at the upper level while we seize control at the lower level and proceed toward the formation of a three-segmented coalition government" (New York *Times,* Jan. 24, 1973, p. 19). The provincial capital of Quang Tri fell before the attack of a conventional—not guerrilla—Communist force during the month of April. When the North Vietnamese army hit, the South Vietnamese army ran. The plan was working well enough for Hanoi to call for the resumption of secret talks on May 2; the meeting was held but produced no movement. Indeed, the ambient reality was being changed so effectively that countermoves became imperative, on one hand to stem the ebb and on the other to return the conflict to the negotiating table before it degraded too far.

Thus, the United States felt impelled to make its contribution to a change in the ambient reality by launching, on May 8, intensive aerial bombardment of North Vietnamese communications in the Hanoi-Haiphong area, along with the mining of Haiphong. The move was filled with risks and with uncertain outcomes, for it was in danger of being so effective as to stop all negotiations, most notably those that were going on at the time with the Soviet Union during Kissinger's and, at the end of the month, Nixon's visits to Moscow, and also with China (for greater details on events and evaluations, see Kalb

1974, pp. 317–35; Szulc 1974, pp. 35–45). The bet was important because the Moscow trips were used for some notable initiatives by Kissinger to get the negotiations moving again. But it was also important, as is often overlooked in the concentration on moves and events, because it showed Hanoi that Saigon's allies were more committed to Saigon than were Hanoi's allies to Hanoi. If, as Nixon's advisers predicted, Russia would only increase its involvement in Vietnam or cancel its invitation to Nixon only if a Soviet ship were hit in Haiphong, Washington could combine the bombing and mining and the visits to Moscow and Peking to make its own offer more attractive by signaling a reduced security point or fall-back position to Hanoi (see Rapoport 1966, pp. 97, 101, and Kissinger 1969, p. 229). Finally, the bombing and mining not only changed the context of reality but also, like the spring offensive to which it responded, it changed the array of potential elements of discussion. Now two new items to negotiate about were present: separate and additional North Vietnamese troops, and several dissociable components of bombing and mining.

At the same time, Kissinger used the same ally of Hanoi to set the negotiation again into motion. It is notable, in terms of the previous comments about communications during negotiations between hostile parties, that some of the messages planted in Moscow involved new offers and new elements, but others consisted of making plain some matters that had been the subject of unclear communications beforehand. Thus, the opening move of the 1972 round of negotiations was an explicit version of the unilateral withdrawal offer coupled with the new element of the North Vietnamese invasion. During his secret visit to Moscow on April 20, Kissinger indicated "that the United States would be willing to accept a cease-fire in place in exchange for the departure of the North Vietnamese forces which entered South Vietnam since the start of the offensive on March 30" (Szulc 1974, p. 36). The detailed proposal was never picked up but its meaning was: "Kissinger was telling Brezhnev that Washington would not demand the evacuation of the estimated 100,000 North Vietnamese who had been in the South prior to the offensive" (ibid.). Kissinger also again insisted on the prime American demand that

Hanoi had always refused—and hence on the whole image of the negotiations: that Hanoi drop the demand for Thieu's removal, at least before any agreement. The second move was made during Nixon's visit, on May 25, when Kissinger indicated that the return of all POWs was not necessarily a precondition for a bombing halt, a major opening of the deadlock on timing that previously had blocked all further discussion. The third move, the same day, was an American mention of a tripartite council representing the Saigon government, neutral elements, and the Vietcong as a successor to the Thieu regime, a proposal more precise than the nine-point Hanoi provision for "a new administration" and the eight-point Washington provision for "an independent body." Szulc (1974, p. 43) reports a notable scene of surprise in Moscow: "Gromyko was so taken aback that he said to Kissinger, 'Let me make quite sure I got right what you said.' Kissinger replied: 'Yes, I'm talking about a tripartite commission.' "

In mid-June, Russian President Podgorny carried the message from Moscow to Hanoi, and once he had left, at the end of the month, the North Vietnamese Politburo met to set policy. The secret talks between Le and Kissinger which began on July 19 produced no moves of substance, but they opened communications and restored the seven- (or nine-) and eight-point proposals to the table. The September 11 session of the official talks in Paris did provide a new element, however, in a new Vietcong document that demanded the end of American support for Thieu but also emphasized the "reality that there exists two administrations, two armies, and other political forces in the South," and that these should "form a provisional government of national concord in the South, comprising three equal components . . . during the period of transition" (*Le Monde*, Sept. 12, 1972). Subsequent press questioning (*Le Monde*, Sept. 14, 19, and 22, 1970) confirmed the fact that the earlier crucial insistence on the immediate removal of Thieu was dropped. Kissinger returned to Paris for renewed secret talks. On September 26, he formally proposed the tripartite electoral commission from the American side and Le proposed an "administrative structure" of three equal parts requiring unanimity for a decision, to operate without replacing Thieu;

the previous week, a leading figure in Hanoi had written in the daily newspaper *Nhan Dan* and broadcast on the government radio that "if the United States really wanted to arrive at a solution to the problem, all the parties could discuss the means and guarantees offered by both sides to prevent one of the three components of the future Saigon government from eliminating the other during the transition period" (*Le Monde,* Sept. 28, 1972). On October 8, Hanoi proposed a draft "agreement on the termination of the war and the re-establishment of peace in Vietnam" calling for a cease-fire in place, followed by complete American withdrawal and return of American POWs within two months, ideas that had already been long discussed. With the termination of the military settlement, the two "administrations" existing in South Vietnam should prepare the political settlement by entering into contact to establish a National Council of Reconciliation and Concord, which would prepare general elections within three months of the cease-fire. Kissinger accepted the draft as the basis for negotiations, which continued over the following three days. By October 12, agreement was reached on a fifty-eight-page draft, which was carried back to Washington and Hanoi. Two remaining questions were left for resolution at a final meeting on October 17, although at that time other details of disagreement also came to light. On October 20, Nixon sent a message to Hanoi expressing appreciation for the goodwill of the other side and indicating that there were some remaining differences but that nevertheless "the text of the agreement could be considered complete." Hanoi gave additional explanations and agreements, which it claims were acknowledged as acceptable, in a message from Nixon on October 22. Two days later, Kissinger was to go to Hanoi to sign the agreement, bring into effect the cease-fire, and end the war.

The military part of the agreement adopted the three elements of Hanoi's October 8 proposal (*Le Monde,* Oct. 27 and 28, 1972). The bombing and mining would end twenty-four hours before signing. The American point on replacements was accepted: Neither South Vietnamese party could receive military personnel from elsewhere, and arms and munitions could be replaced only on a one-to-one basis; in this way the North Vietnamese troops in the South would gradually pass away without ever having been acknowledged (Kissinger 1973, p. 21). This was one of the two hanging questions on October 17; the other was an American desire to leave the release of civilian prisoners in South Vietnam to ulterior negotiations between the two South Vietnamese parties (there were already enough difficulties in getting assent from Thieu to the agreement), a point that the Communists also conceded (*Le Monde*, Oct. 28, 1972). The political part of the settlement provided for the creation, by the two South Vietnamese parties, of a tripartite National Council of National Reconciliation and Concord to solve problems of harmonization and coexistence between the two parties, which would remain in place until it had established new elections, hopefully within three months of the cease-fire. There would be a four-party military commission, a two-party South Vietnamese military commission, and a four-party International Commission of Control and Supervision, to watch over the execution of the agreement, and an international conference on the future of Vietnam to be convened within a month of the cease-fire; there were few details on the functions and composition of these bodies. All foreign parties would withdraw from Laos and Cambodia. New relations, including aid, would be created between Washington and Hanoi.

It is not known what other details were left to be settled between the October 17 meeting in Paris and the signing date two weeks later in Hanoi, besides the two hanging points on military replacements and civilian prisoners. It is clear, however, that, despite the enormous progress made beyond the basic elements that had settled into place over the previous two years, there were a number of imprecisions and loopholes (cf. Kalb 1974, pp. 359 f., 396). The nature of the demilitarized zone (DMZ), the size and powers of the International Commission, the nature of the National Council, and perhaps other points were all elements on which there was a real absence of necessary detail. This is quite a different matter from the solution provided for a number of other points—such as the question of the two armies in the South in the October agreement and a number of other questions in the final agreement—by explicitly leaving the matter to future determination among Vietnamese, which was one of the keys to a successful outcome that Kissinger had foreseen sometime before he became involved in direct negotiations (Kissinger 1969, p. 231).

Nonetheless, Hanoi was fervently—even "maniacally," as Kissinger later put it—attached to a settlement before the American elections. Perhaps deadline bargaining was merely a way of doing business that suited North Vietnamese; it had served them well in Geneva in 1954 (although the deadline was self-imposed on the French), and late concessions have sometimes been seen as a Communist trait. But more relevantly, as in the case of the hopes of removing Thieu, such fixations had a very realistic basis. Hanoi could scarcely have known, but it may well have felt, that Kissinger was at the same time telling Thieu that things would be different after the election and that a tough policy would then be in order. The North certainly believed that Nixon believed that he needed an agreement to wave before the electorate. In addition, the North Vietnamese knew that the spring offensive had not achieved its goal of a political settlement on their terms, that it had not been effective in conventional warfare and had been forced back into guerrilla tactics, that their army had not even been able to hold onto the border provincial capital of Quang Tri and that defenses against the bombing were wearing thin (particularly with a slowdown in Russian supplies).

These two hazards of incompleteness and speed canceled each other out to provide an agreement in a form mutually acceptable to the two negotiating parties by the end of October. The document as it then existed would doubtless have left a number of problems to plague postwar relations in Vietnam and very possibly even to discredit and destroy the peace. Many of these would probably have been discovered and patched over—although not in as good detail as was subsequently to occur—in the final negotiating and initialing meeting in Hanoi on October 24; the site of the meeting in the North Vietnamese capital and its agreed position as the last meeting before signing on October 31 would probably have worked against any last-minute walkouts and in favor of a few final concessions (doubtless more so on the part of Hanoi than of Washington) or at least an agreement not to insist. Other problems would have been handled in the predictably complicated negotiations on the implementing protocols that apparently were to have followed the cease-fire (Kissinger 1973, p. 20) and perhaps even after the American elections, a truly amazing perspective if it was in fact the one envisaged. But the document's remaining and very real weaknesses would probably not have prevented signing by the Foreign Ministers in Paris had it not been for the third hazard, President Thieu.

It would have been very difficult for Nixon, just before the election, to conclude an agreement without Saigon's concurrence. It is very hard to fault Kissinger for keeping Saigon in the dark so long about the negotiations, although it is possible to find some very appropriate observations about the need and value of "let[ting] Saigon get used to the idea that there *would* be negotiations"—and by extension, agreement—in the earlier writings of the principal U.S. negotiator (Kissinger 1969, p. 218, also p. 232). Kissinger was clearly using all possible controls on information to guide negotiations with Hanoi, a fantastically delicate job in itself, but in the process he neglected Saigon.

The problem was not new. Thieu had been neglected until mid-August, when it became impossible to proceed with the idea of a tripartite council without his knowledge. Between the private Paris meetings of mid-August and mid-September, a number of important officials were sent to Saigon to explain things to Thieu and receive his approval, but the answer was adamantly negative. At the end, Kissinger had to request Nixon's permission to go ahead with the tripartite commission regardless of Thieu's objections. Nixon agreed (Szulc 1974, pp. 48–49). It was more than a month later when Thieu actually saw the terms of the agreement, in a draft presented by Kissinger on October 19, less than a week before initialing was to take place in Hanoi. On the following day, and on nearly every day thereafter for the rest of the month, Thieu denounced the proposed agreement, refused to sign, and generally reacted like a caged tiger. By receiving Kissinger in the presence of the South Vietnamese National Security Council and by immediately and repeatedly publishing his reactions, Thieu added commitment to his opposition. The strangely shaped negotiating table suddenly took on a new form: Washington and Hanoi were now trying to sell their agreement to

Saigon. Nevertheless, this new notion of sides is only partially accurate, for the bargaining relation between Washington and Hanoi remained: It now became even more important to keep Hanoi's commitment to the fragile agreement by convincing North Vietnam that Washington's agreement stuck and that the previous bargaining had been in good faith. Yet Washington could not now negotiate with Saigon without in some way changing the terms of its agreement with Hanoi. The next three months were spent bringing Saigon into the agreement.

Saigon's objections concerned the tripartite council, which Thieu feared would become a coalition government; the absence of a cease-fire for Cambodia and Laos as well as Vietnam; the continued presence of North Vietnamese troops; the implicit partition of South Vietnam into two states; the absence of any mention of the DMZ and hence of a recognition of South Vietnam as a sovereign territorial (i.e., bounded) unit; some of the vagueness on crucial points already mentioned; and the absence of any provision for his signature, since the United States was to sign for Saigon, and North Vietnam for the Vietcong in the October version. On October 27, emphasizing the finality of the agreements, Le removed the last point of Thieu's objections by indicating that the agreement would be signed first by the two negotiating parties and then again by the four parties concerned, the "convoluted" procedure finally followed (*Le Monde*, Oct. 29, 1972). The other objections were more difficult to resolve without new negotiations, and the crucial deadline presented by the first Tuesday in November passed. It must be noted that Thieu was not simply being irrationally stubborn in his stand, as he is often portrayed. There is no doubt that he was a terrible annoyance to both sides, an enemy to Hanoi and an ungrateful ally to Washington. But, for all the concessions that he was repeatedly told Hanoi gave, the agreement still represented a threat to his rule. Moreover, in his talks with Kissinger in July and on other occasions, he had been told that after the elections, things would be different and a tough military line would be the theme of American policy, the future scenario that Hanoi also had been led or had led itself to believe. Thus, Thieu felt his fallback position was far better than it turned out to be.

Hanoi's reaction to the deadlock was the same as Washington's at the beginning of the year, but for different reasons in a different situation. By going public on October 25 and revealing a résumé of the agreement, North Vietnam attempted to outweigh Saigon's commitment to opposition with a Hanoi-Washington commitment to agreement. The Vietcong had also given a cease-fire order to at least some of their troops for October 28, which was subsequently canceled before it had time to enter into effect (*Le Monde,* Oct. 29, 1972). On the day after Hanoi's revelation, Kissinger's careful press conference that announced that "peace is at hand" and that "at most three or four days of negotiation" was required was above all designed to reassure Hanoi of Washington's good faith.

Unfortunately, the concrete manifestations were not convincing. The next private talks, to discuss "six or seven minor points," did not take place until November 20. When they did, Kissinger read into the record a document from Saigon demanding sixty-nine changes. Although he retracted half of them the following day and not all of them were of great importance, the impression given was understandably bad, particularly to a set of North Vietnamese negotiators who had, by their training and experience, always had more problems convincing themselves of American good faith and intentions than with technical details. The remaining changes, dealing with the areas of imprecision in the October text, involved serious matters that had either been passed over consciously in the preceding talks or were new to the current discussions. On their side, the North Vietnamese began raising old questions that had previously been decided, strongly exhibiting symptoms of approach-avoidance behavior (see Jensen, in this volume). They then called a week's recess, on November 25, and returned on December 4 with even less enthusiasm for the negotiations. On December 9, the agreement was completed except for the provision on the DMZ; on December 10, fourteen "semantic" changes were introduced by Hanoi; on December 11, these were reduced to two. On December 14, Hanoi again called a recess, leaving a draft protocol on the control commissions, and, the following day, another draft proposing sixteen changes to the basic text. Some of these included retractions of earlier agreements, such as the new demand to link the return of American POWs to the release of political prisoners in

Saigon, a token North Vietnamese troop withdrawal, the replacement of a definition of the DMZ as a provisional border with one permitting free movement into the South, and a return from an agreement on a 5,000-man International Commission to the earlier demand for a 250-man body (New York *Times*, Dec. 20, 1972, Jan. 25, 1973). They also refused to accept the term "administrative structure" as a description of the National Council of National Reconciliation and Concord, reopening the interpretation that it might be a coalition government. Yet during all this time, Hanoi continued to call for immediate signature of the October agreement unaltered, implying that its new or renewed demands were tactical bargaining counters to the new Saigon-Washington points. Hanoi was clearly not interested in further negotiations, but it was interested in maintaining the former agreement.

Washington was not. It is not clear how much of the demand for new terms was the result of a hardening on Nixon's part, of belated awareness of the need to close up the loopholes, or of a last-minute effort to win some of Thieu's demands. In any case, more time was needed to get the agreement on a Laos cease-fire closer to the Vietnam date and to get third parties lined up for the unenviable job of serving on the International Control Commission. It is also hard to tell whether the renewed bombing and mining of North Vietnam that began on December 18 and lasted twelve days over the Hanoi-Haiphong area and nearly a month, until January 15, over the southern part of North Vietnam had any effect on the negotiations or whether the same results would have occurred without it. Certainly Kissinger's safe but implicit suggestion— ". . . there was a deadlock . . . in the middle of December, and there was a rapid movement when negotiations resumed on the technical level on January 3, and on the substantive level on January 8; these facts have to be analyzed by each person for himself"—can have no simple "therefore" read into it. The circumstantial sequence is correct; the causal inference is not proven, although even Kissinger has strong beliefs to the contrary.

The Christmas bombings were not an exercise in reality changing like the May mining or the spring offensive; by all analysis, they were, at best, demonstration bombings designed to impress South Vietnam, and, at worst, frustration alternatives because there was nothing else to do that would restore a deadline. Washington decided to bomb Hanoi until Hanoi and Saigon gave in. Thus, at the same time as the bombing began, Thieu was told that if he did not accept the agreement, he could no longer count on American assistance (Szulc 1974, p. 62; Kalb 1974, p. 415). There was one additional element closer to the nature of the bombings that accrued as a benefit to Saigon, although it is not large enough to cover the delay since October nor the intensity of the Christmas attack. The arms shipments schedule for the Vietnamization policy was nowhere near completion in October, no more than was the North Vietnamese supply program for the Communist units in place in South Vietnam. The three-month delay gave the United States time to rush its weapons deliveries to completion, while the bombing provided interference in the Communists' attempt to do the same thing. But this effect had little to do with the announced purpose of bombing Hanoi into agreement (Kissinger 1973, p. 21). Indeed, if anything, given the closeness of the decision in the North Vietnamese Politburo to propose the October 8 draft and the pattern of past Communist behavior under bombing, it was in great danger of doing just the opposite.

The intensive bombing of the Hanoi-Haiphong area was halted on December 29, and technical talks began five days later, followed by full-scale private negotiations in another five days. "By the morning of January 9, it became apparent that both sides were determined to make a serious effort to break the deadlock in negotiations" (Kissinger 1973, p. 20), and an agreement was arrived at in Paris on January 13, approved in Washington two days later, when Nixon halted all bombing of the North, and accepted in Saigon with doubts and objections on January 17. Kissinger returned to Paris to initial the agreement on January 23, and it was signed and went into effect on January 27.

The additional time had been used to bring a commitment on a truce in Laos down from thirty to twenty days and to get the members of the International Commission ready to go to work immediately, as well as to complete military supplies. In the January negotiations, the ambiguous reference to "administrative structure" in regard to the National Council was finally removed, the sovereignty of South Vietnam and the peaceful coexistence of the two Vietnams on either side of the DMZ were reaffirmed, the International Commission was established with 1,160 men, and the difference between a single and double military commission on the DMZ was split in half. The arrangement on the return of military prisoners was restored, and the civilian prisoners in South Vietnam was left to be negotiated between the two parties in the South, but the responsibility of the United States in promoting the release of the civilians was increased. The DMZ was referred to only as a "provisional military demarcation line . . . not a political or territorial boundary" and the "modalities of civilian movement" across it were to be negotiated "promptly" between the two Vietnams. The continued presence of North Vietnamese troops and the implicit partition of South Vietnam—which were crucial to the basic image—remained in the agreement, as did a number of other minor points that Saigon protested (omission of certain categories of captured South Vietnamese civilians, absence of details on sovereignty of the DMZ, stationing on military commission units in Vietcong as well as government territory). Thus, the major improvement in the January agreement over October was in the provision of new details on a number of important topics. In the process, points of disagreement arose, and Washington generally conceded less than Hanoi did in resolving them. None of the previously agreed points except the size of the International Commission appears to have been changed in the end, although many were retracted and restored in the three months' interval. Perhaps the most positive aspect of the delayed agreements was the fact that the protocols that closed a number of loopholes were agreed to before the cease-fire finally went into effect.

II

Three conditions are necessary for negotiations to take place: identification or the perception of a problem and of a solution to it; stalemate or the inability of the parties to solve the problem by other means; and willingness or the desire of the parties to use negotiations to turn the stalemate and arrive at a solution to the problem. Once negotiations have started, each of the parties tries to manipulate three parameters in the other's view of the field of alternatives: his fallback or no-agreement point (the ambient reality); his offer point (the component elements); and his acceptance or expectance point (the basic image or formula). Each party tries to do this by manipulating these parameters on his own side and, whenever possible, on the other side as well, to bring the latter two pairs into coincidence. The means are extensive in reality, but in concept they are limited. A party may improve his own fall-back position or weaken the other party's, by changing the ambient reality. He may improve his offer or impel the other party to improve its offer, or improve the other party's evaluation of his offer, or, alternatively, seek to show convincingly that he cannot improve his proposals. In the latter case and in other instances as well, he can also seek to alter the other party's acceptance or expectance points. Concessions, compromise, convergence, bargaining, and the like are merely the external manifestations of this process whereby two parties seek to move each other.

In the Vietnam negotiations, Washington began to offer proposals on important elements in order to establish a new image of a settlement—a political reflection of the military stalemate rather than a political decision where no military one had been possible. The two first proposals went hand in hand: Cease-fire in place implied a decision not to press for Vietcong liquidation, and unilateral withdrawal implied a decision not to press for North Vietnamese army withdrawal. In other words, Washington sketched out a deal whereby the Communist forces would be left in place if the Saigon government would be left in place. This was in fact a good deal simply because the reverse would not have been possible: first for the United States because in any case it could not have bought off 145,000 North Vietnamese troops and unnumbered Vietcong by giving over "Thieu-Ky-Khiem," but also for the Communists because it left them better off than at any previous peacetime moment. The third suggestion of concessions had a more procedural meaning: By not asking prior release of POWs, Washington indicated that there were no preconditions for negotiations toward a settlement. Thus, following on a recognized stalemate, the image of a solution and the indication of a means to attain it (including the willingness to do so) were provided in the American communications of 1970 and 1971. This image was essentially a negative one. Washington was indicating that it was not negotiating on Thieu or the North Vietnamese army, but on the conditions for their remaining in place; that it was not negotiating on American withdrawal or on POW exchanges or on a cease-fire, but on the conditions for their taking place; and that it was not negotiating on the future rulership over the South, but on the procedures that would be followed to determine it. In all this list of issues, it was only Thieu and the future rulership who were the subject of disagreement ("only" in the sense of number, not of importance!), the other items all being agreed on before the detailed negotiations ever began.

This is a partially explanatory description of the lay of the land in 1970–71, but the search for explanations may be pushed farther. Washington made a series of apparent concessions because it sought to throw out bait to draw the Communists into a new image of a settlement and at the same time remove major elements from the bargaining. In another sense, it made its proposals at that time because of the impending elections and the success of the military, which made a cease-fire in place acceptable. By making concessions unilaterally early in the exercise it could draw the Communists into making the cessions the United States wanted later on. Eventually this behavior was successful in causing the expected behavior on the other side.

But not immediately. Both sides in early 1972 began a venture into changing the ambient reality in order to improve their fallback position and in the process to add some bargaining items. It is a process for which a conceptual term—such as competition or conquisition—should be established, for it is an important negative corollary to the process of concession. Instead of making reciprocal attempts to move their offer points closer to each other, parties make reciprocal attempts to improve their fallback positions. In Vietnam in 1972, the exercise was not very successful in changing reality—territory held —in either party's favor, although it did add some more items to talk about.

The major move from the North Vietnamese side came in the acceptance of the image of a settlement that Washington had been proposing. It is only in the loosest sense that this may be called a concession, any more than Washington's original moves could properly be described by the same term. The Vietcong's September declaration and Hanoi's October document were rather an adoption of a new definition of expectations, leading to a joint search for implementing details and from which component elements naturally derived. Such a description, however, should not suggest that thereafter the two sides took off on a friendly treasure hunt, hand in hand. The search was painful, wearying, suspicious, and tense, and for two reasons. Each side had to be continually aware of the possibility that the other's acceptance of the new image was a trick, and indeed each side had members back home who were only too willing to remind them of this possibility. Moreover, each side had to be careful lest the other side gain some unequal advantage in the detailed elements, even while still sticking to the general spirit of the underlying image. Since negotiations were not on a simple matter like wages or prices but on very uncomparable details of implementation, each side had to very carefully go over each new detail to discover its implications.

It is more difficult to find the proper terms in which to give an explanation for Hanoi's decision. One has been given in structural terms: "The guessing at the White House is that the 'dove' faction in the Hanoi Politburo prevailed with the argument that a military stalemate had developed, and that Mr. Nixon would be easy to deal with on the eve of the elections last November" (Bernard Gwertzman, New York *Times*, Jan. 26, 1973). Such explanations underline some important aspects, such as stalemate and perception, but they beg the causal question. From this base, one would be pushed to ask further: What caused the "dove" faction to prevail with its argument? One answer, in terms of timing, points to the importance of Podgorny's visit carrying the arguments of the Moscow summit to Hanoi. Another explanation, and a stab at answering this question, could be made in cost/benefit terms. The costs of no-agreement were rising in 1970, with no improvement in the fallback position in hand and a gradual falling away of North Vietnam's allies; the benefits were available for the wresting, for the American commitment to keeping Thieu in office in the short run was firmly demonstrated, but Washington could be expected to pay heavily for that element of the agreement through concessions on the rest.

This answer to the question, Why? is more helpful, since it indicates, Why at that particular time? and also establishes a bridge between the two levels of negotiated values: the basic image and its component elements. But the other elements corresponding to Thieu's maintenance in office had already been conceded by Washington and admitted by everyone but Saigon: maintenance of the Vietcong, maintenance of the North Vietnamese army. The final elements under discussion in late 1972 and early 1973 take us back to an attempt to turn the spirit into words, and not really to concessions. On this measure, the only points on which one side or the other might have been said to have won something more than simply an even, detailed implementation of the basic image were the reaffirmation of the sovereignty of South Vietnam (counterbalanced, it would seem, by the indication that the DMZ is a "provisional military demarcation line") and the American commitment to provide Hanoi with economic aid, never implemented (see Szulc 1974, p. 66).

In this view, it is not clear that the breakoff and bombing of December 1972 had any causative effect on anything, except in the rather vestigial sense of reminding the North about their previous cost/benefit analysis. Yet this is important. If there is any explanatory element in the events of that last month, it lies in the structure of phasing, concession rates, and timing. There just was not enough time to complete the negotiations according to the optimistic schedule of expectations set up by the negotiators. The deadline of October 31, backed by American Election Day, was simply too close to the earlier turning point of October 8. When the false hopes of October were unfulfilled, Hanoi became suspicious that Washington was seeking to pull something over on it and stampede it into an unacceptable agreement. Ironically, Hanoi could accept the incomplete agreement of October, but would not allow Washington to bring in new details under this acceptance in November. Nor was there enough time to bring in Saigon and bring about Thieu—to "get used to the idea . . . [and] confront the fundamental issues explicitly," as Kissinger (1969, pp. 218, 232) wrote earlier. Once October and the election had passed a gesture was needed to restore a meaningful deadline, in one of two forms. Since there was no date to work toward, there had to be a date to work from: The bombing was therefore relevant only in that it provided a "negative deadline," a bombing halt date. It was the most unpleasant of all means of persuasion, an implemented threat, that is of no value in and of itself but that adds value to the cost/benefit analysis only by the promise of its own cessation. When the bombing stopped, the talks started and the last details were agreed to. Agreement was incomplete in October and impossible in November; it was complete and possible in January. Whether bombing was the rational—i.e., appropriate—means of imposing a deadline to enable agreement is a question of process—like the question of Nagasaki—that is not answered simply by the outcome.

The tactics of concession thus flowed directly from the strategy of the basic image, and the major problem was to make sure that it kept flowing. A matrix will help portray the strategic situation in its major components, although—as with the case of most game-theory presentations—it tells little about the details of the tactical exchange. The simple tough/soft matrix from Bartos (in this volume) will do well enough, with the reminder, however, that the values are indicative, not real, and there is no way to make them real in such a complex situation.

|  |  | Hanoi | | | |
|---|---|---|---|---|---|
|  |  | soft | | tough | |
| U.S. | soft | 5/5 | A | B | 2/8 |
|  | tough | 8/2 | C | D | -2/-2 |

Once the possibility of "softness"—i.e., the image of a negotiated solution—was mooted by Washington in late 1970, the public Paris talks served as a forum for Washington's representatives—notably Porter, who was admirably suited for the task—to get across the message that there was a box called A and that any attempt to choose B would land both parties back in D, where they had been all along. At the same time, after Nixon's statement, Kissinger in Paris offered to play on the A-B line. Hanoi's reaction was to choose B, and Washington's response was to return to the C-D line and therefore pick D. In Moscow, Kissinger again offered to play on the A-B line, and this time Hanoi responded with a move to play in the A-C column. But in this position it was vulnerable to Washington's playing C, as Washington had earlier been vulnerable to Hanoi's choosing B. The matrix thus shows very clearly why Hanoi was so suspicious of any false moves by Washington during the exchange on details and why Saigon's monkey wrench so naturally appeared to Hanoi as a shift in strategy and image, a case of bad faith, and not merely some final haggling about details. In this light, perhaps the greatest accomplishment of Kissinger was convincing Hanoi that the Christmas bombing was not the return to a C-D strategy and the D response that it appeared to be, but only a reaffirmation of the mutual choice of A! Such subtleties are beyond the ability of the matrix to portray.

Finally, there are both problems and lessons in an explanation that uses the notion of power. Using the basis (source and use) of the ability of one party to make the other move in an intended direction as the conceptual key to an understanding of the negotiation presupposes that we know each party's innermost predisposition (see White 1971). If we bypass this problem and stick to the public record, or at least the ostensible manifestation of will through action, the interrelation of the power—or causal ability—of the two parties is evident. Washington had the "power" to make Hanoi restudy its cost/benefit accounts and move to Washington's image of a settlement, once Hanoi had already demonstrated its "power" to make Washington restudy its cost/benefit accounts and move to a new image of the settlement closer to Hanoi's.

# PART V
# Sovereign and Other Parties as Negotiators

# INTRODUCTION

This section contains a number of very different chapters whose common characteristic is the involvement of negotiating parties who are not sovereign states. Its purpose is twofold: to see if the concepts and the analyses of sovereign-state negotiators are applicable to other types, and to learn of alternative concepts and analyses that may in turn be useful for the study of negotiations in general. From this point of view, it may not be surprising to find that nonstate parties turn out to be similar enough to diplomatic negotiators to be subject to the same types of analysis, on one hand, but that some significant differences are brought out that tell more about negotiations, on the other.

Although diplomatic negotiations always seem to appear more "serious," as De Felice pointed out, nonstate negotiators face a threat more vital than most diplomats, in that they can be forced out of business. Their livelihood, corporate existence, even life are frequently at stake. As a result, since the risks are so great, the relative scope of power is also extremely broad: The strike, the self-destructing hijacker, the total expropriation are exercises of power relatively comparable to large-scale, if not nuclear, war among states, and yet they are common threats and even events in nonstate negotiations.

Structurally, there are often tremendous imbalances between bargaining nonstate parties, perhaps not so much in their aggregate power bases conceived at some high level of abstraction but rather in the nature of these resources. Labor and management, government and investor, policeman and bandit draw on very different sources for their ability to inflect the other's behavior. In fact, depending on the terms chosen, each member of the three pairs could be described as being infinitely "powerful" toward his opponent, a paradox that shows not balance but difference in power bases.

In communications terms, this imbalance is reflected in real problems in getting the means of persuasion across to the other party, since any degree of commonality in the basic situation of the negotiators that is found among diplomats is frequently absent among nonstate negotiators. Their clienteles are not only different but also of a different type, and it is difficult to put oneself in the other fellow's shoes (see Blake et al. 1972). Indeed, if Schuler's earlier chapter and Kapoor's chapter in this section are any indications, there is less persuasion than simply maneuvering in such encounters, and Baldwin and Fisher's (1973) analyses suggest that in the aberrational case of *"kamakazi* pirate" negotiations, the best hope lies in boxing in the hijacker with structural restraints and then channeling him—like a trapped experimental rat—out a convenient face-saving exit.

Thus the problem of goals, perceptions, and rationality is as much a common thread of the following chapters as is the nonstate nature of one or more of the actors. Baldwin uses a strategic approach to analyze the problem of bargaining under conditions of uncertainty with hijackers, and in the process develops a clearer understanding of complexities in the means of persuasion. Thus, in the early stage of negotiations, the robber has all the threats, but they are generally nongraduated, and if he carries them out he ends the matter rather abruptly. In the later stages, when he is tired and his demands have dropped to simply asylum, he is negotiating to get out from his own threats, and the imbalance is reversed. Thus outcomes are structurally determined unless the cops are able to cut the robbers' communications and actually eliminate the means of persuasion until the passage of time moves negotiations from the first to the second stage.

In Kapoor's analysis of case and context in multinational corporation bargaining, the same element of structural (phase) determination exists in the notion of project life cycle (a phenomenon similar to that noted in the Kenyan negotiations analyzed by Rothchild). Yet within the structural constraints of phasing, communications variables appear to have been the determinant factors in the unsuccessful Bechtel case. In a further extension of the responsiveness proposition noted earlier, *the chances for successful outcome vary directly with the reality of expectations;* perceptions of needs and capabilities so far outran later perceptions of reality that, in analytical terms, it was impossible to pin down offering, acceptance, and threat points for the purpose of bargaining. Such propositions, however, have the reverse drawback of many of the analytical concepts used to describe persuasion: They tell the determinants of breakdown, not the determinants of agreement.

It may seem ironic that the same type of characteristics that dominate business negotiations also appear in collective bargaining. Certainly, one of the major elements in the sixteen-week strike against the New York newspapers in 1962–63 was a lack of precision, realism, and constancy in both expectations and offers during the negotiations, and it led to a prolonged inability to agree, just as it led to a breakdown of Bechtel's negotiations with India. However, whereas Kapoor suggests that the underlying factor in India was a lack of understanding between cultures, Raskin very clearly indicates the sharp personality differences—related in turn to socioeconomic background and past experiences—that lay beneath the negotiating impasse in New York. There is no process or structural model that can capture the problems of ego, mood, and irrationality that the main negotiators exhibited and that posed the biggest challenges to the mayor and his mediators. It is sobering and annoying to theorists and practitioners alike to see the great and unpredictable importance of the complex human factor. But there are other points in the account that do illustrate theoretical or conceptual elements of analysis. Another reason for the delays in agreement was that the strikers' security or threat point (Rapoport 1966, pp. 97, 101) or fallback position, as represented by their strike benefits, was much higher than was the publishers', giving the former more power through their increased ability to hold out. Another element in the unions' threat position was the ability of any one union to go it alone: In a world of coercive deficiency, disunity is strength, even if it does not provide predictable direction. Finally, this account shows one element of detail in the bargaining that is typical of most negotiations but that never appears without an "inside story" about the exchange of propositions: the continual need to find new forms, items of exchange, and reference points for the basic issues. Kheel's formula for trading work hours against overtime and washup time is a good example of the kind of shoehorning that is so often required to restructure the stakes to make them acceptable to both parties.

# 1. BARGAINING WITH AIRLINE HIJACKERS*

## David A. Baldwin, Dartmouth College

Newspaper stories of airplane hijackings have become almost as common as those about plane crashes. The purpose of this chapter is to examine such events in terms of bargaining theory. How adequate is this theory in explaining such situations? Can it prescribe strategies for participants? Even if both answers are negative, our understanding of such situations may be deepened by identifying the discrepancies between theoretical assumptions and the real world. Economists, after all, find the model of pure competition useful even though it rarely corresponds to actual situations.

The main questions addressed here are as follows: Who participates in the bargaining? What goals do they pursue and how? What is different about bargaining with a hijacker? What tactics are relevant to such situations? What are the obstacles to mutually productive bargaining? And what can an analysis of bargaining tell us about better ways of dealing with hijacking?

* The author would like to express his appreciation to Frank Smallwood, Robert Nakamura, Donald McNemar, William Zartman, Joseph Massey, and Denis Sullivan for helpful comments.

## PARTICIPANTS

Several sets of bargaining relationships are involved in the hijacking of a plane. The primary participants include the hijacker or hijackers, the governmental authorities, and the hostages.

How should we label the man who makes hostages of his fellow airline passengers? To call him a terrorist is to imply a senseless commitment to violence that may not be present. Neither "hijacker" nor "kidnaper" carries quite the right connotation; after all, he does not want to steal the plane or its passengers. "Extortionist" or "blackmailer" are better terms, since they imply a threat relationship, a bargaining situation. Bank robbers who seize hostages in a bank vault, Palestinian commandos who seize hostages in Olympic dormitories or foreign embassies, and skyjackers are all engaged in something more like extortion or blackmail than theft. With this caveat in mind we shall bow to convention and reluctantly use the term "hijacker."

Plane hijackers can be divided into four categories: the insane, the mercenaries, the political representatives, and the free-lance revolutionaries. The insane are by definition the least rational, the most erratic in their behavior, and the least consistent in their value systems. The mercenaries are the escaping criminals and those seeking ransom followed by escape. They seek personal gain in what might be viewed as a sort of business transaction. Political representatives act on behalf of established and continuing organizations in pursuit of political goals. Although their organizations may be underground, it is possible to send or receive side payments from the parent organization. Government authorities find this type the easiest to deal with. The free-lance revolutionary, however, is much harder to deal with. No established organization claims him, yet he makes political demands. Should he be treated as a political mercenary or as insane? For the government authorities, deciding on which type of hijacker they are dealing with is of crucial importance. The possibility of side payments, the rationality, and the predictability of the hijacker are all dependent on this decision.

There are three kinds of goals sought by the hijacker. First is control over the immediate environment—asserting and maintaining his control over the crew and passengers; second is whatever external goal is sought—money, release of political prisoners, etc.; third is personal survival.[1] Deciding what priority the hijacker gives to each of these goals as the situation evolves is one of the most important judgments governmental authorities must make.

Governmental authorities always get involved in plane hijackings. It would be ludicrous for a hijacker to say, "Now, don't let the police find out about this." There are novel aspects of plane hijacking, however, that sometimes make it difficult to decide precisely who will speak for the government. If representatives of the Palestinian Liberation Organization hijack an Israeli plane in Chicago, who should handle the negotiations—the FBI, the FAA, the State Department, or the Illinois state police? If the plane proceeds to land in several different countries, the problem is compounded further. As experience with such cases grows, standard operating procedures will undoubtedly be worked out, but it would be a mistake to depict the hijacker as confronted by a single monolithic personification of "governmental authority." This is even more true at the international level, where a political hijacking can involve several governments. For example, when Palestinian guerrillas use a Syrian plane to take their Saudi Arabian hostages out of a French airport while demanding that Jordan release a political prisoner and proceed to land at an airport in Kuwait (cf. events of September 5–8, 1973), the governments involved began to sound like a United Nations roll call.

In bargaining with hijackers, governments pursue three potentially incompatible goals: securing release of the hostages, deterring others from trying the same thing, and punishing the hijacker. Release of the hostages and deterrence of potential future hijackers are far more important than punishment. Except insofar as it affects deterrence, punishment probably matters very little to governments. The incompatibility is between release of the hostages and deterring would-be hijackers. If the only goal were to get the hostages released, large rewards in the form of money and sanctuary could be offered to the hijacker. The government could simply admit that deterrence had failed and proceed to pay the penalty. The reluctance of governments to consider such alternatives indicates the dilemma of trying to secure the release of hostages without encouraging potential future hijackers.

Although hostages are rarely depicted by the media as "participants" in the bargaining process, this probably tells us more about newsmen's concept of bargaining than about the hijacking situation. In the case of a plane in flight, the pilot is clearly a very special kind of hostage. The ability of the hijacker to communicate his demands and threats, the well-being of his other hostages, and his own life depend on the active collaboration of the pilot. In many cases the pilot occupies a unique position as the intermediary between the governmental authorities and the hijacker. In this situation the pilot must bargain on behalf of the authorities while also bargaining on behalf of himself and the passengers. In such a situation much depends on the pilot's ability to estimate the situation—the nature of the demands and threats, the credibility of the threats, the mental state of the hijacker and any changes therein, etc.

Airline pilots like to view their role as analogous to that of a sea captain, and they want the same sort of authority to deal with "unruly passengers" as sea captains have. In testimony on antihijacking legislation before the House Subcommittee on Transportation and Aeronautics, the president of the Air Line Pilots' Association argued in favor of increased latitude for the crew to bargain with the hijacker and for the complete authority of the pilot to "call the shots" (*Hearings* Anti-Hijacking Act of 1973, 93rd Congress, 1st sess., 1973, pp. 310–18). It is not clear how a pilot with a gun at his head may be regarded as "in command" of his plane or how he can "call the shots" without being overheard by the hijacker. Without some means for the pilot to communicate secretly with the ground, it is folly to pretend that the pilot is "calling the shots."[2]

The pilot with a gun at his head is primarily interested in the safety of his passengers and crew; he is much less interested in how the handling of this particular hijacker will affect other would-be hijackers. The reluctance of pilots to turn over control of the situation to governmental authorities may be due to the pilots' perception of this difference in priorities.

The passengers in an airline hijacking are passive hostages relative to the pilot. Their situation is similar to one described by Schelling in *The Strategy of Conflict* (pp. 120–21). In this situation twenty men are held for ransom by one man with a gun and six bullets. Schelling then points out how the inability of the twenty to communicate with one another and to make credible threats and promises puts them at the mercy of their captor.

Bargaining theory usually assumes that participants are rational and that their goals are not subject to change during the bargaining process. One must be wary of these assumptions in analyzing plane hijacking, however. Since the hostages and the hijacker are under tremendous pressure throughout a hijacking, fatigue becomes an increasingly important variable as the situation evolves. Under such circumstances both rationality and motivation are likely to change. Although hostages may become less rational as a result of the pressure and fatigue, their goal of survival is unlikely to change. Unlike the hijacker and the government, they are not juggling priorities among several goals.

The government is less subject to pressure and fatigue. Government spokesmen are playing a bureaucratic role; if one gets tired or "breaks" under the pressure, another can take over. People suffer from fatigue, but governments do not. This asymmetry of the vulnerability of participants to fatigue and pressure may be one reason why a strategy of "waiting the hijacker out" has seemed to work so well.

The hijacker is the man "on the spot." Even if he has helpers, he cannot "take turns" playing the role of hijacker in the same way that bureaucrats can "take turns" playing the role of government spokesman. Most hijackers are unable to create a situation in which the "last clear chance" to avert disaster lies —or appears to lie—with the government. As time wears on, the hijacker probably finds it difficult to convince even himself that the last clear chance is really up to someone else. Even the most rational and most disciplined hijacker must find it hard to cope with the psychological pressure and fatigue. One has only to try to imagine the mental state of a hijacker after forty-eight sleepless hours as he sits in a plane on the ground in Dubai with temperatures in the plane rising above 110 degrees in order to understand why hijackings hardly ever last more than a few days.

## THE BARGAINING SITUATION

Bargaining with hijackers is affected not only by the nature of the participants and their goals but also by the nature of the situation. It is just as important to understand what game is being played as it is to know who the players are. What sort of bargaining situation is this and how does it differ from other kinds of bargaining situations?

### The Concept of Bargaining

Thomas Schelling (1966, p. 136) has rightly complained about the widespread tendency to define "bargaining" or "negotiation" as a formal, verbal, perhaps even face-to-face activity. In order to avoid such a narrow conception, Schelling (1960, p. 5) has suggested using the term "bargaining" to describe all "situations in which the ability of one participant to gain his ends is dependent to an important degree on the choices or decisions that the other participant will make." From this standpoint the bargaining aspects of a situation would include everything that affects the participants' expectations about the capabilities and/or intentions of other participants.

Schelling's general conception of bargaining situations can be subdivided into situations of pure conflict, in which one participant's gain is another's loss, and situations of impure conflict, in which participants have common as well as conflicting interests (cf. Schelling 1960, pp. 83–89). Most airline hijackings fall in the second category, since in most cases all participants in the bargaining process share an interest in avoiding the destruction of the plane and its passengers.

### Bargaining Arena

The arena within which bargaining takes place can be an important factor in a bargaining situation. Airline hijackers and those who seize hostages in bank vaults or embassies are bargaining in a fishbowl with an adversary who is outside the fishbowl and who can change the water in the bowl. There is a crucial difference between the kidnaper demanding ransom from his undiscovered hideout and the hijacker demanding ransom from a Boeing 707. If the kidnaper gets cold feet, he can run away. For the plane hijacker, extracting himself from the situation is much more difficult.

Also, the hijacker's dependence on his adversary for food, water, and fuel—the necessities of life—is rather unusual. This dependency creates the option of direct environmental manipulation by the government. With all of the various kinds of ingenious weapons we are told exist, it is strange that they have not been used. Two factors probably account for this. First, there is uncertainty about the effects of such weapons on such a diverse group as assorted airline passengers. Second, once used, future hijackers may take countermeasures, such as refusing to permit food and water to be brought on board the plane.

### Communication

Although communication is not necessary in *all* bargaining situations, some communication is necessary in a plane hijacking.

### FIGURE 1.
*Diagram of Threat Communication System in Airline Hijacking*

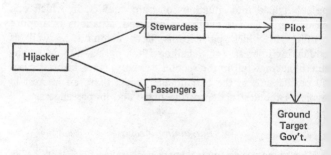

All hijackers threaten violence; few actually use it. Figure 1 diagrams the threat communication system of the typical airline hijacking. During the first stage the hijacker must communicate threats to the stewardess (or some other crew member) and the passengers. Although the passengers are simply told, "Don't interfere or else . . . ," the stewardess must usually be induced to help the hijacker to communicate his threat to the pilot. In order to complete the threat communication process, the pilot must usually pass on the hijacker's threat to the ground. Of course, if all the hijacker wants is a ride to Cuba, then no communication with the ground is necessary, since the pilot can satisfy the hijacker's demand. In most cases, however, the target of the hijacker's threat—the ultimate recipient—is on the ground.

Schelling's *Arms and Influence* (1966) is based on a fundamental distinction between the attempt to structure someone's motives or incentives by such means as threats or promises and the attempt to overcome his strength by brute force. This distinction seems to be missing from much of the discussion of airline hijacking (cf. *Hearings* 1973). Hijackers do not overcome the pilot by brute force in order that they may fly the plane themselves. *The hijacker's stock in trade is threats, not force.* And threats must be communicated in order to be effective.

Proposals to seal off pilots behind armored doors are usually discussed as if the purpose were to protect pilots from brute force rather than threats. The congressman who asks the "expert" witness for his opinion on the effect of sealing off the pilot compartment in order to eliminate the ability of the hijacker to direct particular courses of action to the pilot (*Hearings* 1973, p. 366) has asked a sensible question. Such a question deserves a more thoughtful response than "Well, have you ever seen the front end of an aircraft get someplace without the tail end?" The observation that "very few of the pilots I have talked to have told me that if they knew that the stewardess in the rear of the airplane was going to get her head blown off they would not open that very complicated door" (*Hearings* 1973, p. 366) misses the point. What if the pilot does *not* know that the stewardess is being threatened and has no way of finding out?[3] Preventing threat communication and preventing the use of brute force are not the same thing.

This is not to suggest that armored doors are undesirable. Hijackings are basically matters of threat communication, and countermeasures should be evaluated in that context. The proper question to ask is how the installation of an armored door will affect the hijacker's threat communication system. Such a device would obviously make it harder for the hijacker to monitor the pilot's communications with the ground and would thereby increase the pilot's control over the situation. Armored doors, windows, or two-way mirrors may or may not be useful antihijacking devices; but it is folly to try to evaluate their utility without reference to the hijacker's threat communication system.

## Legitimacy

Legitimate influence attempts are more likely to succeed than illegitimate ones. Mutually productive bargaining is more likely when participants regard each other's demands as legitimate and when each can make legitimate concessions to the other. In a hijacking, however, no legitimacy whatsoever is given to the hijacker's demands by the government. Thus, even the slightest concession by the government is likely to be portrayed in the newspapers as a pact with the devil. Although the hijacker may deny the legitimacy of the government's demands on him, it may be difficult for him to convince himself that the government lacks the right to oppose him. This asymmetry in the distribution of legitimacy in bargaining with a hijacker makes a mutually agreeable outcome very difficult to find.

## Success

The success of a hijacking attempt is difficult to measure. Although such attempts are often labeled "successful" if a hijacker is able to assert and maintain his control over the crew and passengers of an airplane, such a definition is inadequate for understanding the bargaining aspects of a hijacking. If we are to conceive of a hijacking as an influence attempt, we must judge success or failure by the extent to which the target of the influence attempt complies with the hijacker's demands. Often the hijacker makes some outrageous demand and then, when compliance is not forthcoming, proceeds to make progressively more moderate demands until he ends up bargaining for safe passage or asylum in return for release of the hostages. If one judges the success of a hijacker strictly in terms of the degree of compliance with his specific demands, one is likely to conclude that hijackers do rather poorly.

Such a strict evaluation, however, may be misleading, especially if the hijacker was pursuing goals other than those mentioned in his specific demands. The mentally unbalanced hijacker may be trying to impress his family by getting his name in the newspapers. The Palestinian guerrilla may be trying to publicize the Palestinian cause in order to remind Arab governments of its importance. Such goals may be so firmly imbedded in the basic situation that the hijacker himself is only dimly aware of them.

Thus some hijackers are actually making two kinds of threats. The first is an explicit threat that is relatively specific and short-run: "Release the prisoners or we blow up the plane." The second is an implicit threat that is relatively general and long-run: "Get Israel to withdraw from occupied territories or we (or people like us) will continue to harass you by hijacking planes." Although this chapter is mainly concerned with the immediate explicit threats and demands of hijacking situations, the possibility of conceiving of hijackings as tactical moves in a much larger and long-range social bargaining process should be noted.[4]

TACTICS

Both hijackers and governments are confronted with several tactical problems growing out of peculiarities of the bargaining situation. We will examine the general problem of making conditional commitments first; then we will discuss utility of the seemingly relevant distinction between compellent and deterrent threats.

### Conditional Commitments

Commitment tactics are among the most interesting and useful of bargaining tactics. "In bargaining, the commitment is a device to leave the last clear chance to decide the outcome with the other party, in a manner that he fully appreciates; it is to relinquish further initiative, having rigged the incentives so that the other party must choose in one's favor" (Schelling 1960, p. 37). A threat or a promise[5] is a *conditional* commitment, since the maker is committed only under specified conditions.

The efficacy of a threat or promise, however, depends on the user's ability to assure the recipient that the commitment is truly conditional (cf. Schelling 1966, p. 74). A sadist may have no difficulty convincing others of his willingness to carry out his threat, but he may have great difficulty in assuring others that he will refrain from carrying it out if his demands are met. Anyone who is desperate enough (committed enough? crazy enough? dumb enough?) to hijack an airliner will not find it hard to make credible threats to kill some hostages; but he may find it harder to offer credible assurances that he is reasonable and dependable enough to be trusted *not* to kill passengers if his demands are met. The question of how to make binding promises and assurances thus becomes one of the hijacker's stickiest problems.[6]

"Enforcible promises," Schelling (1960, p. 131) points out, "cannot be taken for granted. . . . The problem is compounded when neither party trusts the other and each recognizes that neither trusts the other and that neither can therefore anticipate the other's compliance." The airline hijacker establishes himself in the eyes of the government as a desperate and possibly insane man, a man not to be trusted. None of the traditional methods of binding oneself is available to the hijacker. He cannot make a legal commitment, since he has already demonstrated a willingness to break the law. He cannot stake his future bargaining reputation, since he has a very uncertain future. He cannot exchange hostages, since the government has no hostages comparable to those possessed by the hijacker. If the hijacker is acting as the official representative of an established and continuing organization, of course, the problem is much simpler. Unfortunately, hijackers are usually disavowed by the organizations they claim to represent.[7]

There is a certain irony in the hijacking situation, since nation-states find it almost as difficult to make binding promises as do criminals. The nation-state's claim to sovereignty and the criminal's demonstrated contempt for law both undermine the enforceability of legal commitments. As Schelling (1960, p. 12) reminds us, "Gang war and international war have a lot in common. Nations and outlaws both lack enforceable legal systems to help them govern their affairs."

The difficulty each side has in making promises that the other regards as credible severely limits the utility of such tactics in bargaining with hijackers. If one cannot bind himself, however, it may be possible to unbind one's adversary by either expanding his options or changing the payoffs associated with such options. Schelling (1966, p. 45) notes that an ancient principle of military tactics is never to deprive the enemy of the means to retreat and suggests that this principle "has its counterparts in diplomacy and other negotiations." In bargaining with hijackers the counterpart would seem to be the question of whether to provide or eliminate "safe havens" for hijackers.

Bargaining with hijackers would be much easier if a sanctuary existed—a place that guaranteed safety to any hijacker regardless of race, creed, or nationality. Such a place would make it easier—i.e., cheaper—for the hijacker to change his mind and escape from the situation. The same logic that argues against a mandatory death penalty because it would increase the cost of surrender can be used to argue for a hijacker sanctuary. Why, then, is there virtually unanimous opposition to such a proposal? Even those who favor sanctuary for certain kinds of political hijackers want to be selective in the granting of sanctuary. The reason for opposition to sanctuary probably lies in the supposed effects such a sanctuary would have on deterrence of would-be hijackers. Support for this view was provided by a witness before a congressional committee, who had interviewed a number of hijackers: ". . . of the fifty-two skyjackers I have seen, none would have skyjacked had they known for a certainty that they would be immediately returned to this nation" (*Hearings* 1973, p. 350).[8] The elimination of hijacker sanctuaries is probably a good idea, but it is not a costless idea. The benefits in terms of deterrence must be weighed against the costs of not being able to offer sanctuary to the hijacker after deterrence has failed. In a different kind of world every deterrent measure would enhance both deterrence of future hijackers and defense against actual hijackers. In a different kind of world having one's cake and eating it too would not be incompatible policy options.

## Compellence vs. Deterrence

Schelling (1960, pp. 195–99; 1966, pp. 69–91) suggests that bargaining theorists will find it useful to distinguish between deterrence and compellence.[9] There are, according to Schelling, typical differences between threats intended to make an adversary do something and threats intended to keep him from starting something (1960, p. 195; 1966, p. 69). These differences concern the probability of success, the clarity of the threat, timing, and the difficulty of compliance. The utility of compellence and deterrence as analytical categories will be discussed in terms of the case of airline hijacking.

The deterrence/compellence distinction should be discussed here since certain stages of an airline hijacking provide proto-typical examples of the need for such a distinction. In two almost identically worded passages Schelling (1960, p. 196; 1966, p. 70) argues: "The threat that compels rather than deters often requires that the punishment be administered *until* the other acts, rather than *if* he acts. This is because often the only way to become committed to an action is to initiate it." How better to describe the threat of a hijacker? The mere threat to hijack an airliner may get one put in jail or an asylum, but it is certainly not going to bring about compliance. The hijacker is usually trying to *compel* someone to do some-thing such as provide ransom or release prisoners rather than trying to *deter* someone from doing something. In order to commit himself, the hijacker actually begins to administer the punishment—i.e., holding hostages—before he even com-municates his demands and threats to the ultimate recipient. In many ways an airline hijacker provides the example par ex-cellence of a compellent threat situation.

There are obviously important differences between "Row or I'll tip the boat" and "Row and I'll stop tipping the boat"; there are also important differences between "Release the pris-oners or I'll hijack an airliner" and "Release the prisoners and I'll stop hijacking the airliner." But these differences are obfuscated, not illuminated, by the compellence/deterrence distinction. The difference in these situations is that between a threat and a promise, not that between a compellent threat and a deterrent threat.

Likewise, there is a difference between "Row or I'll tip the boat" and "Row or I'll tip the boat even more than I am already tipping it," and between "Release the prisoners or I'll hijack an airliner" and "Release the prisoners or I'll harm the hostages I have already taken." Here we have two different kinds of threats, but the difference is not that between deterrent and compellent threats; it is that between credible and incredible threats. One tips the boat in order to bolster the credibility of his subsequent threat to tip it further; one hijacks an airliner in order to bolster the credibility of his subsequent threat to harm the passengers; one tips the boat in order to increase the efficacy of his promise to stop tipping the boat; one hijacks an airliner in order to increase the efficacy of his subsequent promise to return the hostages.

To describe hijacking, boat tipping, or blockades as threats is to obscure the dynamics of the situation. It is to distort the concept of threat as a conditional commitment to punish out of all recognition. There is a difference between setting the stage and reading the lines, a difference that is recognized by every stage hand and leading lady. Likewise, there is a difference between creating propitious conditions for making threats and/or promises and actually making threats or promises. After all, a promise to release hostages one has not yet taken is not only incredible, it is also laughable.

There is a difference between trying to discourage the Russians from launching a nuclear attack and trying to encourage the Rhodesians to change their form of government, but describing that difference as the difference between keeping someone from doing something and getting someone to do something is not very helpful. From a purely semantic standpoint, any deterrent threat can be stated in compellent terms, and any compellent threat can be stated in deterrent terms. Thus, we could talk about compelling the Russians to do X (when X is anything except launching a nuclear attack) and about deterring Rhodesians from doing X (when X is continued white dominance). When we describe an influence attempt as deterrence, we usually have in mind a threat that is intended to *reduce* the probability of occurrence of an event that was not very likely to occur in the first place—e.g., nuclear attack, murder, and airline hijacking. When we describe an influence attempt as compellence, however, we usually have in mind a threat intended to *increase* the probability of occurrence of an event that was not very likely to occur anyway. Schelling (1966, p. 100) is quite right in observing that "it is easier to *deter* than to *compel*," but this is more of a truism than an empirical observation. The man who tries to prevent unlikely things from happening will probably succeed; while the man who tries to cause unlikely things to happen will probably fail.

There are nontrivial differences between trying to do hard things, like changing Rhodesia's white-supremacy policies, and trying to do easy things, like getting the Russians not to launch a nuclear attack. Almost all of the differences between compellent and deterrent threats suggested by Schelling can be accounted for by the difference in the autonomous probability[10] of the outcome one is trying to influence. The observation that deterrence threats are more likely to succeed than compellent threats is less profound when one lays bare the implicit assumption that deterrence threats are used for easy tasks, while compellent threats are used for hard tasks. The low probability that an airline hijacker's influence attempt will succeed is not explained by his use of compellent threats, but it is explained by the fact that he has undertaken to bring about an event with a very low autonomous probability of occurrence.

Most of the discussion of the different timing requirements of deterrence and compellence can be reduced to saying that considerable effort will be required to accomplish hard things, while much less effort allows one to accomplish easy things. Why do compellent threats have to be "put in motion to be credible" (Schelling 1966, p. 72)? Because they need a lot of credibility. Why do they need so much credibility? Because they are so unlikely to succeed in the first place!

Schelling (1966, p. 82) also argues that it is likely to be especially difficult to comply with a compellent threat:

> There is another characteristic of compellent threats, arising in the need for affirmative action, that often distinguishes them from deterrent threats. It is that the very act of compliance—of doing what is demanded—is more conspicuously compliant, more recognizable as submission under duress, than when an act is merely withheld in the face of a deterrent threat. Compliance is likely to be less casual, less capable of being rationalized as something that one was going to do anyhow.

Since Schelling uses the term "compellent threat" to refer to situations in which A is trying to get B to do something he is very unlikely to do, and the term "deterrent threat" to refer to situations in which A is trying to get B to do something he was likely to do anyway, the above passage is not surprising. Of course, it is harder to rationalize compliance with compellent threats as something one intended to do anyhow, especially since compliance was something one had no intention of doing. It is much easier to give the appearance of doing what comes naturally if one really is doing what comes naturally. All of Schelling's comments about ease of compliance must be reversed if one compares the compellent threat "Breathe or I'll shoot" with the deterrent threat "Don't breathe or I'll shoot." It is tautological to say that the higher the autonomous probability of B's performance of X, the harder it will be to detect whether B's performance of X resulted from A's influence attempt. Schelling is quite right in saying that compliance is difficult in what he calls compellence situations. This difficulty, however, is not a characteristic of compellent threats; it is a characteristic of the particular type of influence situations that are being labeled "compellent." The difficulty of compliance with a compellent threat disappears if we change the situation from "Stand on your head and whistle 'Yankee Doodle' or I'll shoot" to "Breathe or I'll shoot."[11] Compliance is conspicuous in some compellent-threat situations; in others it is not.

Another difference between compellent and deterrent threats, according to Schelling, is that the former tend to be more ambiguous than the latter. Once again, particular kinds of situations seem to be implied:

> In addition to the question of "when," compellence usually involves questions of where, what, and how much. "Do nothing" is simple, "Do something" ambiguous. "Stop where you are" is simple; "Go back" leads to "How far?" "Leave me alone" is simple; "Co-operate" is inexact and open-ended [Schelling 1966, pp. 72–73].

"Do nothing," however, is not so simple. It leads to "What do you mean; I have to do something, don't I?" "I can't just do nothing?" "Do nothing that will upset me" is more ambiguous than "Get the hell out of here!" "Stop where you are" is not so simple when said by a hijacker to the pilot of a plane at thirty thousand feet! "Leave me alone" is not so simple when said by a tired father to a small child. It invariably leads to "Does that mean I must leave the room or merely that I must stop talking to you?" "Is it all right if I talk to myself?" "How about if I just listen to records?" In such a situation "Leave me alone" is ambiguous; "Go play in the yard" is simple. Even if one accepts the distinction between deterrent and compellent threats, there is no reason to believe that one type of threat is intrinsically clearer than the other.

The alleged greater clarity of deterrent threats carries over to assurances (Schelling 1966, p. 74). Because the assurances associated with compellent threats tend to be ambiguous, they tend to lack credibility. Blackmailers (and hijackers), as Schelling says, "find the 'assurances' troublesome when their threats are compellent"; but blackmailers and hijackers also find assurances troublesome *even when their threats are not compellent*. The credibility of assurances is not a function of the kind of threat being made; the credibility of assurances is a function of the same sorts of things that determine the credibility of threats and promises. The credibility of one's assurance that he will not explode a nuclear bomb if his demands are met grows out of the obvious unpleasantness of such an act, not out of the nature of the threat being made. Sadists, kidnapers, blackmailers, extortionists, and airline hijackers find that the credibility of their assurances is undermined by

he obvious opportunities and incentives they have to renege
on their assurance commitments, regardless of whether they
have made deterrent or compellent threats.

Although the distinction between deterrence and compellence at first appears to be very helpful in analyzing airline
hijacking, further scrutiny raises serious questions not only
about its applicability to this situation but also about the utility
of the distinction. The failure to provide a precise definition of
compellence makes it hard to be sure, but a low probability of
success seems to be inextricably bound up with the implied
definition of this term. It is worthwhile to distinguish between
threats and promises and between influence attempts with a
high probability of success and those with a low probability of
success. Until more precise definitions and more persuasive arguments are produced, however, students of bargaining should
be wary of the distinction between compellence and deterrence.[12]

## CONCLUSION

Although bargaining theory can call attention to some
aspects of airline hijacking that deserve more attention, there
are some very significant differences between the usual assumptions of that theory and the reality of hijacking situations.
Perhaps the most important contribution bargaining theory
can make to understanding hijacking is identification of the
obstacles to mutually productive bargaining between the
hijacker and the government. In the first place, there are
almost no outcomes or bargains that both participants would
regard as legitimate. In the second place, it is very difficult for
either participant to make a binding promise to the other. In
the third place, the government's desire to deter potential future hijackers severely hinders its ability to strike a bargain
with an actual hijacker. And in the fourth place, the value system and rationality of the hijacker are likely to be in doubt
during most of the negotiations.

This last point deserves elaboration because it is the key to
understanding why bargaining theory has difficulty answering
the most important policy questions about how to deal with a
hijacker. Traditional bargaining theory assumes that partici-

pants are rational, that their value systems remain stable du
ing the bargaining process, and that each participant is awa
of the other participants' value systems. In an airline hijackin:
however, there is a reasonable possibility that the hijacker
insane; there is reason to expect his value system to change :
the pressure builds and fatigue sets in; and there is almo:
always considerable ignorance on the part of the governme:
as to the nature of the hijacker's value system. The governme:
must pursue such questions as: Does he know what he wants
If so, what does he want? Can he be expected to evaluate alte:
native options rationally? Some hijackers seem unable even t
formulate coherent demands; others seem to be trying to con
mit suicide; and almost all seem to reorder their priorities :
the situation evolves. In such a situation the government:
policies of trying to find out as much as possible about th
hijacker without irritating him and of watchful waiting appea
quite reasonable.

The uncertainty about the goals and rationality of hijacker
is just as relevant to deterrence as it is to defense. Plainclothe
air marshals, stiff legal penalties, elimination of sanctuarie:
etc., are sensible deterrent measures only if certain assump
tions about the goals and rationality of potential hijackers ar
made. Such measures must be considered in terms of the poss:
bility that potential hijackers might be trying to get themselve
killed, might be seeking a challenge, or might be irrationa
There is no easy solution to the problems posed by such poss:
bilities. It would be a mistake, however, to assume that actua
hijackers are all slightly crazy while potential hijackers are a'
perfectly sane.

It is useful to conceive of airline hijackings as bargaining si:
uations, and bargaining theory can illuminate several aspect
of such situations. This does not mean, however, that potentia
hijackers and potential government antihijacking policymaker
should rely on simpleminded game-theory matrices in makin;
their decisions. We should remind ourselves of Schelling'
warning about the danger of "too much abstractness" in th
study of bargaining: "We change the character of the gam
when we drastically alter the amount of contextual detail tha
it contains or when we eliminate such complicating factors a
the players' uncertainties about each other's value systems. I

is often contextual detail that can guide the players to the discovery of a stable or, at least, mutually nondestructive outcome" (1960, p. 162).

Three avenues of development for future research offer hope for improving our understanding of the bargaining aspects of airline hijacking situations. First, politically motivated hijackings need to be analyzed in the context of theories of bargaining on a societal level (cf. Lipsky 1968; and Nieburg 1969). Second, empirical study of the "contextual detail" of particular kinds of hijacking situations is needed. The Palestinian guerrilla hijackings provide an example of such a category (see appended Cases). And third, further development of the theory of bargaining under conditions of uncertainty will make such theory more applicable to understanding such situations as airline hijacking (see Ikle and Leites 1962; Harsanyi 1962; and Young 1976).

## CASES FROM 1973

### The Arab Hijackers

One important category of airline hijackings deserving of more analysis was that of Palestinian Arabs. Although these cases do not purport to present comprehensive data, they will provide some "thumbnail sketches" of recent Arab hijackings in order to illustrate the kind of analysis that is needed. They will also suggest a paradigm for use in analyzing Arab hijackings as part of a worldwide long-range bargaining process.

#### Case No. 1   July 20–24, 1973

| | |
|---|---|
| Who? | Three Palestinians and one Japanese, described variously as members of "Al-Fatah," "The Japanese Red Army," and "The Sons of Occupied Territories." |
| Arena? | Japanese plane over Europe later landing in Middle East. |
| Hostages? | 123 passengers and 22 crew members—mostly Japanese. |
| Target of demands? | Israel? |

| Type of demands? | Unclear, specific demands never clearly communicated. |
| Threat/promise? | Unclear. |
| Duration? | About forty-eight hours. |
| Outcome? | Plane flown to Libya, hostages released, hijackers captured in escape attempt after destroying plane. |
| Comments: | The remarkable aspect of this hijacking was the inability of the hijackers to formulate specific threats and/or demands. |

## Case No. 2    September 5–8, 1973

| Who? | Five Arabs claiming to belong to Al-Ical (apparently an unheard-of splinter group) |
| Arena? | Saudi Arabia embassy in Paris, then plane to Middle East. |
| Hostages? | Ten French and Arab diplomats and embassy employees. |
| Target of demands? | Jordan. |
| Type of demands? | Release of same Al-Fatah leader Jordan had refused to release in connection with the killing of U.S. diplomats in the Sudan in March 1973. |
| Threat/promise? | To blow up embassy and/or kill hostages. |
| Duration? | About seventy-two hours. |
| Outcome? | Demands steadily moderated from threat to blow up embassy if demands not met by 4:00 P.M., then 6:00 P.M., then 6:30 P.M., then inexact times. Demands finally moderated to safe passage with ultimate surrender in Kuwait. |
| Comments: | Note the lack of "connectedness" (Schelling 1966, pp. 86–90) between demands and threats. Why not the Jordanian embassy? Why choose an embassy in France, which has been a supporter of the Arabs in the Middle East? Why threaten to kill Arab hostages for the Arab cause? |
| | Also, why demand the release of a prisoner that Jordan had already demonstrated intense reluctance to release? It is interesting to note that two weeks later this leader was released as part of a general amnesty for political pris- |

oners in Jordan. That this affront to the Saudi Arabians came on the eve of the October attack on Israel may account for the vigor of the denunciations by Arab governments.

### Case No. 3    November 25–29, 1973

| | |
|---|---|
| Who? | Three Palestinian Arabs. |
| Arena? | Dutch plane over Iraq. |
| Hostages? | 247 passengers released after 24 hours and 11 crew members held until the end. |
| Target of demands? | Netherlands. |
| Type of demands? | Change in Dutch Government's "pro-Israeli" stance. Later on they demanded release of some Palestinian prisoners in Cyprus, but failed to wait for response. |
| Threat/promise? | Return of hostages and plane. |
| Duration? | About ninety-six hours. |
| Outcome? | Dutch Government furnished certain pledges but claimed that they represented no change in Dutch policy. Hijackers surrendered in Dubai in return for safe conduct. |
| Comments: | Dutch Government was able to meet hijackers' demands without admitting that it was doing anything it would not otherwise have done. |

### Case No. 4    December 17–19, 1973

| | |
|---|---|
| Who? | Five Palestinian Arabs. |
| Arena? | Rome airport, then Lufthansa plane to Athens and eventual landing in Kuwait. |
| Hostages? | Thirteen crew members and ground workers —German and Italian. One hostage was deliberately executed to increase threat credibility, which was probably unnecessary, since thirty-one people were killed in the process of taking over the plane. |
| Target of demands? | Greece? |
| Type of demands? | Release of two prisoners in Athens. |
| Threat/promise? | Varied, including shooting hostages one by one, throwing them out in midflight, and crashing the plane in the heart of Athens. |
| Duration? | Thirty hours. |

Outcome?          Greek prisoners not released. Surrender i
                  Kuwait in return for promise of "free pas
                  sage."

Comments:         The trivial nature of the demands togethe
                  with the timing—the eve of the opening o
                  Arab-Israeli peace talks in Geneva—sugges
                  that the hijackers' real goal was broader than
                  release of two prisoners. This sort of multipl
                  bargaining might be diagramed as in Figure :
                  below.

Figure 2 illustrates how a hijacker's demands may allow him te
bargain on many levels. Not only is he bargaining via the pilot anc
ground contact point with the immediate specific target of his influence attempt but also via the media with third parties, supporters
of his cause (if any), and with his ultimate targets. Thus the pattern
of messages may be intended as follows:

To specific target:      Release two prisoners!
To intermediate target:  Don't forget the Palestinians!
To ultimate target:      Yield or else!
To third parties:        See how committed and desperate we are?
                         You may be next!
To supporters:           Don't despair!

FIGURE 2.
*Communication Channels for Explicit and Implicit Demands*

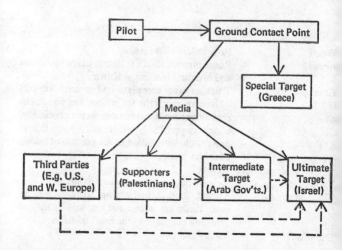

The dotted lines indicate possible channels by which pressure on target nations may result from the hijackers' demands. Such messages might take the following form:

From third parties: This is irritating to us; do you suppose there is anything you could do?

From supporters: Do you see what powerful (committed, crazy, etc.) friends we have?

From specific target: Sorry to do this but you can see what a bind we are in.

From intermediate target: We would like to be more conciliatory but the Palestinians won't let us.

Although the details of such an analytical scheme may be faulty, the general idea is to facilitate discussion of Arab hijackings in the broader political context of the Arab-Israeli dispute. (For a more sophisticated schematic representation of the process of bargaining via protest action, see Lipsky 1968, p. 1,147.)

## NOTES

1. Psychiatrists who have interviewed plane hijackers believe that many of them have suicidal desires and are trying to get themselves killed (*Hearings* 1973, pp. 258, 351, 365). Changing the probability of personal survival is still a goal for such a hijacker; however, he wants to lower it rather than increase it.
2. There is some possibility of developing standardized codes for sending and receiving instructions on hijacking. These would have to be kept very simple, however. There would be no room for subtlety or complexity; they would have to be confined to such commands as code words for "board," "stay away," and "don't give me all the fuel I ask for." See *Hearings* 1973, pp. 313–41.
3. "It is not invariably an advantage, in the face of a threat, to have a communication system in good order . . ." (Schelling 1960, p. 18). For discussions of proposals for physical modification of cockpit doors see *Hearings* 1973, and Aggarwala, Fenello, and Fitz-Gerald 1971.
4. On political protest as part of a broader social bargaining process, see Lipsky 1968 and Nieburg 1969.
5. The following definitions are used in this chapter: A "threat" is a conditional commitment to punish; a "promise" is a conditional commitment to reward; and an "assurance" is a conditional commitment not to punish or not to reward. See Baldwin 1971a, 1971b, 1971c.

6. "It is not always easy to make a convincing, self-binding prom
ise. Both the kidnaper who would like to release his prisoner, an
the prisoner, may search desperately for a way to commit the latte
against informing on his captor, without finding one" (Schellin
1960, p. 43).

7. The Arab hijackers may be a special case. At first glance the
appear to be free-lance revolutionaries, since they usually claim t
be members of some heretofore unheard-of splinter group of th
Palestinian Liberation Organization and since they are usuall
disavowed by the alleged parent organization. Further scrutiny
however, suggests that the "free-lance revolutionary" classificatio
may be misleading. Even if such hijackers do not receive specific in
structions from the PLO, they may receive tacit approval and en
couragement from the actions and words of the PLO. No direc
communication would even be necessary; the news media coul
furnish sufficient communication channels for the existence of a
"implicit organization." If enough people share a set of commo
goals, they may be able to co-ordinate their activities through read
ing about each other in the newspapers and without establishin
direct formal communication links. Thus, when Arab hijacker
demand a change in Austrian policy in return for release of hos
tages, it is difficult to explain Austrian compliance, since the hostage
will be released *before* Austrian compliance is complete. Two ex
planations might be considered. First, Austrian compliance may b
more apparent than real. And second, the existence of an implici
loosely knit organization of potential Arab hijackers lent some cred
ibility to the implicit threat of more hijackings if Austria failed t
give any sign of compliance. However that may be, there is at leas
reason to suspect a degree of tacit collaboration among Ara
hijackers that makes one have reservations about classifying then
as "free-lance revolutionaries."

8. The deterrent value of eliminating the possibility of sanctuary i
understandable if one assumes that potential hijackers are rationa
and hope to survive their hijacking attempt. It is disconcerting, how
ever, to find the same expert witness who claims that he has neve
met a skyjacker who would not have been deterred by the absence
of possible sanctuary describing skyjackers as "a nutty bunch" whe
have an unusually high level of suicidal intent (*Hearings* 1973, pp
350–65).

9. For Schelling this amounts to a distinction between deterren
threats and compellent threats. Deterrent and compellent promise
are virtually ignored by Schelling. Cf. Baldwin 1971a, 1971b
1971c.

10. The autonomous probability of the outcome X is defined as the

obability that X would have occurred in the absence of any attempt by A to make it occur. Thus, the autonomous probability of in a situation in which A is trying to influence B to do X is the obability that B would have done X anyway. See Deutsch 1968, . 26–27, 128; and Baldwin 1971a, 1971b, 1971c. Strictly speaking, e autonomous probability of B's performance of X is not the me as the probability of success of A's attempt to get B to do X. high autonomous probability need not indicate a high probability success for A, and a low autonomous probability does not necessrily mean that it will be hard for A to get B to do X. B's strong slike of A may make him reluctant to do X if he knows A wants m to; likewise, B's respect for A may make B eager to do X after e learns of A's desire. Other things being equal, however, it is genally harder to make unlikely events occur than it is to make likely ents occur. For purposes of this chapter, therefore, it will be arbiarily assumed that influence attempts aimed at bringing about low tonomous probability outcomes have a low probability of success, hile influence attempts aimed at bringing about high autonomous obability outcomes have a high probability of success.

. "Breathe or I'll shoot" is actually just a variation of "Act norally or I'll shoot"—a compellent threat often found in TV dramas picting the criminal hiding in the closet while the prisoner anvers the doorbell.

. The closest Schelling comes to a precise definition of comellence is in *Arms and Influence*, pp. 70–71. He cites Singer's 963) distinction between "persuasion" and "dissuasion" approvgly but rejects it because of the adjectives associated with such a istinction. For a discussion of Singer see Baldwin 1971d.

I suspect that psychologists may have some persuasive arguments to why it is useful to distinguish between deterrence and comellence. Schelling does not present such arguments, however.

# 2. INTERNATIONAL BUSINESS-GOVERNMENT NEGOTIATIONS: A STUDY IN INDIA

*Ashok Kapoor, New York University*

## BACKGROUND

Late in 1963, Bechtel Corporation began exploring with the government of India a crash program to produce 1 million tons of fertilizer in India by constructing five standardized plants, each with 200,000 tons' annual capacity.[1] In August 1964, a committee of senior officials from the Ministries of Finance, Petroleum and Chemicals, and Food and Agriculture authorized Bechtel to submit by late December 1964 a detailed feasibility study on the production and distribution of approximately 1 million tons per annum of nitrogen in urea and complex fertilizers. The schedule for project development was submission of a specific proposal by early January 1965; approval in principle by March 1965; final approval of specific terms of investment by July 1, 1965.

In September 1964, top Bechtel executives, together with Lucius Clay of Lehman Brothers, visited India to hold general discussions with senior government officials about the terms of investment. Their meetings were highly publicized in the Indian press, which emphasized the Americans' pleasure with the enthusiastic response and the constructive attitude displayed by the government. However, at this time, some influential officials opposed the project for one or more of the following reasons: It would result in foreign control over a significant portion of India's indigenous fertilizer manufacturing capacity; India did not need the quantity of fertilizers proposed; it would be impossible to market such a large quantity of fertilizers; the United States Government, through the embassy and the Agency for International Development (AID), was too closely associated with the project.

By October 1964, Bechtel and Lucius Clay had organized to conduct the feasibility study and to develop the terms of a proposal. The participating companies were: Texaco, Esso Standard Eastern, Shell Oil Company, Allied Chemical, and Food Machinery Corporation. Members of the consortium agreed that participation in the feasibility study would not commit them to participation in a proposal to the Indian Government and that for the time being the names of the members would not be disclosed.

By December 1964, Mobil Oil Company joined the consortium, while Esso and Shell withdrew; several members were skeptical about being able to agree among themselves on terms of a proposal and about the capacity of the Indian market to absorb the proposed fertilizer output; and the oil companies insisted on securing the right to sell crude oil as a condition for participation. By February 1965 the conflict within the consortium had become pronounced; members were concerned about the feasibility of the project; Mobil Oil Company withdrew.

In late January 1965 the consortium developed the general terms of a proposal whereby the consortium would commit itself for two plants, with three additional plants to be undertaken at a later date as market demand developed. The meetings in January-February between Bechtel executives and Indian officials disclosed many areas of conflict. The Indian officials were strongly critical of the summary report on the feasibility study. Bechtel was informed by the Indian Government that the American International Oil Company and the National Iranian Oil Company had been awarded a site at Madras to build a fertilizer-refinery complex in collaboration with the government.

As a result of these meetings and at the insistence of the oil companies, in late February the consortium developed a modified four-plant proposal, which included a petroleum refinery at a site at Haldia.

In March, Bechtel executives representing the consortium met again with the government committee. It soon became obvious that the two sides still had many areas of difference, the most pronounced ones being the consortium's requirements for crude oil supply rights, guaranteed rate of return on investment, and 50 per cent equity interest. An increasing number of officials (including many who had originally been enthusiastic supporters of the project) began to doubt the seriousness of the consortium's interest in developing an acceptable proposal.

By April 1965, the consortium (now known as the Western Industrial Corporation) informed the Indian Government of its intent to bid for a 50,000-barrels-per-day refinery and a 200,000-tons-per-year fertilizer plant at Haldia, and that it would continue its negotiations for the fertilizer project only if it were awarded crude oil supply rights through the Haldia refinery. However, a detailed proposal was not submitted because of internal disagreement on the nature and terms of a proposal.

Because of serious doubts about the proposal, the Indian Government announced that May 15 would be the deadline for negotiations with the consortium. Publicity in the Indian press remained at a high level and was critical of the Indian and the U.S. governments, but particularly of the consortium.

In the first half of May, Bechtel executives returned to India for a final round of negotiations with a new and high-powered government committee. The major conflict areas were discussed without reaching agreement. The government offered alternative approaches to the conflict areas, including the question of crude oil supply rights. Bechtel transmitted these suggestions to the consortium members, who remained uninterested. Therefore, Bechtel informed the Indian Government in late May that the consortium was withdrawing the fertilizer proposal.

## IMPORTANCE OF NEGOTIATIONS

Governments (particularly in developing countries) are
·laying a growing role as regulators, planners, and participants
n the development of their countries. This role will increase in
he future, especially in the developing countries (see Kapoor
974, Kapoor and Boddewyn 1973, Kapoor and Grub 1972,
ind Fayerweather 1973a). The effectiveness of foreign en-
erprise will depend upon its ability to interact effectively with
he host government. And increasingly, the large international
:nterprises, including those from the United States, will have
o pay far greater attention to cultivating effective relations
vith the home government.[2] The main characteristic of inter-
ational business that has emerged in the 1960s and the 1970s
ind promises to grow in importance in the coming years is the
undamental significance of effective relations between inter-
ational enterprise, host governments, and home governments
f they are to develop meaningful and lasting exchange of
·esources.[3]

The importance of international business-government rela-
ions has been reflected in the growing body of literature that
ias emerged in the field (see Behrman 1971, Kapoor and
3oddewyn 1973, Fayerweather 1969 and 1973a, Kapoor 1966,
1970a, 1970b, 1974, Mikesell 1971, and Vernon 1972). A
;rowing number of scholars in international relations are be-
;inning to study the general subject of international enterprise,
vith particular emphasis on the business-government rela-
ions dimension (see Buertis et al. 1971, Modelski 1972, and
Iuntington 1973). Additionally, a growing number of schol-
irs of business administration are beginning to study specific
limensions of the subject of business-government relations. In
:hort, the subject has been recognized as one of critical impor-
:ance in international business and is attracting growing
·esearch activity in the United States and in other countries.[4]

Although there is a large body of literature on decision-
naking and negotiations, there is very little on the subject of
nternational business negotiations. Yet, negotiation represents
)erhaps the most effective and lasting means of reconciliation
)f conflict between international enterprise and host countries

(see Hanner 1965, Williams 1965, Van Zandt 1970, Curtis an
Okita 1971, Thorelli 1966, Fayerweather 1973a, Gabriel 1972
Moran 1973, and Kapoor in Kapoor and Grub 1972). Th
subject of international business negotiations has been studie
in detail to a very limited extent (see Kapoor 1970b, i
Kapoor and Boddewyn 1973, and in Behrman, Boddewyn, an
Kapoor 1974, Fayerweather 1973a, Mikesell 1971, and Pinel
1973). However, greater interest in this subject is bein
expressed by scholars in international business (Buertis et al
1971) and international relations (Zartman 1971).

NEGOTIATION CHARACTERISTICS

## Organization Variables

*Precedent orientation.* A foreign-investment proposal is con
sidered by the foreign company and the host government with
reference to past proposals and expectations for the future. To
what extent and why were decisions on the massive fertilize
program precedent-oriented?

Some of the major decision areas for the Indian Govern
ment were the consortium's requirement for an assured rate o
return on investment, crude oil supply rights, and extent o
foreign ownership interest. The Indian Government's evalua
tion of these terms was significantly influenced by the extent to
which they would be both in keeping with terms granted in the
past and desirable as precedents for other investors in the fu
ture. When precedents existed (majority foreign ownership i
collaboration with the Indian private sector and foreign man
agement control in collaboration with the Indian Govern
ment), the government was willing to meet the consortium'
terms. Though the consortium maintained that the fertilize
proposal was an unprecedented project, its terms of investmen
reflected a strong adherence to precedents. The oil compan
members, unlike the other members of the consortium, insiste
on crude oil supply rights and a significant equity interes
because these stipulations were in keeping with the petroleun
industry's practice in investing overseas.

Precedents can come from the recent or distant past. Bu

what time constitutes the appropriate "statute of limitations" for precedents? Both the Indian Government and the consortium stressed those recent instances of investment as precedents that were likely to offer them better terms of investment. In justifying a decision, a precedent-oriented approach is safer than a nonprecedented approach. In formulating terms of investment, both the foreign companies and the host government should attach particular importance to relatively recent precedents where they exist.

Other writers have noted the orientation of organizations toward weighing precedents in reaching decisions. Cyert and March (1963, pp. 101–13) state that "organizations accept precedents as binding and look at standard operating procedures as constraints in any problem-solving situation." Aharoni (1966, p. 41) also notes the precedent orientation of companies in the foreign-investment decision process where "many previous 'policies' are taken as given and become constraints in the decision process." Kapoor (1974, conclusions) stresses the importance of precedents, especially in decision-making of governments.

As reflected in the fertilizer proposal, negotiators view their decisions in relation to their impact on current and future negotiations. Schelling (1960) states that the advantage in negotiations "goes to the party that can persuasively point to an array of other negotiations in which its own position would be prejudiced if it made a concession in this one." As demonstrated in the fertilizer proposal, when the same two parties are to negotiate other topics either simultaneously or in the future, Schelling states that a special case of interrelated negotiations occurs:

> The logic of this case is more subtle; to persuade the other that one cannot afford to recede, one says in effect, "If I concede you here, you would revise your estimate of me in our other negotiations; to protect my reputation with you I must hold firm." The second party is simultaneously the "third party" to whom one's bargaining reputation can be pledged.[5]

*Commonalty of goals.* Do groups place greater emphasis on achieving their short-term goals instead of long-term goals? Is agreement on terms of investment more likely if the short-term goals of groups are similar? The term "goals" as used here refers to the objectives of the different groups (actors) associated with a proposal; "means" refers to the respective preferences of the different groups (actors) on the method used to achieve these objectives; "short-term" refers to the period of time an actor—corporate executive or government official—expects to remain in a particular assignment and to the time period used to measure a group or an actor's performance.

Groups in the consortium and the government place greater emphasis on achieving their respective short-term goals. The Ministry of Finance saw in the fertilizer proposal a means for achieving its short-term goals of improving the foreign investment climate in India and increasing the country's indigenous fertilizer manufacturing capacity. The Ministry of Petroleum and Chemicals' (P & C) short-term goal was to achieve a rapid expansion of indigenous fertilizer manufacturing capacity, but through proposals that were likely to become a reality; if P & C emphasized one proposal to the exclusion of others, and if the proposal failed to materialize, it would have seriously adverse repercussions on the ministry in general and on its key officials in particular. The Ministry of Food and Agriculture's short-term goal was to secure fertilizer immediately from indigenous or foreign sources in order to increase food production, because F & A's performance would be assessed by the improvements it demonstrated in domestic food production.

The consortium's emphasis on short-term goals is reflected in the various terms of investment it was seeking, but particularly in its requirement of an assured return on investment in five years. An important, if not fundamental, consideration for many of the consortium members was the effect their identification with the fertilizer proposal or acceptance of certain terms of investment would have on their existing projects and current negotiation for projects in India and elsewhere in the world.

Within and between the consortium and the Indian Government there was a significant commonalty of long-term goals that could be achieved through the fertilizer proposal; India's long-term foreign private investment climate would be improved; foreign investors would secure a foothold in the developing Indian economy; food production would be greatly increased through the use of fertilizers; relationship between the Indian and U.S. governments would be improved. These long-term objectives were of a broad nature and did not violate any of the specific short-term goals of the actors, with the result that the various actors could readily subscribe to them.[6]

Foreign companies and the host government should recognize that the terms of investment that are sought or granted are evaluated particularly for their impact on the short-term goals of the participating groups.

*Expectations.* Does an actor or a group's optimism or pessimism for a proposal shift significantly with time? If so, is the expectation magnified in terms of optimism or pessimism, and if so, why?

The expectations of various groups within both the consortium and the Indian Government fluctuated significantly, and in almost all cases, the expectations were magnified in terms of optimism or pessimism. In September 1964, the Indian Government, the United States embassy, the Agency for International Development, and Bechtel and Clay displayed a highly favorable reaction toward the fertilizer proposal, as reflected in the favorable publicity accompanying Bechtel and Clay's visit to India. However, such a magnified expression of an optimistic mood—high expectation—for the fertilizer proposal at the time was not based on any concrete evidence in terms of a specific proposal.

Both the Indian Government and the consortium also demonstrated magnified pessimism—low expectation. The generally optimistic mood toward the fertilizer proposal lingered in the Indian Government from September through early January 1965, and thereafter rapidly deteriorated into a pessimistic one because of strong dissatisfaction with the summary report, limited prospects of reduction of fertilizer prices through the fertilizer proposal, the consortium's reaction to the award of the Madras site to the American International Oil Company, U. S. Ambassador at Large Harriman's stormy meeting with the Indian Finance Minister, and the consortium's requirements for crude oil supply rights.

The consortium's high expectations of September 1964 were

replaced in January 1965 with concern and outright pessimism about the fertilizer proposal. Esso and Shell, two companies with vast experience in India, withdrew; the members discovered many areas of conflict among themselves, including the nature and contents of the summary report. Thus, by late January 1965, the consortium had a low expectation of its ability to emerge with a proposal that would be approved by the Indian Government within the framework for negotiations established by Bechtel Corporation.

The consortium's low expectation for achieving the fertilizer proposal was reflected in its response to the alternative suggestions on the conflict areas offered by the Indian Government in May 1965. Though the alternative suggestions appeared to be in the direction of the terms being sought by the consortium, the consortium members did not view them to be promising because of their conviction that the fertilizer proposal could not be realized. However, the Indian Government's alternative suggestions would have been interpreted quite favorably by the consortium if they had been presented at a time when the consortium was still optimistic about the massive fertilizer proposal. The negotiation process is strongly affected by the respective expectation frameworks of the participating groups, which can be understood through insight into the organizational, environmental, and personality factors that influence the framework.[7]

*Commitment.* Decision-making units in both the Indian Government and the consortium comprised a number of participants. In the process of negotiation, any one member of the unit could offer a commitment for a certain course of action (the term "commitment" is aptly defined by Aharoni [1966, pp. 122–41, esp. p. 123] as representing "a state of mind, a feeling that guides action, not a legal obligation"). But both within the Indian Government and the consortium, commitments by individual members of decision units did not always lead to group commitments, particularly in instances when the size of the decision-making unit was large, when it contained a number of diverse interests, or when the decisions had significant economic and political consequences. For example, the Indian Finance Minister's alleged understanding with Bechtel and Clay that his government would not award fertilizer plant sites to other manufacturers was a significant decision, which made achievement of the country's fertilizer manufacturing targets dependent on the outcome of this one proposal. Such a decision called for the participation and approval of the Ministry of Petroleum and Chemicals, other ministries, and other political and economic interests. Consequently, the Finance Minister's alleged commitment was not supported by the Indian decision unit on the fertilizer proposal. In fact, the approach to decision-making in Prime Minister Shastri's administration was to emphasize consensus;[8] Shastri sought to achieve "collective responsibility, collective leadership, and collective approach" to a decision.[9]

The consortium's decision-making unit consisted of a number of participating companies. Bechtel and Clay had supposedly reached an understanding with the Indian Government in September 1964 on some major issues of investment. However, the consortium members refused to adhere to Bechtel and Clay's understandings with the Indian Government because the issues were central to their evaluation of the fertilizer proposal and could not be decided by any one member of the decision unit.

The more important decisions are made not by any one participant in a decision unit but by the entire unit. Almost all the Indian decisions were group decisions: the approval of the feasibility study; the award of the Madras site to the American International Oil Company; the response to the consortium's crude oil supply rights; the decision to continue negotiations with the consortium after the meetings in March. The group approach to decision-making, a tradition in the Indian Government, was reinforced by the economic and political importance of the massive fertilizer proposal to the various ministries associated with the proposal. The consortium used a group approach in making decisions on the feasibility study, the nature and terms of the bid for the Haldia refinery, and withdrawal of the proposal in May 1965.[10]

### Information Variables

*Face-to-face interaction.* Face-to-face interaction between groups is of course one of the most important means of communication in negotiations. The objective here is to comment on the frequency and effectiveness with which it is used.[11]

Internal consortium and Indian Government decisions on all major issues were largely based on face-to-face interaction between members of the respective decision units. Negotiations between the consortium and the Indian Government was also largely based on formal face-to-face meetings between January and May, resulting in approval of the feasibility study. There were in addition frequent less formal face-to-face interactions between individual consortium negotiators and various members of the Indian Government decision unit.

Both the consortium and the Indian Government stressed face-to-face interaction for the following reasons: Communication on a face-to-face basis was likely to be more effective than other means of interaction, such as letters or intermediaries; it offered an opportunity to assess the subjective factors affecting a decision; and it permitted gathering on-the-spot information on specific and general reactions toward a proposal.

A notable characteristic of the fertilizer proposal that applies to almost all cases of foreign investments in India is that face-to-face interaction between the consortium and the Indian Government took place almost exclusively in India. If some members of the host government's decision-making unit had visited the U.S.A. for face-to-face interactions with the consortium's decision-making unit, would the Indians have gained a better and faster understanding of the nature and direction of the consortium's terms of investment? Would it have conveyed to the consortium India's continued and serious interest in the fertilizer proposal? Were the visits to India by the consortium's negotiators of sufficient duration to permit effective discussion of a proposal as complex and significant as the fertilizer proposal?

There are two themes in the foregoing questions. First, the Indian Government would have been more effective in its negotiations if it had sent one or more senior officials for negotiations in the United States.[12] Such an action would have reaffirmed the importance attached by the Indians to the fertilizer proposal in the eyes of the consortium. By taking the initiative in this manner, the Indian Government would have created a particularly favorable impression with the consortium because the latter did not expect it to make such a move. Also, while in the United States Indian negotiators could have explored different sources of information and intelligence on the true intent and progress of the consortium.

The second theme is of time and continuity of presence of the consortium's negotiators in India. The duration of stay on each visit by consortium negotiators was limited.[13] Additionally, the consortium had not established some sort of an office in India to suggest a long-range presence in the country. Both these features had an adverse effect on the negotiations.

*Publicity.* Frequently foreign-investment proposals are accompanied by significant publicity. What is the impact of such publicity on the negotiation process? The fertilizer proposal experience suggests that publicity accompanying a foreign-investment proposal invariably has an adverse effect on the negotiation process between the foreign investor and the host government. ("Publicity" is defined here as comments about the fertilizer proposal made by Indian officials, newspaper correspondents and editors, members of Parliament, and other individuals or groups that were disclosed to the public largely through the press.)

The publicity had adverse effects on the negotiation process: It exposed the Indian Government's decision-makers to public scrutiny—a development that was not conducive to carefully considered and private judgment of the pros and cons of the proposal; it gave the project far greater economic and political significance than warranted by the facts of the case; Indian decision-makers were extremely cautious in their approach toward the fertilizer proposal because each action and decision was subjected to extensive public report and comment; there are always some groups in any society, particularly one as large and diverse as India, that are against a proposal because it is associated with a particular country, company, or concept; the fertilizer proposal led to this kind of reaction—it was American, it was big, therefore it was bad and had to be criticized.

Publicity is a major tool in negotiation, and frequently one or both parties in a negotiation will purposely disclose

"confidential" information. Press reports frequently contained
details on discussions between the Indian Government and the
consortium that could have been secured only through members of the negotiating/decision-making units who chose to
present selected aspects of the discussions to the public. These
disclosures helped the Indian negotiators by permitting them to
demonstrate to the consortium's negotiating unit the adverse
public reaction to the terms that the consortium was seeking.

Schelling (1960, p. 28) observes that representatives of
governments and other organizations

> . . . seem often to create a bargaining position by public
> statements, statements calculated to arouse a public opinion
> that permits no concessions to be made. If a binding public
> opinion can be cultivated and made evident to the other
> side, the initial position can thereby be made visibly
> "final."[14]

Publicity should be avoided at least until a final agreement has
been reached between the foreign investor and the host government. However, both the foreign investor and the host government should realize that, particularly in the case of large
foreign-investment proposals, leaks to the press cannot be
completely prevented. Therefore, each negotiating unit should
develop its own program for the management of communication—at what stage of negotiations, under what circumstances,
and by what means information should be released to public
media.[15]

*Informal communication.* Informal communication is an
off-the-record expression of views on a face-to-face basis between members of opposing negotiation or decision-making
units. In the fertilizer proposal negotiations, the frequency and
role of informal communication were quite limited; almost the
entire negotiation process was on a formal basis (for the
record) due to the importance of the proposal, the publicity attached to it, and the diversity of interests represented in the Indian Government decision unit.

However, informal communication can play a highly
significant role in facilitating the negotiation process.[16] Since
such discussions take place between representatives of oppos-

ing groups who are fairly well known to each other, they permit a more relaxed and open expression of views than is possible at a formal meeting, and in the process, important dimensions of the decision-making framework are disclosed. An important side benefit is that such communication permits the negotiators to "get things off their chest," which is of important therapeutic value in a tense situation.

*Specification of terms.* The negotiation process is affected by the extent to and pace at which opposing groups specify their terms of investment. The Ministry of Finance realized from the very beginning that the consortium would seek crude oil supply rights as a condition for participating in the fertilizer proposal. However, Finance did not ask Bechtel and Clay to specify their stand on this issue. Presumably the Ministry of Petroleum and Chemicals was aware that the consortium would seek crude oil supply rights, yet it also did not seek a specification from the consortium. Finance's strategy in not seeking a specification was that the price of crude oil was declining and that if specification of terms was delayed, the Indian Government would be able to secure better terms. Moreover, Finance did not wish to state its conviction that the consortium would seek crude oil supply rights because various groups in India would then reject the fertilizer proposal immediately. Bechtel and Clay were aware that crude oil supply rights would have to be granted to the consortium, but they did not raise this point with the Indians at their meetings in September 1964.

The entire negotiation process reflects a fundamental difference in approach between the Indian Government and the consortium. The consortium insisted that agreement should be reached in principle on major decision areas before discussing the details of each area, and the host government maintained the opposite approach. The consortium did not wish to enter into detailed discussions because it feared endless negotiation and was also afraid that once the Indian Government learned the details of the fertilizer proposal, it would use them in negotiations with other prospective investors. The Indian Government, on the other hand, insisted that it could not commit itself to an agreement in principle (for example, on equal equity interest) without first discussing the details and consequences of such an agreement. Each group was stressing an approach most likely to promote its interests.

Failure to vocalize certain terms does not mean that such terms are not important to one or both groups.[17] Failure to raise an important issue is in itself an important communication; however, to be able to interpret it in this manner requires a thorough understanding of the organizational, environmental, and personality factors of particular interests in a decision unit.

### ASSESSMENT AND ADDITIONAL RESEARCH

#### Assessment

The foregoing discussion has highlighted several variables that influence the process and the outcome of negotiation. But which was the most important variable in the fertilizer proposal negotiation? Each group used highly exaggerated expectations at the beginning, when the proposal was initially presented and generally reviewed. Yet these expectations were not based on hard facts and figures. The consortium members knew, based on their experience in India and in other parts of the world, that the real requirements of the project would result in significant deflation of the high expectations that had been generated at the outset. The Indian Government on its side had had considerable experience in negotiating for large projects and was acutely aware of the large gap that exists between what is initially discussed with foreign companies and what is the final scope and orientation of a project. Yet, both groups persisted in promoting exaggerated expectations, because in this way they hoped to provide momentum to the project, increase the credibility of the entire concept of the fertilizer proposal, encourage companies that were wavering to join the project, and attempt to reduce opposition to it. Of course, the key promoters of the massive fertilizer proposal from the consortium, the Indian Government, and the U.S. embassy had become personally involved in the outcome of the project.

However, as study, discussion, and negotiation on the specific characteristics of the project progressed, the real needs and conditions of the fertilizer proposal could no longer be sidestepped, and it became rapidly apparent that the initial expectations were grossly exaggerated. Given the high level of initial expectation, the subsequent reckoning with reality caused a sharp deflation effect, resulting in stronger charges and countercharges between the consortium and the Indian Government than would have been the case if the real dimensions of the project had been recognized from the beginning. However, even when the fertilizer proposal was definitely "inoperative" as a concept or as a practical project, neither the Indian Government nor the consortium stressed the role of high initial expectations as a major reason for the subsequent difficulties in the process of negotiations. Rather, both parties attempted to explain the outcome by reference to specific physical parameters of the project such as crude oil supply rights, ownership level, and provision of foreign exchange.

However, the high expectations for the fertilizer proposal were partly due to the unprecedented nature of the project, as there were no other similar projects in India with which it could be compared. A basic theme of the approach to negotiation adopted by both the Indian Government and the consortium was to stress the positive (expectations) in the hope that it would create a mood that would overcome the very real problems that were bound to arise if the project ever moved beyond the stage of negotiations for initial investment to the stage of project implementation and operations.

*Planning in international business negotiation.* The variables highlighted in the foregoing discussion assist in explaining some of the characteristics and processes of negotiation. The subject of international business negotiation is extremely complex in nature. However, in order to achieve the stated objectives in a negotiation, it is imperative that the negotiators recognize the major forces that influence the outcome. In fact, in the heat of battle the tactical aspects are often emphasized without sufficient regard for the broader considerations. By using greater planning, both the consortium and the Indian Government could have achieved their respective objectives faster and with a far lower element of surprise than proved to be the case.[18]

The concept of investment life cycle (hereafter called ILC) offers an approach to planning for international business negotiation. Figure 1 highlights the essential characteristics of the concept. The major features of ILC are:

- It refers to a project in a country and not to a foreign company's range of projects in the same country.
- It focuses on the theme of contributions made by the foreign company and the host country. The value assigned to contributions is subjectively determined.
- It states that over time with respect to a project in a country, the negotiations strength of the foreign company will decrease vis-à-vis the host country. The changes in strength can be generally anticipated and planned for in order to benefit from the standpoint of negotiation strength.
- It states that the values assigned are composed of both economic and noneconomic considerations.
- It states that changes in negotiation strength require changes in the attitudes of corporate executives and government officials.

The major benefits of investment life cycle in planning for negotiation are stressing the key themes of contribution, encouraging decision-makers to review their project from the standpoint of contribution to negotiation strength, and assisting in simplifying a highly complex situation.

However, ILC does not specify the shape of the curve except that it will decline for the company; does not indicate the pace of the decline except that host governments will attempt to hasten it; does not indicate the length or duration of each stage of ILC; does not offer quantitative formulas but is based on subjective judgment of the decision-makers; and does not forecast in a specific but general sense.

The stages of ILC are highlighted in Figure 1. However, additional stages could be added, such as negotiation leading to initiation of a project and negotiations for re-entry into a country after a forced or voluntary divestment. The specific characteristics of a project will determine the type of ILC breakdowns used by decision-makers in estimating negotiation strength.

## FIGURE 1:
*Investment Life Cycle*

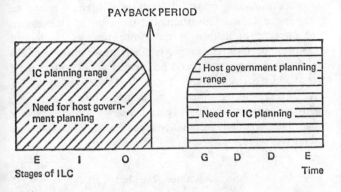

Negotiation Strength

Generally IC* possesses
positive strength

Host government begins
to become aware of positive
strength

PAYBACK PERIOD

IC planning range

Host government planning
range

Need for host govern-
ment planning

Need for IC planning

E      I      O            G    D    D    E
Stages of ILC                                            Time

E=Entry;     I=Implementation;     O=Operations;     G=Growth;
D=Decline;     D=Divestment;     E=Expropriation.
             Other stages can be added.

*International company

At present, use of investment life cycle by companies and
by governments is far more implicit and *ad hoc* in nature than
it is explicit and systematic. To the extent that companies use
ILC, the time horizon is largely through the stage by which the
company expects payback of its original investment. This point
generally occurs between the operations and growth stages.
Governments, on the other hand, appear to place emphasis on
the postoperations stages, when the costs of the project are
brought into sharper focus. However, companies need to place
greater emphasis on those same stages, because in the
preoperations stage their strength is inherently greater. Governments need to place greater weight on the preoperations
stages, since their strength in the postoperations stages tends to
increase. The basic theme that applies both to companies and

to governments is the need to adopt a time framework in planning for international business negotiation that accommodates the life cycle of the investment.

The ILC concept applies to the massive fertilizer proposal even though it terminated at the entry stage. The dimension of time had a bearing on the respective negotiation strengths of the Indian Government and the consortium. In the beginning the consortium was powerful because of what it hoped to achieve; the Indian Government could not have developed such a package on its own. However, over time, as the concept adopted some concrete shape, the host government realized that the original concept that it had valued would no longer be promoted by the consortium. Therefore, in the eyes of the Indian Government, the consortium no longer offered a unique, highly valued contribution. This change of attitude rapidly reduced the negotiation strength of the consortium vis-à-vis the Indian Government.

### Additional Research

The respective approaches to negotiation used by the Indian Government and the consortium were determined by a collectivity of issues, events, and moods being engendered through and by a number of actors functioning within a complex, interrelated, and dynamic environment. Aharoni's observation (1966, pp. 45–46) on the foreign-investment decision process is quite applicable to international business-government negotiation.

In summary [the negotiation process] is a very complicated social process, involving an intricate structure of attitudes and opinions, social relationships both inside and outside the firm, and the way such attitudes, opinions, and social relations are changing. It contains various elements of individual and organizational behavior, influenced by the past and the perception of the future as well as the present. It is composed of a large number of decisions, made by different people at different points in time. The understanding of the final outcome of such a process depends on an understanding of all its stages and parts.

The points explored in this chapter offer at best a glimpse of some of the characteristics of international business negotiations with governments. Additional research is needed on each of these (and other) characteristics. Some of the more promising approaches for research on the subject are: in-depth case studies analyzing the dynamics of negotiations between foreign companies and host governments; an effort to develop a conceptual framework as we gain greater understanding of the subject; and a determined effort to achieve an interdisciplinary approach by collaborating with scholars from the fields of politics, international relations, and game theory.

## NOTES

1. The case summary is based on Kapoor 1969. For a detailed discussion and analysis of the Bechtel case see Kapoor 1970b.
2. The Hartke-Burke legislation, tax reforms aimed to reduce benefits to international enterprises, congressional hearings under way or planned, and strong criticism of oil companies as a result of the energy crisis are only some of the developments necessitating closer interactions between U.S. companies and the U. S. Government. Charges of price fixing, hoarding, and excessive profits have been levied by the Japanese Government against large Japanese companies, which is an important development especially in a country where the ruling political party (Liberal Democratic party) has been viewed as a spokesman for big Japanese business.
3. This triangular relationship is the main conclusion of Behrman, Boddewyn, and Kapoor 1974.
4. Traditionally, Japanese business and government have been very close to each other, with interchange of views on all major decisions. See Eugene J. Kaplan, *Japan—The Government-Business Relationship: A Guide for the American Businessman* (Washington, D.C.: Bureau of International Commerce, U. S. Department of Commerce, U. S. Government Printing Office, 1972), and Chitoshi Yanaga, *Big Business and Japanese Politics* (New Haven, Conn.: Yale University Press, 1970).
5. In negotiating for sale of its fertilizer plant in the Philippines, Esso's approach was strongly influenced by the effect on its current and future negotiations for the company's petroleum refining and marketing operations in the Philippines. See Kapoor 1974 for a detailed case study of Esso Fertilizer and Agricultural Chemicals (ESFAC).

6. The same characteristic is present in the negotiations for Chrysler's joint venture with Mitsubishi in Japan, Esso's divestment of a fertilizer plant in the Philippines, Esso's joint venture with the Indian Government for a lubricant plant in India, and the international oil companies' negotiation with the Organization of Petroleum Exporting Countries leading to the agreement in Teheran in 1971; for a detailed discussion of each case, see Kapoor 1974. The foreign company stresses the long-term economic benefit/loss of foreign investment in negotiating with host governments; see Behrman, Boddewyn, and Kapoor 1974.

7. The expectations of negotiators have a direct and significant bearing on other characteristics of negotiations. For example, the commitment offered by a government is valued more if the foreign company believes that the government is serious about a particular project.

8. Michael Brecher, *Nehru's Mantle: The Politics of Succession in India* (New York: Frederick A. Praeger, 1966), pp. 105–6.

9. Ibid., p. 67; also see p. 92. The entire study is a fascinating account of decision-making in the Indian Government. The emphasis on consensus in government decision-making is demonstrated also in Japan. "Politicians and political parties do not lead. They wait, hoping for a national consensus on the issues confronting them before they are forced to act. To Westerners this way of operating may seem strange, but it is in keeping with a fundamental, perhaps subconscious, Japanese drive toward agglomeration, 'clustering'"; see Carl and Shelly Mydans, "What Manner of Men Are These Japanese?" *Fortune* (Apr. 1969), p. 101. For an excellent study see Chie Nakane, *Japanese Society* (Berkeley: University of California Press, 1970).

10. Aharoni (1966, p. 17) makes a similar observation; he states that the decision "whether or not to invest abroad is made by a group of individuals in an organization, not by an individual" (also see pp. 35 and 143). The same point is highlighted in Kapoor 1974.

11. Lall 1966, p. 333, elaborates on the importance of such communication to negotiations between nation-states.

12. Unfortunately, governments, particularly in developing countries, seldom take the initiative to control the site of negotiation. At times, especially during the preliminary stages, it is desirable to shift the site to the country of origin of the foreign company; for additional comments see the concluding chapter in Kapoor 1974.

13. In negotiations between American International Oil Company and the Indian Government for the Madras fertilizer and refinery projects, the chief AIOC negotiator made over fifty visits to India during an eighteen-month time period. On one visit, the AIOC ne-

gotiator arrived in Chicago on a direct flight from New Delhi, discussed the project with the board of directors, and took a flight on the same day to return to New Delhi.

14. The use of the press by opposing groups to improve their respective negotiating positions is vividly demonstrated in Ford 1954; see pp. 64–65 and p. 107 in particular. The role of the press in favor of or against a proposal is demonstrated in the debates on the antimonopoly law in Japan; see Chitoshi Yanaga, op. cit., pp. 163–64. Yanaga also discusses how the Filipino delegation used the press in negotiating the reparation settlement with Japan; see p. 219.

15. For additional comments see Kapoor 1974, especially the ESFAC case in the Philippines and the concluding chapter, which discusses the dimension of publicity in relation to stages of project life cycle.

16. Lall 1966 offers many examples of informal communications for their role in the international negotiation process. Informal communications are of critical importance, especially in negotiating with Japanese. See the case study of the Chrysler-Mitsubishi joint venture in Kapoor 1974 and Van Zandt 1970.

17. However, at times the negotiators simply overlook incorporating an issue into the negotiation (and draft agreements) because of the pressures of time, the desire to reach agreement, and the recognition that not all issues of conflict can be anticipated.

18. For a detailed discussion of one approach to planning, see Kapoor 1974.

# 3. THE NEWSPAPER STRIKE: A STEP-BY-STEP ACCOUNT*

## A. H. Raskin, The New York Times

"This is a history of failure—the failure of men and machinery, of politics and personalities, of miscalculated maneuvers and misjudged aspirations." That epitaph for the city's longest and costliest newspaper strike comes from a ranking official of the Publishers' Association of New York City. A top unionist makes a virtually identical evaluation, then adds almost prayerfully: "This should be the strike to end all newspaper strikes."

Why did it happen? Why did it take so long to settle and so much longer to end? What are the chances that the settlement will usher in an era of durable labor-management peace on the newspapers in the country's communications capital? New Yorkers, baffled by sixteen weeks of hearing little more than that negotiations were on or off, may find some clue to the answers in the untold story of what went on while more than 600 million daily and Sunday papers were unprinted.

The story began with the words, "It's too late," spoken at 1:56 A.M. on December 8, 1962, in a negotiating room at the

* © 1963 by The New York Times Company. Reprinted by permission from The New York Times (Apr. 1, 1963).

New Yorker Hotel by John J. Pilch, vice president of the International Typographical Union. He and Bertram A. Powers, president of Big Six, the union's New York local, were rejecting a plea made by Stephen I. Schlossberg, special assistant to the director of the Federal Mediation and Conciliation Service, to "stop the clock." Seven minutes later Theodore Newhouse, associate publisher of the Newhouse chain, knocked at the door to announce that pickets already were on the march.

The clock had started ticking 12 years before when the New York Newspaper Guild won a 73-day strike at the New York *World-Telegram,* primarily through the strength it gained from a newly forged "blood brotherhood" with nine other newspaper unions. These unions, representing printers, pressmen, and other mechanical employees, forced the paper to suspend by refusing to cross picket lines set up by the reporters, copy editors, and clerical employees in the Guild.

The effectiveness of this union alliance, perfected over the years, prompted the publishers to weld a united front of their own as a protection against "divide and conquer" strikes and the pyramiding of union demands. The result was a bargaining system under which a contract negotiated with one union fixed a pattern for all the unions, and a strike called against one paper generated an employer-enforced blackout of all the papers.

The calendar thrust the Guild into the role of union ball-carrier in the biennial negotiations. Its agreements expired on October 31, while those of the major printing crafts ran out on December 7. A chief goal of the strike of the Big Six printers was to establish a single expiration date for all the contracts so that the printers' union would no longer have to accept a follow-the-leader status in negotiating on wages and job security for its 2,980 members in newspaper composing rooms.

Long before the strike showdown there had been a joint recognition by the publishers and all the unions that they were at the end of the road on the old negotiating pattern and that Guild settlements would no longer be accepted on a take-it-or-leave-it basis. Officers of the ten unions and the Publishers' Association had met in April, May, and August in a vain effort to establish a co-ordinated mechanism for reaching contracts covering all 17,761 unionized newspaper workers before the October 31 Guild deadline.

The Publishers' Association is an organization of the publishers of the city's nine major daily papers. It negotiates as a unit with the nine craft unions representing newspaper employees. The Newspaper Guild of New York, representing editorial and commercial department employees, negotiates with individual newspapers.

With no general contract in prospect, the Guild called a strike at the *News* on November 1. When the other unions respected its picket lines, the members of the Publishers' Association met to order a citywide shutdown. A telephoned request from Secretary of Labor W. Willard Wirtz, who was about to fly to New York on instructions from President Kennedy, caused them to scrap the order.

During his mediation of the eight-day *News* tieup, Mr. Wirtz met secretly with Mr. Powers and Harry Van Arsdale, Jr., president of the New York City Central Labor Council, in an attempt to insure that the one-newspaper suspension in November would not be followed by an all-newspaper suspension in December.

However, any hope that the Guild accord at the *News* could be broadened to take in the craft unions evaporated when the Officers' Committee for Newspaper Union Unity, made up of the officers of the 10 unions representing newspaper employees, voted six to four not to authorize the Guild to submit a tentative settlement formula to the strikers for ratification. The Guild, noting that Big Six printers were already committed to ignore any Guild formula, disregarded the unity group's injunction and accepted a two-year contract providing package benefits of $8.50 a week and retention of the October 31 expiration date.

Guild leaders, in signing individual agreements on these terms with each newspaper, warned the publishers that the other unions would not regard the money provisions as a standard and that the Guild would support them if they struck for more. This warning was made even more explicit by Secretary Wirtz before he returned to Washington. At a meeting in the apartment of Richard E. Berlin, president of the Hearst Corporation, at 835 Fifth Avenue, Mr. Wirtz stressed the danger of a Big Six strike in what one publisher later described as "terms far more solemn and far more urgent than any we had ever heard from our own professionals."

Direct negotiations between the printers and the publishers had gotten under way July 26, three months ahead of the usual timetable, but little came of the talks. The dullness of the sessions did not delude either side; the fuse of potential conflict was sputtering too loud to be unremarked. The union, founded more than a century ago, was fighting to restore itself to a front position among the printing crafts. It complained that it had slipped far behind the parade in wages and working conditions, a complaint sharpened by fears that automation would make the craft obsolete.

The employers were plagued by problems of both cost and precedent. Most of the New York newspapers do not make ends meet on circulation and advertising. Only the New York *Times* and the *News* are consistent moneymakers; the others operate on subsidies from chains or individual owners. The worry on the publishers' side was the level at which a money package might push one or more newspapers into extinction. A parallel worry was how many restraints the union might seek to impose on the increased efficiency that new technology permitted.

Both negotiating teams recognized that the standards set here on economic and noneconomic matters would have a compelling effect on contract terms and on the survival of newspapers in most major cities. It was the fatefulness of these considerations that made both sides wary, even though the union had not called an official strike on any New York newspaper since 1883. The only interruption in that period had been a "voluntary vacation" started by Big Six members in 1919 in violation of ITU orders. Intended to achieve a 44-hour week, the outlaw walkout petered out in failure.

### THE NEGOTIATORS

Mr. Powers headed the union committee. His opposite number on the publishers' side was Amory H. Bradford, vice president and general manager of the New York *Times*. The two men had developed a regard for each other's intelligence and capacity while serving as cotrustees of the printers' pension and welfare funds several years before. Their mutual admiration did not last long.

The 41-year-old union president is tall, dapper, with whitish-blond hair, an earnest manner, and no talent for small talk. A printer at 17 (his formal education ended after two years in high school), he served as vice president of Big Six for eight years before being elected its president by a vote of 5,080 to 3,511 in May 1961. A year or so earlier he had contemplated quitting the local to become a federal mediator because he saw little chance of climbing any higher on the union ladder.

One of the army of government peacemakers who got to know him well in the endless hours of round-the-clock negotiations after December 8 describes Mr. Powers as "honest, clean, democratic—and impossible."

Another government official calls him "cold, ambitious, and utterly incapable of setting any realistic priorities for himself," then observes that he was "so superior to anyone he had to negotiate against that it was like matching Sonny Liston with a Golden Glove champion."

His critics in other unions denounce him as a "rule-or-ruin" type bent on modeling himself into a counterpart of the John L. Lewis of the 1930s. They say his goal is to become head of a national fusion of all printing unions. To his defenders such ambitions do not seem excessive, though they deny they are what makes him run. Pro-Powers unionists term him "incomparably the ablest and most forward-looking of the men in the graphic arts unions."

Mr. Bradford, two inches taller than the union chief and nine years older, is handsome, articulate, and aloof. Descendant of a distinguished New England family, he worked his way through school at Phillips Academy at Andover, Massachusetts, Yale, and Yale Law School. In the Army in World War II, he rose from private to captain. Later he served in the State Department and practiced corporation law before joining the *Times* in 1947.

One top-level mediator said Mr. Bradford brought an attitude of such icy disdain into the conference rooms that the mediator often felt he ought to ask the hotel to send up more heat. Another mediator, who called Mr. Bradford the possesor of the keenest mind on the management side, said he operates on a "short fuse."

Long in advance of the 1962 negotiations the executive committee of the Publishers' Association nominated Mr. Bradford to serve as chairman of the scale committee that would bargain with Big Six in behalf of all the papers. The choice was unanimously approved by the newspaper owners. They admire his independence and assurance, although they are occasionally galled by his imperiousness. His designation to direct talks with the printers represented a mark of special trust since it was recognized that these were the year's most ticklish negotiations and that their outcome might involve life or death for some papers.

## THE POSITIONS

Between July and the eve of the strike in December, Big Six moved down in its demands from an initial asking figure of $98 a week in contract gains for each worker to an only slightly less stratospheric total of $83. The employers' sole money offer in that period was an $8.00 package, coupled with a call for union concessions on automation and work practices.

Behind the ritualistic screen of formal negotiations, Mr. Bradford and F. M. Flynn, president of the *News*, undertook off-the-record explorations intended to determine whether there was any genuine possibility of obtaining a contract consistent with the publishers' idea of how much they give without pushing financially weak papers into bankruptcy. These attempts to learn whether their "ceiling" and Mr. Powers' settlement "floor" were anywhere near level proved fruitless. As the last day approached, Mr. Bradford said to the union chief: "I guess you've decided to strike first and negotiate later."

Nevertheless, at 6:00 P.M. on December 7, with the deadline only eight hours off, Mr. Bradford expressed to other members of the publishers' group his opinion that there would be no walkout. His judgment reflected the sentiment of most of the labor relations experts attached to the employers' negotiating committee. At 6:35 P.M. the committee sought to get the

bargaining into high gear by making a package offer of $9.20 a
week, $.70 above the Guild settlement, but they never got an
opportunity to put the extra sweetening into the pot that night.
Mr. Powers left almost at once to attend a session of the Unity
Committee representing all the unions.

He returned at 10:10 P.M. to announce the local's rejection
of the package, then left again without making a coun-
terproposal. While he was away, the publishers got to the lip of
an agreement with the Newspaper and Mail Deliverers' Union,
which had a "no contract, no work" walkout set for midnight.

The deliverers, satisfied that an accord was at hand, stopped
the clock and at 1:00 A.M. asked the Unity Committee to give
clearance for acceptance of an offer of $10.07 a week in
wages, welfare, and vacation benefits. The committee voted
authorization by a five to four vote, with Mr. Powers leading
the opposition. When Joseph Baer, the drivers' president, said
he felt obliged to recommend that his committee approve the
offer anyway, Mr. Powers retorted: "Whatever you do, we're
going to go out at 2:00 A.M. unless we get an offer that meets
our needs." Challenged by Mr. Baer to say what such an offer
must contain, the printers' head declared that he would not tell
either the Unity Committee or the publishers. "Let them make
me a good enough offer" was all he would say.

Finally, at 1:45 A.M., Mr. Powers led the printers' four-
man team back to meet with the employers and announced in
a quavery voice that he was prepared to submit a coun-
terproposal. He read it very fast—so fast that he had to go
through it a second time to let the publishers scribble notes on
what he was seeking.

The revised demands came to $38, more than four times the
package the employers had offered seven hours before. Mr.
Powers wound up his recital by emphasizing that the local's
proposal was put forward as a basis for further negotiation.
The publishers were too stunned to respond. Mr. Schlossberg,
the mediator, noted that not much negotiating could be done
in the few minutes still left, but his suggestion to stop the clock
was vetoed by the union. When Mr. Newhouse arrived with
word that the strike had begun, Mr. Bradford led the publishers out of the room.

The strike call was confined to printers at the New York

imes, the *News*, the *Journal-American*, and the *World-elegram and Sun*. Mr. Powers said the union would not nolcst five "marginal" papers—the *Herald Tribune*, the *Post*, ie *Daily Mirror*, the Long Island *Star-Journal*, and the Long sland *Press*—to assure a continued flow of news and to safe-uard their financial position against the hazards of a long eup.

Mr. Bradford called the selective strike "a deliberate device o whipsaw the struck papers into making excessive conces-ions" for a settlement that would then become binding on all he metropolitan publishers. At 5:00 A.M. four of the un-truck papers announced that they were suspending publica-ion. The fifth, the Long Island *Press*, cut off its circulation in Queens, but kept putting out its Nassau and Suffolk County editions.

Underlying the shutdown were issues more complex than he money gap. Chief among them were these:

*Common expiration date.* Both the printers and the publish-ers agreed that stability would be enhanced if all the newspa-per labor contracts ran out at the same time. They disagreed on what the date should be. Mr. Powers insisted that it had to be October 31, 1964, the date already fixed in the contracts the papers had signed with the Guild. The publishers wanted December 7, 1964, and then shifted to a date two years from whenever the printers returned to work. The October date, coming on the eve of a presidential election and at the start of the pre-Christmas advertising season, promised maximum eco-nomic leverage for the union. By December 7, only one week of peak advertising would be at stake before the post-Christmas slack that extends through most of January and February.

*Automation.* The publishers sought the right to have all their Stock Exchange and other financial tables set into type automatically through the use of Teletypesetter tape supplied by the Associated Press or United Press International. They offered a contractual guarantee that no regular employees would lose their jobs through the introduction of the new process. The union, fearful that the change would be a first step toward the use of computers to displace Linotype opera-tors, asked that a share of the savings made possible through tape go into a special fund for retraining, early retirement payments, or supplemental unemployment benefits. The employers objected, saying that publishers in all other big cities already had a union green light for much more extensive application of tape without any special fund.

*Shorter workweek.* The printers wanted their basic work time cut from 36¼ hours a week to 35, the standard already in force for the Guild. They said the reduced work schedule could be effected without extra cost or loss of productive time through the voluntary surrender by the printers of 15 minutes a day of washup and toilet time. The publishers resisted on the ground that there was no real assurance the printers would actually stop taking the washup time and that the spread of the change to other crafts would drive up costs by as much as $9.00 a week.

In addition, Big Six asked for an increase of $10.55 a week the first year and $8.45 the second in its old wage of $141, bigger night-shift pay differentials, an increase in paid sick leave from one day a year to five, and higher employee contributions to the pension and welfare funds to offset increased premium costs for benefits established two years before.

Public officials of all kinds, all parties, and all degrees of experience in labor matters offered a helping hand—with uniform lack of success. . . . One reason . . . was notice by the publishers that they wanted only arbitration, not recommendations that could become a jumping-off point for higher union demands. Another reason was the union's adamancy against either arbitration or fact-finding. Mr. Powers told the Labor Secretary that he regarded both as forms of government dictation alien to free collective bargaining. He said his hostility would not abate even if the presidential panel were composed of Mr. Meany [of the AFL-CIO], Mr. Van Arsdale, and Walter P. Reuther, president of the United Automobile Workers.

### FIRST REAL MOVE

The first substantial movement on the bargaining front came in total secrecy at Gracie Mansion on December 30, the Sunday before New Year's Day. Mr. Van Arsdale had met privately with several ranking publishers on Friday and had expressed confidence that a pact could be worked out if both sides dropped some of their frozen attitudes.

He proposed that he and the mayor, acting as mediators, sit with Mr. Powers and Mr. Bradford to seek a meeting of minds on every point. The Gracie Mansion session began at 10:30 A.M. and ended at 2:30 A.M. the next day. The understanding on both sides was that everything proposed or accepted would be washed out if the session ended without a full agreement.

At one stage the prospect for an accord appeared so bright that the discussion centered on how soon Mr. Powers could assemble the Big Six members for a ratification vote and how long after that it would require to get the presses rolling again.

Encouraged by indications that the publishers might give way on the 35-hour week and other key issues, the union president scaled down his package demand to $16.42 a week, less than half the figure he set when the countdown for the walkout was under way December 8. Mr. Bradford asked: "How do we fit that into a $10 bill?"

When it became plain that the publishers were unprepared to go more than a few cents above the money that was available on the day the strike began, the talks collapsed. Mr. Van Arsdale, disappointed at the employers' refusal to make any substantial improvement in their prestrike offer, told union associates the next day that he would not walk one block in any direction from then on to be helpful in settling the tieup.

With the situation back in a state of drift, Secretary Wirtz decided on January 6 to join with Governor Rockefeller and Mayor Wagner in a new approach. They appointed three judges to a Board of Public Accountability to examine the strike's causes and determine how well the parties were discharging their duties to the public.

Those on the board were retired Federal Judge Harold R. Medina of the Second Circuit of the United States Court of Appeals; retired Justice David W. Peck, former presiding justice of the Appellate Division of the State Supreme Court, First Department; and Joseph E. O'Grady, then a Criminal Court judge.

Up to then a good deal of polite sparring had been going on

between the Republican governor and the Democratic Labor Secretary and mayor. The two Democrats had taken the lead in settlement efforts, but Mr. Rockefeller let both sides know almost daily that he was ready to step in if they got nowhere. When Mr. Wirtz proposed the three-judge panel, the governor suggested that it be created under a 1941 state law empowering the industrial commissioner to name boards of inquiry with subpoena power. The federal official frowned on this project, and Mr. Rockefeller went along with the initial idea for three-way sponsorship, even though he suspected that the lack of subpoena power might handicap the panel.

Mr. Powers boycotted the board's hearings, but seven of the nine other newspaper unions took part. The report of the three judges put most of the blame for the shutdown on the printers' leaders. It accused them of having plotted a long strike to compel the newspapers to yield or face economic extinction. "The printers' strike which occasioned the shutdown of all the newspapers was not a move of last resort to which the printers were driven after a full exploration of the possibility of settlement," the board asserted. "It was a deliberate design formed by the printers' representatives as the opening gambit in negotiations."

A separate supplemental report by Mr. O'Grady, the only member of the panel with extensive labor experience, took a somewhat different view from the one to which he had subscribed in the unanimous main report. He observed that the employers had been trying to break it and that he had no fault to find with the appropriateness of either position.

At the board's behest, federal, state, and city mediators opened a new round of negotiations between the printers and the publishers on January 12. The employers raised their pre-strike offer of $9.20 a week by about $1.00 to bring it into line with the tentative settlement they had reached with the deliverers an hour before the printers quit.

The union pruned $1.00 off the wage part of its December 8 demands, leaving the total still at least $10 a week above the $16.42 figure Mr. Powers had unveiled in the off-the-record conversations at Gracie Mansion two weeks earlier. This retrogression caused a further dampening in the publishers' hopes for an agreement with Big Six, and they turned actively to efforts to crack the union front.

The aim was to induce the other printing crafts to break away from the Powers leadership and negotiate contracts in their own right. Out of this, the publishers hoped, would come sufficient pressure on Big Six to oblige it to enter into parallel settlements or risk a refusal by the other unions to continue honoring its picket lines.

The pressmen, who had been close to an agreement on December 8, negotiated all through the night of January 8 without arriving at a settlement. After that there were sporadic moves inside the Unity Committee to bypass Big Six in contract talks, but no union ever got a tempting enough offer to make it want to take the lead, and none was prepared to instruct its members to walk through the printers' lines.

The official mediation talks with Big Six became so ineffectual that the publishers began referring to the federal, state, and city peacemakers as "Winken, Blinken, and Nod." Almost every day some new overture would come from a would-be architect of an agreement outside the formal negotiations. . . .

On January 24, the ball passed to Albany, where Governor Rockefeller proposed a bill to set up a State Commission of Public Concern to recommend terms for settling disputes in vital industries. The measure was scheduled for swift passage in the Republican-controlled legislature, with the understanding that the commission's first order of business would be the newspaper strike.

The Rockefeller bill was very much in Mayor Wagner's mind when he met for lunch the following noon with Mr. [Theodore W.] Kheel [impartial chairman of the New York transit industry], who had just helped settle the Atlantic and Gulf Coast longshore strike as a member of a presidential panel, and Mr. O'Grady, who had quit the bench a few days before to become chairman of the Transit Authority. Mr. Kheel left the luncheon table at the Algonquin Hotel to phone Secretary Wirtz about back-to-work developments on the docks. He asked the Cabinet officer what he thought the mayor could usefully do in the news blackout. The reply was: Call all the publishers and all the unions to City Hall and tell them to roll up their sleeves and get to work on a settlement. Mr. Kheel said he thought the suggestion was "terrific." So did the mayor when it was relayed to him.

Late that afternoon Mr. Wagner sent telegrams informing everybody that he was intervening as mediator and that he expected them to co-operate in continuous negotiations at City Hall until the walkout was over. The publishers got their telegrams on their return from a private meeting with the governor, at which they had informed him they had no use for his bill. Their initial reaction to the mayor's intervention was no more cordial. In fact, Mr. Bradford telephoned the mayor at once and told him his action was the most foolish he had ever taken. Mr. Wagner flashed back that he was mayor and would do the things he deemed necessary to protect the community interest.

When the invitation to go to City Hall came up for official consideration at the Publishers' Association that evening, Mr. Bradford reported that the association's executive committee (made up of ranking administrative and labor relations officials) was overwhelmingly against acceptance. Its members believed that the talks would prove a waste of time and that the mayor, with Mr. Kheel and Mr. Van Arsdale as his principal advisers, would lean so far in favor of the printers that the cost of settlement would rise to even more forbidden heights.

The publishers themselves overruled these objections. The owners of the papers and the heads of the big chains said it was unthinkable on public-relations grounds for the press to say no to the mayor when all the dailies had been shut down for so long. Confronted with their unanimous decision to be represented at City Hall, Mr. Bradford put on his hat and coat and said he was not going. The next day he was persuaded to change his mind.

That weekend marked the start of what became, in the mayor's words, 60 days of "Late Late Shows." Management and union negotiators greeted the dawn on an average of two or three times each week, and almost always the mayor and Mr. Kheel were there to blink at the wintry sun, snow, or sleet with them. Both sides came to City Hall with meager enthusiasm. Their first insistence was a guarantee by Mr. Wagner that he would not make any settlement recommendations of his own. Their second was that the talks be off the record. The wall of secrecy was made so tight that even the other members of the Unity Committee were denied information about the precise positions of the printers and the publishers.

The first few days at City Hall were unusually fruitful. Mr. Powers indicated he would drop his pressure for an extra welfare contribution, thus cutting his minimum asking price to $13.75. The employers raised their money offer to $11.04, but the increase was hitched to a 26-month contract. Since all their calculations of what they could afford were based on a yardstick of $.42 in new labor costs for each month, this was merely a new twist on the contract they had offered the deliverers on December 8.

Progress was made on the issue of using Teletypesetter tape for stock tables, even though the reluctance of the publishers to acknowledge specifically the printers' right to a share of savings presented an unresolved semantic hurdle. Just when a new optimism was taking hold, the talks started moving backward again on the 35-hour week.

Mr. Kheel, seeking to ward off a fresh impasse, came up with a novel formula for neutralizing the cost of the shorter week through a blend of overtime and washup time. Mr. Powers pronounced it ingenious but too complicated to sell to the members. Despite this objection, the mediator tried it out on the publishers. He bade them get out their pencils because it would be hard to understand.

At this Mr. Bradford told the mayor that he was sick and tired of the whole proceedings and could see no reason why the publishers had to keep wasting time by coming to City Hall. "If that's the way you feel," Mr. Kheel exclaimed, "why don't you leave? Because if you don't I will. I certainly have got better things to do."

The other members of the employer committee—Mrs. Dorothy Schiff, publisher of the *Post;* Walter N. Thayer, president of the *Herald Tribune;* and Mr. Flynn—did not join in the Bradford complaint. But after they had gone, Mr. Kheel notified the mayor that he was pulling out. The next day Orvil E. Dryfoos, president and publisher of the *Times,* visited the mediator at his home and assured him that the employers wanted him to stay. Mr. Kheel, in turn, told Mr. Dryfoos that it was very important that Mr. Bradford also remain in the negotiations.

Despite the decision of both men to stay on the job, the momentum went out of the City Hall talks in the second week. Part of the explanation was that Mr. Powers backtracked on some of the commitments he had seemed willing to volunteer on the use of tape and on money. These retreats impelled Mr. Kheel to describe him as "a jitterbug bargainer—he giveth and he taketh away." Throughout the negotiations, complaints were frequent from mediators, the employers, and other unionists that Mr. Powers changed his mind so often on what he was prepared to do that no valid assessment of his goals ever could be made.

Another explanation for the slackening of the Wagner mediation efforts was that the parent, ITU, had scheduled a national referendum among its 115,000 members on a 3 per cent wage assessment to replenish its defense fund, emptied by the cost of benefits for the New York and Cleveland strikers. The fund was already more than $2,000,000 in debt to ITU locals for loans made to prevent a suspension of benefit payments. A referendum in mid-October to prepare for the walkouts by raising the fund's minimum reserve from $500,000 to $5,000,000 had been defeated by a margin of 53,880 to 21,524. With the new vote set for February 6 and with the union's solvency dependent on approval, there was a general feeling at City Hall that no settlement could be expected until the referendum was over.

During this period of drift, ill feeling between Mr. Powers and some of his associates on the Unity Committee kept bubbling to the surface. Leaders of the other unions charged that Big Six was deliberately stalling in the negotiations because even the prospect of an early settlement might undermine support for the assessment. Mr. Powers replied that all the delay was on the publishers' side and that he was as eager as ever for an agreement.

One night, when a long wait for Mr. Powers to emerge from a session with the employers had left the committee's nerves edgy, its members spotted him walking down the corridor with his overcoat on. Joseph Baer of the deliverers' union, a stocky, muscular man, a head shorter than Mr. Powers, rushed out to stop his exit. He caught him near the rotunda, blocked his passage with a restraining hand, and upbraided him for not having the courtesy to inform the other unions what had happened. Mr. Powers turned back quietly and assured the group that the only reason he had not come in was that nothing of moment had developed at the long meeting.

Irritations also made themselves felt in the publishers' councils, but they were mostly over the slowness with which agreement came on any shift in bargaining position, even on minute issues. The head of one morning newspaper said to another, as they left a particularly enervating session at the Publishers' Association: "That was like trying to move around in a barrel of molasses." However, differences on basic matters were infrequent. "If Powers had come in for a slow landing and tempted us more, he might have created more division," one executive observed later. "He was always too far away."

The February 6 referendum resulted in authorization of the assessment by 62,913 to 21,869. The union benefits, coupled with the availability after the strike's eighth week of state unemployment insurance payments, gave the average striker an assured income of just over $120 a week. This was comparable to his normal take-home pay when working. The newspapers had received an estimated total of $2,250,000 in strike insurance payments in the early stages of the shutdown, but these payments had ceased before the union referendum. The *News* did not share in the insurance payments.

With the union vote no longer a hazard, the mayor asked Elmer Brown, president of the ITU, to come to New York to take a personal hand in the negotiations. Preparations were made for a climactic effort to end the tieup over the weekend of February 8–11. . . .

The weekend wound up in failure at 9:00 A.M. Monday after a 20-hour session. The breaking point came when Mr. Kheel tried to sweep aside the logjam on hours by getting the publishers to consider a 32-month agreement, with the cut in the workweek to come in the last year. The publishers had a split vote, but their rules require unanimity. The Hearst and Scripps-Howard chains, concerned about the impact of a

35-hour schedule on their papers in other cities, exercised their veto.

Mr. Brown, returning to the union headquarters in Colorado Springs, pronounced the mayor's efforts "completely unprofitable and a waste of time." He invited Governor Rockefeller to send William J. Ronan, his executive secretary of the State Mediation Board, out to Colorado for conferences with Mr. Powers and other ITU officials. On their return Mr. Ronan called Mr. Thayer at a vacation resort in Nassau and said he thought he could succeed in getting peace talks moving again. The two men met in New York February 17, but nothing came of the new Rockefeller effort. At the same time another Republican, Senator Jacob K. Javits, arranged a series of conferences with leaders on both sides. Nothing came of these talks either. . . .

### THE FIRST BREAK

The first important power shift of the strike came on February 28 when Mrs. Schiff announced that the *Post* would resume publication on Monday, March 4. She explained that she believed the tieup had gone on long enough, that she saw no evidence of a quick settlement, and that she felt the city should have at least one regular newspaper. Mr. Powers, who was at her side when the announcement was made, emphasized that the *Post* had no commitment to pay its printers retroactive wage increases or to duplicate the benefits of the general settlement, whenever it came.

The *Post,* with a customary circulation of 335,859, increased its press run to nearly 800,000 by starting its presses early. Macy's and several other large advertisers kept their ads out of the paper, but it did not lack for other advertising. The resumption of publication was almost blocked by a manning dispute with the deliverers, but this was speedily ironed out.

The specific spur for Mrs. Schiff's decision to resign from the Publishers' Association and break the publishers' solid front was the association's refusal to appoint Mr. Orenstein, her labor counsel, to a new negotiating committee. She had won her own appointment to a similar committee a few weeks earlier after an exchange with Mr. Bradford. She said she felt he ought to serve with Mr. Bradford, Mr. Thayer, and Mr. Flynn. The committee head replied: "There is no rule of the Publishers' Association that says the *Post* has to be represented on every subcommittee."

"Yes," Mrs. Schiff replied, "and there is no rule that says the *Post* has to be a member of the Publishers' Association."

When the negotiating group was recast to comprise Mr. Bradford; Eugene Buttrill, vice president of the *Herald Tribune;* and John J. Green, assistant business manager of the *World-Telegram and Sun,* the association stood firm on the exclusion of any additional members.

Even though this was the immediate cause of Mrs. Schiff's departure, a more basic impellent was her abandonment of hope for a settlement. Every few days she would get a call from Mr. Thayer on back-scene developments. His standard opening was, "Fasten your seat belt, I have news for you." Then would follow an equally standard, "Absolutely nothing happened."

On February 27, the night before her resignation, she voiced her despair to the mayor while he was meeting with a group of publishers at Gracie Mansion. "This situation is intolerable," she exclaimed. "Isn't there anything the Democratic party and the entire labor movement can do to make reason prevail?" The mayor looked blank. He said he did not even know which party Mr. Powers belonged to. Mrs. Schiff informed him that the union chief had rung doorbells for John F. Kennedy in 1960. Earlier in the strike she had attempted to persuade Secretary Wirtz to set up a meeting between the President and Mr. Powers, but he took no action on the suggestion.

When Mrs. Schiff announced at the Publishers' Association that she was resigning, she said she was going into the next room to telephone Mr. Powers and make arrangements to resume publication. No one said anything, but Mr. Dryfoos followed her into the adjacent room. He suggested that by not telling the union head she had resigned, she might be able to learn from him what his rock-bottom settlement price was and thus help to promote a general settlement. Acting on this suggestion, Mrs. Schiff talked with Mr. Powers at some length before telling him that she was out of the association. However, he declined to disclose what his lowest price was. He said

he had told it only to the mayor and Mr. Kheel. It was th
$13.75 figure he had put forward at the start of the City Hal
talks a month before.

The Schiff defection and the arrival of the heavy Easter ad
vertising season injected a new intensity into the mayor'
revived negotiations. Mr. Kheel, who had repeatedly cautioned
both sides that any split in either front would have a disruptiv
effect on the negotiations, told Mr. Flynn that he viewed th
*Post* as having "gone through the publishers' picket lines" in
the same manner as if the Guild had gone through the printers
lines. He added, however, that the action would change noth
ing in the City Hall approach. Mr. Brown returned to New
York and assumed command on the union side. The talks were
transferred to the Commodore Hotel, and the mayor and Mr
Kheel spent endless hours putting together the intricate mosaic
of a contract that would satisfy both sides.

The semantic problems were even more troublesome than
the problems of substance. On the use of Teletypesetter tape
the publishers were willing to let an arbitrator decide how
much payment should be made and to let the union decide
how the money should be used. But they did not want an ex
plicit declaration of the principle of sharing or the formal es
tablishment of a fund.

The language on the pivotal problem of a common expira
tion date was no less tricky. Mr. Powers did not want to be
charged with renegotiating the Guild contract after all his ob
jections to having the Guild negotiate the Big Six contract. So
the proposals Mr. Kheel drafted for the mayor relied on an
affirmation by the Unity Committee of the desirability of a sin
gle date in recommending that all unions seek contracts expir
ing two years from the return to work.

After a week of behind-the-scenes exploration, Mr. Kheel
worked from 10:00 A.M. until 11:00 P.M. March 7 at his
office, 477 Madison Avenue, polishing the Wagner proposals
to what he hoped would prove the point of irresistibility. He
carried an armful of copies to the Commodore, and the mayor
called in both sides to consider them and let him know
whether they were acceptable. The package called for a total
of $12.63 a week in wage and fringe payments, an improve
ment of roughly $2.50 over what could have been had without

strike. The principal money items were a $4.00 weekly raise
he first year and $4.00 more the second; an increase of $2.00
1 the night-shift bonus and $4.00 in the late-night, or lobster,
hift bonus, and an increase in paid sick leave from one day a
ear to three.

On all three of Mr. Powers' key issues of principle, the
nion achieved breakthroughs. It got its 35-hour week, in re-
urn for the sacrifice of 15 minutes of daily washup time. The
hange was to become effective the second year. The common
xpiration date was ordered, although not on the October 31
ate the local had wanted. The use of Teletypesetter tape was
imited to AP and UPI tables of transactions on the New York
nd American Stock Exchanges, about two thirds of the mate-
ial the publishers had hoped to include. A joint committee
vas to study the savings and decide what payments should be
nade, with an arbitrator to take over if no agreement was
eached.

At 1:45 A.M. the publishers returned and said, "We will
accept if the union accepts." Things did not go as smoothly on
he union side. The executive council of the ITU unanimously
:ndorsed the Wagner package and informed the local commit-
ee that it would do everything in its power under the consti-
ution to persuade the Big Six membership to vote yes. Asked
)y one local committee man whether this meant strike benefits
vould be cut off if the contract were turned down, Mr. Brown
eplied, "You read the book and you'll see. It's all there." No
)ne had to check the constitution to be aware there was a section authorizing a cessation of benefits.

Nonetheless, by 2:20 A.M. it was clear the international
:ould not budge Mr. Powers and his group. They were
unanimous in rejecting the proposals. Mr. Brown reported the
disagreement to the mayor, then the three international
)fficers left for their own hotel. The local committee was about
to get its coats when the mayor and Mr. Kheel called in Mr.
Van Arsdale. "This is crazy," the leader of the city
AFL-CIO said. "He'll destroy himself and the whole labor
movement. He has all his issues of principle. How much more
can he want?"

Then began a 90-minute effort to satisfy Mr. Powers and
David W. Crockett, vice president of Big Six, that the contract

was a fair one and should be accepted. "Maybe you're enjoy-
ing this strike too much and don't really want to settle this
thing," was as close as Mr. Van Arsdale came to reproach. At
the end the two local officials went back to their committee,
and after an hour-long argument all but one of the seven negotiators joined in recommending the mayor's package.

### RATIFICATION AND COMPARISON

The rigors of that tussle proved an accurate index of what
was to follow in winning membership ratification of the Big
Six pact and in getting the nine other unions under contracts
embodying the basic ingredients of the printers' money
formula.

Insurgent elements in Big Six, led by Thomas W. Kopeck,
its secretary-treasurer, derided the economic benefits as too
niggardly and the protective clauses as too weak. In an initial
vote at Manhattan Center on March 17, they upset the contract by a 64-vote margin, 1,621 to 1,557. That meant the
mayor and Mr. Kheel had to start again on what they called
"the twelfth resurrection of Humpty Dumpty," with no certainty that all the pieces would still fit together.

A complicated ballet, in which the employers, the international union leaders, and the mayor all had precise parts to
play, worked with computerlike accuracy under Mr. Kheel's
stage management. Its aim was to convince the Big Six rank
and file that they would not get another penny in contract
benefits if the strike went 100 days more. Even arranging the
second vote for Madison Square Garden on Sunday involved a
midnight call by the mayor that had to evoke just the right
response from the Garden management or the strike would
have dragged on another week.

The man at the other end of the phone was Irving Felt, president of the Graham Paige Corporation, which owns the Garden. The mayor told him he had to know at once whether the
Garden would be available Sunday, then just 72 hours away,
or Big Six would not have the requisite time to notify its
members. He explained that there was no other auditorium big
enough to guard against the overcrowding that had kept
hundreds of ITU members from voting the previous Sunday.

Within 15 minutes Mr. Felt called back with word that there
`as to be an ice hockey game in the arena that night but that
ie union could use it if it were out by 4:00 P.M. When Mr.
.heel relayed to Mr. Powers the news that the huge hall was
vailable, he added: "Remember the platform on which you
`ill be standing is built over ice, and it's mighty thin ice." The
eballot on voting machines supplied by the city brought
atification by 2,562 to 1,763.

For the other unions, collective bargaining turned into col-
:ctive comparison and ultimately into collective confusion.
.he stereotypers, the mailers, the deliverers, and all the other
rafts evaluated every offer with slide-rule care to make sure
hat it added up to exactly the $12.63 in total benefits the
rinters had received. What started as a rebellion against pat-
ern bargaining moved inexorably toward a new pattern, with
*ig Six replacing the Guild in the pace-setter role.

However, variations developed behind the $12.63 façade.
ome unions took four weeks of paid vacation after one year
*f service, in preference to the cut in hours. Others applied
ome of their money for welfare. The Guild, the only union
vith a contract already signed, could have torpedoed every-
hing if it had clung to its October 31, 1964, expiration date.
*ut it swung to the new date in the interest of uniformity and
n return for a pay increase of $4.13 a week in the five-month
xtension period.

In the pulling and hauling for new contracts the Unity Com-
nittee was again turned into a forum for recriminations.
Unionists who had spent weeks criticizing Big Six for
ndifference to the total welfare of the newspaper workers
.cted, in the words of one committee member, "as if they
:ould wait five more weeks to bring their own agreements to
:ruition." "This whole thing ought to be settled over in the
psychopathic ward," Mr. Van Arsdale told his associates while
he bickering was at its height at a March 14 meeting. Mr.
Kheel was equally caustic in a report to the mayor. "These
inion fellows are like Janus," he said. "They have eyes in the
front of their head, and in the back of their head. They see
what the other fellow got and what he is going to get, and they
want it all."

The most serious hitch came over a relatively microscopic

problem involving hours for 371 photoengravers, the highest-paid in all the printing trades. Their president died in mid-strike, and a successor, Frank McGowan, was elected March 1. He decided to battle for four weeks of paid vacation and a cut in hours instead of following the lead of the stereotypers, the pressmen, the mailers, and the deliverers in taking the first and giving up the second. When the employers balked on the ground that this demand would not fit inside the $12.63 tent, the engravers retorted that they were ready to stay out forever to establish the principle that the cost of the shorter workweek should not be charged against the basic money package.

The engravers' stand stirred a tempest in the Unity Committee on March 24, the day the printers were voting to ratify their pact. When Mr. Powers urged Mr. McGowan to consider the impact of his holdout on all the 17,000 idle newspaper unionists, the engravers' chief answered: "You had a 100-day strike; now I'm entitled to a 100-day strike." "And then I'll take a third 100-day strike," Thomas Murphy, executive vice president of the Guild, asserted disgustedly.

The next day, with the engravers the only union still unready to go back to work, Robert E. Clune, president of the pressmen, telephoned City Hall to inform the mayor that if the McGowan union got shorter hours as a no-cost item he would pull the pressmen out on strike. At this point the mayor and Mr. Kheel saw Humpty Dumpty teetering for what could be his fatal fall, just when everything had appeared rosiest.

Again the mayor decided that a recommendation was the best way out. In last Tuesday's predawn hours, he came up with a formula under which the $12.63 package would have to cover everything the engravers got in wages, vacations, hours, and other benefits. The mayor left to an arbitrator the task of determining how much cost, if any, would be entailed in the introduction of the 35-hour week, with the understanding that the expense would be subtracted from the wage allowance for the second year.

The employers accepted the formula, but the union committee was unhappy about leaving anything to arbitration. Mr. Powers emerged at this juncture as an evangel of peace. He spent many hours with the engravers' committee, and the mayor's aides credit him with much of the responsibility for a decision by the engravers' leadership to stay inside the $12.63 limit, even though it meant sacrificing a general 35-hour week. That removed the last roadblock, except for the necessity of a ratification vote. Unfortunately, this proved anything but a formality.

A package based on the mayor's formula and recommended by the local officers was voted down 191 to 111 at a membership meeting last Wednesday in the New York School of Printing. The session got under way two hours late, principally because of haggling between the union officers and a publishers' subcommittee over detailed contract language. By the time Mr. McGowan got to the hall, many of the engravers had fortified themselves for the meeting by trips to nearby bars. Rebellion asserted itself in boos and heckling when the union president expressed his view that the contract was "very fair" and that all the other unions were waiting on its acceptance so their members could return to work. James J. McMahon, president of the New York Stereotypers' Unions, sought to address the engravers to warn them that they would have to "go it alone" if they turned down the formula. Twice he was forcibly ejected.

## CONCLUSIONS

What conclusions emerge from this welter on the whys of the strike? Many informed outside observers, including those closest to the settlement efforts, give low marks to both the publishers and the unions on their handling of the situation.

The peacemakers found particularly disturbing the lack of dependable channels for the confidential exchange of bargaining positions in an industry that was among the first in the country to establish union-shop relations. "Both sides had their own version of the 'Gromyko veto,'" one mediator observed. "The publishers, with their requirement that all decisions had to be unanimous, could always agree on saying no but rarely could agree on saying yes. On the union side, no craft could make a settlement without a majority vote of the Unity Committee, but any single union was free to shut down everybody by going on strike or staying on strike, regardless of how everybody else felt about it." In a telephone conversation with

the President several days after Mr. Kennedy's censure of Mr.
Powers, Mayor Wagner made plain his own belief that neither
management nor labor had much to boast about in adroitness
at the bargaining table. "Both sides deserve each other," was
the mayor's estimate.

Those who undertook the frustrations of conciliation doubt
that there ever was a real chance of averting a walkout on
December 8. One basis for this belief is the campaign Mr.
Powers began more than a year earlier to indoctrinate his
members with the notion that only a long strike could "swing
the pendulum so that we might obtain those things that belong
to us."

Here are other factors cited by mediators to explain why the
strike proved so intractable:

[1] The submission of "pie in the sky" demands by the
union developed exaggerated expectations among the strikers
and helped engender the disappointment reflected in the initial
rejection of the Wagner formula.

The publishers inadvertently added to this rank-and-file
disappointment by overadvertising Mr. Powers' official asking
price. Long after he had cut his off-the-record figure in half,
the publishers kept pointing to his formal call for a $38
package. At one stage, the union chief admonished Mr. Bradford: "You've got people so convinced I want $38 that if I get
$34 my members will say, 'Where's the other $4.00?'"

[2] Reversals of bargaining position by the Big Six leader
caused him to lose the trust of many he had to deal with in
management and labor. He was accused of making commitments one day and reneging on them the next. His written
statement of what he wanted after two weeks in City Hall
called for a higher cash package than he had offered to settle
for at Gracie Mansion 40 days earlier.

[3] Miscalculations by the publishers led them astray on
whether the strike would begin at the deadline and on whether
they could chip other unions away from the Powers banner.
The ITU never had authorized a walkout immediately on expiration of a contract, and this gave rise to management
confidence that Big Six would stay at work after the 2:00
A.M. countdown. When this proved wrong, hope shifted for

many weeks to the possibility that other unions could be induced to cross the printers' picket lines.

[4] High union strike benefits, reinforced by state unemployment insurance, diminished the printing craftsmen's incentive for settling. The printers had a strike income just over $120 a week. For photoengravers the rate was $137.50 a week until mid-March, when the parent union cut off its $25 weekly contribution. This brought the engravers' stipend to $112.50. Strike insurance was a less substantial prop for the publishers because it was limited as to both amount and duration.

[5] The reluctance of both sides to go along with any government fact-finding procedure prevented the emergence early in the blackout of recommendations that might have ended the stoppage. Secretary Wirtz and the mayor were deterred from naming such panels by objections from both groups. Governor Rockefeller was the only one with a clear statutory warrant, under the 22-year-old state law authorizing the appointment of boards with subpoena power, but similar objections were addressed to him. His proposed bill for a State Commission of Public Concern was shelved, under combined fire from labor and management.

What of the future? In the closing days of the tieup, the mayor told the publishers that they would have to get over the attitude that everything could be handed down in lordly fashion from on high. He advised them to make labor relations a front-office job, 365 days a year, and not leave it to functionaries at contract time. In separate talks with union leaders, the mayor stressed his conviction that an overhaul of their bargaining machinery was needed to guard against whipsaw tactics that would imperil the survival of marginal newspapers and to insure that each union would have a direct voice in establishing contract conditions without an endless chain of strikes.

Industry leaders are already discussing privately what changes ought to be made in their negotiating machinery to improve the chances of lasting peace. One possibility under consideration is the designation of a top-level professional chairman to represent the association in future contract bargaining. This would be a permanent, full-time post, with the new official unconnected with any newspaper. "Our professionals miscalculated on every major point," is the lament of one pillar of the association. "Every time they were unanimous, they were wrong. Always their approach was 'Give 'em nothing—and do it retroactively.'"

The unions also are doing some reassessment, although the hostilities that turned the Unity Committee into a battleground may take many months to heal. "Every union leader was a De Gaulle saying, 'I am out to protect France,'" one member of the committee says. "We were each out to protect our own union. Now it is time to recast the committee so it will be a vehicle for advancing the interests of all our members." . . .

Friction developed in the first week of March when the Wagner-Kheel settlement efforts reached fruition. At that point Mr. Powers made no secret of his resentment at the extent to which the Big Six committee had been superseded by Mr. Brown in the behind-the-scenes maneuvers preceding issuance of the mayor's recommendations. However, cooperation was restored when the two unionists joined forces in seeking to quell rank-and-file uprisings against ratification of the contract.

The initial falling out between the local and the international over whether the Wagner formula was good enough stemmed principally from Mr. Powers' unhappiness over not getting four extra days of paid sick leave, instead of two. Mr. Brown's view was that it would be foolhardy to prolong the strike indefinitely over an item that represented only $1.25 a week in additional gains in the contract's second year. In the end the argument that swung Mr. Powers was that the union had won a substantial victory on all three of its key issues of principle—the 35-hour week, the common expiration date and the automation payments—and that this was the real measuring rod of success. "It was the first time in three months that Powers showed any ability to differentiate between what was important and what was trivial," says one of his Unity Committee colleagues. "Perhaps it is a hopeful augury, especially since once he switched he became the fellow who almost single-handed put this agreement across."

Most observers think the turning point in the negotiations

came after the seventy-fifth day, with the President's call for "independent determination," the supporting demands for recommendations addressed to the mayor by the Guild, the deliverers, and the paper handlers, and the assumption of direct command of the printers' negotiations by Mr. Brown.

However, there is virtual unanimity that the indispensable element in nursing the agreement through all its dismal moments of near collapse was provided by the mayor, with the aid of Mr. Kheel and Mr. Van Arsdale. "Nobody sufficiently appreciates Wagner's ability to take a beating when he feels it is necessary to keep the city going," a high federal official commented this week. "His patience is inexhaustible. He didn't browbeat the parties as Fiorello La Guardia would have done, and he didn't go on TV to read the comics. But he did stick with this through all the frustrations and affronts that came from both sides and finally he made it come out right."

Two developments are likely to determine whether more harmonious industry-union relations grow out of this excursion into what one management lawyer terms "collective bargaining reduced to the absurd." One is how speedily the two sides move to set up a joint industry board to deal with the vexing problems of new technology in a field in which the traditional dividing lines between the printing crafts are fast being erased. The other is how successful the unions are in submerging their internal wrangles and creating a new bargaining council. . . .

Creating a bargaining council is regarded by most of the unions as desirable, but only the most tentative discussion has yet been held of how to accomplish such a fusion. What is sought is some counterpart of the New York Hotel Trades Council, through which separate unions representing maids, waiters, electricians, bellmen, engineers, elevator operators, and other hotel crafts have for many years conducted joint contract talks with all the city's large hotels. One distinctive feature of the hotel union setup is that no strike can be called without the unanimous concurrence of all the crafts. This is the opposite of the practice in the unity committee, where each union makes its own decision on whether to go out. . . .

In general, the City Hall architects of the present back-to-work formula see some hope that the current backwash of discord will be replaced by a more cordial environment for future co-operation. Their hopes are buoyed by the record in the steel industry, which came out of the 116-day strike of 1959 with little indication that either side had learned anything constructive from the costly struggle. Yet steel is now pioneering in new human-relations machinery for solving the problems of automation with fairness for stockholders, workers, and consumers.

# PART VI
Explanation and Prediction

# INTRODUCTION

Explanation and prediction are similar exercises. The contents of this collection have so far focused on analytical explanations of outcomes, but it would be inaccurate to suggest that whatever success they have means that prediction is around the corner. The reasons are important. It may be that negotiations are theoretically unpredictable, or simply that present theory is not very useful for predicting. The two judgments are expressed by Bartos and Hamermesh, respectively, in the following chapters, and the two are very different matters.

Theoretically, one major problem to prediction is symmetry, but another is its reverse, cultural relativism. Both problems were recognized and reflected in the school of Renaissance diplomacy writing that continued down to Nicolson (1964). The problem of symmetry is that if both parties know the theory, the outcome is either stalemate or nontheoretical. Bartos deals with the first problem in his chapter, Hamermesh with the second. The outcome is stalemate if the theory is an explanation of rational outcomes in maximal terms, such as D'Ossat's maxim, De Felice's advice, or Bartos' own propositions on toughness, since in trying to do best, both sides check each other's efforts. The outcome is nontheoretical if the theory is an explanation of rational outcomes in minimax terms, such as Nash's point or Cross's concession rates provide, because parties try to deviate from, not conform to, cataclysmic models and because the theoretical units are difficult to find in the real world. In a word, bargainers are not minimaxally rational, but outcomes cannot be maximal for both sides. Or again in other terms, neither justice nor power alone determines negotiated outcomes.

The cultural problem is the reverse because it makes no claims about the universal rationality of parties, but rather suggests that they act within set codes that are culturally determined. Like Jensen and Kapoor, Bartos found that there are national styles that condition not only what one does but also what one learns by doing, inserting an important intervening variable into the Skinnerian interpretation of negotiation as a learning process (see Schild 1968, Cross 1969). A common-sense explanation is easily comprehensible: We distrust countercultural learning because it goes against the grain, and even if it "proves" successful, we "know" that even more success would be achieved by doing the same thing the culturally "right" way (just as we would distrust findings that a gun could best hit a target if used backward, because "backward" is the "wrong" way for a gun to be used). The argument between the universalists and the cultural relativists is an old one in social science, and like other religious wars its greatest lesson is that both sides are wrong when they insist on their exclusive merit, and both are right when combined with the other. As a result, until a pervasive world culture has been achieved, intercultural negotiations should be tested for a cultural variable in the explanation of outcomes, a point De Callières knew when he talked about Spanish idiosyncrasies and Nicolson formulated more typologically when separating shopkeepers from warriors.

The second reason for poor predictability is of an entirely different order. Theory about negotiation is still not well developed, either in abstract terms or *a fortiori* in terms that can be used to explain real outcomes. Concepts that can be operationalized, relationships of observed regularity, hypotheses about causal influences—all need more work. Especially, more attention is needed to the type of article of Hamermesh, Baldwin, and Jensen in this collection, who try to use and test more abstract concepts and propositions for the interpretation of reality, as well as the sort of work done by most of the other authors who develop terms and relations out of concrete cases. To be sure, the idea of theoretical unpredictability can be cited to discourage further work in explanatory theory of negotiation. But the notion of theoretical inadequacy leads one to suspect that current theory is not sufficiently developed to leave us with theoretical unpredictability as the last word!

# 1. HOW PREDICTABLE ARE NEGOTIATIONS?*

*Otomar J. Bartos, University of Colorado*[1]

Undoubtedly, many students of negotiation are interested in their subject because negotiation is one of the outstanding mechanisms by which social and political conflicts can be resolved. Their hope is that a close and detailed study of the process of negotiation will yield information which will help to ease some of the world's more threatening tensions. In this paper we shall discuss some of the reasons why reaching this goal is more difficult than may seem at first glance.

## THE PROBLEM

In order to explore the reasons why the results of empirical study of negotiation may not always help to resolve social conflicts, let us consider the conditions under which we may advise a practicing negotiator on how to proceed. Such advice is justified only if we can demonstrate that one who follows it

* "How Predictable Are Negotiations?" by Otomar J. Bartos is reprinted from *Journal of Conflict Resolution* XI (Dec. 1967), No. 4, pp. 481–95, by permission of the publisher, Sage Publications, Inc.

will fare—in one way or another—better than one who ignores it. But can we always give such advice?

The theory of games, codified by Von Neumann and Morgenstern (1947), provides a framework for one such justification. The argument may be paraphrased as follows: "While I cannot predict exactly what will happen if you follow the (optimal) strategy I recommend, I can guarantee that you will receive at least a certain minimal payoff no matter what your opponent does." If a negotiator accepts this provision and is satisfied with the certainty of a minimal payoff, all is well. But he may not be satisfied with this minimum. Furthermore—and this is an even greater problem—relatively few conflicts of interest can be conceptualized as games with optimal strategies.

We shall now attempt to show that negotiations can be readily conceptualized as games having optimal strategies only if the behavior of the opponent is predictable, and that the behavior of the opponent in such games *cannot* be predicted.

## Optimal Strategies of Negotiation

After a thorough analysis of material dealing with bargaining and negotiation, Walton and McKersie (1965) conclude that a typical negotiation consists of two phases, the problem-solving and the bargaining. The problem-solving phase (the early phase of the negotiation process) serves mainly to establish the alternative solutions for the problem at hand as well as to define the payoff functions over these alternatives. The bargaining phase then functions to isolate one set of possible solutions as *the* solution.

While the problem-solving phase has intriguing dilemmas of its own, of primary interest to the theory of negotiation is the bargaining phase: if it is assumed that the possible outcomes and the associated payoffs are already defined, how should one behave in order to get the best possible deal? Walton and McKersie argue—and we agree—that the most important strategic variable of the bargaining phase is "toughness," the degree to which a negotiator is reluctant to make concessions to his opponent. As a result, the strategic aspects of bargaining can be represented most simply by a game which offers each player two choices, to be tough or to be soft. However, most negotiations occur within certain limitations, the most prominent of them being the deadline: the agreement has to be reached within a more or less definite period of time. Consequently, it is possible—and convenient as well—to define "toughness" as a strategy which, if pursued by *both* parties, leads to a failure to reach an agreement within the allotted period of time. Assuming for simplicity's sake that failure to agree has the payoff of zero for each party, the strategic aspects of a negotiation may be thus illustrated by the following payoff matrix:

|              |       | Negotiator 2 |       |
|--------------|-------|--------------|-------|
|              |       | Soft         | Tough |
|              | Soft  | 5,5          | 2,8   |
| Negotiator 1 |       |              |       |
|              | Tough | 8,2          | 0,0   |

The payoffs are clearly arbitrary, but certain of their aspects are not. For example, notice that it pays to be tough when the opponent is soft, but not when he is tough also.

The above game is reminiscent of the Prisoner's Dilemma, but differs from it in one important respect: the traditional criteria of rationality[2] are insufficient to define its optimal strategies. Hence it is anybody's guess how the game should be played. Notice, however, that if either one of the two players knows the probability that his opponent will be soft, $q$, then the principle that expected payoff should be maximized is sufficient to define an optimal strategy. Consider, for example, the row player. If he expects his opponent to be soft with probability $q$, then his expected payoff is

$$E(v) = \begin{bmatrix} 5 & 2 \\ 8 & 0 \end{bmatrix} \begin{bmatrix} q \\ 1-q \end{bmatrix} = \begin{bmatrix} 3q+2 \\ 8q \end{bmatrix}$$

That is, if he is soft his expected payoff is $3q+2$; if he is tough it is $8q$. The principle that expected payoff should be maximized means that he should be soft if $3q+2 > 8q$, that is, if $q > 2/5$. If $q < 2/5$, he should be tough; if $q = 2/5$ he may as well toss a coin to decide which way to play. But notice that whether he should be soft depends "inversely" on the probability that the opponent will also be soft: if the probability that his opponent will be soft is large ($q > 2/5$), he should be tough; if it is low ($q < 2/5$), he should be soft. In other words, *one should be soft against an opponent likely to be tough, tough against an opponent likely to be soft.*

Does this recommendation apply to most negotiations? This clearly depends on whether payoff matrices such as the one given here are adequate representations of the strategic aspects of negotiation. It is impossible even to begin considering this problem here. At the very least, however, this representation illustrates why optimal strategies of negotiation may be definable only if the opponent's behavior is predictable.

## Grounds for Unpredictability

Let us assume that it is indeed true that optimal strategies of negotiation can be defined only if the opponent's behavior is predictable. We shall now show that there are compelling reasons for believing that it is in fact not predictable. Two main reasons may be mentioned, one "logical," the other "empirical."

The logical reason is quite simple. It starts from the observation that negotiations are to a large extent *symmetrical:* whatever is true of me is usually also true of my opponent. In particular, if my opponent's behavior is predictable in the sense that I can specify probability $q$ that he will be soft, then my own behavior must also be predictable, and it will be possible to specify probability $p$ that I will be soft. However, if both $p$ and $q$ are known, then the game is already solved and to ask what I should do becomes a purely academic question: irrespective of what behavior might be to my advantage, I will do what I must—I will be soft with probability $p$. If, on the other hand, we insist on assuming that one is free to make a choice (that probability $p$ cannot be defined on *a priori* grounds), then we cannot assume that probability $q$ can be defined either. Thus, because of the symmetrical nature of negotiations, either it is possible to define an optimal strategy but not to use it (when behavior is assumed to be predictable), or else no optimal strategy can be defined (when men are assumed to be free to control their own behavior).

The "empirical" reason is somewhat more involved. To start with, one could argue that the usual bases on which a behavioral scientist predicts behavior (such as social class, sex, age, personality) are not applicable to negotiation since a professional negotiator does not speak for himself but rather for the organization he represents. But now recall our argument that the game-theoretical approach, which defines optimal strategies on the basis of payoff alone, breaks down when applied to negotiation, because here optimal strategies *cannot* be defined from payoffs alone. If this is the case, then a negotiator whose only motivation is to represent the interest of his organization (which define the payoffs of the game) would behave in a completely unpredictable manner. If we wish to maintain that his behavior is predictable, then we must trace it to such personal characteristics as background.

Moreover, the fact that considerations other than payoff influence negotiation is recognized in the literature. Speaking about international negotiations, Ikle (1964) notes that professional negotiators are highly concerned about their reputation, believing that a reputation for being soft could ruin their effectiveness. Sawyer and Guetzkow (1965), also speaking about international negotiations, discuss the "national character" of the negotiator and maintain that different nations have different styles of negotiation. Whether these differences are due to unique personal idiosyncrasies of the negotiators or to characteristics shared by a whole nation, it is perhaps clear that standard sociological variables such as sex, age, nationality, race, religion, and personality should be related to such variables of negotiation as toughness. Our argument, of course, is that only if such variables are in fact related to toughness can we hope to define optimal strategies of negotiation.

Our previous work with experimental negotiation suggests that some degree of relationship between toughness and background does exist: "well-adjusted" subjects (those scoring high on the California Personality Inventory) tend to be softer than "poorly-adjusted" ones, Caucasians softer than Japanese, older subjects softer than younger, and so on. But it was precisely these results which led to our present query: what significance is there in the finding, for example, that Caucasians tend to be softer than Japanese? What conclusions about the optimal strategy of negotiation can be drawn from this observation?

The most immediate reaction to this finding is in line with our previous discussion: since Japanese are tougher than Caucasians, and since one should be soft against a tough opponent, it follows that one should be softer against a Japanese than against a Caucasian.

But at this point the logical argument reappears in full force: if I am going to take advantage of the relationship between nationality and toughness, why should my opponent not do the same? Suppose that I am a Caucasian about to negotiate with another Caucasian. Expecting my opponent to be soft (because he is Caucasian), I turn tough. But now my opponent, expecting me to be soft because I am a Caucasian, turns tough also. Then the whole basis on which my strategy was defined disappears and my strategy is no longer optimal—both of us may be so tough that we cannot reach an agreement in the allotted time.

Thus, ironically, publication of scientific findings of this kind may influence the negotiation process itself and, in so doing, render the original finding inapplicable. No longer will each negotiator be guided by his *own* nationality as was originally reported. In fact, if everybody utilizes this finding, everybody will end up being guided by the nationality of his *opponent!*

This argument could be pursued further to show how scientific research into negotiation renders itself invalid, but it seems more profitable to consider a possible objection. One could argue that we have shown merely that certain relationships hold only under certain conditions, that our original findings apply only to "naive" negotiators, those who are not familiar with the laws that govern their own behavior. For the informed negotiator we have to postulate different laws—that is all. In other words, we have not shown that negotiating behavior is unpredictable, merely that it is conditionally predictable.

But let us consider this argument: is it reasonable to assume

hat I will ever have access to the information I need in order
to predict? If I am about to negotiate, can I really find out
what knowledge my opponent has about the laws governing
negotiating behavior? For example, how can I find out whether
he believes that I will behave in accordance with my own reputation rather than trying to adjust my behavior to his reputation? Can I be expected to be able to read my opponent's
mind?

The assumption concerning predictability can be pushed so
far that it loses practical significance. It is of considerable
practical importance that I can predict my opponent's behavior from a knowledge of his background, for such information
is readily available. But it becomes trivial to insist that my opponent's behavior is predictable if the information on which
the prediction must be based is practically inaccessible. I can
predict, for example, that most professional negotiators will
behave in accordance with the instructions they receive from
the organization they represent, but of what use is this to me if
these instructions are a well-kept secret?

Thus we are inevitably drawn to the conclusion that negotiating behavior is highly intractable, that it is in principle
unpredictable, and that empirical research can offer little help
in clarifying it. But against this conclusion stands an equally
inescapable fact: many negotiators do in fact use strategies
and they do in fact reach agreement in a fairly large number
of cases. How can this be explained?

### Grounds for Predictability

So far we have implicitly assumed that the negotiators are
fully rational and that they see the futility of trying to define
optimal strategies. But it is quite conceivable that many expert
negotiators are rational in a limited sense only, in the sense
that they will try to maximize their expected payoff, defined on
the assumption that the opponent will behave in a certain way.
Let us then imagine that most negotiators predict their opponents' behavior although, as we have shown, this approach
leads to paradoxical results—the presumably optimal strategy
would not be optimal in fact, and the negotiator would find his
expectations contradicted by experience.

We would expect that the user of an unsuccessful strategy will be curious to know why his presumably optimal strategy did not work. And *to the extent to which he is curious and analyzes the problem intelligently, his behavior is likely to change from session to session.* He may see that the negotiation situation is so indeterminate as to permit a large number of quite different strategies, and then proceed to use all of them more or less randomly; or, perhaps not possessing such penetrating insight, he may honestly try to learn by the mistakes he made previously. He may note that his opponent was not as soft as his reputation had indicated, and decide that the next time he will pay less attention to reputation. Following this reasoning he will adopt a different strategy and hence his behavior will be different.

But how long can we expect a person to continue such a search in session after session, repeatedly facing the unpredictable nature of negotiation? We know that men invent certainty where there is none. For example, most gamblers believe they have a system which guarantees success even in games of chance in which it is easy to prove that no such system can exist. Thus we would expect that negotiating behavior would tend to stabilize into a rather predictable pattern.

In what sense is this pattern predictable? Primarily in the sense in which a gambler's behavior is predictable: once we know what his system is, we can predict that he will follow it. But can we predict which system he will develop?

There is some evidence that *different* systems of belief tend to develop with respect to negotiation. For example, Jensen (in this volume) found that, during the disarmament negotiations following the Second World War, the American delegates made most of their concessions early, while the Russians made theirs late. This difference in behavior is probably related to a difference in beliefs: American culture tends to emphasize cooperativeness and good will, and thus American negotiators tend to believe that this "American formula" will be successful in negotiation. The Russian culture, on the other hand, tends to emphasize revolutionary toughness and willingness to fight for what they believe is right, and this attitude of toughness may "spill over" into negotiation situations.

Thus, in a sense, we are back to where we started when we

und that Caucasians tend to be softer negotiators than are apanese: we are now arguing that different cultural systems ay develop different styles of negotiation. We have made ome progress, however. We can now argue that such ifferences will tend to be stable to the extent to which the ne-otiator has *beliefs about the negotiation process itself.* A Jap-nese who is not a professional negotiator (and hence does ot have definite beliefs about negotiation) may start negotiat-ng in a different manner from that of a Caucasian, but as he ains first-hand experience (rather than indoctrination about ow a Japanese should negotiate), his behavior may change nd the original differences in approach between Caucasians nd Japanese may tend to disappear. A Japanese who *is* a pro-essional negotiator (who has been taught how a Japanese hould negotiate), however, is unlikely to change his style, ven if this style brings him repeated failures. Men do not eadily question their customs even if these customs happen to vork to their personal disadvantage.

## Role of Research

This analysis leaves several important questions unan-wered. It suggests that we should expect that the behavior of n unexperienced negotiator will vary from negotiation to ne-otiation, and that of a professional negotiator will tend to be redictable because he will follow his culture's beliefs about egotiation. But it is rather disturbing to have to conclude that egotiating behavior can stabilize in just about *any* form. What appens, for example, when the beliefs of professional negotia-ors are challenged again and again? When Americans negoti-te repeatedly with Russians and when each side finds that its pproach simply does not work? Can we predict how—or vhether—their beliefs will be changed?

It is for this reason that experiments with *un*experienced ne-otiators are of considerable interest: we can attempt to study he range within which negotiation can vary. Are there some imitations to this variation? Does a subject tend to stabilize at a certain level of toughness no matter what his background characteristics may be?

In this chapter we shall explore the range of variation in negotiating behavior. We shall now discuss experiments in which subjects were informed (not necessarily truthfully) whether their opponents were soft or tough, investigating the impact of such information upon their behavior.

## EXPERIMENTS IN NEGOTIATION

The experiments on which this chapter is based have been described in considerable detail elsewhere (e.g., Bartos 1974). For this reason, we shall give only the barest outlines of the manner in which they were conducted and analyzed.

The experiments were conducted as part of a continuing research into negotiation, designed to stimulate real-life negotiations. Three types of design have been used, each at a different level of reality. Of interest here is the so-called "team" design, in which two two-man teams are pitted against each other.

Our subjects were students at the University of Hawaii who volunteered to participate. Once a student had volunteered, he was put through a training session to acquaint him with the role he was to play and with the "feeling" of what negotiation was going to be like. Once he was trained, he was paired with another subject to form a team, which then went through two experiments, meeting the same opposing team each time.

The objective of the experiment was to make the subjects feel and act as diplomats or politicians meeting to resolve some difficult problems. Table 1 represents a payoff matrix which was the basis of one of the two experiments. Note that one team represented Communist China, the other the United States, and that their agenda included five proposals which such a conference might be expected to consider. Furthermore, the payoffs were defined in a reasonably realistic manner, giving a nation a high payoff for a proposal which seemed to be in its national interest, a low payoff otherwise. The realism of the payoffs was helpful for our purposes, but it was not essential. As is usually the case in real life as well, our experimental negotiators played a dual role. Not only did they defend the interests of their nations, but in so doing they also were defending their own private interests: the number designating a given payoff also represented dollars the team would ceive if the corresponding proposal was agreed to. In other ords, the subjects were instructed not only to defend their national interests but also to try to make as much money for emselves as possible.

## TABLE 1

*One of the Two Payoff Matrices Used in the Experiments*

| | | (Communist) China | United States |
|---|---|---|---|
| otal disarmament | 1 | 12* | −9 |
| Nuclear test ban | 2 | −1 | 4 |
| nternational inspection stations | 3 | −2 | 5 |
| JN police force | 4 | −10 | 13 |
| Destruction of nuclear weapons | 5 | 20 | −17 |

*Payoffs are in dollars. For example, if both sides agreed on "total disarmament," China would gain $12, USA would lose $9.

Their task was made difficult, however, by the fact that they ould make money only if they reached an agreement within a mited period of time. Specifically, the experiment always arted with a speech by Communist China, followed by a peech by the United States. Speaking alternately, each team as allowed to make twelve speeches,[8] after which three more inutes were allowed in which to reach an agreement. If by e end of the three minutes no agreement was reached, each am received zero payoff.

An agreement could involve one or more of the five proposals on the agenda. In fact, any one of the 31 combinations that an be made from the five proposals could constitute an greement. Thus there were 32 possible outcomes, including 1 agreements and one "failure to agree." The payoff from greement on a combination of proposals for a given team was omputed by adding together the payoffs for all of the individual proposals comprising the agreement. Thus, for example, China could make as much as $32.00 (if agreement on total isarmament and destruction of nuclear weapons was eached), or as little as −$13.00 (losing thirteen dollars by greeing to a nuclear test ban, international inspection, and JN police force).

In order to increase the realism of the experiments, *each*

*team knew only its own payoffs,* and was not allowed to reveal at any time what they were. Thus the negotiators were able to use that important weapon of bargaining—misrepresentation of own interests. However, since the roles played were fairly realistic, any too blatant misrepresentation was made only at the risk of arousing distrust and suspicion in the opponents.

## Special Instructions

Of crucial interest to this chapter is the question whether toughness depends on the beliefs a negotiator has formed about his opponents. Is it true, as we might expect if the subjects were using the "limited rationality" of maximizing their expected payoffs, that they will be soft if they expect their opponents to be tough and vice versa? For this reason we divided our experiments into two groups, "control" and "experimental." The experimental group received instructions designed to generate certain beliefs about opponents' toughness. The following instructions were read privately to each team in the experimental group, just before negotiation began:

> It is our policy in these experiments to tell you something about the composition of the other team. As you know, we have administered personality questionnaires and observed your behavior in the training session. Using this information, we have composed three types of teams, "tough," "normal," and "cooperative:" the "tough" teams are composed of students who can be expected to be tough bargainers (who expect to make a great deal of money) and hence are reluctant to make concessions; the "cooperative" teams are composed of those who are likely to be willing to settle for almost any payoff and hence are prone to make concessions readily; the "normal" teams are composed of those who fall in between the two extremes.
>
> The team opposing you is: (tough, cooperative).
>
> Your team is: normal.
>
> Feel free to utilize this information in whatever way you wish in planning your strategy.

In all cases the subjects were told that their own team was "normal." However, half of these teams were told that their

ponents were "tough," and the other half that they were
ooperative." This information about the opposing team was
tended to be true in about one half of the cases, false in the
her half. However, an *ex post facto* check revealed that we
tually tended to give the subjects *wrong* information.

The experimental group consisted of 40 teams. The control
oup, identical with the experimental group in all respects ex-
pt that it did not receive the above special instructions,
nsisted also of 40 teams. The subjects were volunteers from
aduate and undergraduate courses in sociology, political
ience, and psychology. Their pay for this work was chiefly
e money they made as a result of the agreement they
ached.

### Analysis of the Data

As was indicated in our early discussion, the rate at which
e negotiator makes concessions is an important strategic
ariable of negotiation. Several ways of measuring this rate
iggest themselves. However, we decided to use one which is
uite simple and yet has the virtue of utilizing maximum data:
e so-called mean demand.

To understand the computation of "mean demand," it
ould be recalled that each team delivered a series of "en-
orsements," each endorsement consisting of one or more pro-
osals (which the team was recommending for agreement).
ince each proposal had a definite payoff for the team making
e endorsement, it is obvious that each endorsement was an
implicit) demand, the value of which was precisely the total
ayoff for the speaker associated with the endorsed proposals.
he "mean demand" is simply the average of all the demands
given team made during the experimental session. It is
erhaps clear that a team with a high mean demand tended to
ake high individual demands—that is, it was making few
oncessions. To simplify our discussion, we shall say that our
ean demand measured the toughness of the team: the higher
he mean demand of a team the tougher it was said to be
and the fewer the concessions it tended to make).

Toughness was the dependent variable of our analysis. Our
bjective was to predict variation in toughness from the negoti-

ator's background: his age, sex, race, and personality. Age
sex, and race as independent variables are self-explanatory, bu
personality deserves a few comments. We used as our measure
the California Personality Inventory (CPI), a well-tested
diagnostic device which enables the administrator to score the
subject with respect to 18 specific personality traits. We com
bined the 18 traits into one single score, the mean of the 18
scores. We felt that this was permissible because the 18 scores
tend to be interrelated, and hence he who scores high on one
tends to score high on all. We termed those who had a high
mean CPI score *"well-adjusted,"* because of the following
statement by the author of the CPI: "If nearly all scores are
above the mean statement score line, the probabilities are that
the person is one who is functioning effectively both socially
and intellectually. Conversely, if most scores are below the
mean, the chances are good that the individual is experiencing
significant difficulties in his interpersonal adjustment" (H. G.
Gough, *California Personality Inventory* [Palo Alto, Cal.:
Consulting Psychologists Press, 1960], p. 15).

### FINDINGS

Frequencies of the various outcomes are shown in Table 2.
Table 3 shows correlations between toughness (as measured
by mean demand) and the background variables of age, sex,
race, and personality. The coefficients in the first column
belong to those subjects who were given no special instructions
about their opponents' toughness (control group); the second
column belongs to those who were given such information
(experimental group). It should be added that each correlation is a weighted average[4] of four distinct correlations: since
each team participated in two experiments, two correlations
were computed for each team; since each experiment consisted
of two teams, each role thus was characterized by four
coefficients of correlation.

Our first and most compelling interest is in noting whether
the information we gave to the subjects affected their behavior
in any way. Somewhat to our surprise, it seemed to make
almost no difference *what* we told the subjects, but the fact of
*telling* did make considerable difference. Note that the teams

## TABLE 2
### Proposals, Payoffs, and Outcome Frequencies

| Out-come | Proposals Included | Payoff to China | Payoff to United States | Number of experiments ending in the outcome $C^a$ | $E^b$ | $T^c$ |
|---|---|---|---|---|---|---|
| 0 | — | 0 | 0 | 0 | 0 | 0 |
| 1 | 1 | 12 | −9 | 0 | 0 | 0 |
| 2 | 2 | −1 | 4 | 0 | 0 | 0 |
| 3 | 3 | −2 | 5 | 0 | 0 | 0 |
| 4 | 4 | −10 | 13 | 0 | 0 | 0 |
| 5 | 5 | 20 | −17 | 0 | 0 | 0 |
| 6 | 1, 2 | 11 | −5 | 0 | 0 | 0 |
| 7 | 1, 3 | 10 | −4 | 0 | 0 | 0 |
| 8 | 1, 4 | 2 | 4 | 0 | 0 | 0 |
| 9 | 1, 5 | 22 | −26 | 0 | 0 | 0 |
| 10 | 2, 3 | −3 | 9 | 0 | 0 | 0 |
| 11 | 2, 4 | −11 | 17 | 0 | 0 | 0 |
| 12 | 2, 5 | 19 | −13 | 0 | 0 | 0 |
| 13 | 3, 4 | −12 | 18 | 0 | 0 | 0 |
| 14 | 3, 5 | 18 | −12 | 0 | 0 | 0 |
| 15 | 4, 5 | 10 | −4 | 0 | 0 | 0 |
| 16 | 1, 2, 3 | 9 | 0 | 0 | 0 | 0 |
| 17 | 1, 3, 4 | 0 | 9 | 0 | 0 | 0 |
| 18 | 1, 4, 5 | 2 | −13 | 0 | 0 | 0 |
| 19 | 1, 2, 4 | 1 | 9 | 2 | 0 | 2 |
| 20 | 1, 2, 5 | 31 | −22 | 0 | 0 | 0 |
| 21 | 1, 3, 5 | 30 | −21 | 0 | 0 | 0 |
| 22 | 2, 3, 4 | −13 | 22 | 0 | 0 | 0 |
| 23 | 2, 3, 5 | 17 | −8 | 0 | 0 | 0 |
| 24 | 2, 4, 5 | 9 | 0 | 0 | 0 | 0 |
| 25 | 3, 4, 5 | 8 | 1 | 5 | 5 | 10 |
| 26 | 1, 2, 3, 4 | −1 | 13 | 0 | 0 | 0 |
| 27 | 1, 2, 4, 5 | 21 | −9 | 0 | 0 | 0 |
| 28 | 1, 3, 4, 5 | 20 | −8 | 0 | 0 | 0 |
| 29 | 2, 3, 4, 5 | 7 | 5 | 15 | 12 | 27 |
| 30 | 1, 2, 3, 5 | 29 | −17 | 0 | 0 | 0 |
| 31 | 1, 2, 3, 4, 5 | 19 | −4 | 0 | 0 | 0 |

[a] Control group (no instructions).
[b] Experimental group (with instructions).
[c] Total (both groups).

who were told that their opponents were tough turned out to be just as tough themselves as those who were told that their opponents were soft: the correlation $r = -.05$ is not statistically significant at the .05 level. However, for those who were given information about their opponents (no matter what it was) the role of background was the reverse of that for subjects who were given no such information. Note that, in the control group, women, Caucasians, and those with well-adjusted personalities tended to be *soft* ($r = -.10, -.33,$

TABLE 3
*Zero-Order Correlation Between Background and Toughness*

| Background variables | Toughness (mean demand) in: | |
| --- | --- | --- |
| | Control group (without information) | Experimental group (with information) |
| Own age | −.12 | −.11 |
| Own sex (being female) | −.10 | .06 |
| Own race (being Caucasian) | −.33* | .22* |
| Own personality (being well-adjusted) | −.25* | .18 |
| Own information (opponent said to be tough) | − | −.05* |
| Own previous toughness | .46* | .52* |
| Opponent's age | −.02 | −.17 |
| Opponent's sex (female) | .16 | .36* |
| Opponent's race (Caucasian) | .15 | −.18 |
| Opponent's personality (well-adjusted) | .09 | −.25 |
| Opponent's information (team said to be tough) | − | .27* |
| Opponent's previous toughness | −.03 | .10 |
| Opponent's "current" toughness | −.29* | −.15 |
| Number of cases | 80 | 80 |

*Significant beyond the .05 level.

25). In the experimental group, however, subjects with these ne background characteristics (women, Caucasians, and ll-adjusted individuals) tended to be *tough* ($r = .06, .22,$ 3). These differences are significant well beyond the .05 el, and thus there is little doubt that they exist.

It appears that the three background variables (sex, race, d personality) act as an integrated system which is of con- lerable importance in determining toughness. This impres- n is further supported when we note how our subjects acted when these three variables were defined as describing *ponent's* background. With one exception (sex in the ex- rimental group), the three variables again are related in a nilar fashion to toughness. In the control group, subjects ided to become *tough* when the opponent was a woman, Caucasian, or well-adjusted ($r = .16, .15, .09$). In the experi- ental group, however, the same traits tended to make the bjects *soft:* they were softer against a Caucasian than against non-Caucasian ($r = -.18$), and softer against a well- ljusted than against a poorly-adjusted opponent ($r = -.25$).

Given the similar effect the three background variables seem produce, it becomes of considerable interest to untangle this stem and isolate the influence of each of the three variables. nis can be accomplished by computing partial coefficients of rrelation instead of the zero-order correlations shown in ible 3. We computed such partial correlations by using a sys- m of ten independent variables[5] shown in Table 4. Each efficient shown in that table is partial in the sense that it rep- sents relationship between a given pair of variables oughness and one of the ten variables) when the remaining ne variables are controlled for. Thus each correlation in ible 4 shows the impact (upon toughness) for each variable l by itself.

It is interesting to note—although not of primary impor- nce to our discussion—that sex has a different impact upon ughness when considered alone than when other influences e permitted to interfere. Table 4 shows that "womanhood" ads to toughness under control conditions ($r = .40$), to ftness under experimental conditions ($r = -.28$); Table 3, 1 the other hand, shows that women tended to be soft under ormal conditions ($r = -.10$) and tough under experimental

## TABLE 4
*Partial Correlations Between Background and Toughness*

| Background variables | Toughness (mean demand) in: | |
| --- | --- | --- |
| | Control group (without information) | Experimental group (with information) |
| Own sex (being female) | .40* | −.28* |
| Own race (being Caucasian) | −.09 | .28* |
| Own personality (being well-adjusted) | −.32* | .37* |
| Own information (opponent said to be tough) | — | .31* |
| Own previous toughness | .34* | .30* |
| Opponent's sex (female) | .46* | .59* |
| Opponent's race (Caucasian) | .14 | −.34* |
| Opponent's personality (well-adjusted) | −.27* | −.49* |
| Opponent's information (team said to be tough) | — | −.13 |
| Opponent's "current" toughness | −.49* | .22 |
| Number of cases | 80 | 80 |

*Significant beyond the .05 level.

conditions ($r = .06$). Thus we conclude that to maintain that women are softer than men under normal (control) conditions is correct but misleading: women are softer not because they are women but because they are other things as well; when "womanhood" is considered by itself, we find that it leads to toughness under normal (control) conditions.

Of primary interest to us, however, is the observation that the reversal effect, noted in Table 3, holds in Table 4 as well: *introducing information about the opponent reverses the relationship between background and toughness.* We see in Table 4 that lacking such information a man, a Caucasian, or a well-

djusted subject tends to be soft; with such information he
ends to be tough.

Let us pursue further the impact of introducing information
bout an opponent's toughness. We see that providing such in-
ormation caused a difference in two additional aspects: it
hanged the manner in which our subjects reacted to their op-
onent's real behavior, and also the way in which they reacted
o their opponent's racial background. To see the first change,
bserve that normally (under control conditions) our sub-
ects followed the strategy we identified earlier as optimal: the
ougher their opponent, the softer they were themselves ( $r =$
-.29 in Table 3, $r = -.49$ in Table 4). When the subjects are
nformed about their opponents, however, the influence of the
pponent's actual behavior decreases ( $r = -.15$ in Table 3),
erhaps is even reversed ( $r = .22$ in Table 4). To see the
hanges involving race, note that when they lacked informa-
ion our subjects tended to be tough against Caucasians ( $r =$
-.15 in Table 3, $r = -.14$ in Table 4); with information they
ended to be tough against non-Caucasians ( $r = -.18$ in
Table 3, $r = -.34$ in Table 4).

But we must not emphasize only the changes resulting from
ntroducing additional information; some relationships were
*not* altered. For example, our subjects tended to be tough
against women and against poorly adjusted opponents under
both conditions, and toughness tended to be a stable trait: the
eams which were tough in their first session tended to be
ough in the second as well ( $r = .46, .52$ in Table 3, $r = .34,$
30 in Table 4). Thus we see that certain aspects of the negotiation process were not altered by introduction of new informa-
ion.

Finally, we observe that while the data in Table 3 suggest
hat the nature of the information given out had almost no
effect, Table 4 suggests that it did exert some effect after all.
When the impact of this information is isolated from all other
influences, we obtain a positive (and significant) correlation
$r = .31$, suggesting that if we inform a team that their opponents are tough negotiators, they tend to become tough also;
if we tell them their opponents are soft, they too become soft.
However, we cannot put too much faith into this finding, since
the coefficient $r = .31$ is an average of four greatly different

coefficients, two of which are negative. It seems safer to conclude that our subjects did not quite know how to handle information concerning their opponents.

## CONCLUSIONS

The main objective of this chapter is to demonstrate that negotiating behavior, under some circumstances, is quite unstable; that it is very easy to alter the relationship between a negotiator's background and his performance. For this reason we performed experiments in which some negotiators were told that their opponents were tough, others that they were soft, and still others were given no information at all. What do our findings show?

### Interpretation of Findings

We were right in arguing that the relationship between background and performance is—with inexperienced negotiators at least—quite unstable: the introduction of information completely *reversed* the relationship between a negotiator's sex, race, and personality and his toughness. For those who are weary of *ex post facto* explanations, let it be said that the arguments given in the early parts of the chapter were formulated long before we knew the results of the experiments. In fact, we designed the experiments to test the implications of these arguments.

Yet our findings are not exactly as we expected them to be. Not only did we expect that information about the opponent's toughness would alter the relationship between the negotiators' backgrounds and their toughness, but we had expectations also about the *kind* of change this would produce. We believed that we would find a negative relationship between information and toughness: that a team which was told that its opponents were tough would become soft; a team informed that its opponents were soft would become tough. This we believed because, as shown earlier, such a strategy is optimal under the conditions we created in our experiments.

But of course, we were wrong. No clear-cut relationship of this kind appeared; there were even intimations that the relaonship might in fact be just the reverse. How can we account or these findings?

Unfortunately we cannot offer a completely satisfactory explanation. In a way, we have succeeded in making our point nly too well: behavior in negotiation is so unpredictable that ve cannot even offer a very satisfactory explanation of why ertain relationships exist. However, we can guess what may lave been happening.

In the first place, we tend to think that our subjects did not eact to our instructions in the way we thought they would, imply because they did not believe what we told them. College students become so suspicious of the various tricks used by experimenters that they take all instructions with a grain of salt. For this reason, we believe, the subjects were simply confused and showed a great variation in response.

The second point has to do with the reversal effect: we have o explain why being Caucasian, well-adjusted, and male led to oftness under normal (control) conditions and to toughness under experimental conditions. Our explanation takes as its point of departure the argument we made earlier in this chapter, namely that differences in negotiating behavior tend to be associated with *cultural* differences. And we ask whether the CPI, our personality measure, in ascertaining the adjustment of our subjects, is not ascertaining adjustment to our American culture. We believe that this is what the CPI measures in part, since a high scorer is said to function "effectively both socially and intellectually." Social effectiveness (as the term is used here), we believe, is a typical American value, and amounts to the requirement that one be cooperative. Thus it is hardly surprising to find that those who "function effectively socially" are just that—cooperative in real life as well as under our control conditions. For the same reason, we find that Caucasians also are cooperative (soft) under normal conditions, because in all probability they subscribe to the value of cooperativeness more readily than do students of Oriental background.

But why do the well-adjusted and the Caucasians become tough under experimental conditions? Our explanation is quite tentative, but perhaps the reader will find it plausible. We suggest that our instructions to participants in effect destroyed the moral superiority of cooperativeness, creating a *morally neutral climate,* and that in this new climate new guide-lines were needed.

Our intention when reading the instructions to the experimental group was to tell them what behavior to expect of their opponents. It seems to us now, however, that what we really did was to give the subjects the idea that it is all right to be tough! This we did, we believe, by equating the three modes of negotiation (tough, normal, and cooperative), thereby treating them as morally equivalent. We conjecture that this hint was enough to destroy the slight moral superiority of cooperativeness and to create an atmosphere in which morality no longer served as a guide.

Given this lack of moral guidance in the experimental group, the subjects had to search for new values against which to plan their behavior. And we supplied such a value: again and again we urged them to try to make as much money as possible. Thus it seems reasonable to assume that the main difference between the control group and the experimental group was that in the control group the ascendant values were cultural, while in the experimental group they were utilitarian (maximizing own payoff).

Two more points must be made before our explanation is complete. First, toughness is more likely to maximize payoff than is softness[7] and, second, those subjects scoring high on the CPI were effective not only socially but also intellectually ("intelligent"). Being "intelligent," the high scorers were likely to discover that toughness was a good strategy and to put this strategy into effect. Thus we find that, under experimental conditions, the well-adjusted tended to be tough.

However, this explanation is satisfactory to us only when we consider personality as a factor. When we start considering race and sex, we are on much less firm ground: why are Caucasians tougher under experimental conditions? And why does "womanhood" lead to toughness under normal conditions, softness in experimental situations? Is it not true that women are supposed to be soft and submissive (under normal circumstances), not tough?

Our very tentative answer is that this is not altogether true. We can argue that cooperativeness is an attitude for which a man has considerable need in the business world, but one for

hich a woman has little need in her role as a mother. Fur-
hermore, there is evidence that American women are in fact
ess cooperative than men: Rapoport and Chammah (1965)
emonstrated this in their experiments with the Prisoner's
Dilemma.

In the second place, we can argue that American culture—
erhaps like that of any highly industrialized nation—has a
eculiar duality about it. As Williams has emphasized, Amer-
cans are expected to be both cooperative and competitive.
Perhaps our Caucasian subjects looked upon the normal (con-
rol) negotiations as situations calling for cooperation. When
his interpretation of the situation was altered by our instruc-
ions (under experimental conditions), the other side of
American culture appeared with a vengeance, and the latent
competitiveness of the Caucasian was revealed.

## Some Implications

Inevitably, we shall have to answer questions about the general implications of our results. What do they suggest for fu-
ure research? What implications do they have for the practi-
ioner of the art of negotiation? The key to whatever relevance
our discussion may have is the argument that a negotiator's
*beliefs* play a crucial role in negotiation. The implications for
both the theory and the practice of negotiation stem from that
argument.

The notion that the beliefs of a negotiator are of considerable importance is hardly new. But what may not always
have been clearly understood is the dependence of these beliefs
upon group support: only when a negotiator inherits his beliefs
from the culture of his society can we expect these beliefs to
manifest stability which, in turn, renders his behavior predictable. If his beliefs lack such cultural support, then they may be
extremely unstable and render his behavior highly unpredictable.

It is unfortunate that the very nature of our analysis
prevents us from being able to offer any advice to professional
negotiators and diplomats. If our analysis is correct, these professionals follow their own codes of behavior and nothing we
could offer or suggest would change them. But what we can do

—or at least attempt to do—is subject these very codes to careful scrutiny, suggesting modifications if necessary. And it follows from our argument that nothing less than the creation of a new subculture may suffice if we are to attain the goal of alleviating some of the dangerous conflicts which beset the modern world.

Nor can we say what this new code should be, except that somehow it should have the support of both logical and empirical research. We certainly cannot hope to be very successful in introducing a new code into a profession unless we can show that in some very real sense it is better than the old one. Such a proof, in order to be universally appealing, will have to rest upon concepts such as rationality used by the theory of games. However, we have also argued that it is not possible to define optimal strategies of negotiation using the traditional meaning of rationality. Hence it may ultimately be necessary to develop a new meaning of rationality, one which somehow is supported by empirical research.

Thus, ultimately, the most tangible implication of our discussion is somewhat negative: there are good ways of studying conflict, and there are bad ways. Specifically, it does not seem profitable to conduct simple experiments with subjects who are not professional negotiators and generalize from their behavior to that of professionals, if the most important ingredient, the code, is missing from the experiments. What can be legitimately studied in such experiments is the process of professionalization, the development of norms and beliefs about negotiation itself. Do subjects from different cultural backgrounds converge toward the same normative system? Can the development of different systems be fostered? Perhaps it is precisely this kind of experimentation which will ultimately lead to the new concept of rationality that seems to be needed.

## NOTES

1. The author wishes to express his thanks to Wilberta Woodson and Dennis McLaughlin for their help in performing the experiments and analyzing the data. The research was conducted under Air Force Office of Scientific Research grant AFOSR–62–314 and

ith the assistance of the Social Science Research Institute, Univer-
y of Hawaii. This article is a modified version of a paper of the
me title produced by the Social Science Research Institute as
'orking Paper No. 3, 1966.

By "traditional" criteria of rationality we mean the requirement
at the player should always act so as to maximize his (expected)
ayoff. Although there are those who object to even this
quirement, it nevertheless enjoys much greater acceptance than
e requirements we would have to impose upon "rationality" if we
ere to solve the above game.

After each team had delivered three speeches, negotiation was
ljourned to allow the teams to chart future strategy.

Each coefficient of correlation was transformed into a z-score,
eighted by the number of cases involved, and then converted back
ito a correlation coefficient.

Age and opponent's previous toughness were omitted from Table
since Table 3 shows that either variable is related to toughness in
significant manner.

Above all, women tend to score higher on CPI (be "better
ljusted") than men. It seems to be this adjustment of women
hich accounts for their tendency to be soft negotiators. Once this
ictor is removed, however, the "true" nature of womanhood ap-
ears in Table 4—it appears as a variable leading to toughness
ither than softness.

The correlation between being tough and receiving high payoff
as $r = .68$ for the control group, $r = .13$ for the experimental
roup.

# 2. WHO "WINS" IN WAGE BARGAINING?*

*Daniel S. Hamermesh, Princeton University*

"It is regrettable that a strike had to be called . . . against the General Motors Corporation. The company held out no other choice. . . . The offers [by GM] were made to seem expensive because of the sheer size of this most mammoth of industrial corporations; actually, the corporation's contract proposals were far short of providing equity for each General Motors worker."

> Leonard Woodcock,
> in *News from UAW*,
> September 14, 1970.

"The UAW always starts with fantastic demands. They usually are deliberately vague about some of the important demands. . . . The strangest and most unfortunate thing about the negotiations is the absence of any collective bargaining by the union of economic issues."

> Earl Bramblett (GM),
> in Bureau of National Affairs,
> *Daily Labor Report*,
> September 15, 1970.

* Reprinted with permission from *Industrial and Labor Relations Review* XXVI (July 1973), No. 4, pp. 1, 146–49. Copyright © by Cornell University. All rights reserved.

Bargaining theory contains very few interesting propositions that can be tested empirically. Hicks's model (1932, pp. 140–58) suggests that the final outcome of the collective bargaining process will lie somewhere between the maximum the employer will offer to avoid a strike and the minimum the union will accept without a strike. While its analysis of union and management resistance is useful, the indeterminacy of the wage settlement makes the model useless for predictive purposes.

Cross (1969) links uncertainty concerning the opponent's rate of concession to the bargainer's own rate of concession and thus explicitly introduces into the theory the possibility that mistaken expectations on either side can produce a strike or lockout. He also implies that one bargainer's offers should be most responsive to his opponent's demands at that point in time when he realizes the seriousness of his opponent's intentions. In labor negotiations, this point in time is likely to be the period directly preceding the expiration of the old contract, so we should expect a flurry of bargaining at this time. This implication is verified by observing most collective negotiations, but beyond this it holds little interest for empirical research.

Only the models of Zeuthen (1930) and Nash (1950) contain an interesting and potentially verifiable empirical hypothesis. Both imply that the union and management will settle at that point which maximizes the product of the increments to their utilities. If both sides in the negotiations have identical utility functions and there is no bluffing, the outcome of bargaining will be to "split the difference" between the extreme points of the core. If we construct data representing the initial union demand, the initial employer offer, and the final settlement and make some assumptions about the net amount of bluffing and the shape of the utility functions, we should be able to provide some evidence concerning whether the parties do "split the difference." The result of this test should be of interest even apart from its implications for bargaining theory, for it provides the first direct evidence on the relation of wage settlements to demands and offers.[1]

An alternative way of considering our test of the Nash result is to view it instead as a measure of the relative amount of bluffing by unions and management. If we accept the validity of the "split the difference" model, any deviation of the final settlement from the Nash point can be seen as a measure of differential bluffing. This interpretation is in a sense the complement of the other; either one assumes the absence of asymmetries in bluffing and tests the "split the difference" model, or one assumes the validity of that model and tests for differential bluffing. A simultaneous test of the Nash hypothesis and bluffing asymmetries cannot be conducted with data that reflect only offers and demands.

One difficulty with the Nash model is that its results are defined in the utility space, while the only data available measure compensation in money terms. In order to test the model, one must assume that both sides have identical utility functions whose sole content is compensation per employee and which are linear over the range of compensation discussed during bargaining. (These amount to the assumptions of the simplest model of Zeuthen.) We cannot, therefore, distinguish between a failure to verify the implications of the complete model due to its inapplicability to collective bargaining and a failure due to the inappropriateness of the assumption that each side has this unusual utility function. Whatever our results, they must be qualified by possibilities such as the employment effect of the wage increase entering the union leaders' utility function.

## THE DATA

The data cover forty-three negotiations concluded between September 1968 and December 1970.[2] Of these, twenty-five were teacher negotiations, nine involved firefighters or policemen, and nine covered miscellaneous occupations. Data were constructed on the previous wage paid, the union's initial demand, the employer's initial offer, and the final settlement. Our data cover only wages; no attempt was made to reduce other forms of compensation and work rules to their monetary equivalents because of the difficulty of finding methods of calculation on which both sides agree (Hamermesh 1970).

By necessity our data cover only negotiations in the public sector, for only there is the employer's offer a matter of public record. In the private sector, it is impossible, in all but a few cases, to find data on the employer's response to the union's initial demand. In any event, the public sector data are more easily analyzed, for there are few long-term contracts in this sector and thus it is not necessary to devise methods of compressing a number of deferred and cost-of-living increases into one figure representing the wage package. Furthermore, the demand for labor is likely to be relatively inelastic in this sector. Our failure to include the employment effect in the union leaders' utility function should bias our results less than it would in a test based on private sector data.

The raw data are used to compute $\dot{W}_D$, the percentage wage increase initially demanded; $\dot{W}_E$, the increase initially offered by the employer; and $\dot{W}_S$, the increase finally settled upon. All of these figures are calculated at an annual rate of increase, so that, for example, if a particular contract is to last two years, the percentage increase is divided by two. The following are the means and the standard errors of the means of the designated variables: $\dot{W}_D$ ($\bar{x} = 22.85$, $\sigma_{\bar{x}} = 2.10$); $\dot{W}_E$ ($\bar{x} = 8.28$, $\sigma_{\bar{x}} = .77$); $\dot{W}_S$ ($\bar{x} = 11.95$, $\sigma_{\bar{x}} = .94$).

## TESTING THE MODEL

To test the "split the difference" model, we employ the null hypothesis:
$$Z = [\dot{W}_D - \dot{W}_S] - [\dot{W}_S - \dot{W}_E] = 0.$$
The mean of $Z$ is 7.23, indicating that, on the average, the final settlement lies much closer to the employer's initial offer than to the union's initial demand. The $t$-value of the test of the null hypothesis is 3.83, so that we can reject the hypothesis that $Z$ equals zero.[3] Our result thus implies either that (1) the two parties' utility functions are not identical and linear with respect to wage increases; or (2) the amount of bluffing by the union is greater than by the employer; or (3) the "split the difference" theory of bargaining is inapplicable.

The first of these possibilities cannot be rejected, but there is no reason to assume (as one must, to rationalize our results) that the public employer's utility decreases more in response to a given percentage wage increase than the union leader's utility is increased by the same wage increase. For the reasons

described previously, it is always difficult to distinguish be
tween the second and third possibilities; this difficulty i
especially severe in analyzing negotiations in the public sector
where the pressure of public opinion may force employers to
offer an acceptable increase at the beginning of negotiations
There may thus be very little room for bluffing by state and
local governments. Public employee unions, on the other hand
have an incentive to engage in bluffing in negotiating their first
few contracts. After several rounds of negotiations, their relative bargaining power may force them to lower their demands
as their threats become less credible. Since negotiations between public employers and unions have begun only quite
recently, however, the unions may still be bluffing more than
employers.[4] The third possibility is simply that the difference is
not split equally.

On one level, our results show that public employee unions
only receive approximately one fourth of the difference between their wage demands and the amounts public employers
offer them. In this superficial sense, public management might
be said to "win" in collective negotiations. On a deeper level,
however, this conclusion cannot be supported, since we do not
know the minimum increase for which union leaders are
willing to settle, and since we expect more bluffing by unions
than by employers in the public employment sector.

This study demonstrates the severe problems involved in
using existing bargaining theory to derive and test propositions
about behavior in nonexperimental situations. Any empirical
test is likely to be confounded both by the existence of asymmetries in bluffing and by the possibility that the utility functions of the parties differ in makeup and are not linear with
respect to observable monetary quantities. One must conclude
that the likelihood that current theory can help us to reach
concrete conclusions based on tests using data on the collective
bargaining process is small indeed.

## NOTES

1. De Menil 1971 attempts an indirect test of the Nash hypothesis
using a model relating wage inflation to productivity per worker.
2. These data were all culled from issues of Bureau of National

Affairs, *Government Employee Relations Report* (Washington: B.N.A., various years) and were the only ones available for this period which had all the required information. Great care was taken to ensure that the initial demands and offers used were actually the first made by each side, but there is the possibility that the basic material failed to report the earliest publicized demand (offer) in some cases. An appendix listing these data is available on request from the author.

3. The variable $Z$ was regressed against dummies for occupation, for the type of public employee relations law, and for the occurrence of a strike. None of these could explain any significant degree of variation in $Z$.

4. The fact that differential bluffing is sufficient in our sample to place one side beyond its threat point is demonstrated by the high proportion of cases (thirty-two out of forty-three) in which some work stoppage occurred after the initial demand and offer were made.

# VII. BIBLIOGRAPHY

\* indicates theoretical, methodological, or experimental works.

Abel, Elie. 1963. *The Missile Crisis*. New York: Bantam.

Aggarwala, N.; Fenno, N. J.; and Fitzgerald, G. F. 1971. *Air Hijacking*, International Conciliation. No. 585, Carnegie Endowment.

Aharoni, Yair. 1966. *The Foreign Investment Decision Process*. Cambridge, Mass.: Harvard Business School.

Alger, Chadwick F. 1972. "Negotiation, regional groups, interaction and public debate in the development of consensus in the UN General Assembly," *The Analysis of International Politics*, ed. James Rosenau and Maurice East. New York: The Free Press.

Allard, Sven. 1970. *Russia and the Austrian State Treaty*. University Park, Pa.: Pennsylvania State University Press.

Allison, Graham T. 1969. "Conceptual Models and the Cuban Missile Crisis," *American Political Science Review* LXIII, No. 3, pp. 69–718.

———. 1971. *Essence of Decision*. Boston: Little, Brown.

\*Atherton, Wallace. 1973. *Theory of Union Bargaining Goals*. Princeton, N.J.: Princeton University Press.

\*Axelrod, Robert. 1970. *Conflict of Interest*. Chicago: Markham.

\*Bacon, Francis. 1597. *On Negotiation*.

Bagdikian, B. H. 1963. "Press Independence and the Cuban Crisis," *Columbia Journalism Review* I, No. 4, pp. 5–11.

Baldwin, David A. 1965. "The International Bank in Political Perspective," World Politics XVIII, No. 1, pp. 68–81.

*——. 1971a. "Thinking About Threats," Journal of Conflict Resolution XV, No. 1, pp. 71–78.

*——. 1971b. "The Costs of Power," Journal of Conflict Resolution XV, No. 2, pp. 145–55.

*——. 1971c. "The Power of Positive Sanctions," World Politics XXIV, No. 1, pp. 19–38.

*——. 1971d. "Inter-nation Influence Revisited," Journal of Conflict Resolution XV, No. 4, pp. 471–86.

*Bartos, Otomar J. 1974. Process and Outcome of Negotiations. New York: Columbia University Press.

*Bass, B. 1966. "Effects on the Subsequent Performance of Negotiators of Studying Issues or Planning Strategies Alone or in Groups," Psychological Monographs LXXX, No. 6.

Bechhoefer, Bernard F. 1959. "Negotiating the Statute of the International Atomic Energy Agency," International Organization XIII, No. 1, pp. 38–59.

——. 1961. Postwar Negotiations for Arms Control. Washington, D.C.: The Brookings Institution.

Behrman, Jack N. 1971. U. S. International Business and Governments. New York: McGraw-Hill.

——; Boddewyn, Jean; and Kapoor, Ashok. 1974. Governmental Relations of U. S. International Companies. Washington, D.C.: U. S. Department of State.

Bell, Coral. 1962. Negotiating from Strength. London: Chalto & Windus.

*Bell, Roderick; Edwards, David; and Wagner, R. H. (eds.). 1969. Political Power. New York: The Free Press.

*Berelson, Bernard and Steiner, Gary A. 1964. Human Behavior. New York: Harcourt, Brace & World.

*Blake, R. and Mouton, J. 1961. "Comprehension of Own and of Outgroup Positions Under Inter-Group Competition," Journal of Conflict Resolution V, No. 3, pp. 304–10.

*Blake, Walter et al. 1972. "Application of Judgment Theory and Interactive Computer Technology to Labor-Management Negotiations," Industrial Relations Research Proceedings, pp. 195–201.

Blalock, Hubert M., Jr. 1967. Toward a Theory of Minority-Group Relations. New York: John Wiley.

Blood, Robert O., Jr. 1960. "Resolving Family Conflicts," Journal of Conflict Resolution IV, No. 2, pp. 209–19.

*Boulding, Kenneth. 1956. The Image. Ann Arbor: University of Michigan Press.

*——. 1959. "National Images and International Systems," *Journal of Conflict Resolution* III, No. 1, pp. 120–31.

*——. 1962. *Conflict and Defense*. New York: Harper & Row.

*Braithwaite, R. B. 1955. *Theory of Games as a Tool for the Moral Philosopher*. New York: Cambridge University Press.

Brecher, Michael. 1973. "Images, Process and Feedback in Foreign Policy: Israel's Decision on German Reparations," *American Political Science Review* LXVII, No. 1, pp. 73–102.

Browne, Joy. 1973. *The Used Car Game: A Sociology of the Bargain*. Lexington, Mass.: Heath.

Buertis, David et al. 1971. *Multinational Corporation—Nation State Interaction: An Annotated Bibliography*. Philadelphia: Foreign Policy Research Institute.

Burgoon, Beatrice M. et al. 1970. "Effects of the Structure of Collective Bargaining in Selected Industries," *Industrial Relations Research Proceedings*, pp. 491–517.

Burns, E. L. M. 1969. "The Nonproliferation Treaty: Its Negotiation and Prospects," *International Organization* XXIII, No. 4, pp. 788–807.

Camps, Miriam. 1959. *The Free Trade Area Negotiations*. London: Political and Economic Planning, Occasional Paper 2.

——. 1964. *Britain and the European Community 1955–63*. Princeton: Princeton University Press.

Chamberlain, Neil W. 1951. *Collective Bargaining*. New York: McGraw-Hill.

Chayes, Abraham; Ehrlich, Thomas; and Lowenfeld, Andreas (eds.). 1969. *International Legal Process*. Boston: Little, Brown.

*Cheng, Pao Lun. 1968. "Wage Negotiation and Bargaining Power," *Industrial and Labor Relations Review* XXI, No. 2, pp. 163–81.

*Coddington, Alan. 1966. "A Theory of the Bargaining Process: Comment," *American Economic Review* LVI, pp. 522–33.

*——. 1968. *Theories of the Bargaining Process*. Chicago: Aldine.

*——. 1972. "On the Theory of Bargaining," *Expectations and Uncertainty in Economics*, eds. D. F. Carter and J. Ford. Oxford: Basil Blackwell.

*——. 1973. "Bargaining as a Decision Process," *Swedish Journal of Economics* LXXV, pp. 397–405.

Coombs, D. 1970. *Politics and Bureaucracy in the European Community*. London: Political and Economic Planning.

Coplin, William D. 1969. *The Functions of International Law*. Chicago: University of Chicago Press, esp. Chap. III.

*Coser, Lewis. 1967. *Continuities in the Study of Social Conflict.* New York: The Free Press.

*Cowen, E. 1952. "The Influence of Varying Degrees of Psychological Stress on Problem-Solving Rigidity," *Journal of Abnormal and Social Psychology* XXXXVII, No. 2 supplement, pp. 512–20.

*Cross, John G. 1969. *The Economics of Bargaining.* New York: Basic Books.

*Curry, R. L., Jr. and Wade, L. L. 1968. *A Theory of Political Exchange.* Englewood Cliffs, N.J.: Prentice-Hall.

Curry, R. L., Jr. and Rothchild, Donald. 1974. "On Economic Bargaining Between African Governments and Multinational Companies," *Journal of Modern African Studies* XII, No. 2, pp. 173–89.

Curtis, Gerald L. and Okita, Saburo. 1971. "The Textile Negotiations," *Columbia Journal of World Business* VI, No. 1, pp. 72–78.

*Cyert, M. and March, James G. 1963. *A Behavioral Theory of the Firm.* Englewood Cliffs, N.J.: Prentice-Hall.

*Dahl, Robert. 1955. "Hierarchy, Democracy and Bargaining in Politics and Economics," *Research Frontiers in Politics and Government.* Washington: Brookings Institution.

*——— and Lindblom, Charles. 1963. *Politics, Economics and Welfare.* New York: Harper & Row.

Davis, David H. 1972. *How the Bureaucracy Makes Foreign Policy.* Lexington, Mass.: Heath.

Davison, W. Phillips. 1958. *The Berlin Blockade.* Princeton: Princeton University Press.

Dean, Arthur. 1966. *Test Ban and Disarmament.* New York: Harper & Row.

*De Callières, François. 1963 (1716). *On the Manner of Negotiating with Princes,* trans. A. F. Whyte. Notre Dame, Ind.: Notre Dame University Press.

*De Mably, Abbe. 1767. *Des principes de negociation.* La Haye.

*De Menil, George. 1971. *Bargaining: Monopoly Power vs. Union Power.* Cambridge, Mass.: The MIT Press.

Deney, Nicole. 1962. "Les États-Unis et le Barrage d'Assouan," *Revue Française de Science Politique* XII, No. 2, pp. 361–98.

Dennett, R. and Johnson, Joseph (eds.). 1951. *Negotiating with the Russians.* New York: World Peace Foundation.

De Rivera, Joseph. 1968. *The Psychological Dimension of Foreign Policy.* Columbus, O.: Charles E. Merrill.

*Deutsch, Morton. 1974. *Resolution of Conflict.* New Haven, Conn.: Yale University Press.

*Deutsch, Karl W. 1963. *Nerves of Government.* New York: The Free Press.

*——. 1968. *The Analysis of International Relations.* Englewood Cliffs, N.J.: Prentice-Hall.

Diesing, Paul. 1965. "Bargaining Strategy and Union-Management Relationships," *Human Behavior and International Politics,* ed. J. David Singer. Chicago: Rand McNally.

Dommen, Arthur. 1964. *Conflict in Laos.* New York: Praeger.

D'Ossat, Cardinal Arnaud. 1698. *Lettres.* Paris: Boudot.

Douglas, Ann. 1957. "The Peaceful Settlement of Industrial and Intergroup Disputes," *Journal of Conflict Resolution* I, No. 1, pp. 69–81.

——. 1962. *Industrial Peacemaking.* New York: Columbia University Press.

*Druckman, Daniel. 1973. *Human Factors in International Negotiations.* Beverly Hills, Calif.: Sage Publications.

Duperron, Cardinal. 1633. *Les Ambassades et negociations.* Paris: Martin Collet.


*Edgeworth, Frances Y. 1881. *Mathematical Physics.* London: Kegan, Paul, repr. Kelly (1967).

*Edmead, Frank. 1971. *Analysis and Prediction in International Mediation.* New York: UNITAR Study PS-2.

Ellsberg, Daniel. 1972. *Papers on the War.* New York: Simon and Schuster.

*Evan, William M. 1962. "Role Strain and the Norm of Reciprocity in Research Organizations," *American Journal of Sociology* LXVIII, No. 3, pp. 346–54.


Fall, Bernard. 1969. *Anatomy of a Crisis.* Garden City, N.Y.: Doubleday.

Fayerweather, John. 1966. "Nineteenth-century Ideology and Twentieth-century Reality," *Columbia Journal of World Business* I, No. 1, pp. 77–84.

——. 1969. *International Business Management.* New York: McGraw-Hill.

—— (ed.). 1973a. *International Business-Government Affairs.* Cambridge, Mass.: Ballinger.

——. 1973b. *The Mercantile Bank Affair.* White Plains, N.Y.: International Arts and Sciences Press.

*Festinger, Leon. 1957. *A Theory of Cognitive Dissonance.* New York: Row Peterson.

Fisher, Roger. 1969. *International Conflict for Beginners*. New York: Harper & Row.

———. 1973. *Dear Israelis, Dear Arabs*. New York: Harper & Row.

*Foldes, Lucien. 1964. "A Determinate Model of Bilaterate Monopoly," *Econometrica* XXXI, No. 2, pp. 117–31.

Ford, Alan. 1954. *The Anglo-American Oil Dispute of 1951–52*. Berkeley, Calif.: University of California Press.

*Forehand, G. and Gilmer, B. 1969. "Environmental Variation in Studies of Organizational Behavior," *Readings in Organizational Behavior and Human Performance*, eds. L. Cummings and W. Scott. Homewood, Ill.: Irwin-Dorsey.

Forward, Nigel. 1971. *The Field of Nations*. Boston: Little, Brown.

Friedheim, Robert L. 1965. "The 'Satisfied' and 'Dissatisfied' States Negotiate International Law," *World Politics* XVIII, No. 1, pp. 20–41.

Frye, W. R. 1961. *Disarmament*. New York: Foreign Policy Institute.

Gabriel, Peter. 1972. "MNCs in the Third World," *Harvard Business Review* L, No. 4, pp. 93–102.

George, Alexander; Hall, David K.; and Simons, William E. 1971. *The Limits of Coercive Diplomacy*. Boston: Little, Brown.

Gross, Leo. 1962. "Some Observations on the International Court of Justice," *American Journal of International Law* LVI, No. 1, pp. 33–63, esp. pp. 40–42.

Halperin, Morton. 1974. *Bureaucratic Politics and Foreign Policy*. Washington: The Brookings Institution.

*Hamermesh, Daniel. 1970. "Wage Bargains, Threshold Effects and the Phillips Curve," *Quarterly Journal of Economics* LXXXIV, No. 3, p. 507.

Handelman, John R.; Shapiro, Howard B.; and Vasquez, John A. 1973. *Introductory Case Studies for International Relations: Vietnam, Middle East, Environmental Crisis*. Chicago: Markham.

Hanner, F. T. 1965. "Business Investment Negotiations in Developing Countries," *Business Horizons* VIII, No. 4, pp. 97–103.

*Harsanyi, J. C. 1956. "Approaches to the Bargaining Problem Before and After the Theory of Games," *Econometrica* XXIV, No. 1, pp. 144–57.

*———. 1962. "Bargaining in Ignorance of the Opponent's Utility Function," *Journal of Conflict Resolution* VI, No. 1, pp. 29–38.

Haskel, Barbara G. 1974. "Disparities, Strategies and Opportunity Costs: The Example of Scandinavian Economic Market Negotiations, *International Studies Quarterly* XVIII, No. 1, pp. 3–30.

Henig, S. 1971. *The External Relations of the European Community.* London: Political and Economic Planning.

*Hicks, John. 1932. *The Theory of Wages.* New York: Macmillan.

Hilsman, Roger. 1967. *To Move a Nation.* Garden City, N.Y.: Doubleday.

*Holsti, K. J. 1963. "The Use of Objective Criteria for the Measurement of International Tension," *Background* VII, No. 2, pp. 77–96.

*Holsti, Ole R. 1964. "An Adaptation of the 'General Inquirer' for the Systematic Analysis of Political Documents," *Behavioral Science* IX, No. 4, pp. 382–87.

*Holsti, Ole R. 1969. "The Belief System and National Images," *International Politics and Foreign Policy,* ed. James Rosenau. New York: The Free Press.

Holsti, Ole. 1972. *Crisis, Escalation and War.* Montreal: McGill-Queen's University Press.

*——; Brody, Richard A.; and North, Robert C. 1964. *Theory and Measurement in Interstate Behavior.* Stanford, Calif.: Stanford University (mimeo).

——; Brody, Richard A.; and North, Robert C. 1968. "Perceptions and Action in the 1914 Crisis," *Quantitative International Politics,* ed. J. David Singer. New York: Holt, Rinehart & Winston.

*—— and North, Robert. 1965. "History as a 'Laboratory' of Conflict," *Social Science and Human Conflict,* ed. Elton B. McNiel. Englewood Cliffs, N.J.: Prentice-Hall.

*Homans, G. C. 1961. *Social Behavior.* New York: Harcourt, Brace & World.

Horelick, Arnold L. 1964. "The Cuban Missile Crisis," *World Politics* XVI, No. 3, pp. 363–89.

Huntington, Samuel. 1973. "Transnational Organizations in World Politics," *World Politics* XXV, No. 3, pp. 333–68.

*Ikle, Fred C. 1964. *How Nations Negotiate.* New York: Harper & Row.

*—— and Leites, Nathan. 1962. "Political Negotiation as a Process of Modifying Utilities," *Journal of Conflict Resolution* VI, No. 1, pp. 19–28.

Jacobsen, Kurt. 1970. "Sponsorship Activities in the UN Negotiating Process," *Cooperation and Conflict* V, No. 4, pp. 241–69.

Jacobson, Harold Kahn and Stein, Eric. 1966. *Diplomats, Scientists and Politicians.* Ann Arbor: University of Michigan Press.

Jakobson, Max. 1961. *The Diplomacy of the Winter War*. Cambridge, Mass.: Harvard University Press.

*Janis, I. and Terwilliger, R. 1962. "An Experimental Study of Psychological Resistances to Fear-Arousing Communications," *Journal of Abnormal and Social Psychology* LXV, No. 6, pp. 403–10.

Janis, Irving. 1972. *Victims of Groupthink*. Boston: Houghton Mifflin.

Jensen, Lloyd. 1965. "Military Capabilities and Bargaining Behavior," *Journal of Conflict Resolution* IX, No. 2, pp. 155–63.

*Jervis, Robert. 1969. "Hypotheses on Misperception," *International Politics and Foreign Policy*, ed. James Rosenau. New York: The Free Press.


Kalb, Marvin and Bernard. 1974. *Kissinger*. Boston: Little, Brown.

Kapoor, Ashok. 1966. "Foreign Collaborations in India," *Idea* X, No. 2, pp. 213–58 and No. 3, pp. 351–87.

——. 1969. "A Consortium That Never Was," *Columbia Journal of World Business* IV, No. 5, pp. 63–70.

——. 1970a. "Business-Government Relations Become Respectable," *Columbia Journal of World Business* V, No. 4, pp. 27–33.

——. 1970b. *International Business Negotiation: A Study on India*. New York: New York University Press (paperback, Princeton: Darwin Press).

——. 1974. *Planning for International Business Negotiation*. Cambridge, Mass.: Ballinger.

—— and Boddewyn, Jean (eds.). 1973. *International Business-Government Relations*. New York: American Management Associations.

—— and Grub, P. D. (eds.). 1972. *The Multinational Enterprise in Transition*. Princeton: Darwin.

Karrass, Chester L. 1970. *The Negotiating Game*. New York: World.

Kelman, Herbert (ed.). 1965. *International Behavior*. New York: Holt, Rinehart & Winston.

Kennedy, Robert. 1969. *Thirteen Days*. New York: New American Library.

Kissinger, Henry A. 1964. *A World Restored*. New York: Grosset & Dunlap.

——. 1969. "The Viet Nam Negotiations," *Foreign Affairs* XLVII, No. 2, pp. 211–34.

——. 1973. "News Briefing on Vietnam Cease-Fire," *New York Times* (Jan. 25).

Kitzinger, Uwe. 1973. *Diplomacy and Persuasion.*

Klaiber, Wolfgang. 1973. *Era of Negotiations.* Lexington, Mass.: Heath.

Kolkowicz, Roman. 1963. "Conflicts in Soviet Party-Military Relations," RAND memo RN-3760-PR. Santa Monica, Calif.: Rand.

*Kuhn, H. W. 1962. "Game Theory and Models of Negotiation," *Journal of Conflict Resolution* VI, No. 1, pp. 1–4.

*——— and Tucker, A. W., eds. 1953. *Contributions to the Theory of Games* II. Princeton, N.J.: Princeton University Press.

Lall, Arthur. 1964. *Negotiating Disarmament.* Ithaca, N.Y.: Cornell University Center for International Studies.

*———. 1966. *Modern International Negotiations.* New York: Columbia University Press.

———. 1968. *How Communist China Negotiates.* New York: Columbia University Press.

Larson, David L. 1963. *The "Cuban Crisis" of 1962.* Boston: Houghton Mifflin.

*Lasswell, Harold D. 1930. *Psychopathology and Politics.* Chicago: University of Chicago Press.

Lee, James A. 1966. "Cultural Analysis in Overseas Operations," *Harvard Business Review* XXXXIV, No. 2, pp. 106–14.

*Lindblom, Charles. 1955. *Bargaining: The Hidden Hand in Government,* research memo 1434-RC. Santa Monica, Calif.: Rand.

———. 1965. *The Intelligence of Democracy: Decision-Making Through Mutual Adjustment.* New York: The Free Press.

*Lipsky, Michael. 1968. "Protest as a Political Resource," *American Political Science Review* LXII, No. 4, pp. 1,144–58.

*Lockhart, Charles. 1974. *The Efficacy of Threats.* Beverly Hills, Calif.: Sage Publications.

Love, Kenneth. 1969. *Suez.* New York: McGraw-Hill.

*Mabry, Bevars duPre. 1965. "The Pure Theory of Bargaining," *Industrial and Labor Relations Review* XVIII, No. 4, pp. 479–502.

*———. 1966. *Labor Relations and Collective Bargaining.* New York: Ronald Press.

*March, James G. and Simon, Herbert. 1958. *Organizations.* New York: John Wiley & Sons.

*Marlowe, D.; Gergen, K. J.; and Doob, A. N. 1966. "Opponent's Personality, Expectation of Social Interaction, and Interpersonal Bargaining," *Journal of Personality and Social Psychology* III, No. 2, pp. 206–13.

Marshall, Howard and Natalie. 1971. *Collective Bargaining.* New York: Random House.

Martens, Baron Charles de. 1837. *Guide Diplomatique.* J-P Aillaud.

*McGrath, Joseph E. and Julian, James W. 1963. "Interaction Processes and Task Outcome in Experimentally Created Negotiation Groups," *Journal of Psychological Studies* XIV, No. 3, pp. 117–38.

*Midgaard, Knut. 1970. *Communication and Strategy.* Oslo: Universitetsforlaget.

*———. 1973. "Teori om internasjonale forhandlinger," *Internasjonal Politikk,* No. 2, pp. 453–73, No. 4, pp. 923–46.

———; Stenstadvold, Halvor; and Underdal, Arild. 1973. "An Approach to Political Interlocutions," *Scandinavian Political Studies* VIII, pp. 9–36.

Mikesell, Raymond F. 1971. *Foreign Investment in the Petroleum and Mineral Industries.* Baltimore, Md.: The Johns Hopkins University Press.

Miller, Linda B. (ed.). 1968. *Dynamics of World Politics: Studies in Resolution of Conflict.* Englewood Cliffs, N.J.: Prentice-Hall.

Modelski, George (ed.). 1972. *Multinational Corporations and World Order.* Beverly Hills, Calif.: Sage Publications.

*Moffitt, J. and Stagner, R. 1956. "Perceptual Rigidity and Closure as Functions of Anxiety," *Journal of Abnormal and Social Psychology* LII, No. 3, pp. 354–58.

*Monat, Jonathan S. 1971. "Determination of Bargaining Power," *Personnel Journal* L, No. 7, pp. 513–20.

Moran, Theodore H. 1973. "Transnational Corporations," *International Organization* XXVII, No. 2, pp. 273–89.

Moskow, Michael H. 1970. *Collective Bargaining in Public Employment.* New York: Random House.

*Murray, H. 1938. *Exploring Personality.* New York: Oxford University Press.


*Nash, John. 1950. "The Bargaining Problem," *Econometrica* XVIII, No. 1, pp. 155–62.

Newhouse, John. 1967. *Collision at Brussels.* New York: W. W. Norton.

———. 1973. *Cold Dawn.* New York: Holt, Rinehart & Winston.

Nicolson, Harold. 1954. *The Evolution of Diplomatic Method.* London: Constable.

*———. 1964. *Diplomacy.* New York: Oxford University Press.

*Nieburg, H. L., 1969. *Political Violence*. New York: St. Martin's Press.

Nierenberg, Gerard I. 1973. *Fundamentals of Negotiating*. New York: Hawthorn.

Nogee, Joseph. 1960. *The Diplomacy of Disarmament*. New York: Carnegie Endowment.

———. 1965. *Neither War nor Peace: The Soviets at Geneva*. Cambridge, Mass.: The MIT Press.

——— and Spanier, John. 1962. *The Politics of Disarmament*. New York: Praeger.

*North, Robert C. 1962. "International Conflict and Integration," *Intergroup Relations and Leadership,* ed. Muzafer Sherif. New York: John Wiley & Sons.

———; Brody, Richard A.; and Holsti, Ole R. 1964. "Some Empirical Data on the Conflict Spiral," *Peace Research Society Papers*, pp. 1–14.

*Osgood, Charles E. 1962. "Studies on the Generality of Affective Meaning Systems," *American Psychologist* XVII, No. 1, pp. 10–28.

———. 1963. *An Alternative to War or Surrender*. Urbana: University of Illinois Press.

*———; Suci, J.; and Tannenbaum, Percy H. 1957. *The Measurement of Meaning*. Urbana: University of Illinois Press.

Pachter, Henry M. 1963. *Collision Course*. New York: Praeger.

Pecquet, A. 1737. *Discours sur l'Art de Negocier*. Nyon Fils.

*Pen, Jan. 1952. "A General Theory of Bargaining," *American Economic Review* XLII, No. 1, pp. 24–42.

*Pennock, J. Roland (ed.). 1972. *Coercion: Nomos XIV*. Chicago: Aldine-Atherton.

Peters, Edward. 1955. *Strategy and Tactics in Labor Negotiations*. New London, Conn.: National Foreman's Institute.

Pinelo, Adalberto J. 1973. *The Multinational Corporation as a Force in Latin American Politics: A Case Study of the International Petroleum Company in Peru*. New York: Praeger.

Preeg, Ernest H. 1970. *Traders and Diplomats*. Washington, D.C.: The Brookings Institution.

Randle, Robert. 1970. *Geneva 1954*. Princeton, N.J.: Princeton University Press.

———. 1973. *The Origins of Peace*. New York: The Free Press.

*Rapoport, Anatol. 1960. *Fights, Games & Debates*. Ann Arbor, Mich.: Michigan University Press.

*——. 1966. *Two-person Game Theory*. Ann Arbor, Mich.: Michigan University Press.

—— and Chammah, A. M. 1965. *Prisoner's Dilemma*. Ann Arbor, Mich.: Michigan University Press.

Richardson, Lewis F. 1960. *Arms and Insecurity*, eds. Nicolas Rashevsky and Ernesto Trucco. Pittsburgh: Boxwood Press.

*Riker, William H. 1967. "Bargaining in a Three-person Game," *American Political Science Review* LXI, No. 3, pp. 642–56.

Robertson, T. 1965. *Crisis: The Inside Story of the Suez Conspiracy*. New York: Atheneum.

*Rosenau, James N. 1966. "Pre-Theories and Theories of Foreign Policy," *Approaches to Comparative and International Politics*, ed. R. Barry Farrell. Evanston, Ill.: Northwestern University Press.

Rothchild, Donald. 1973. *Racial Bargaining in Independent Kenya*. New York: Oxford University Press.

Rusk, Dean. 1955. "Parliamentary Diplomacy–Debate vs. Negotiation," *World Affairs Interpreter* XXVI, No. 2, pp. 121–38.


*Sawyer, Jack and Guetzkow, Harold. 1965. "Bargaining and Negotiation in International Relations," *International Behavior*, ed. Herbert C. Kelman. New York: Holt, Rinehart & Winston.

Scheinman, Lawrence and Wilkinson, David (eds.). 1968. *International Law and Political Crises*. Boston: Little, Brown.

*Schelling, Thomas C. 1960. *The Strategy of Conflict*. Cambridge, Mass.: Harvard University Press.

*——. 1966. *Arms and Influence*. New Haven, Conn.: Yale University Press.

*Schild, E. O. 1968. "The Shaping of Strategies," *Simulation Games in Learning*, eds. Sarane Boocock and E. O. Schild. Beverly Hills, Calif.: Sage Publications.

Schlesinger, Arthur. 1965. *A Thousand Days*. Boston: Houghton Mifflin.

*Schopenhauer, Arthur. 1896. *The Art of Controversy*. London: George Allen & Unwin.

*Sells, S. 1963. "Dimensions of Stimulus Situations," *Stimulus Determinants of Behavior*, ed. S. Sells, Chaps. XXX–XXXI. New York: Ronald Press.

*Shackle, G. L. S. 1957. "The Nature of the Bargaining Process," *Theory of Wage Determination*, ed. John Dunlop. New York: St. Martin's Press.

*Sharp, Gene. 1973. *The Politics of Nonviolent Action*. Boston: Porter Sargent.

*Sherif, Muzafer. 1966. *In Common Predicament*. Boston: Houghton Mifflin.

*Shubik, Martin. 1964. *Game Theory and Related Approaches to Social Behavior*. New York: John Wiley & Sons.

*Siegel, Sidney and Fouraker, Lawrence, 1960. *Bargaining and Group Decision-making*. New York: McGraw-Hill.

*Simmel, Georg. 1955. *Conflict*, trans. Kurt H. Wolff. New York: The Free Press.

*Singer, J. David. 1963. "Inter-nation Influence," *American Political Science Review* LVII, No. 2, pp. 420–30.

Smith, David M. (ed.). 1974. *From War to Peace*. New York: Columbia University International Fellows Program.

*Smith, M. 1950. "The Phenomenological Approach to Personality Theory," *Journal of Abnormal and Social Psychology* VL, No. 3, pp. 516–23.

Smoker, P. 1969. "A Time-Series Analysis of Sino-Indian Relations," *Journal of Conflict Resolution* XIII, No. 2, pp. 172–91.

*Snyder, Richard. 1958. "A Decision-Making Approach to the Study of Political Phenomena," Reprint PS-266. Indianapolis, Ind.: Bobbs-Merrill.

*Snyder, Richard C. et al. (eds.). 1962. *Foreign Policy Decision-Making*. New York: The Free Press.

*Snygg, D. and Combs, A. 1949. *Individual Behavior*. New York: Harper & Brothers.

*———. 1950. "The Phenomenological Approach and the Problem of Unconscious Behavior," *Journal of Abnormal and Social Psychology* VL, No. 3, pp. 523–28.

Sorensen, Theodore C. 1963. *Decision-Making in the White House*. New York: Columbia University Press.

Spector, B. I. 1975. *The Effects of Personality, Perception and Power on the Bargaining Process and Outcome*. Doctoral Dissertation, New York: New York University Press.

Steinbruner, John D. 1974. *The Cybernetic Theory of Decision*. Princeton: Princeton University Press.

*Stevens, Carl. 1958. "On the Theory of Negotiation," *Quarterly Journal of Economics* LXXII, No. 1, pp. 77–97.

*———. 1963. *Strategy and Collective Bargaining*. New York: McGraw-Hill.

Stone, Jeremy. 1967. *Strategic Persuasion*. New York: Columbia University Press.

*Stone, Philip J. et al. 1962. "The General Inquirer," *Behavioral Science* VII, No. 4, pp. 484–94.

*Suci, George J. 1957. "An Investigation of the Similarity Between the Semantic Space of Different Cultures." Southwest Project for Comparative Psycholinguistics.

Suhrke, Astri. 1973. "Bargaining Between Unequal Partners." International Studies Ass'n. Annual Meeting.

*Swingle, Paul (ed.). 1970. *The Structure of Conflict*. New York: Academic Press.

Szulc, Tad. 1974. "How Kissinger Did It," *Foreign Policy*, No. 15, pp. 21–69.

Tanter, Raymond. 1974. *Modeling and Managing International Conflict: The Berlin Crisis*. Beverly Hills, Calif.: Sage Publications.

Thorelli, H. B. 1966. "The Multinational Corporation as a Change Agent," *Southern Journal of Business*, No. 1, pp. 1–9.

*Towers, B. (ed.). 1972. *Bargaining for Change*. Davlin.

Underdal, Arild. 1972. *Forhandlingene om norsk medlemskap i EF*. Institute for Political Science, University of Oslo.

———. 1973. "Multinational Negotiating Parties," *Cooperation and Conflict* VIII, Nos. 3–4, pp. 173–82.

*Valavanis, Stefan. 1958. "The Resolution of Conflict When Utilities Interact," *Journal of Conflict Resolution* II, No. 2, pp. 156–69.

Van Zandt, Howard F. 1970. "How to Negotiate in Japan," *Harvard Business Review*, pp. 45–56.

Vatcher, William. 1958. *Panmunjom*. New York: Praeger.

*Verba, Sidney. 1961. "Assumptions of Rationality in Models of the International System," *World Politics* XIV, No. 1, pp. 93–117.

Vernon, Raymond. 1972. *Sovereignty at Bay: The Multinational Spread of U. S. Companies*. New York: Basic Books.

*Von Neumann, John and Morgenstern, Oskar. 1947. *Theory of Games and Economic Behavior*. Princeton: Princeton University Press.

Wadsworth, James. 1962. *The Price of Peace*. New York: Praeger.

Walder, Francis. 1959. *The Negotiators*. New York: McDowell, Obolensky.

*Walton, R. E. and McKersie, R. B. 1965. *A Behavioral Theory of Labor Negotiation*. New York: McGraw-Hill.

*———. 1966. "The Theory of Bargaining," *Industrial and Labor Relations Review* XIX, No. 3, pp. 414–24 and "Reply," B. P. Mabry, *ibid.*, pp. 424–35.

Weintal, Edward and Bartlett, Charles. 1967. *Facing the Brink*. New York: Scribner's Sons.

Whetten, Lawrence L. 1974. *The Canal War: Four-power Conflict in the Middle East*. Cambridge, Mass.: The MIT Press.

*White, D. M. 1971. "Power and Intention," *American Political Science Review* LXV, No. 3, pp. 749–59.

Wiklund, C. 1970. "The Zig-zag Course of the Nordek Negotiations," *Scandinavian Political Studies* V, pp. 307–35.

Williams, Simon. 1965. "Negotiating Investments in Emerging Countries," *Harvard Business Review* XXXXIII, No. 1, pp. 89–99.

Wohlstetter, Albert and Roberta. 1965. *Controlling the Risks in Cuba*, Adelphi Paper 17. London: Institute for Strategic Studies.

*Wright, Quincy. 1957. "Design for a Research Proposal on International Conflict and the Factors Causing Their Aggravation or Amelioration," *Western Political Quarterly* X, No. 2, pp. 263–75.

———. 1964. "The Cuban Quarantine of 1962," *Power and Order*, eds. John G. Stoessinger and Alan F. Westin. New York: Harcourt, Brace & World.

Young, Kenneth T. 1968. *Negotiating with the Chinese Communists*. New York: McGraw-Hill.

Young, Oran. 1968. *The Politics of Force*. Princeton, N.J.: Princeton University Press.

——— (ed.). 1976. *Bargaining*. Urbana: University of Illinois Press.

Zartman, I. William. 1964a. "The Moroccan-American Base Negotiations," *Middle East Journal* XVIII, No. 1, pp. 27–40.

———. 1964b. "Les relations entre la France et l'Algerie depuis les Accords d'Evian," *Revue française de science politique* XIV, No. 6, pp. 1,087–113.

———. 1971. *The Politics of Trade Negotiations Between Africa and the EEC: The Weak Confront the Strong*. Princeton, N.J.: Princeton University Press.

*———. 1974. "The Political Analysis of Negotiation: How Who Gets What and When," *World Politics* XXVI, No. 3, pp. 385–99.

*———. 1975. "Negotiations: Theory and Reality," *Journal of International Affairs* IX, No. 1, pp. 69–77.

*Zeuthen, Frederick. 1930. *Problems of Monopoly and Economic Warfare.* London: Routledge & Sons.

Zimbardo, Philip and Ebbeson, Ebbe. 1969. *Influencing Attitudes and Changing Behavior.* Chicago: Addison, Wesley.

Zoppo, C. E. 1961. *The Issue of Nuclear Test Cessation at the London Disarmament Conference of 1957.* RM-2821-ARPA. Santa Monica, Calif.: Rand.

# INDEX

R1